Advances in Digital Multimedia Broadcasting

Volume III

Advances in Digital Multimedia Broadcasting
Volume III

Edited by **Alicia Witte**

CLANRYE
INTERNATIONAL

New Jersey

Published by Clanrye International,
55 Van Reypen Street,
Jersey City, NJ 07306, USA
www.clanryeinternational.com

Advances in Digital Multimedia Broadcasting: Volume III
Edited by Alicia Witte

International Standard Book Number: 978-1-63240-049-9 (Hardback)

Printed in the United States of America.

Contents

Preface

Multimedia is a combination of different types of media such as audio, video, text, animations, graphics, images, and interactive media. This field of computer technology is widespread in the present world due to its use in communication, entertainment, and academics. Multimedia involves presentation of data using multiple principles, concepts, and theories. A very important aspect of multimedia is digital broadcasting, which one can observe on television, internet, radio, cell phone communication etc. Multimedia has gained unimaginable importance over the last few decades. It has gained relevance in the field of computer science, especially in programming and communication technology.

Digital multimedia has also gained considerable importance in medical sciences, engineering, education, entertainment etc. Digital multimedia broadcasting is a technique used to distribute data over a large area by processing and transmitting the data using computer science tools. It converts data into digital forms such as bits, and then transmits the same using tools of electronics and physics.

This book has contributors from several countries, all of them leading experts in their field. All the chapters have been thoroughly written and reviewed, ensuring that the views of the contributors have been preserved in a uniform format. This effort would not have been possible without the kind cooperation of our contributors, who patiently went through revisions of their chapters. I convey my heartfelt thanks to all contributors and to the team at the publishing house for their encouragement and excellent technical assistance as and when required.

Editor

Design and Implementation of a Mobile Multihop WSN for AGV System

Jiaqi Zhang, Molin Jia, Noriyoshi Yamauchi, and Takaaki Baba

Graduate School of Information, Production and Systems, Waseda University, 2-7 Hibikino, Wakamatu-ku, Kitakyushu-shi, Fukuoka 808-0135, Japan

Correspondence should be addressed to Jiaqi Zhang, jackyzhang@fuji.waseda.jp

Academic Editor: Dimitrios Katsaros

A system data sharing protocol of mobile WSN named synchronous dynamic multihop data sharing protocol (S-DMDS) is presented for automated guided vehicle (AGV) system. It is a cross-layer protocol designed from route layer to MAC layer. By adopting a concept of system data sharing, it is possible to make each node exchange the data timely with all the other nodes. It is also a topology-agnostic protocol which has no knowledge of neighbors, routes, or next hops. From the results of the 16-nodes simulation, S-DMDS protocol is proved to be efficient exchange data timely between the devices of AGV system in mobile multihop situation. Moreover, it also shows that S-DMDS significantly outperforms NST-AODV with investing about 41.6% system sharing delay as well as 80% RAM consumption. At last, 5-node experiment indicates that S-DMDS can work well in real environment.

1. Introduction

In recent years, wireless sensor networks (WSNs) technology becomes an emerging field in a wide range of applications such as industrial environment [1]. In addition, with the development of AGV system, the application combining WSN technology with AGV system becomes more widespread. Benefits of wireless technologies are fairly obvious: WSN facilitates installation and maintenance of AGV system and eliminates expensive cables and save costs; in addition, AGV system can easily be reconfigured. One potential dominant technology, which seems to be really effective for the industrial application, is the IEEE802.11 standard [2–5]. Its main drawback still remains in cost, particularly if simple WSNs are considered. Other cheaper technologies such as IEEE802.15.4 [6] and Bluetooth [7] (IEEE802.15.1) are already important actors in the market. However, IEEE802.15.4 does not have a good performance when it is applied to a multi-hop mesh network, although it supplies for such a function. And the serious beacon collision occurs in the beacon mode and the hidden node problem still exists in no-beacon mode. Moreover, both IEEE802.15.4 and Bluetooth need at least one coordinate node to manager

the whole network. At the same time, solutions based on the work of the IEEE 802.15.4 group, like WirelessHART and ISA SP100, have been presented, but devoted to process control [8]. They are able to manage very large mesh network but overall "information rate" is low within 1 node/s or less.

Furthermore, routing in WSNs is an also very challenging task due to the inherent characteristics that distinguish these networks from other wireless networks like mobile ad hoc networks or cellular networks. Most of the network architectures assume that sensor nodes are stationary. However, some devices may change their position rapidly in AGV system leading to the dynamic network topology. Routing messages from or to moving nodes is more challenging since route stability becomes an important issue.

Some mobile route algorithms proposed by MANET [9, 10] can adapt dynamic topology. Ad hoc On-demand Distance Vector routing (AODV) is one of the most studied routing protocol among them. AODV is a reactive routing protocol. When a node requires a route, it initiates a route discovery procedure broadcasting Route Request (RREQ) messages. When a node receives a RREQ, if either it has a valid route entry to the demanded destination or it is the destination itself, it creates and sends a Route Reply

(RREP) message back to the originator node. Every node maintains route entries with forward and backward next hop information that expires after a specified time if the path becomes inactive (i.e., it is not used for data transmission). However, full version of AODV is mainly proposed for implementation of laptop or PDA platform. It costs so much hardware resources that simple WSN node cannot supply. Therefore some simple version of AODV [11–15] is proposed for low cost application. Not So Tiny-AODV (NST-AODV) [16] is a typical one. It is implemented into MICAz [17] platform which use a 2.4 GHz IEEE 802.15.4 radio interface with a 250 kbps data rates. Although it has been proved to be efficient for point to point transmission, it may not be so suitable for AGV system. Since AGV system requires each device should obtain the information of all the other devices in time. It needs a mobile multi-hop data sharing WSN shown as Figure 1, which is not a conventional transmission style that is from source node to destination node.

S-DMDS protocol is proposed to provide multi-hop data sharing communication between mobile AGV nodes with reasonable low cost. It adopts a data sharing concept that each device can get an interface to communicate with the whole system. Via this interface, any node can get the system state in time.

This paper is structured as follow. In Section 2, AGV system scenario is introduced. Then, the protocol principle including software structure, data update processing and time division multiple access (TDMA) mechanism is described in Section 3. After that, the implement hardware (WHM-4) is introduced in Section 4. A series of performance evaluations are provided in Section 5. Finally, conclusion of the paper is made in Section 6.

2. AGV System Scenario

Recently, AGV system is widely used in many automatic systems. Due to the increasing demand for mobility and capability of work in harsh environment, the use of wireless sensor network (WSN) is gaining its importance.

In the scenario shown as Figure 2, establishing a mobile multi-hop wireless sensor network, we plan to control the AGV vehicle to carry cargos and register cargo information automatically in order to achieve unattended management in a storehouse. In the system, there are several AGV vehicles used for carrying cargos; some ground equipments for stacking goods; a charger is used for the AGV power supply and a monitor is also provided to let manager watch and control the whole system. The total number of devices in the AGV system is 16-node.

All the devices in the AGV system should detect their own state (such as location information of AGV and devices on the ground) through sensors and share their state or command information to the others via wireless network. For example, carrying command from devices on the ground should be delivered to the suitable AGV to execute. And traffic control must be executed by AGV itself intelligently in the case of intersection, dead-end road, and so forth.

For the wireless sensor network, the conditions and features of AGV system scenario are summarized as follow.

(1) considering AGV vehicles are moveable, the topology of the network changes rapidly;

(2) the real time system data sharing is necessary;

(3) data transmission between every two nodes of the network may be multi-hop;

(4) high network stability is required;

(5) since power of wireless sensor module is supplied by devices of AGV system, the power consumption problem is not so important in this scenario.

S-DMDS protocol is designed for the AGV system. In the following section, S-DMDS is described in detail.

3. S-DMDS Protocol

S-DMDS is a protocol of system data sharing. To realize system data sharing, each node is arranged to broadcast a data sharing frame (DSF) regularly as shown in Figure 3 which is an interface between each node and the whole system. Since the DSF consists of every node's information in the network, each node can realize data exchanging with all the other nodes by reading and writing the DSF. Hence, mobile multi-hop network can be easily realized on simple wireless sensor nodes.

DSF is a data sharing media to collect the sharing information from all of the nodes. As shown in Figure 4, the structure of DSF consists of two main parts: head and data. Frame head is used for declaring the length and class of the frame, and it also includes sending node id. The purpose of the frame head is to realize a synchronous mechanism which integrates the main idea of [18, 19].

Since S-DMDS protocol employs TDMA as media access method to ensure each transmission to be successful. So it requires that once receiving DSF, each node needs to calculate next broadcast time slot by comparing the sending node id with its own id. Then the node can be synchronized again and again after receiving DSF.

The following equations describe the detailed relationship:

If my id > sending id

Broadcast time

$$= \text{current time} + (\text{my id} - \text{sending id}) \times \text{time slot}, \quad (1)$$

If my id < sending id

Broadcast time

$$= \text{current time} + (16 + \text{my id} - \text{sending id}) \times \text{time slot}. \quad (2)$$

Data part of DSF is composed of all nodes' sharing data. Besides, each node's information also consists of two parts, one is the sequence number, and the other is the sharing information. The function of sequence number will be explained in the next section.

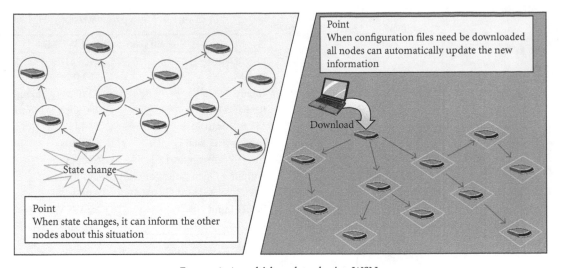

FIGURE 1: A multi-hop data sharing WSN.

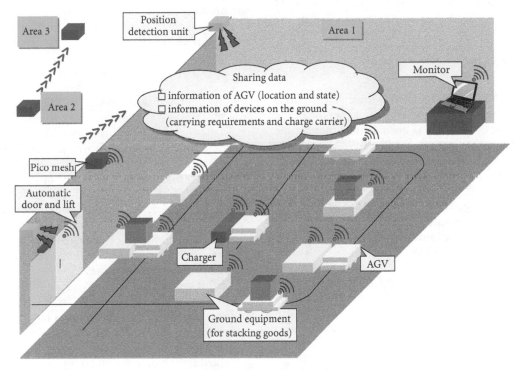

FIGURE 2: AGV system scenario.

When the network is working, every nodes broadcast data sharing frame (DSF) regularly in order to share their information to the whole network. When DSF is broadcasted in the network, any node receiving DSF can get other nodes information and store the information in its memory. Meanwhile, each node can also update its own corresponding unit in DSF when some information needs to be transmitted. Then in the next transmission time, it can make the other nodes know its new information by broadcasting DSF from its memory.

The modules' software structure is shown in Figure 5. After stating, each node will keep on waiting for receiving DSF except when it turns to broadcast time. If it receives

a new DSF, it will employ a data update process to update the information into its memory. If a node reaches broadcast time, it will enter the synchronous adjustment process to calculate its own broadcast time before broadcast.

In the following two parts, data update process and node synchronous process are explained, respectively.

3.1. Data Sharing Update Process.

This process works when a new DSF has been received as shown in Figure 6. The value of Sequence Number (Seq No) indicates whether the node information is new or not. And whenever any node updates the information of its corresponding unit

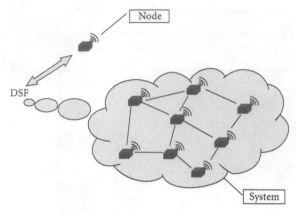

FIGURE 3: Data sharing mode.

TABLE 1: Main parameters of WHM-4.

Main parameters of WHM-4		
Frequency		2405 MHz–2480 MHz
Bandwidth		75 MHz
Channel Step		5 MHz (16 channels maximum)
RF Baud Rate		250 kbps Maximum
Micro-controllers		TI-MSP430
Input	Digital Logic	4 Inputs
	Analog A/D	6 Inputs
Output	Open Collector Output	2 Outputs
I/F	RS232	3 pins
Power input		1.5 V/3 V External power supply
Board Size		38 mm × 55 mm × 20 mm

in DSF, the corresponding Sequence Number will be increased by 1 to indicate that the information is the newer one.

Such purpose is to make sure that the receiving nodes can recognize whether the information of other nodes received is newer one by comparing Seq No.

3.2. Synchrosnous Mechanism. S-DMDS arrange each node to broadcast DSF at every broadcast cycle. In sending time sequence, broadcast cycle time has been divided into N time slots per broadcast cycle as shown in Figure 7. N is defined as the total number of the network. Each node could be allocated to its id's corresponding broadcast time slot to broadcast DSF after joining the sending time sequence. For example, node1 is arranged into 1st time slot to broadcast its DSF. Between every two broadcast time, it also adds a guard interval to make sure that previous node broadcast is finished before next node starts to broadcast. Besides, it can also make up the clock offsets problem.

However, it should be noticed that S-DMDS protocol allows only one time reference node to start broadcasting DSF at first. Otherwise, the synchronous system will be out of order. An example is given to explain the synchronous process in detail.

3.3. Synchronous Process. In the example, network topology is shown in Figure 8. Node1 is selected to be the time reference node. At first, the other nodes will keep on silence until receiving DSF. (Receiving DSF means the node joined the network group). After reference node1 starting to broadcast, node3, node4, and node15 can receive it and then calculate their broadcast time according to rule defined by (1) and (2). Because node3 has the nearest ID to node1 among them, it will broadcast DSF immediately. Thus, Node6 can receive the frame meanwhile it is also arranged to the sending temporal series. Following this rule, after several cycle all the nodes which can receive DSF are added to the system sending temporal series one by one. At last the synchronous process is over. Then every node can maintain the synchronous time table periodically once they receive DSF.

3.4. Prototype of S-DMDS Protocol. To show that by adopting S-DMDS how node can share their data to each other in one broadcast cycle time, a prototype is presented. As show in Figure 9, there are 4 nodes in this scenario. Node3 is a movable node as well as it cannot community with node1 directly.

At first stage, the scenario looks like as state 1, node1 is selected as a time reference node, and according to the sending temporal series, node1 will first start broadcasting, it sends DSF to its neighbor node2 and node4. Then node2 and node4 can get the information of node1.

After that, the scenario turns to state2, node2 starts to broadcast DSF which consists of the information of node1 and node2 to its neighbor node such as node1, node3 and node4. So node3 and node4 get the information of node1 and node2, meanwhile node1 and node4 can get the new information of node2. When the scenario turns to state3, node3's location changed. Therefore, Node3 ran out of node2's communication range, meanwhile, it ran into node4's communication range.

In this way, when Node3 broadcasts DSF, only node4 can receive the DSF which consists the information of node1, node2 and node3. At this time node4 has obtained all nodes' information. After node4 broadcasts DSF, all the nodes in this scenario can get the other nodes' information. Namely, the initial system data sharing is finished.

4. Implement Platform

A wireless sensor module named as WHM-4 developed by IPS of Waseda University is utilized for implementing S-DMDS protocol. The appearance of WHM-4 is shown in Figure 11. WHM-4 is a low-power consumption wireless module employing IEEE802.15.4 (2.4 GHz) radio interface, where every channel supports up to 250 kbps data rates. The power of RF module is 1.5 mA (3.3 V). The largest transmission range of WHM-4 is about 50 meters. The other main parameters of WHM-4 are shown in Table 1.

A TDMA schematic diagram is used to describe the AGV system with 16-node as shown in Figure 10. Then length of DSF (K) is defined as 340 bytes consisting of 320 bytes for storing the sharing data of 16-node and 20 bytes for control

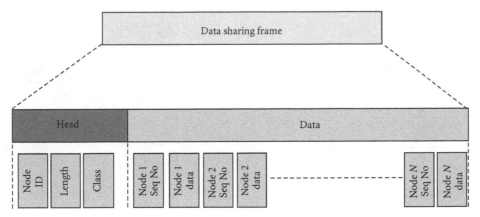

FIGURE 4: Structure of DSF.

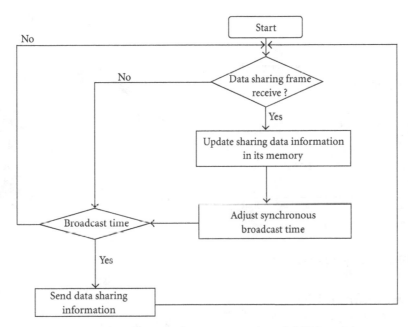

FIGURE 5: Flow chart of software structure in each WSN module.

information. Obviously, the length of each node sharing data is 20 bytes in DSF.

Therefore, each DSF transmission (Δt) takes about 10 ms and a guard interval (Tg) is kept into 10 ms for node to adjust broadcast time as well as avoiding clock offset. Each node broadcasts DSF every 320 ms (Tc) according to the sending sequence. Namely, Tc is the broadcast cycle.

5. Performance Evaluation

The evaluation scenarios are composed of 16 WHM-4 modules accorrding to the requirement of AGV system. First, a throughput analysis is provided to evaluate the network capacity. And then a simulation of 16-node scenario is presented by using C++ simulation programs based on parameters of WHM-4 hardware. By doing such a simulation, the performance of S-DMDS in 16-node AGV system can be evaluated. At final part of this section, a five nodes experiment is shown to prove S-DMDS protocol can work well in real environment.

5.1. Throughput Analysis. The throughput of the network is defined as how much data is successfully delivered in unit time. Because each node sent same size package regularly and by adopting TDMA that each transmission is successful without any collision as shown in Figure 10, the throughput of network is defined as

$$\text{Throughput} = \frac{N \times K}{\text{Tc}}. \tag{3}$$

In S-DMDS algorithm, $\text{Tc} = N * (\Delta t + \text{Tg})$, and we define K as length of DSF ($K = 340$ bytes). Hence the network throughput becomes

$$\text{Throughput} = \frac{K}{\Delta t + \text{Tg}}. \tag{4}$$

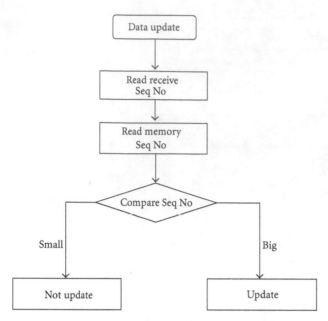

FIGURE 6: Data sharing update process flow chat.

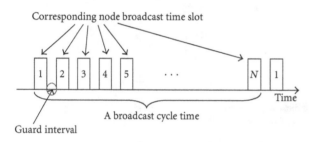

FIGURE 7: TDMA sending sequence.

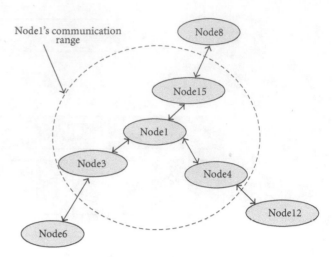

FIGURE 8: An example of synchronous process.

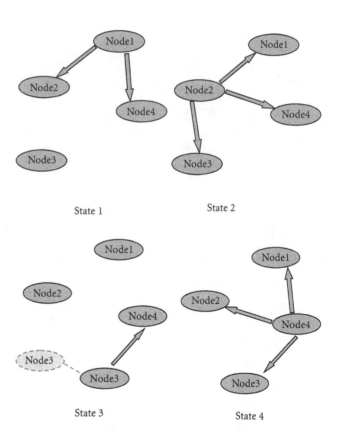

FIGURE 9: Data sharing process of the algorithm.

Because Δt and Tg are determined by the speed of RF module and K is a constant, if the speed of RF module is fixed, the throughput becomes a constant value. In 16-node circumstance, a 2.4 G RF module of 125 kps transmission speed is adopted, so the network throughput is 136000 bits/sec.

5.2. Simulation of System Sharing Delay. To evluate the system sharing delay in multi-hop situation, three different scale of network are established including the network of single-hop, 3-hop and 6-hop (6-hop is the largest network scale in 16-node circumstance). And a mobile situation is also included to indecate how S-DMDS performs.

Before doing the simulation, all nodes store only its own sharing data in its memory before broadcasting. System sharing delay (Tssd) means that how long all nodes can obtain system sharing data from all the other nodes. The network hops scale is assumed as minimum number of hops between two farthest nodes in network (e.g., from node1 to node 16, it takes 3-hops, so it means 3-hop networks in Figure 12).

5.2.1. Single-Hop Scale. For testing system sharing delay in single-hop network, node is allowed to communicate

with all the others directly. And some mobile nodes are allowed to exchange their position to simulate mobile scenario as shown in Figure 13. The result shows that Tssd is about 320 ms (Tc) no matter whether nodes moved or not. In Figure 10, Tssd is the time at which the 16th nodes finish broadcasting DSF. Therefore, it can be summarized that in single-hop network, all nodes can share data to each other only within one Tc (Tssd = Tc). It can fully satisfy the timely transmission required by AGV system.

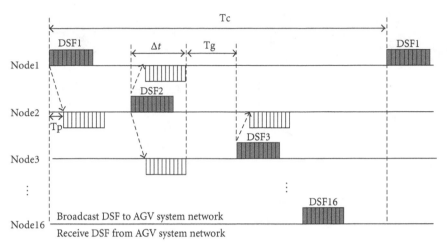

Tc: a whole system broadcast cycle
Δt: a DSF transmission time
Tg: guard interval
N: total number of nodes
Tp: processing time

FIGURE 10: TDMA Schematic Diagrams of 16-node Scenario.

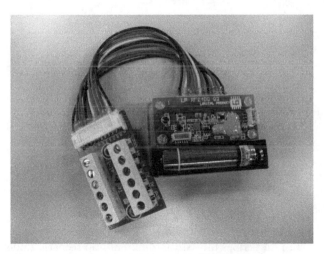

FIGURE 11: Appearance of WHM-4.

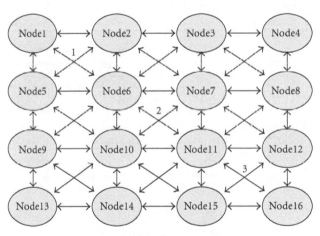

FIGURE 12: Topology A of 3-hop network.

5.2.2. Three-Hop Scale. To evaluate the Tssd performance in 3-hop networks, Topology A of 16-node network is established as shown in Figure 12. (e.g., node1 can only communicate with node2, node5 and node6). In order to simulate the mobile situation, some nodes' positions exchanged as shown in Figure 13, then the network topology turns to Topology B.

First, the simulations proved that after mobile nodes swapped their positions like Figure 13, S-DMDS protocol can adapt the topology change as usual without any additional cost. Thus, S-DMDS is proved to be efficient to deal with mobile situation.

From the result summarized in Figure 14, two cases represented by Topologies A and B indicate how long each node can obtain the sharing data from all the other nodes in 3-hops network. The maximum peaks of two cases represent the Tssd for the two networks, respectively. Those results suggest that the S-DMDS can provide very low system sharing delay of the network. In Topology A, it is only about 780 ms. A more interesting phenomena is that under the Topology B, the Tssd further decreases to around 640 ms. Meanwhile, sharing delay for each node becomes more balanced. Therefore, it means that system sharing delay in Topology B is better than that in the Topology A. After trying many times simulations, it is proved that under the Topology A the network takes the longest sharing delay in 3-hops scenario. The main reason causes by the following points:

The TDMA sending sequence arranges node to broadcast DSF from Node1 to Node16. Therefore, it is more efficient for the node of small ID like node1 to share its data with large ID node. (In Topology A, sharing data of node1 can be shared

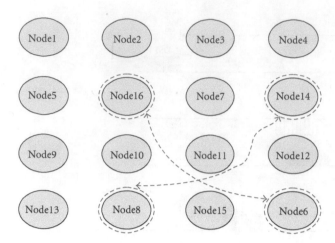

FIGURE 13: Mobile scenario (after exchanging positions of node 6 and node16 as well as the positions of node8 and node14, the network topology turns to Topology B).

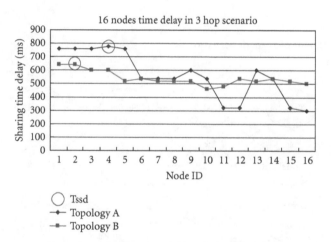

FIGURE 14: Sharing time delay in 3-hop scenario.

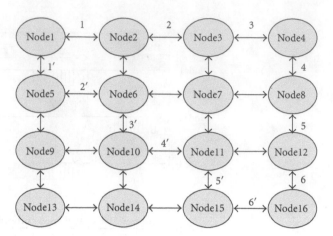

FIGURE 15: Topology A of 6-hop network.

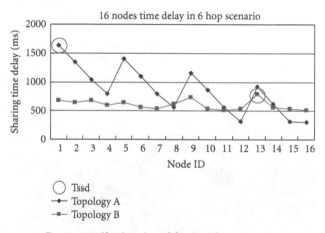

FIGURE 16: Sharing time delay in 6-hop scenario.

In summary, the influence caused by node position swapping in 6-hop scenario is larger than that in 3-hops scenarios.

with all the other nodes in one Tc). In contrast, the sharing data of large ID node takes more time to be transmitted to small ID node. Besides, under Topology A, the nodes of large ID are arranged to gather together so that it leads to a delay overlap.

Hence, 3-hop scale simulation indicates that the largest Tssd is 780 ms.

5.2.3. Six Hops Scale.
Transmission range has been set so that each node can only communicate with its neighbor node as shown in Figure 15 (e.g., node1 can only communicate with node2 and node 5), thus, network scale becomes 6-hops. Obviously, this scenario is the largest scale of 16 node network. Like 3-hop network, two scenarios are represented by Topologies A and B, respectively, in 6-hops scale. From the result described in Figure 16, the maximum Tssd is around 1.6 s.

With the network changing from 3-hop to 6-hop, the Tssd of both topologies increases. However, the increment under Topology A is much larger than that under Topology B.

5.2.4. Sharing Delay Analysis in Mobile Multi-Hop Scenarios.
Figure 17 describes the Tssd in different hop scenario under Topologies A and B, respectively. Tssd rises rapidly following the increase of network hops. Moreover, Tssd under Topology A can be significantly decreased owing to the mobile situation realized under Topology B.

5.3. Comparison Simulation with NST-AODV.
To explain how efficient S-DMDS can realize system data sharing, a comparison simulation with NST-AODV is provided. NST-AODV is a simple version of AODV based on IEEE802.15.4 for low cost device to realize mobile multi-hop wireless network.

5.3.1. A Discussion of Algorithm Complexity.
Table 2 provides a general comparison of the two protocols. Since NST-AODV is proposed for point to point transmission, it needs to establish and maintain dynamic route table for mobile scenario as well as adopt many route control packets to coordinate each transmission.

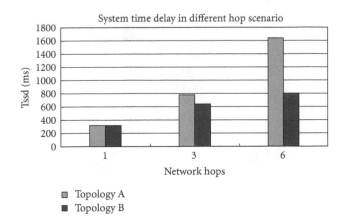

FIGURE 17: Relationship between network hops and system sharing delay in deferent topology.

TABLE 2: Comparison between S-DMDS with NST-AODV.

	NST-AODV	S-DMDS
Purpose	Point to point transmission	System data sharing
Dynamic routing table	Discovery and maintenance	No need
Media access	CSMA/CA	TDMA
Route control packet	RERR, RREQ, RREP	No need
RAM consumption	692 + 131 bytes	660 bytes

However, S-DMDS does not need such a complex process, because it is a topology-agnostic protocol. Therefore, NST-AODV takes more RAM consumption than S-DMDS. Besides, S-DMDS adopt TDMA as the media access method which is more stable than CSMA/CA, because AGV real time system is sensitive to packet loss.

5.3.2. Simulation in Static Scenario. NST-AODV is implemented into MICAz mote which has a same physical layer as WHM-4. [16] also gives a detailed performance evaluation of NST-AODV: to discovery route, it costs average 10 ms per hop; after route has been found, it also takes roughly 10ms per hop to execute an end to end transmission; when an active route changes, it takes around 50 ms to find a new route; and so forth.

In the simulation, both NST-AODV and S-DMDS are applied to finish system data sharing of 127 bytes in the 3-hops network of 16-node shown as Figure 12. Moreover, in NST-AODV, an additional delay will be caused (about 200 ms per node) once there are more than two nodes attempt to start discovery route or broadcast data at same time. To avoid data collision, node is assumed to share data one by one in simulation scenario.

The simulation result shown in Table 3 indicates that S-DMDS takes roughly 28.5% total sharing delay of NST-AODV in initial sharing situation and 38% total delay of NST-AODV in general situation. In initial situation, NST-AODV needs each node take 10 ms per hop to establish a

TABLE 3: Simulation result of system sharing delay in state scenario

	NST-AODV (Tssd_N)	S-DMDS (Tssd_S)	Ratio (Tssd_S/Tssd_N)
initial system sharing delay	9120 ms	2600 ms	28.5%
general system sharing delay	4560 ms	2060 ms	45.2%

TABLE 4: Simulation result of system sharing delay in mobile scenario.

	NST-AODV (Tssd_N)	S-DMDS (Tssd_S)	Ratio (Tssd_S/Tssd_N)
initial system sharing delay	9320 ms	2480 ms	26.6%
general system sharing delay	4760 ms	1980 ms	41.6%

route table of 15-node. And then each node spends another 10 ms per hop to share its data to the other 15-node. 16-node take about 9120 ms to share data. In same situation, S-DMDS only need about 780 ms for 16-node to share data to all the others at first round.

At this moment, S-DMDS can only share 20 bytes data because of DSF definition, so it needs approximate another 6 Tc to continue sharing the rest of data.

In general sharing situation, since NST-AODV can skip route discovery operation, it can reduce the system sharing delay down to 4560 ms. And S-DMDS only needs slightly less than 7 Tc (about 2060 ms) to finish system data sharing. Overall, S-DMDS is proved to perform much better than NST-AODV in terms of system data sharing.

5.3.3. Simulation in Mobile Scenario. In order to evaluate the performance in mobile scenario, node positions are allowed to be exchanged as shown in Figure 13. Table 4 shows the result of system sharing delay in mobile scenario.

After 4 nodes changes position, NST-AODV needs about 200 ms to recover the route. In contrary, as previous discussion in Section 5.2.2, the system sharing delay of S-DMDS will decrease after topology changes to the Topology B shown as Figure 13. Moreover, the change extent of S-DMDS is smaller than that of NST-AODV. Therefore, S-DMDS outperforms NST-AODV in mobile situation.

The simulation result proves that S-DMDS is much better than NST-AODV for system data sharing in 3-hop network of 16-node. Since topology changes rapidly in AGV system, S-DMDS takes around 41.6% system sharing delay of NST-AODV in most cases.

5.4. The Experiments of 5 Nodes Based on WHM-4. To prove S-DMDS can work in reality, 5-node experiments are provided. The length of DSF is defined as 78 bytes, so each DSF transmission (Δt) takes slightly less than 5 ms and a guard interval (Tg) is set as 15 ms in 5-node experiments. The broadcast cycle (Tc) changes to be around 100 ms. To evaluate the performance of S-DMDS in real

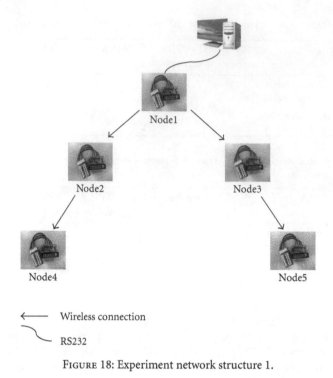

Wireless connection

RS232

Figure 18: Experiment network structure 1.

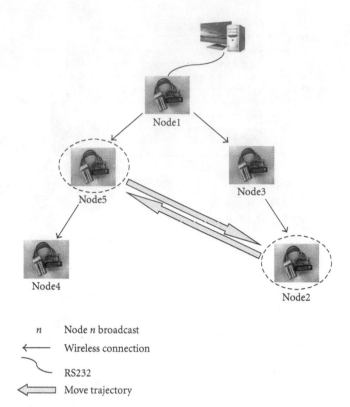

n Node n broadcast

Wireless connection

RS232

Move trajectory

Figure 19: Experiment network structure 2.

implementation, two experiment scenarios are provided including 2 hops mobile transmission scenario and 4 hops system data sharing scenario.

5.4.1. Two Hops Mobile Transmission Experiment. Two-hop transmission with two mobile nodes experiment is shown in Figure 18. (other nodes take max 2 hops to receive node1's sharing data) Node1 is connected with the PC by RS232. By using wireless communication, node1 can send the new sharing data from the PC to the other nodes such as node2 and node3. Then node2 and node3 will transform the sharing data to node4 and node5, respectively.

To test performance of S-DMDS in case of mobile situation, the positions of node2 and node5 are exchanged to simulate the dynamic topology. So the network structure turns to the structure 2 shown in Figure 19, and the results of the above two experiments are summarized in Figure 20 to explain how much time each node takes to receive the sharing data from node 1.

By doing the experiments, first, S-DMDS is proved to be really implemented into WHM-4 to build a mobile multi-hop network. Secondly, a node such as node1 is very efficient to share its sharing data to all the other nodes in the network. In addition, when the locations of node2 and node5 changed, the network can work normally without any influence.

5.4.2. System Data Sharing Experiment of Four Hops. A four-hop network scenario is provided to evaluate the system sharing delay in real multi-hop situation shown as Figure 21.

Figure 22 shows the time delay of each node receiving the data from node1 and node 5. To share node1's data, it only needs 1 broadcast cycle, but to share node5's data it needs 3.2 broadcast cycle.

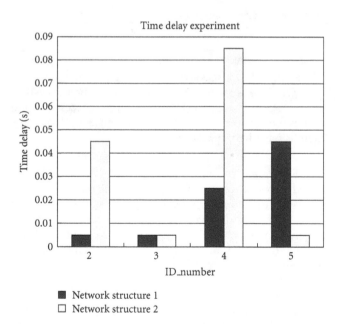

■ Network structure 1
□ Network structure 2

Figure 20: Experiment result of two-hop network.

Because after node1 broadcasted the data, node2, node3 and node4 start to broadcast one by one. So the data from node1 can be sent to node5 in one broadcast cycle. Before the middle nodes (such as node 2, node 3 and node 4) broadcast DSF, they also input their sharing data to the DSF, therefore, each node can get previous nodes' data. So node5 can obtain all the nodes' sharing data. And then the data from node5

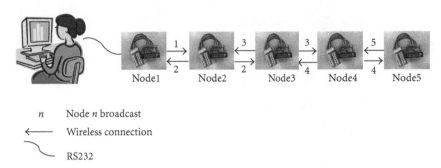

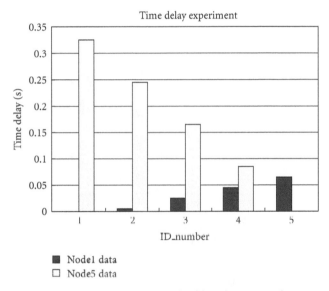

n Node n broadcast

←   Wireless connection

⌐   RS232

FIGURE 21: Four hops transmission experiment.

FIGURE 22: Experiment result of four-hop network.

maximum Tssd in 3-hop and 6-hop network is 780 ms and 1.6 s, respectively. Furthermore, Tssd can be significantly decreased in the mobile situation. Therefore, the Tssd of S-DMDS is low enough to satisfy AGV system in dynamic multi-hop situation. In addition, the results of comparison simulation show that compared with NTS-AODV, S-DMDS takes only about 41.6% system sharing delay as well as 80% RAM consumption. At last, 5-node experiment proved S-DMDS can work well in real environment.

In conclusion, S-DMDS protocol is an outstanding solution to compose mobile multi-hop WSN with simple wireless senor module for AGV system.

Acknowledgments

The authors would like to sincerely thank Mr. T. Tsuji and Mr. T. Otawa of Logic Product Corporation.

starts to be delivered to node1. Because it is the last node in broadcast cycle, the data needs wait about 0.08 s to be sent to node4. By parity of reasoning, it needs roughly 0.32 s to deliver node5's data to node1. At this time, all the nodes have kept the other nodes' data, thus, the system data sharing has been realized.

6. Conclusion

To realize a mobile wireless sensor network for AGV system that provides each device exchange its state information timely with all the others, S-DMDS protocol is proposed. The proposed protocol is implemented by simple wireless module with low calculation overhead. It adopts a regularly broadcasted DSF as a data exchange media to realize data sharing of whole system faster than conventional approaches. Moreover, dynamic topology will not influence the performance of network. TDMA is employed so that S-DMDS can provide stable and efficient accessing without transmission collision.

S-DMDS protocol has been implemented into WHM-4 hardware module which will be equipped to the devices of AGV system. 16-node simulation results indicate that

References

[1] T. S. Rappaport, "Indoor radio communications for factories of the future," *IEEE Communications Magazine*, vol. 27, no. 5, pp. 15–24, 1989.

[2] A. Willig, M. Kubisch, C. Hoene, and A. Wolisz, "Measurements of a wireless link in an industrial environment using an IEEE 802.11-compliant physical layer," *IEEE Transactions on Industrial Electronics*, vol. 49, no. 6, pp. 1265–1282, 2002.

[3] P. Ferrari, A. Flammini, D. Marioli, and A. Taroni, "IEEE802.11 sensor networking," *IEEE Transactions on Instrumentation and Measurement*, vol. 55, no. 2, pp. 615–619, 2006.

[4] C. Koulamas, S. Koubias, and G. Papadopoulos, "Using cut-through forwarding to retain the real-time properties of profibus over hybrid wired/wireless architectures," *IEEE Transactions on Industrial Electronics*, vol. 51, no. 6, pp. 1208–1217, 2004.

[5] H. Ye, G. C. Walsh, and L. G. Bushnell, "Real-time mixed-traffic wireless networks," *IEEE Transactions on Industrial Electronics*, vol. 48, no. 5, pp. 883–890, 2001.

[6] "IEEE 802.15.4-2003 MAC and PHY specifications for low-rate wireless personal area networks," 2003.

[7] "BT SIG, Specification of the Bluetooth System," 2004, http://www.bluetooth.org/.

[8] T. Lennvall, S. Svensson, and F. Hekland, "A comparison of WirelessHART and ZigBee for industrial applications," in *Proceedings of the 7th IEEE International Workshop on Factory Communication Systems (WFCS '08)*, pp. 85–88, May 2008.

[9] D. Johnson, D. Maltz, and J. Broch, "The dynamic source routing protocol for mobile ad hoc networks," IETF MANET Working Group, draft-ietfmanet-dsr-03.txt, November 1999.

[10] C. E. Perkins and E. M. Royer, "Ad-hoc on demand distance vector routing," IETF MANET Working Group, draft-ietfmanet-aodv-05.txt, March 2000.

[11] K. Kim, S. D. Park, G. Montenegro, and S. Yoo, "6LoWPAN ad hoc on demand distance vector routing (LOAD)," draft-daniel-6lowpan-load-adhocrouting-01, IETF Internet Draft (Work in progress), July 2005.

[12] G. Montenegro, "AODV for IEEE 802.15.4 networks," draft-montenegro-lowpan-aodv-00, IETF Internet Draft (Work in progress), July 2005.

[13] I. Chakeres and L. Klein-Berndt, "AODVjr, AODV simplified," *Mobile Computing and Communications Review*, vol. 6, no. 3, pp. 100–101, 2002.

[14] "TinyAODV implementation, TinyOS source code repository," http://cvs.sourcefourge.net/viewcvs.py/tinyos/tinyos-x/contrib/hsn/.

[15] C. E. Perkins, E. Belding-Royer, and I. Chakeres, "Ad hoc on-demand distance vector (AODV) routing," draft-perkins-manet-adovbis-01, IETF Internet Draft (Work in progress), February 2004.

[16] C. Gomez, P. Salvatella, O. Alonso, and J. Paradells, "Adapting AODV for IEEE 802.15.4 mesh sensor networks: theoretical discussion and performance evaluation in a real environment," in *Proceedings of the International Symposium on a World of Wireless, Mobile and Multimedia Networks (WoWMoM '06)*, pp. 159–167, June 2006.

[17] "MOTE-KIT2400 Datasheet," http://www.xbow.com/.

[18] J. Elson, L. Girod, and D. Estrin, "Fine-grained network time synchronization using reference broad-casts," in *Proceedings of the 5th symposium on Operating systems design and implementation (OSDI '02)*, December 2002.

[19] M. Maroti, B. Kusy, G. Simon, and A. Ledeczi, "The flooding time synchronization protocol," in *Proceedings of the Second International Conference on Embedded Networked Sensor Systems (SenSys '04)*, pp. 39–49, November 2004.

2

Fast Detection Method in Cooperative Cognitive Radio Networks

Zhengyi Li, Lin Liu, and Chi Zhou

Department of Electrical and Computer Engineering, Illinois Institute of Technology, Chicago, IL 60626, USA

Correspondence should be addressed to Chi Zhou, zhouc@ece.iit.edu

Academic Editor: Hsiao Hwa Chen

Cognitive Radio (CR) technology improves the utilization of spectrum highly via opportunistic spectrum sharing, which requests fast detection as the spectrum utilization is dynamic. Taking into consideration the characteristic of wireless channels, we propose a fast detection scheme for a cooperative cognitive radio network, which consists of multiple CRs and a central control office. Specifically, each CR makes individual detection decision using the sequential probability ratio test combined with Neyman Pearson detection with respect to a specific observation window length. The proposed method upper bounds the detection delay. In addition, a weighted K out of N fusion rule is also proposed for the central control office to reach fast global decision based on the information collected from CRs, with more weights assigned for CRs with good channel conditions. Simulation results show that the proposed scheme can achieve fast detection while maintaining the detection accuracy.

1. Introduction

In the traditional management of licensed spectrum, users usually pay and have the exclusive access of spectrum with a certain level of Quality of Service (QoS) guarantee. On one hand, the spectrum is getting more and more crowded as the number of wireless devices increases drastically. However, on the other hand, the utilization of spectrum at any given time is low. Figure 1 shows a measurement of 30M–3GHz spectrum utilization. We can see that a lot of spectrum bands are vacant. Therefore, it would be efficient to allow unlicensed users to share spectrum with licensed users by using a vacant frequency band.

Cognitive Radio technology is developed to utilize these white spaces intelligently [1, 2]. FCC Spectrum Policy Task Force published a new spectrum management policy, open access or license exempted model, in 2002, to allow unlicensed user to use the opportunistic spectrum. As the transition from analog to digital television is complete, there are vacant channels (white spaces) in every media market [3]. Accordingly, the FCC announced a Notice of Proposed Rule Making (NPRM) on 13 May 2004, which proposed "to allow unlicensed radio transmitters to operate in the broadcast TV spectrum at locations where that spectrum is not being used". Seen as the secondary user, the cognitive radio (CR) must avoid interfering with primary user (PU), that is, licensed user, while sharing the licensed band with the PU. Therefore, cognitive radio needs to sense the spectrum to detect the existence of PU, identify the white spaces of spectrum, and adapt its transmission to one of the white spaces to avoid interfering with PU.

Detecting the vacant bands of the spectrum is the very first step but very crucial in Cognitive Radio technology. There are three major digital signal processing techniques that could be used to detect the existence of PU: matched filtering, energy detection, and cyclostationary feature detection [4, 5]. Among those, energy detector has been used widely due to its simplicity and easy implementation [6]. As a radio device, a single CR may suffer severe shadowing or multipath fading with respect to primary transmitter so that it cannot detect the existence of PU even in its vicinities. In addition, there exists a hidden-node problem, in which a CR may be too far from the PU to detect the existence, but close to the primary receiver to interfere with the reception if transmited. Cooperative sensing provides a solution to the challenges mentioned above [7, 8]. In cooperative sensing, multiple cognitive radios cooperate to reach an optimal global decision by exchanging and combining individual local sensing results. Allowing multiple CRs to cooperate, cooperative sensing can increase the detection probability, reduce the detection time, and achieve the diversity gain [9–18].

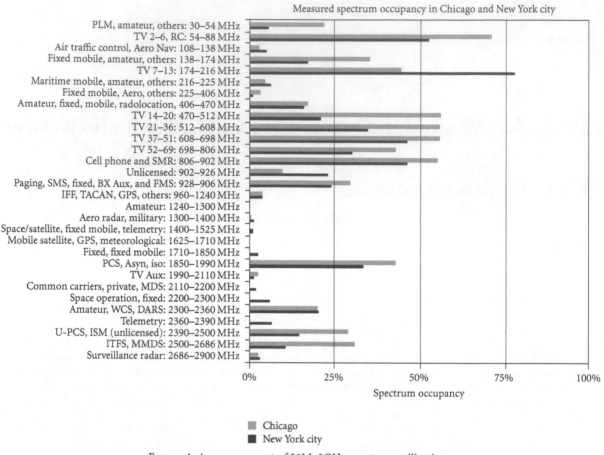

FIGURE 1: A measurement of 30M–3GHz spectrum utilization.

Due to the fading and noisy wireless channel, a large number of samples are needed for accurate detection. However, the spectrum utilization is dynamic, which requests fast detection to enable opportunistic sharing. In this paper, we propose a fast detection scheme in a cooperative cognitive radio network, which consists N CRs and a central control office. Each CR makes individual detection decision and then forwards its decision and the average signal to noise radio (SNR) to the central control office, which will make a global detection decision based on the collected data from CRs in the network. Then the central control office broadcasts the global detection decision to all the CRs. The proposed scheme consists of two folds: the first is to propose Sequential Probability Ratio Test (SPRT) method with a truncated window to upper bound the detection time at individual CR, while satisfying the detection accuracy requirements; the second is to propose a weighted K out of N fusion rule, which assigns more weights for CRs with good channel conditions, at the central control office to speed up the global decision making by using less number of individual decisions. Simulation results show that the proposed scheme can achieve fast detection while maintaining the detection accuracy.

The remaining contents are organized as follows. In Section 2, we discuss the system model. Section 3 presents the proposed fast detection scheme. In Section 4, simulation results are presented. In the end, we give the conclusion.

2. System Model

We consider a cognitive network, which consists of N CRs and a central control office. Each CR is equipped with an energy detector to individually detect the existence of PU by measuring the received SNR. Once the detection decision is reached by a CR, the CR transmits its decision along with the average received SNR to the central control office for global decision making. Serving as a fusion center, the central control office applies some fusion rule to its collected data and reach the global detection decision. Then the central control office broadcasts the global detection decision to all the CRs. Widely adopted Ad hoc On-demand Distance Vector (AODV) routing protocol [19] is used over a default clear channel for information exchange between the CRs and the central control office. The default channel may be selected among several predetermined channels.

In this paper, we use the log-normal shadowing path loss model:

$$P_r(d) = P_0(d_0) + 10 \cdot n \cdot \text{Log}(d_0 \setminus d) + X(0, \delta), \quad (1)$$

where $P_r(d)$ is the received signal power at distance d, $P_0(d_0)$ is the received power at the reference point d_0, n is the path loss exponent, and $X(0, \delta)$ is normal shadowing random variable with zero mean and δ standard variance in dB.

We summarize the major notations which will be used in the paper in Table 1.

3. Fast Detection Scheme

In this section, a fast detection scheme is proposed and discussed in details. SPRT with truncated window is proposed for individual detection, followed by a weighted K out of N fusion rule for the central control office to reach quick global decision.

3.1. Individual Detection. Fast and accurate individual detection is a must. To achieve desired detection accuracy, multiple samples need to be taken due to the time-varying wireless links. One approach is to take a certain amount of samples and then make a one-time decision, such as Neyman Pearson method [20]. Another approach is sequential detection, that is, the detection decision criterion will be checked whenever one new sample is taken, such as Sequential Probability Ratio Test (SPRT) [21]. Neyman Pearson method has a fixed detection delay, while SPRT usually takes less-detection time on average but may take long delay though with small probability. We propose to combine these two approaches together to take advantages of the two. Specifically, we propose to impose a truncated window to SPRT so that the detection delay is bounded. When the number of the samples is less than the window size, original SPRT is used to do the sequential detection. If the sequential detection cannot reach decision when the window size is reached, Neyman Pearson method will be used to make the final decision. The proposed SPRT with truncated window achieves smaller detection delay compared with SPRT and Neyman Pearson method.

3.1.1. Sequential Probability Ratio Test. We define two hypotheses, specified as follows:

$$H_0: \text{the primary user does not exist,}$$
$$H_1: \text{the primary user does exist.} \tag{2}$$

When a CR observes a new sample from energy detector, it will compute the cumulative sum of the log-likelihood ratio. We assume all samples are i.i.d. Let y_i be the received power from the ith observed sample, and then the log-likelihood ratio for the sample is

$$l(y_i) = \ln \frac{pdf(y_i \mid H_1)}{pdf(y_i \mid H_0)}. \tag{3}$$

When H_0 is true, that is, the PU does not exist, y_i is just the noise power. When H_1 is true, that is, the PU does exist, y_i is the received signal power plus the noise power. Let $\text{noise}(i)$ be the AWGN noise for the ith sample with zero mean and variance δ_n^2. Then y_i is normal distributed

$$\text{If } H_0 \text{ is true: } y_i = \text{noise}(i) \sim \text{Normal}(0, \delta_n^2),$$
$$\text{If } H_1 \text{ is true: } y_i = u + \text{noise}(i) \sim \text{Normal}(u, \delta_n^2), \tag{4}$$

where u is the signal power. Therefore, the log-likelihood ratio for the sample is

$$l(y_i) = \frac{u y_i}{\delta_n^2} - \frac{u}{2\delta_n^2}. \tag{5}$$

TABLE 1: Notation table.

λ_0, λ_1:	two stopping bounds in SPRT
$P_{m,\text{sprt}}$:	miss-detection probability in SPRT
$P_{d,\text{sprt}}$:	detection probability in SPRT
$P_{f,\text{sprt}}$:	false alarm probability in SPRT
$P_{d,\text{NP}}$:	detection probability in NP
$P_{f,\text{NP}}$:	false alarm probability in NP
P_{dd}:	detection probability in SPRT-TW
P_{ff}:	false alarm probability in SPRT-TW
$P(H_0)$:	statistic probability of H_0
$P(H_1)$:	statistic probability of H_1
w:	window size
I_i:	individual decision
α_i:	assigned weight value
SNR_i:	received SNR of the ith CR
d_0:	reference distance
n:	path loss exponent
$P_0(d_0)$:	received power at reference distance
P_{rc}:	confidence probability

The cumulative sum of the log-likelihood ratio can be written in the sequential way as

$$L(Y_i) = L(Y_{i-1}) + l(y_i), \tag{6}$$

where

$$L(Y_0) = 0. \tag{7}$$

It can be also written as

$$L(Y_i) = \sum_{k=1}^{i} l(y_k). \tag{8}$$

According to (5), we have

$$L(Y_i) = \sum_{k=1}^{i} l(y_k) = \frac{u}{\delta_n^2} \sum_{k=1}^{i} y_k - \frac{iu}{2\delta_n^2}. \tag{9}$$

The cumulative sum of the log-likelihood ratio will be compared with two stopping bounds, λ_0 and λ_1, to make decision. When the cumulative sum $L(Y_i)$ is larger than λ_1, we accept H_1 hypothesis and the detection process stops. If the cumulative sum $L(Y_i)$ is less than λ_0, we accept H_0 hypothesis and the detection process also stops. However, when $L(Y_i)$ lies between these two bounds, a new sample will be taken and the cumulative sum will be updated and compared with the bounds. The sequential detection process continues until it stops.

These two stopping bounds are set to satisfy the required miss-detection probability $P_{m,\text{sprt}}$ and false alarm probability $P_{f,\text{sprt}}$. They can be approximated as [21]

$$\lambda_0 \approx \ln \frac{P_{m,\text{sprt}}}{1 - P_{f,\text{sprt}}},$$
$$\lambda_1 \approx \ln \frac{1 - P_{m,\text{sprt}}}{P_{f,\text{sprt}}}. \tag{10}$$

Let T be the detection time. We could obtain expected detection time:

$$E(T \mid H_1) = \frac{\left(1 - P_{m,\mathrm{sprt}}\right)\lambda_1 + P_{m,\mathrm{sprt}}\lambda_0}{E(l(y_i) \mid H_1)},$$

$$E(T \mid H_0) = \frac{\left(1 - P_{f,\mathrm{sprt}}\right)\lambda_0 + P_{f,\mathrm{sprt}}\lambda_1}{E(l(y_i) \mid H_0)}. \tag{11}$$

3.1.2. Proposed SPRT with Truncated Window. The sequential detection process is random and may take a very long time before it stops. In order to put an upper bound on the detection time, we impose a truncated window with size w to SPRT. If SPRT cannot stop within w samples, instead of taking more samples, we apply Neyman Pearson (NP) method to reach immediate decision while achieving certain false alarm probability $P_{f,\mathrm{NP}}$ and detection probability $P_{d,\mathrm{NP}}$ with w samples.

The proposed SPRT with truncated window (SPRT-TW) scheme is summarized as follows:

$$L(Y_i) \geq \lambda_1: \text{Accept } H_1,$$

$$L(Y_i) \leq \lambda_0: \text{Accept } H_0,$$

$$\lambda_0 < L(Y_i) < \lambda_1 \text{ and } i < w: \text{Continue sampling},$$

$$\lambda_0 < L(Y_i) < \lambda_1 \text{ and } i = w: \text{Apply NP method}. \tag{12}$$

Therefore, the individual detection probability P_{dd} and the individual false alarm probability P_{ff} for the proposed SPRT-TW could be written as, according to Bayes' Rule,

$$P_{dd} = P_{d,\mathrm{NP}}(w) \cdot P(T > w) + P_{d,\mathrm{sprt}} \cdot P(T \leq w),$$

$$P_{ff} = P_{f,\mathrm{NP}}(w) \cdot P(T > w) + P_{f,\mathrm{sprt}} \cdot P(T \leq w), \tag{13}$$

where $P(T > w)$ is the probability that the CR does not reach a decision within window size w samples and $P(T \leq w)$ is the probability that the CR reaches a decision within window size w. According to the rule of total probability, the two probabilities can be expressed as

$$P(T > w) = P(T > w \mid H_1) \cdot P(H_1)$$
$$\qquad\quad + P(T > w H_0) \cdot P(H_0),$$

$$P(T \leq w) = P(T \leq w \mid H_1) \cdot P(H_1)$$
$$\qquad\quad + P(T \leq w \mid H_0) \cdot P(H_0) \tag{14}$$

where $P(H_0)$ and $P(H_1)$ are statistical probabilities for the two hypothesis and

$$P(T > w \mid H_1) = \prod_{i=1}^{w} P(\lambda_0 < L(Y_i) \leq \lambda_1 \mid H_1),$$

$$P(T > w \mid H_0) = \prod_{i=1}^{w} P(\lambda_0 < L(Y_i) \leq \lambda_1 \mid H_0), \tag{15}$$

$$P(T \leq w \mid H_1) = 1 - P(T > w \mid H_1),$$

$$P(T \leq w \mid H_0) = 1 - P(T > w \mid H_0).$$

From (9), $L(Y_i)$ is the sum of normally distributed random variables. Therefore, $L(Y_i)$ follows normal distribution

If H_0 is true: $L(Y_i) \sim \text{Normal}(-b, a^2 i \delta_n^2)$,

If H_1 is true: $L(Y_i) \sim \text{Normal}(aui - b, a^2 i \delta_n^2)$, $\tag{16}$

where

$$a = \frac{u}{\delta_n^2},$$

$$b = \frac{iu^2}{2\delta_n^2}. \tag{17}$$

The expected detection delay for SPRT-TW could be obtained:

$$E(T \mid H_1) = 1 \cdot P(T \leq 1 \mid H_1)$$

$$\qquad + \sum_{i=2}^{w} i \cdot P(T > i - 1 \mid H_1) P(T = i \mid H_1)$$

$$\qquad + w \cdot P(T > w \mid H_1) P_{d,\mathrm{NP}}(w),$$

$$E(T \mid H_0) = 1 \cdot P(T \leq 1 \mid H_0)$$

$$\qquad + \sum_{i=2}^{w} i \cdot P(T > i - 1 \mid H_0) P(T = i \mid H_0)$$

$$\qquad + w \cdot P(T > w \mid H_0) P_{f,\mathrm{NP}}(w), \tag{18}$$

where

$$P(T > w \mid H_1) = 1 - P(\lambda_0 < L(Y_w) \leq \lambda_1 \mid H_1),$$

$$P(T > w \mid H_0) = 1 - P(\lambda_0 < L(Y_w) \leq \lambda_1 \mid H_0). \tag{19}$$

Based on (13)–(17), the expected delay could be obtained easily.

3.2. Weighted K out of N Fusion Rule. Data fusion is a technique used to efficiently combine the data for decision making. Due to its simplicity and effectiveness, K out of N fusion rule has been widely used in many applications including cognitive radio [7, 22]. We could also apply the K out of N fusion rule in the central control office to reach the global detection decision. Similar to [23], the global decision rule could be specified as

$$\sum_{N} I_i \geq K: \text{Accept } H_1,$$

$$\sum_{N} I_i < K: \text{Accept } H_0, \tag{20}$$

where I_i is the indicator of individual detection decision for CR_i. $I_i = 1$ if CR_i accepts H_1 and $I_i = 0$ if CR_i accepts H_0.

The above K out of N fusion detection rule implies that each data has the same credibility as others by simply adding the individual detection decisions together. However, this is not true in wireless communication systems. For example, suppose two CRs correctly detect the existence of the PU with one CR located very close to the PU and the other located far away from the PU. The nearby CR receives strong signal and quickly detects the PU, while the far-away CR receives very weak signal and takes much longer time to reach the decision. Obviously, the detection decision from the nearby CR is more reliable, which is not taken into account in the original K out of N fusion rule. Therefore, we propose a weighted K out of N fusion rule by assigning bigger weight to the CR with good signal reception (i.e., good channel condition). Then the global decision rule is specified as

$$\sum_N \alpha_i I_i \geq K: \text{Accept } H_1,$$
$$\sum_N \alpha_i I_i < K: \text{Accept } H_0, \tag{21}$$

where α_i is the weight for individual decision of CR_i. There are many ways to design the weight α_i to reflect the credibility of individual decision. In this paper, as an example, we design the weight as a linear function of received SNR

$$\alpha_i = A \cdot SNR_i + B, \tag{22}$$

where A and B are some constants.

In the weighted K out of N fusion rule, the individual detection decisions under good channel conditions are given more weights in the global decision making. Therefore, the global decision making requests a small number of CRs if those CRs have good channel condition or a large number of CRs if they have bad channel condition. Since those CRs with good channel condition also have smaller detection time using SPRT-TW and consequently their decisions arrive at the central control office faster, the global detection time can be reduced when most CRs have good channel condition.

4. Simulation Results

In this section, we first consider the individual detection performance for each CR, and then evaluate the weighted K out of N fusion rule for global detection. For the log-normal shadowing path loss model, the shadowing random variable $X(0, \delta)$, adds the randomness to the results, which complicates the illustration and insight discussion. Therefore, in the simulation for the individual detection, we first consider the log-distance path loss model without fading and then generalize it to slow fading scenario. The simulation results in the no fading scenario help understand the whole innovative fast detection scheme. Throughout simulation, we set the following parameters: the noise follows normal distribution with zero mean and the noise power set as -120 dBm; the path loss exponent $n = 4$; $P_0(d_0)$ is set as 20 dBm; reference distance is set $d_0 = 1$ m; the statistic probabilities $P(H_0) = P(H_1) = 0.5$.

4.1. Individual Detection Scenario 1: No Fading. With no fading, the path loss model is simplified to the log-distance path loss model and the average received signal power is

$$u = P_r(d) = P_0(d_0) + 10 \cdot n \cdot \text{Log}(d_0 \setminus d). \tag{23}$$

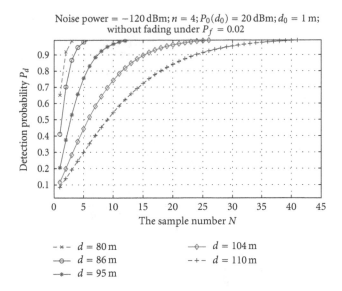

Noise power $= -120$ dBm; $n = 4$; $P_0(d_0) = 20$ dBm; $d_0 = 1$ m; without fading under $P_f = 0.02$

$-*-$ $d = 80$ m	$-\diamond-$ $d = 104$ m
$-\circ-$ $d = 86$ m	$-+-$ $d = 110$ m
$-*-$ $d = 95$ m	

FIGURE 2: Traditional NP method: under fixed $P_{f,NP} = 0.02$.

CRs with longer distance to the PU receive weaker signal power, therefore, the distance can be used to represent the received signal strength or the received SNR.

Note that the detection performance depends on the window size w and received signal power u. Intuitively, the larger the window size is, the better the detection performs; the stronger the received signal power u is, the better the detection performs. We first examine the performance of traditional Neyman Pearson (NP) method when varying the number of samples (i.e., the window size w in SPRT-TW). We fix the false alarm probability for NP method as 0.05. Figure 2 shows how the detection probability of NP method varies with the number of samples for CRs at different distance from the PU. It is shown that the detection probability increases as the number of samples increases and the CR with smaller distance (i.e., stronger signal) achieves higher detection probability for any given number of samples. As shown in Figure 2, the traditional NP method needs up to 42 samples to reach 0.99 detection probability for CRs at the distance 110 m.

We set the two stopping bounds of SPRT based on the miss-detection probability $P_{m,sprt} = 0.01$ and false alarm probability $P_{f,sprt} = 0.02$ and simulate the proposed SPRT-TW. Figure 3 shows how the detection probability P_{dd} of SPRT-TW varies with the window size for CRs with different distance. Figure 3 has the same trend as Figure 2. Shown in Figure 3, the CR at distance 110 m (received SNR is 58.343 dB) takes most window size $w = 18$ to meet 0.99 detection probability while the CR located at $d = 80$ m (received SNR is 63.8764 dB) only needs 2 samples on average to reach the same detection probability. Compared with the NP method, SPRT-TW takes less samples to reach the same detection probability (e.g., 42 samples for NP method and 18 samples for SPRT-TW at the same CR at $d = 110$ m).

Figure 4 shows the corresponding false alarm probability P_{ff} of SPRT-TW as the window size varies. It is shown that

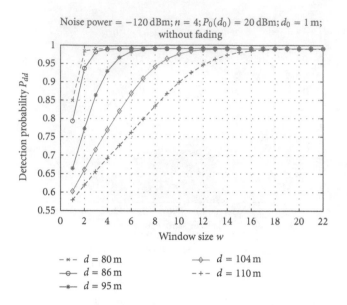

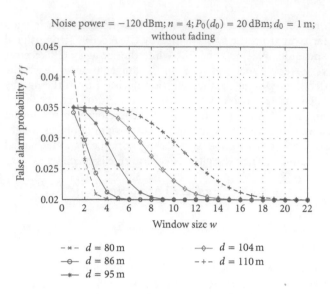

FIGURE 3: Detection probability P_{dd} versus Window size.

FIGURE 4: False alarm probability P_{ff} versus Window size

P_{ff} decreases with the window size and the CR at the smaller distance achieves smaller P_{ff} for any given window size. Shown in Figure 4, the CR at $d = 110$ m needs window size $w = 20$ to reach 0.02 false alarm probability, which takes only 4 window size for the CR at $d = 80$ m.

From Figures 3 and 4, we see that the window size needs to be carefully selected to meet the desired detection performance. In addition, the selection of window size also depends on the channel condition (i.e., received SNR). In order to minimize the detection delay, we need to select the minimum window size w that can meet the performance requirements.

We further compare the detection delay among NP method, SPRT, and our proposed SPRT-TW. Figure 5 shows that the NP method needs the longest delay and our proposed SPRT-TW has smallest delay. The simulation results validate that our SPRT-TW is indeed a fast detection scheme compared to NP method and original SPRT.

4.2. Individual Detection Scenario 2: Slow Fading.

In this section, we consider the log-normal shadowing path loss model, shown in (1). Because of the random fading factor $X \sim N(0, \delta(\text{dB}))$, we define a confidence probability Prc,

$$\text{Prc} = P(P_r(d) > \varepsilon), \qquad (24)$$

where the $P_r(d)$ is received power and ε is the power threshold. Prc describes how much confidence we have when the receive power is stronger than the power threshold. In the simulation, we set $\delta = 8$ dB for shadowing and $n = 4$ for path loss exponent.

We set the threshold power as -56.1236 dBm and plot how the confidence probability varies with distance in Figure 6. It is shown that the confidence probability decreases with distance. To achieve 0.9 confidence level, the CR has to locate closer than 45 m from the PU. Without fading, however, the CR can locate at far as $d = 80$ m to receive

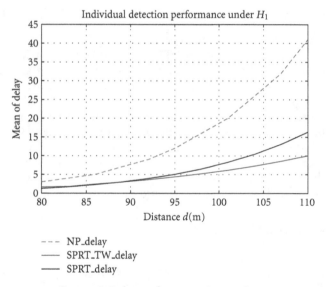

FIGURE 5: Delay performance Comparison.

-56.1236 dBm power. Therefore, the CR at $d = 45$ m under fading condition should use the same window size as the CR at $d = 80$ without fading. We also try various threshold power and identify the distances for no fading scenario and fading scenario which use the same window size to achieve similar detection performance. The results are shown in Table 2 under 0.9 confidence level. It is shown that the fading has negative impacts for the detection performance.

4.3. Weighted K out of N Fusion Rule.

In this section, we compare our proposed weighted K out of N fusion rule with the original K out of N fusion rule. From [23], we know that K is usually chosen as $N/2$ to minimize the total error probability, shown in Figure 7.

We randomly generate $N = 100$ CRs according to a uniform distribution at the distance from the PU ranging

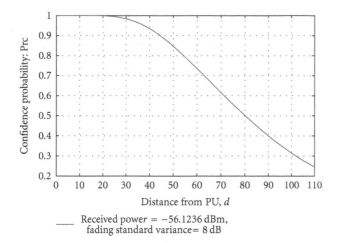

FIGURE 6: Confidence probability under threshold -56.1236 dBm versus Distance d.

TABLE 2: Comparing the distance from PU under fading and no fading.

Threshold power (dBm)	No fading	Slow fading
-56.1236	80 (m)	45 (m)
-57.3799	86 (m)	47 (m)
-59.1089	95 (m)	52 (m)
-60.6813	104 (m)	57 (m)
-61.6557	110 (m)	62 (m)

from 80 m to 110 m. We use the linear weight function to assign the weight to each CR. For fair comparison, we set the values A and B such as the expectation of weights is equal to 1 but the variance of the weights can vary. Figures 8 and 9 show the weight assigned for the CRs at different distance with the mean weight as 1 but the weight variance as 0.5 and 0.02, respectively. It is shown that the nearby CR is assigned with higher weight compared to the far-away CR due to the good channel condition. In addition, the weights for CRs at different distances differ more when the weight variance is larger.

We compare the minimum number of individual decisions needed to reach the global decision. We pick $K = N/2 = 50$ so that the total error probability can be minimized in the original K out of N Fusion Rule. For the original fusion rule, each individual decision is treated the same with weight 1, therefore, minimum 50 individual detection decisions with all positive detections are needed. In the weighted fusion rule, the individual decision is treated differently. To minimize the number of individual decisions, we need to include the CRs with the best channel conditions (i.e., the CRs closest to the PU). Example results are shown in Table 3. It is shown that the weighted fusion rule needs less minimum number of individual decisions. In addition, the more the weight variance is, the less number of individual decisions the fusion needs. Since those decisions come from the CRs with best channel conditions and consequently arrive at the

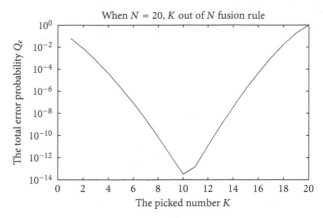

FIGURE 7: Total error probability versus value K when $N = 20$.

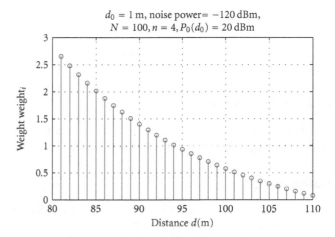

FIGURE 8: Assigned weight for CRs at different distance when weight variance = 0.5.

TABLE 3: Comparing the original and the weighted fusions.

$N = 100$	Original fusion	Weighted fusion
variance = 0	$M = 50$	$M = 50$ (same as the original)
variance = 0.02	$M = 50$	$M = 44$
variance = 0.5	$M = 50$	$M = 26$

central control office quickest, the global decision can be reached quickly without waiting for more decisions.

5. Conclusion

In this paper, we have proposed a fast detection scheme, SPRT-TW for individual detection and weighted K out of N fusion rule for global detection, for cooperative cognitive radio networks. It is shown that the proposed SPRT-TW takes the least detection time compared with traditional NP detection method and the original SPRT and the weighted fusion rule in general takes less numbers of individual decisions (consequently faster) to reach the global decision compared to the original fusion rule. Our scheme takes into consideration the characteristic of wireless channels. For the

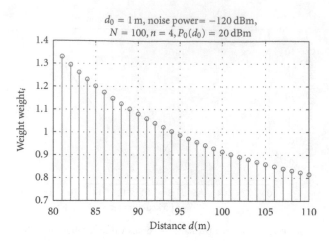

FIGURE 9: Assigned weight for CRs at different distance when weight variance = 0.02.

future work, we will try to derive the optimal design for the weight assignment.

Acknowledgments

This paper was supported by AFOSR under Grant FA9550-09-0630 and by NSF under Grant CNS 0619693.

References

[1] J. Mitola, *Cognitive Radio*, Licentiate thesis, KTH, Stockholm, Sweden, 1999.

[2] S. Haykin, "Cognitive radio: brain-empowered wireless communications," *IEEE Journal on Selected Areas in Communications*, vol. 23, no. 2, pp. 201–220, 2005.

[3] M. A. Sturza and F. Ghazvinian, "White Spaces Engineering Study: can cognitive radio technology operating in the TV white spaces completely protect licensed TV broadcasting?" New America Foundation Wireless Future Program, working paper no.16, January 2007.

[4] K. Watanabe, K. Ishibashi, and R. Kohno, "Performance of cognitive radio technologies in the presence of primary radio systems," in *Proceedings of the 18th Annual IEEE International Symposium on Personal, Indoor and Mobile Radio Communications (PIMRC '07)*, September 2007.

[5] D. Cabric, S. M. Mishra, and R. W. Brodersen, "Implementation issues in spectrum sensing for cognitive radios," in *Proceedings of the of the 38th Asilomar Conference on Signals, Systems and Computers*, pp. 772–776, November 2004.

[6] F. F. Digham, M.-S. Alouini, and M. K. Simon, "On the energy detection of unknown signals over fading channels," in *Proceedings of the International Conference on Communications (ICC '03)*, vol. 5, pp. 3575–3579, May 2003.

[7] E. C. Y. Peh, Y.-C. Liang, and Y. L. Guan, "Optimization of cooperative sensing in cognitive radio networks: a sensing-throughput tradeoff view," in *Proceedings of the IEEE International Conference on Communications (ICC '09)*, pp. 1–5, June 2009.

[8] G. Ganesan and Y. Li, "Cooperative spectrum sensing in cognitive radio networks," in *Proceedings of the 1st IEEE International Symposium on New Frontiers in Dynamic Spectrum Access Networks (DySPAN '05)*, pp. 137–143, November 2005.

[9] J. N. Laneman, D. N. C. Tse, and G. W. Wornell, "Cooperative diversity in wireless networks: efficient protocols and outage behavior," *IEEE Transactions on Information Theory*, vol. 50, no. 12, pp. 3062–3080, 2004.

[10] G. Ganesan and Y. Li, "Cooperative spectrum sensing in cognitive radio—part I: two user networks," *IEEE Transactions on Wireless Communications*, vol. 6, no. 6, pp. 2204–2213, 2007.

[11] G. Ganesan and Y. Li, "Cooperative spectrum sensing in cognitive radio—part II: multi-user networks," *IEEE Transactions on Wireless Communications*, vol. 6, no. 6, pp. 2214–2222, 2007.

[12] G. Ganesan and Y. Li, "Agility improvement through cooperative diversity in cognitive radio," in *Proceedings of the IEEE Global Telecommunications Conference (GLOBECOM '05)*, vol. 5, pp. 2505–2509, 2005.

[13] Z. Jiang, X. Zhengguang, W. Furong, H. Benxiong, and Z. Bo, "Double threshold energy detection of cooperative spectrum sensing in cognitive radio," in *Proceedings of the 3rd International Conference on Cognitive Radio Oriented Wireless Networks and Communications (CrownCom '08)*, pp. 1–5, 2008.

[14] J.-W. Ho, M. Wright, and S. K. Das, "Fast detection of replica node attacks in mobile sensor networks using sequential analysis," in *Proceedings of the 28th Conference on Computer Communications (INFOCOM '09)*, pp. 1773–1781, June 2009.

[15] Z. Quan, S. Cui, and A. H. Sayed, "Optimal linear cooperation for spectrum sensing in cognitive radio networks," *IEEE Journal on Selected Topics in Signal Processing*, vol. 2, no. 1, pp. 28–40, 2008.

[16] L.-H. He, X.-Z. Xie, X.-T. Dong, and T. Zhou, "Twice-cooperative spectrum sensing in cognitive radio systems," in *Proceedings of the International Conference on Wireless Communications, Networking and Mobile Computing (WiCOM '08)*, 2008.

[17] K. B. Letaief and W. Zhang, "Cooperative communications for cognitive radio networks," *Proceedings of the IEEE*, vol. 97, no. 5, pp. 878–893, 2009.

[18] A. Ghasemi and E. S. Sousa, "Collaborative spectrum sensing in cognitive radio networks," in *Proceedings of the 1st IEEE International Symposium on New Frontiers in Dynamic Spectrum Access Networks (DySPAN '05)*, pp. 131–136, November 2005.

[19] RFC 3561: Ad hoc On-Demand Distance Vector (AODV) Routing, The Internet Society, July 2003.

[20] J. Neyman and E. Pearson, "On the problem of the most efficient tests of statistical hypotheses," *Philosophical Transactions of the Royal Society of London*, pp. 289–337, 1933.

[21] K. P. Varshney, *Distributed Detection and Data Fusion*, Springer, New York, NY, USA, 1997.

[22] W. Wenzhong, Z. Weixia, Z. Zheng, and Y. Yabin, "Detection fusion by hierarchy rule for cognitive radio," in *Proceedings of the 3rd International Conference on Cognitive Radio Oriented Wireless Networks and Communications (CrownCom '08)*, pp. 1–5, May 2008.

[23] W. Zhang, R. K. Mallik, and K. B. Letaief, "Cooperative spectrum sensing optimization in cognitive radio networks," in *Proceedings of the IEEE International Conference on Communications (ICC '08)*, pp. 3411–3415, 2008.

3

Design of an IPTV Multicast System for Internet Backbone Networks

T. H. Szymanski[1, 2] and D. Gilbert[1]

[1] Department of Electrical and Computer Engineering, McMaster University, Hamilton, ON, Canada L8S 4K1
[2] Bell Canada Chair in Data Communications, McMaster University, Hamilton, ON, Canada L8S 4K1

Correspondence should be addressed to T. H. Szymanski, teds@mcmaster.ca

Academic Editor: Daniel Negru

The design of an IPTV multicast system for the Internet backbone network is presented and explored through extensive simulations. In the proposed system, a resource reservation algorithm such as RSVP, IntServ, or DiffServ is used to reserve resources (i.e., bandwidth and buffer space) in each router in an IP multicast tree. Each router uses an Input-Queued, Output-Queued, or Crosspoint-Queued switch architecture with unity speedup. A recently proposed *Recursive Fair Stochastic Matrix Decomposition* algorithm used to compute near-perfect transmission schedules for each IP router. The IPTV traffic is shaped at the sources using *Application-Specific Token Bucker Traffic Shapers*, to limit the burstiness of incoming network traffic. The IPTV traffic is shaped at the destinations using *Application-Specific Playback Queues*, to remove residual network jitter and reconstruct the original bursty IPTV video streams at each destination. All IPTV traffic flows are regenerated at the destinations with essentially zero delay jitter and essentially-perfect QoS. The destination nodes deliver the IPTV streams to the ultimate end users using the same IPTV multicast system over a regional Metropolitan Area Network. It is shown that all IPTV traffic is delivered with essentially-perfect end-to-end QoS, with deterministic bounds on the maximum delay and jitter on each video frame. Detailed simulations of an IPTV distribution system, multicasting several hundred high-definition IPTV video streams over several essentially saturated IP backbone networks are presented.

1. Introduction

Multimedia traffic such as IPTV and video-on-demand represent a rapidly growing segment of the total Internet traffic. According to Cisco [1, 2], global Internet traffic is nearly doubling every 2 years, and global capacity will have to increase 75 times over the decade 2002–2012 to keep up with the demand. Furthermore, video-based traffic such as IPTV [3] will represent 90% of global network loads in 2012. The US Federal Communication Commission (FCC) has required that all TV broadcasts occur in digital format in 2009, and the growing fraction of multimedia traffic threatens to overwhelm the current Internet infrastructure. According to [4], "*The United States will not be the first country to complete the transition to digital television... Luxembourg, the Netherlands, Finland, Andorra, Sweden, and Switzerland have all completed their transitions, utilizing the*

Digital Video Broadcasting—Terrestrial (DVB-T) standard. Transitions are now under way in more than 35 other countries." According to Cisco [5]: "*With the deployment of these new IPTV services, existing network infrastructures will be pushed to their limits.*" The congestion problems are already visible: "*Video is clogging the internet. How we choose to unclog it will have far-reaching implications*" [6]. Recognizing the problems, the US National Science Foundation initiated a major project called "*Global Initiative for Network Investigations*" (GENI), which is open to a complete "*clean slate*" redesign of Internet if necessary, in an attempt to address the problems [7, 8]. In summary, new technologies which support the efficient multicasting and broadcasting of multimedia services such as IPTV are essential.

In this paper, the design of an IPTV multicast system for Internet backbone networks is presented and explored through extensive simulations. An IPTV multicast system was first proposed in [9] based upon a theoretical foundation established in [10, 11]. Extensive simulations where presented for an 8-node multicast tree in [9], however the design or simulation of a multicast system for a real IP network topology was not presented.

In this paper, the design of a realistic IPTV multicast system for several real backbone IP networks described in [12] is presented. Exhaustive simulations confirm that the system can deliver several hundred IPTV packet streams over the Internet backbone networks with essentially zero delay jitter, essentially zero packet loss rate, and essentially-perfect end-to-end QoS for every provisioned multicast tree. In the proposed system, a resource-reservation algorithm such as RSVP, IntServ, or DiffServ is used to reserve resources such as buffer space and transmission capacity in each multicast router in each multicast tree. Each IP router then uses a recently proposed *Recursive Fair Stochastic Matrix Decomposition* scheduling algorithm [9, 10] to schedule the IPTV traffic streams through the router while meeting rigorous QoS guarantees, under the constraint of unity speedup.

Internet routers can use three basic switch architectures, the *Input-Queued (IQ)* switch, the *Output-Queued (OQ)* switch, or the *Combined Input and Crosspoint Queued (CIXQ)* switch. OQ switches can achieve optimal throughput but they require an internal speedup of O(N), which renders them impractical for large sizes. *Combined Input and Output Queued (CIOQ)* switches have also been proposed. These switches can also achieve 100% throughput, but they also require a speedup typically by a factor of 2 or 4, which is difficult to realize and which increases costs. CIXQ switches can also achieve 100% throughput with simpler scheduling algorithms, but they require many crosspoint queues in the switching matrix which increase costs. To minimize costs, many high capacity routers exploit some form of Input Queueing. Figure 1 illustrates a packet-switched IP router using an $N \times N$ *Input-Queued* (IQ) switch architecture. Each input port has N "*Virtual Output Queues*" (*VOQs*), and the switch has a total of N^2 *VOQs*. Figure 2 illustrates a packet-switched IP multicast tree, which consists of a tree of packet-switched IP routers as shown in Figure 1.

Many IP routers exploit a fixed-sized cell switching architecture. Variable-sized IP packets containing video data arrive at the input ports. Each IP packet is disassembled into small fixed-sized cells, which are stored in the appropriate *VOQ* at the input side of the switch. Typical cells can be between 64 and 256 bytes in length. At each input port j, each $VOQ(j,k)$ stores cells destined for output port k. The fixed-sized cells are scheduled for transmission across the switch in a series of time slots. The variable-sized IP packets are reconstructed at the output side of the router and are then transmitted to the next router in the multicast tree. In each time slot, a scheduling algorithm is used to compute a set of up to N cells to transfer across an IQ switch, subject to two constraints: (1) each input port transmits at most 1 cell from its N *VOQs*, and (2) each output port receives at most 1 cell from any *VOQ*. The set of cells to transmit per time slot can be represented as a permutation.

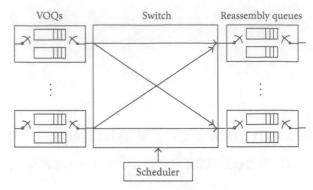

FIGURE 1: IQ switch.

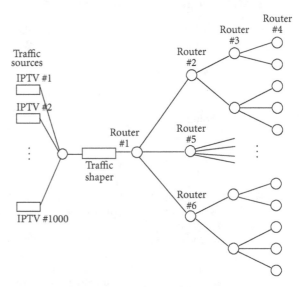

FIGURE 2: 2. IPTV Multicast tree.

Scheduling for IQ switches is known to be a difficult problem [13–27]. The difficulty is compounded when Quality-of-Service (QoS) constraints are added to the scheduling problem. It is has been shown that effective IPTV delivery requires low jitter [28–30]. The selection of a set of N cells to transfer per time-slot in an IQ switch is equivalent to finding a matching in a bipartite graph. Assuming link rates of 40 or 160 Gbps, the durations of a time-slot for a 64-byte cell are 12.8 and 3.2 nanoseconds, respectively. Therefore, schedulers for IQ switches must compute new bipartite graph matchings very quickly, typically at rates of 100–300 million matchings per second. Existing switch schedulers can be classified into two classes: (1) "*Dynamic schedulers*" which compute new bipartite matchings in every time-slot without any a priori knowledge of the long-term traffic demands on the switch, and (2) "*Guaranteed-Rate (GR) schedulers*" which periodically compute a sequence of F matchings to be used in F consecutive time slots called a "*scheduling frame*". The schedules can be reused repeatedly, and the schedule is recomputed when the long-term traffic demands of the switch are modified.

It is known that dynamic schedulers for IQ switches can achieve 100% throughput, if a *Maximum Weight Matching*

(*MWM*) algorithm is used to compute the matching for each time-slot, where the largest queues receive preferential service [13]. However, the *MWM* algorithm has complexity $O(N^3)$ work per time-slot and is considered intractable for use in real IP routers [13]. Therefore, existing dynamic schedulers typically use sub optimal heuristic schedulers, such as Parallel Iterative Matching or iSLIP [14]. However, due to the severe time constraints all heuristic schedulers have sub optimal throughput efficiencies and exhibit significant delay and jitter at high loads. The iSLIP algorithm used in the Cisco 1200 series routers is an iterative heuristic scheduler which can achieve throughput efficiencies as high as 80% for non uniform traffic patterns. However, the average queuing delay per cell can approach several thousand time slots at high loads, and the delay jitter can be equally high.

In this paper, a recently proposed *Recursive Fair Stochastic Matrix Decomposition* algorithm is used to schedule multicast IPTV traffic in each router in an IP multicast tree in a fully saturated IP network, and the performance is examined through extensive simulations. A resource-reservation protocol such as RSVP, IntServ, or DiffServ is used to maintain a traffic rate matrix for each IP router. (We note that while DiffServ does not use explicit resource reservation, DiffServ does use class-based weighted fair queueing, which effectively reserves bandwidth for each Diffserv traffic class.) Each traffic rate matrix is doubly sub stochastic or stochastic, and specifies the guaranteed traffic rates between every pair of *Input-Output* (IO) ports of the router. The traffic matrix in each router can then be mathematically decomposed to yield a sequence of bipartite graph matchings or permutations. Each matching configures the switch for one time-slot, and the sequence of matchings is guaranteed to deliver the IPTV stream through the IP router while providing rigorous QoS guarantees, under the constraint of unity speedup.

The *Recursive Fair Stochastic Matrix Decomposition (RFSMD)* algorithm proposed in [10] converts an admissible traffic rate matrix for a router into a quantized (integer) matrix with integer-valued elements, assuming a scheduling frame of length F time slots. The algorithm then recursively partitions the quantized matrix in a recursive and relatively fair manner, yielding a sequence of permutation matrices, also called permutations. The resulting sequence of permutations forms a "*frame transmission schedule*", for transmitting cells through the packet-switched IP router. The sequence of permutations in a frame transmission schedule can be repeatedly reused, as long as the traffic rate matrix remains unchanged. When the traffic rate matrix is updated by the RSVP, IntServ, or DiffServ algorithm, the frame transmission schedule can be recomputed. The RFSMD algorithm, along with appropriate traffic shaping at the sources, rigorously guarantees that every provisioned traffic flow achieves near-minimal delay and jitter and essentially-perfect end-to-end QoS, for all networks loads up to 100%. By "essentially-perfect QoS", we mean that every provisioned traffic flow can be delivered with zero packet loss rate, nearminimal end-to-end delay and zero network-introduced delay jitter. Theoretical bounds on the delay, jitter and QoS are presented in [10, 11] and are summarized in Section 4 of this paper.

In this paper, we apply the RFSMD scheduling algorithm to the problem of multicasting real IPTV traffic through multicast trees in several real IP backbone networks, to explore the feasibility of large-scale IPTV multicasting in IP networks.

Section 2 describes video traffic model. Section 3 describes some prior guaranteed-rate scheduling algorithms. Section 4 describes the low-jitter RFSMD scheduling algorithm in more depth. Section 5 describes the IP backbone networks and the IPTV multicast trees, and presents detailed simulation statistics. Section 6 contains concluding remarks.

2. Video Traffic Model

Cisco Systems estimates that several hundred video channels requiring up to 1 Gbps bandwidth may be distributed over the IP backbone to support emerging IPTV applications [5]. To gather realistic data for our simulations, a high-definition video stream entitled "*BBC Blue Planet*" available at the University of Arizona [31] website was processed. The video stream includes 61 K video frames which arrive at the rate of 24 video frames/sec. The minimum, mean, and maximum video frame sizes are 81, 21 K, 495 K bytes respectively, illustrating a very bursty behaviour.

We assume these video frames are disassembled into fixed-sized 64-byte cells before transmission into the IP multicast tree. These video frame sizes correspond to a mean of 328 cells per video frame, with a minimum and maximum of 2 and 7,735 cells per video frame, respectively. The single video stream has a compression ratio of 151, with a mean bit rate of about 4 Mbps, and a peak bit rate of 95 Mbps. To simplify the terminology, define this data to represent a single "*video channel*". A "*video stream*" consists of the aggregation of 1 or more video channels.

The Arizona website [31] provides video frame size statistics for a few high-definition video channels. In this paper, we assume 100 high-definition video channels are to be multicast in each multicast tree, each with a 4 Mbps average rate, for an aggregate stream traffic rate of approximately. 404 Mbps. To achieve the statistics for the 100 video channels used in our network simulations, the data for the video "*BBC Blue Planet*" was reused in a circular manner, with a randomly selected starting video frame for each channel.

Table 1 lists some properties of the single video channel and several aggregated video traffic streams. In Table 1, the ratio of the peak-to-mean rates is an indication of the burstiness of the traffic. The single channel has a peak-to-mean ratio of 23.5, indicating a high degree of burstiness. Referring to Table 1, the aggregated stream of 100 channels has an aggregate data rate of 404 Mbps, with a peak rate of 700 Mbps. The ratio of peak-to-mean rates is 1.73, indicating a considerable reduction in burstiness.

Figure 3 illustrates visually the effect of aggregation of multiple video channels on the burstiness of the aggregated video stream. Figure 3 illustrates the instantaneous normalized bandwidth versus time for the same aggregated streams. The mean rate of each stream has been normalized to 1, and the reduction in burstiness when many video channels are aggregated is evident.

TABLE 1: Statistics on aggregated traffic.

Channels	Mean Rate(Mbps)	Max Rate	Max/Mean	Standard Deviation	10% extra cap delay (sec)
1	4.04	95	23.5	6.68	97.1
10	40.4	165	4.08	21	45.4
100	404	700	1.73	69	4.35

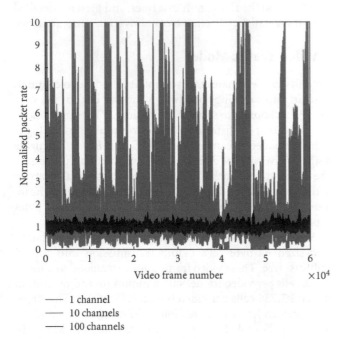

—— 1 channel
—— 10 channels
—— 100 channels

FIGURE 3: Burstiness of aggregated traffic.

Assume that video frames for any one video channel arrive at the root of a multicast tree at the fixed rate of 24 video frames per second. The arrival rate of video frames for the aggregated stream of 100 channels is therefore 2,400 video frames per second. The arriving traffic is quite bursty, as shown in Figure 3.

In this paper, we assume an *Application-Specific Token Bucket Traffic Shaper (ASTS)* module [9, 11] is used at the source to smoothen incoming bursty IPTV traffic to conform to an appropriate mean traffic rate with bounded burstiness. Cells are allowed to depart the ASTS at the maximum rate of 440 Mbps, when cells are available. The ASTS will introduce an *application-specific* delay at the source which is independent of the network. Referring to Figure 2, assume that the 100 video channels are available at the root of each IP multicast tree for distribution. The aggregated stream of 100 channels has an average data rate of 404 Mbps, and each IP multicast tree must be provisioned to support this traffic. In this paper, we assume that each IP multicast tree is provisioned such that the average data rate of the aggregated video stream consumes 90% of the provisioned tree link capacity, thereby providing 10% excess bandwidth for bursts. Therefore, each IP multicast tree must be provisioned to support about 440 Mbps of guaranteed rate traffic on every link in the tree. Given the line rate of 40 Gbps, the use

of 64-byte cells, and a scheduling frame of length $F = 1\,K$, then each time-slot reservation represents a bandwidth of approximately 40 Mbps. Therefore, a guaranteed rate of 440 Mbps requires the reservation of 11 cells per scheduling frame, or about 1% of the line rate. However, each backbone network has multiple IPTV multicast trees, between 9 and 16 trees in our simulations, so the fraction of multicast traffic on each link will be typically between 4% and 7% of the link capacity in our models. When bursts of cells arrive at the ASTS module, these cells will be temporarily stored, and will be released into the network at an average rate of 400 Mbps and a maximum data rate of 440 Mbps.

Referring to Figure 2, the router no.1 is the root of a multicast tree and implements a 1-to-3 multicasting of the cells. There are many nodes in an IP multicast tree, distributing content to potentially millions of end-users (i.e., households). Each destination node of the multicast tree has an *Application-Specific Playback Queue (ASPQ)* [9, 11] which receives the fixed-sized cells corresponding to the aggregated video stream. The purpose of the ASPQ is to filter out residual network-introduced jitter and reconstruct the original bursty video frames. The destination nodes in an Internet backbone network may represent a Central Office in a city. The Central Office node must deliver the IPTV streams to the ultimate end-users, which are the residential homes or mobile phones, and so forth, over a regional Metropolitan Area Network. The delivery of the IPTV traffic over the regional Metropolitan Area Network can use the same IPTV multicast design described in this paper. Therefore, bursty IPTV traffic flows can be delivered to the ultimate end-users in a hierarchical manner, with essentially zero delay jitter, with essentially zero packet loss rates and with essentially-perfect end-to-end QoS.

IP networks typically transmit variable-sized IP packets. Packets are typically disassembled into fixed-sized cells at the input size of each IP router, and IP packets are reassembled at the output size of the IP router, before they are transmitted to the next IP router. The use of variable-sized IP packets typically leads to delays associated with disassembling and reassembling IP packets in each IP router. In this paper, we assume an IP/MPLS technology, where all IP packets carrying video data have a fixed size, for example 64 bytes, 1024 bytes, or 1500 bytes. IP packets are disassembled once at the ingress router and reassembled once at the egress router of an MPLS domain. This assumption eliminates the need to repeatedly disassemble and re-assemble variable-sized IP packets at each IP router within one domain, and removes the packet reassembly delay in each IP router. However, the main results hold even if large fixed-sized packets are used (i.e., 1500 bytes), or if variable size packets are used. In this case, the packet reassembly delay must be added to each router. The important point is that all variable queueing delays and jitter have been removed.

3. Prior Guaranteed-Rate Scheduling Algorithms

Several schemes have been proposed for scheduling guaranteed-rate (GR) traffic through an IQ packet switch, which are briefly reviewed. All of the schemes discussed in this section assume that every router maintains a traffic rate matrix, which specifies the requested traffic rates between all IO pairs in the router.

In the Birkoff von-Neuman (BVN) scheme proposed in [17, 18], a doubly stochastic traffic rate matrix is decomposed into a sequence of permutation matrices and associated weights. Each matrix represents a switch configuration, that is, a matching or permutation of input ports onto output ports. These matrices are then scheduled to appear in proportion to their weights using the GPS or WFQ algorithm, to determine the sequence of switch configurations which meet the GR traffic requirements. Each switch configuration is used to configure the packet switch for one time-slot. Best-Effort IP traffic can then use any switching capacity not used by GR traffic. The BVN decomposition can achieve 100% throughput through a router, that is, it does not introduce "*speedup*" at any router, However, the BVN decomposition has a time complexity of $O(N^{4.5})$ in a serial processor and is generally considered too slow for use in real-time packet-switched IP routers.

An algorithm to schedule traffic through an IQ packet-switched IP router, while attempting to minimize the "*service lag*" amongst multiple competing IP flows and to minimize the speedup, was developed at MIT [16]. A doubly stochastic traffic rate matrix is first quantized to contain integer values and then is decomposed into a series of permutation matrices and associated weights, which then must be scheduled. With speedup $S = 1 + sN$ between 1 and 2, the maximum service lag (defined ahead) over all IO pairs is bounded by $O((N/4)(S/(S - 1)))$ time slots. According to [16]; "*with a fairly large class of schedulers a maximum service lag of $O(N^2)$ is unavoidable for input queued switches. To our knowledge, no scheduler which overcomes this $O(N^2)$ has been developed so far. For many rate matrices, it is not always possible to find certain points in time for which the service lag is small over all IO pairs simultaneously.*"

A greedy scheduling algorithm which attempts to minimize the delay jitter amongst simultaneous competing IP flows through an IQ packet switch was developed at Bell Labs [19, 20]. The traffic demand is specified in an $N \times N$ traffic rate matrix. The low-jitter GR traffic is constrained to be a relatively small fraction of the total traffic. The delay and jitter minimization problem is first formulated as an integer programming problem. The traffic rate matrix must be decomposed into a set of permutation matrices and associated weights, such that each traffic flow is supported by exactly one permutation in the set. This

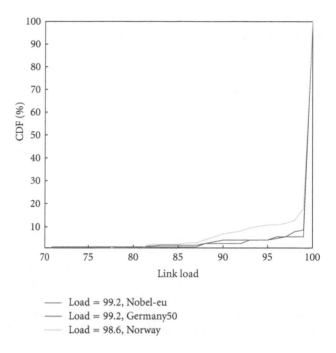

— Load = 99.2, Nobel-eu
— Load = 99.2, Germany50
— Load = 98.6, Norway

FIGURE 4: Average link loads.

matrix decomposition problem was shown to be NP-HARD. They then formulate a greedy low-jitter decomposition with complexity $O(N^3)$ time. The resulting schedule requires a worst-case speedup of $O(\log N)$, which renders it costly in practice. Hard analytic bounds on the jitter were not available.

A heuristic scheduling algorithm for scheduling packets in an IQ switch was developed at the UCR [21]. The algorithm attempts to decompose an admissible integer traffic rate matrix into the sum of integer matrices, where the maximum row or column sums of the matrices represent a decreasing geometric sequence. The authors establish a jitter bound which grows as the switch size N increases, and identify an open problem "*to determine the minimum speedup required to provide hard guarantees, and whether such guarantees are possible at all*" [21].

In summary, there is a considerable body of recent research into mathematical scheduling algorithms based upon the decomposition of traffic rate matrices. Unfortunately, tractable scheduling algorithms which achieve stability within the capacity region or which achieve bounded delays or jitter under the constraint of unity speedup, in one IP/MPLS router or a network of IP/MPLS routers, are unknown.

4. The Recursive Fair Stochastic Matrix Decomposition Algorithm

An $N \times M$ packet switch has N input and M output ports, and an associated traffic rate matrix. Each input port j for $0 \le j < N$ has M Virtual Output Queues, one for each output port $k, 0 \le k < M$. The guaranteed-rate traffic requirements for an $N \times N$ packet switch can specified in a doubly sub stochastic or stochastic traffic rate matrix Λ:

$$\Lambda = \begin{pmatrix} \lambda_{0,0} & \lambda_{0,1} & \cdots & \lambda_{0,N-1} \\ \lambda_{1,0} & \lambda_{1,1} & \cdots & \lambda_{1,N-1} \\ \cdots & & & \cdots \\ \lambda_{N-1,0} & \lambda_{N-1,1} & \cdots & \lambda_{N-1,N-1} \end{pmatrix},$$

$$\sum_{i=0}^{N-1} \lambda_{i,j} \le 1, \quad \sum_{j=0}^{N-1} \lambda_{i,j} \le 1. \qquad (1)$$

Each element $_{j,k}$ represents the fraction of the transmission line rate reserved for guaranteed-rate traffic between IO pair (j,k). The transmission of cells through the switch is governed by the frame transmission schedule, also called a "frame schedule". In an 8×8 crossbar switch with $F = 128$ time slots per frame, the minimum allotment of bandwidth is $1/F = 0.78\%$ of the line rate, which reserves one time-slot per frame on a recurring basis. Define a new quantized traffic rate matrix R where each traffic rate is expressed as an integer number times the minimum quota of reservable bandwidth:

$$R = \begin{pmatrix} R_{0,0} & R_{0,1} & \cdots & R_{0,N-1} \\ R_{1,0} & R_{1,1} & \cdots & R_{1,N-1} \\ \cdots & & & \cdots \\ R_{N-1,0} & R_{N-1,1} & \cdots & R_{N-1,N-1} \end{pmatrix},$$

$$\sum_{i=0}^{N-1} R_{i,j} \le F, \quad \sum_{j=o}^{N-1} R_{i,j} \le F. \qquad (2)$$

Consider two classic underlying theories from the field of graph theory and combinatorial mathematics, summarized in [10, 16–21]. Theorem 1 states that any integer matrix with a maximum row or column sum of F can be expressed as the sum of F permutation matrices. Theorem 2 states that any doubly sub stochastic or stochastic matrix can be decomposed into a convex set of permutations matrices and weights. All of the matrix decomposition algorithms reviewed in Section 3 attempt to exploit the above 2 theorems. They all are based upon the decomposition of a given traffic rate matrix into a convex set of constituent permutation matrices and associated weights, such that the weighted sum of the permutation matrices equals the original traffic rate matrix. Unfortunately, problems in combinatorial mathematics are difficult to solve efficiently, due to the large number of combinations that must be considered in any solution. As shown in Section 3, the problem of scheduling traffic to achieve zero jitter in minimum time is NP-HARD. All the algorithms reviewed in Section 3 (except for the BVN algorithm) require the introduction of "*speedup*" to the switches to achieve a decomposition, which limits their practical applicability. The BVN decomposition does not require a speedup, but its complexity is $O(N^{4.5})$ on a serial processor, which is considered intractable given that current Internet routers must compute decompositions at the rates of 100–300 million permutation matrices per second.

The *Recursive Fair Stochastic Matrix Decomposition* algorithm presented in [10] is an efficient deterministic

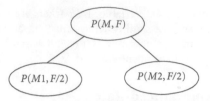

FIGURE 5: Recursive problem P(M,F) of scheduling of matrix M into a scheduling frame with F time slots.

algorithm to decompose an admissible traffic rate matrix into a sum of permutation matrices under the constraint of unity speedup. Let $P(M,F)$ denote the problem of scheduling an admissible quantized traffic rate matrix M into a scheduling frame of length F time slots, as shown in Figure 5. In particular, an integer matrix M with a maximum row or column sum of F must be partitioned into two integer matrices $M1$ and $M2$, each with a maximum row or column sum of $F/2$. More specifically, the scheduling problem $P(M,F)$ must be recursively decomposed into 2 smaller scheduling problems $P(M1,F/2)$ and $P(M2,F/2)$, such that the integer matrices $M1 + M2 = M$, where $M1$ and $M2$ are admissible integer traffic rate matrices, and for all j and k where $0 \le j \le N$ and $0 \le k \le N$, then $M1(j,k) \le M2(j,k) + c$ and $M2(j,k) \le M1(j,k) + c$ for $c = 1$. This step of partitioning an integer matrix into 2 integer matrices is a problem in combinatorial mathematics. The RFSMD algorithm achieves the decomposition by transforming one combinatorial problem into another combinatorial problem with a recently proposed solution. In particular, the problem of decomposing an integer matrix relatively fairly into 2 integer matrices is transformed into the problem of routing permutations in a rearrangeably nonblocking switching network [10]. An efficient algorithm for the combinatorial problem of routing permutations in rearrangeable networks was proposed in [10].

The recursive nature of the RFSMD algorithm yields a very efficient decomposition. The decomposition of an $N \times N$ integer matrix with a maximum row or column sum of F can be accomplished in $O(NF \log (NF))$ time. The decomposition yields F permutations or bipartite graph matchings, which can configure the switch for F time slots. The computational complexity for each computed permutation of N elements is therefore $O(N \log (NF))$ time on a serial processor, which is near optimal.

The RFSMD algorithm also partitions each matrix M relatively fairly, so that the two smaller matrices $M1$ and $M2$ differ by at most 1 in any position. As a result, the traffic in the original scheduling problem is scheduled relatively fairly over the 2 smaller scheduling problems. This relatively fair recursive partitioning leads to a bound on the maximum jitter for any traffic flow, and a bound for the *maximum normalized service lead* or *maximum normalized service lag* for any scheduled traffic flow (these terms are formally defined in the next paragraphs). The bounded normalize service lead/lag can be used to create bounds on the end-to-end QoS for every scheduled traffic flow, as will be shown ahead.

One step in the decomposition for a 4×4 matrix operating at 99.2% load with unity speedup is shown in (3). Given an $N \times N$ switch and a fixed scheduling frame length F, the *RFSMD* matrix decomposition algorithm [10] bounds the *normalized service lead* and *service lag* for the aggregated traffic leaving any *node* to $\leq k \cdot IIDT$ time slots for constant K, where $IIDT$ represents the "*Ideal Interdeparture Time*" for cells belonging to the aggregated traffic leaving an edge. Furthermore, the bound applies to all individual competing traffic flows traversing each edge, provided that cells are selected for service within each VOQ according to a GPS scheduling algorithm

$$
\begin{bmatrix} 106 & 222 & 326 & 345 \\ 177 & 216 & 303 & 326 \\ 459 & 232 & 183 & 147 \\ 282 & 352 & 211 & 178 \end{bmatrix} = \begin{bmatrix} 53 & 111 & 163 & 172 \\ 88 & 108 & 152 & 163 \\ 230 & 116 & 91 & 74 \\ 141 & 176 & 105 & 89 \end{bmatrix}
$$
$$
+ \begin{bmatrix} 53 & 111 & 163 & 173 \\ 89 & 108 & 151 & 163 \\ 229 & 116 & 92 & 73 \\ 141 & 176 & 106 & 89 \end{bmatrix}. \qquad (3)
$$

Each smaller scheduling problem contains approximately one half of the original time-slot reservation requests, and has as smaller scheduling frame of length $F/2$ time slots to realize these reservation requests, as shown in Figure 5. Repeated application of the relatively fair recursive partitioning results in a sequence of partial or full permutation matrices which determine the IQ switch configurations, called the frame transmission schedule. Due to the relatively fair recursive partitioning, the service a traffic flow receives in each half of the frame schedule will be relatively fair, and the delay jitter will be relatively small.

Several of the following definitions from [10] will be useful to interpret the simulation results to be presented in Section 6.

Definition 1. A "*Frame transmission schedule*" of length F is a sequence of partial or full permutation matrices (or vectors) which define the crossbar switch configurations for F time slots within a scheduling frame. Given a line rate L, the frame length F is determined by the desired minimum quota of reservable bandwidth = L/F. To set the minimum quota of reservable bandwidth to $\leq 1\%$ of L, set $F \geq 100$, that is, $F = 128$.

Definition 2. The "*Ideal Interdeparture Time*" denoted $IIDT$ (i, j) of cells in a GR flow between IO pair (i, j) with quantized rate $R(i, j)$ time-slot reservations in a frame of length F, given a line rate L in bytes/sec and fixed-sized cells of C bytes, is given by: $IIDT(i, j) = F/R(i, j)$ time slots, each of duration (C/L) sec. (The subscripts will be suppressed when possible.)

Definition 3. The "*Ideal Service Time*" (ST) of cell $0 \leq c \leq R(i, j)$ in a GR flow between IO pair (i, j) with an *Ideal Interdeparture Time* of $IIDT(i, j)$ is given by $ST = j*IIDT(i, j)$ time slots.

Definition 4. The "*Received Service*" of a flow with quantized guaranteed rate $R(i, j)$ at time-slot t within a frame of length F, denoted $Sij(t)$, equals the number of permutation matrices in time slots $1 \ldots t$, where $1 \leq t \leq F$, in which input port i is matched to output port j.

Definition 5. The "*Service Lag*" of a flow between input port i and output port j, at time-slot t within a frame of length F, denoted $Lij(t)$, equals the difference between the requested quantized GR prorated by t/F, and the received service at time-slot t, that is, $Lij(t) = Sij(t) - (t/F)Rij(t)$. A positive Service Lag denotes the case where the received service is less than the requested service, that is, a cell arrives later than its ideal service time. A negative Service Lag is a Service Lead, where the received service exceeds the requested service, that is, a cell arrive sooner than its ideal service time. The *normalized service lead/lag* for a flow f equals the service lead/lag for flow f divided by the IIDT for flow f.

Consider a discrete time queueing model, where time is normalized for all flows and is expressed in terms of the IIDT for each flow. The following notations presented in [11] are used. The cumulative arrival curve of a traffic flow f is said to conform to $T(\lambda, \beta, \delta)$, denoted, $A_f : T(\lambda, \beta, \delta)$ if the average cell arrival rate is λ cells/sec, the burst arrival rate is $\leq \beta\lambda$ cells/sec, and the maximum normalized service lead/lag is δ. A similar notation is used for cumulative departures and cumulative service. In any IP router, the cumulative departure curve for f is said to "*track*" the cumulative service curve for f when cell departures are constrained by the scheduled service opportunities. This situation occurs when flow f has queued cells at $VOQ(j,k)$.

The following four theorems were established in [11]. Assume each traffic flow is admitted to an IP/MPLS network subject to an *Application-Specific Token-Bucket Traffic Shaper Queue (ASSQ)*, and has a maximum normalized service lead/lag of K cells. The traffic rate matrix for each router is updated by a resource reservation protocol such as RSVP, IntServ, or DiffServ. Each *IP router* is scheduled using the proposed *RFSMD* algorithm with a maximum normalized service lead/lag of K cells. We assume fixed size cells, with any reasonable cell size, however similar bounds apply for the case of variable-sized IP packet.

Theorem 1. *Given a flow f traversing VOQ(j,k) over an interval $t \in [0, \tau]$, with arrivals $A_f : T(\phi(f), \beta, K)$, with service $S_f : T(\phi(f)\beta, K)$ and $Q(0) \leq O(K)$, then $Q(t) \leq O(K)$.*

Theorem 2. *When all queues in all intermediate nodes have reached steady state, the maximum end-to-end queueing delay of a GR flow traversing H routers is $O(KH) \cdot IIDT$ time slots.*

Theorem 3. *In the steady state, the departures of traffic flow f at any IQ router along an end-to-end path of H routers are constrained by the scheduling opportunities, and will exhibit a maximum normalized service lead/lag of K, that is, $S_f : T(\phi(f)\beta, K)$. The normalized service lead/lag of a flow is not cumulative when traversing multiple routers.*

Theorem 4. *A traffic flow which traverses H IQ routers along an end-to-end path can be delivered to the end-user with zero network-introduced delay jitter, when a playback buffer of size $4K$ cells is employed, that is, $S_f : T(\phi(f)\beta, K)$.*

According to Theorem 4, a bursty IPTV traffic flow which traverses H IQ routers along an end-to-end path can be delivered to the end-user with *zero network-introduced delay jitter*, when an appropriately-sized Application-Specific Token-Bucket Traffic Shaper Queue and Application-Specific Playback Queue are used, as described in Section 3.

Theorem 1 states that the number of cells buffered for any flow in any router in any network is limited to a small number for all loads up to 100%. Theorem 2 states that all end-to-end traffic flows will never experience any congestion, excessive delay or throughput degradation. Every end-to-end flow experiences a small but effectively negligible queueing delay at each router compared to current router technologies. Theorem 3 states that the normalized service lead/lag is not cumulative when traversing multiple routers in any network. Theorem 4 states that every end-to-end traffic flow can be delivered at every destination router with essentially-perfect end-to-end Quality of Service. In particular, a bursty IPTV traffic flow transmitted through an IP network using the RFSMD scheduling algorithm can be perfectly regenerated at every destination route, with zero packet loss rate and zero delay jitter. These 4 theorems demonstrate that traffic flows can be scheduled to achieve essentially-perfect end-to-end QoS in any Internet topology for all loads up to 100%. The simulation results reported in Section 6 will demonstrate these 4 theorems.

5. Backbone Topologies

The *Survivable Network Design Library (SNDlib)* is a library of telecommunication network designs [12]. The library contains data for 22 IP backbone networks and several optimization problems for each network. The SNDlib provides a series of real IP network topologies appropriate for reproducible case studies. In this paper, simulation results for three of the SDNlib networks are presented. We have followed the node placement and link assignments described by SNDlib, although we have made our own assumptions about the IPTV broadcast tree construction, session demands, and link capacities.

We selected the NOBEL-EU, GERMANY50, and the NORWAY network models from [12], as shown in Figure 6. The NOBEL-EU network covers Europe and has 28 nodes and 41 edges. It is a reference network originating from the European project NOBEL, where a detailed cost model was developed for various kinds of SDH and WDM equipment [12]. The GERMANY50 has 50 nodes and 88 edges provided by T-Systems International AG, and is an extension of the NOBEL-GERMANY network. The NORWAY network has 27 nodes and 51 edges and represents a backbone network from Norway.

We developed several heavily loaded IPTV *traffic specifications* for each network. In each traffic specification, one-third of the highest degree nodes are selected as roots of the IPTV multicast trees. For example, in the NOBEL-EU network with 28 nodes there are 9 multicast trees, each broadcasting 100 IPTV traffic streams. To generate each traffic specification, a 2-step process was used. In the first step, the IPTV multicast trees where routed into the network. N/3 nodes with the highest degrees were selected as roots for the N/3 trees. Each multicast tree was then routed to every other node in the network, using a shortest distance spanning tree computed using Dijkstra's algorithm. Many links in the network, especially those in the center of the topology, carry traffic from each of the all N/3 multicast trees. In the second step, background traffic was added in an iterative manner between randomly selected pairs of nodes, to essentially saturate the network. In our traffic specifications, we achieve link loads of approx. 99%. In each iteration, a random pair of nodes was selected, and a shortest delay path between the nodes was computed using an OSPF routing algorithm. A traffic rate was selected for the flow to nearly saturate the end-to-end path, and the flow would be confirmed. As the network load approaches 100%, it becomes increasingly difficult to route any additional flows, as all links approach saturation. Therefore, in the last iteration, multiple 1-hop traffic flows are added between neighboring nodes to effectively saturate the network, so that every link has a load of approximately 99%. Referring to Figure 4, the link loads used in our 3 network simulations are 99.2%, 99.2%, and 98.6%.

Each traffic specification represents an extremely heavy load, not likely to be encountered in practice. A resource reservation protocol such as RSVP, IntServ, or DiffServ was then used to reserve buffer space and bandwidth along each router and link in the network. These reservations result in the creation of an admissible traffic rate matrix for every router in the network. The traffic rate matrices for each router where then scheduled using the RFSMD algorithm. The network was then simulated, to gather statistics on the end-to-end QoS for every traffic flow, including IPTV multicast traffic and background traffic.

Numerous traffic specifications were generated, routed and simulated for the three selected network topologies. Figure 6 illustrates typical multicast trees in the 3 topologies examined in this paper, that is, the NOBEL-EU, NORWAY, and the GERMANY50 topologies. All of network simulations indicated essentially identical results, so we present the detailed simulations of one traffic specification over two networks, the NOBEL-EU and GERMANY50 networks. The NOBEL-EU network has 28 nodes, 41 links, and 9 IPTV multicast trees, each multicasting 100 IPTV channels to all other nodes. The selected traffic specification results in 321 traffic flows in the NOBEL-EU network, with an average distance of 5 hops and a maximum distance of 14 hops. The average link load is about 99%. The GERMANY50 network has 50 nodes, 88 links, and 16 IPTV multicast trees, each multicasting 100 IPTV channels to all other nodes. The selected traffic specification results in 693 traffic flows in the GERMANY50 topology, with an average distance of 5 hops and a maximum distance of 18 hops.

The roots of the IPTV multicast trees are illustrated as a bold circle in Figure 6. The IPTV multicast trees are

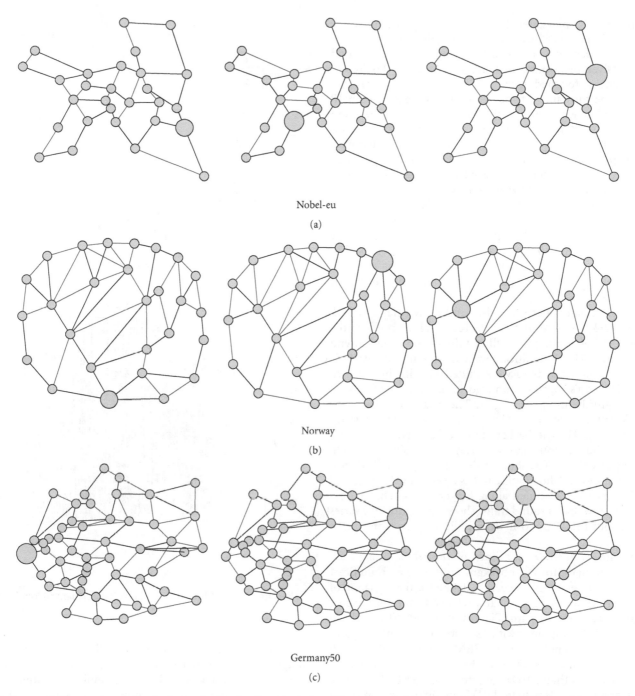

Nobel-eu

(a)

Norway

(b)

Germany50

(c)

FIGURE 6: Three network topologies, each showing three typical multicast trees. Bold nodes are the roots of IPTV multicast trees.

routed according to Dijkstra's shortest path algorithm. As a result, links near the center of the network will tend to carry more IPTV traffic than those near the edge. Each multicast tree for a given source node is not unique, since in many cases each tree has several equal length shortest paths from which to select an edge. In our traffic specifications, a typical link will devote between 4% and 7% of its allocated bandwidth of 40 Gbps to IPTV multicast data, with a maximum of 20%. The remaining bandwidth is used for background traffic between randomly selected pairs of nodes.

6. Results of IPTV Multicasting

Assume an IP/MPLS backbone network with 40 Gbps links, with a scheduling frame length $F = 1.024$ (where 1 Gbps denotes 2^{30} bps and 1 Mbps denotes 2^{20} bps). The minimum quota of reservable bandwidth is one time-slot reservation per scheduling frame, or equivalently 4 Mbps. The provisioned GR rate of 440 Mbps per multicast tree established in Section 2 requires 11 time-slot reservations per scheduling frame. Each IP router in Figure 6 must reserve and schedule 11 cell transmissions per scheduling frame between the appropriate IO pairs, per IPTV multicast tree. In our traffic specifications, every incoming and outgoing link in each IP router is essentially saturated with additional background traffic. Given this worst-case load, the IP routers should find it challenging to schedule the traffic to meet QoS guarantees.

The performance of the IP multicast trees in each IP backbone network was evaluated using a discrete-event simulator written in the C programming language, with over 20,000 lines of code. The simulator was written with the help of four graduate students, with funding provided by the Ontario Centers of Excellence. (Several independent simulators were actually written, to verify the experimental results.) The simulations were run on a large cluster-based supercomputing system in the Dept. of ECE at McMaster University, with 160 dual processing nodes running the LINUX operating system. Each dual-processor node has a clock rate of 1-2 GHz and between 1-2 GB of memory. A central dispatcher assigns tasks to processors to exploit parallelism.

Figure 7 illustrates the end-to-end delay (lifetime) PDF for (a) background traffic and (b) for multicast traffic in the GERMANY50 topology. Recall that there are 693 end-to-end paths and 16 IPTV multicast trees in this traffic specification. The multicast trees were routed first in the network using Dijkstra's shortest path algorithm, and therefore they have relatively low path lengths. The end-to-end delay for multicast traffic shown in Figure 7(b) varies from 1 IIDT up to about 9 IIDT. The background traffic is point-to-point, and was routed along shortest-delay paths using the OSPF routing algorithm. The shortest-delay paths generally do not equal the shortest-hop paths, and as a result the background traffic tends to be routed along longer paths. The end-to-end delays for background traffic shown in Figure 7(a) varies from about 1 IIDT up to 40 IIDT, indicating that some paths are very long.

Figure 8 illustrates the jitter of the traffic along each end-to-end path, for both background traffic and multicast traffic. The jitter along one path is defined as the deviation of each cell's delay along that path, relative to the mean value of the delay along a path. Figures 8(a) and 8(b) apply to the NOBEL-EU topology with 321 end-to-end paths. Figures 8(c) and 8(d) apply to the GERMANY50 topology with 693 end-to-end paths. Observe that 99% of all traffic flows arrive with less than 3 IIDTs of jitter, and 100% of all traffic flows arrive with less than 4 IIDTs of jitter. Observe from Figure 8 that the jitter for all point-to-point traffic and all multicast traffic is small and bounded by 4 IIDT, and the bound is network independent. These experimental results are consistent with the 4 theorems summarized in this paper. In [10], Theorems 5 and 8 establish that all jitter is bounded by 4 IIDT. Therefore, the experimental results in Figure 8 are perfectly consistent with the theorems in [10, 11].

Figure 9 illustrates the PDF for the distribution of the number of cells queued in each IP router in the GERMANY50 topology, for background traffic and multicast traffic. There are 3,465 individual plots in Figure 9, equal to 693 end-to-end paths passing through 5 routers on average. The number of cells queued per traffic flow in each router is small, less than 2 cells on average per multicast output

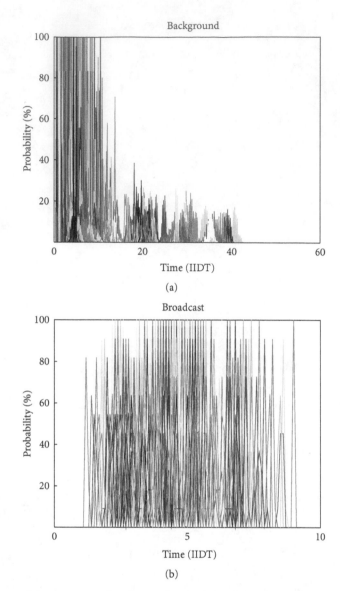

FIGURE 7: PDF of End-to-End Delay for Germany50 topology.

port. No router buffers more than 7 cells per flow per unicast output, as shown in Figure 9(a). No router buffers more than 3 cells per aggregated flow per multicast output port, as shown in Figure 9(b). The multicast cells are stored in a multicast queue, which is separate from the VOQs in each router. Figure 9 indicates that the cells move at a relatively consistent rate through the IP network. These experimental results are consistent with the 4 theorems summarized in this paper. In particular, Theorem 1 in [11] establishes that all queue sizes are bounded by a small number of cells (16 cells for these networks). Therefore, the experimental results in Figure 9 are perfectly consistent with the theorems in [10, 11]. The amount of memory required for buffering is several orders of magnitude lower when compared to traditional IP routers, as the next section will demonstrate.

Figure 10 illustrates the end-to-end delay for the IPTV multicast traffic, as a function of the excess bandwidth selected for each multicast tree. Recall that in our traffic

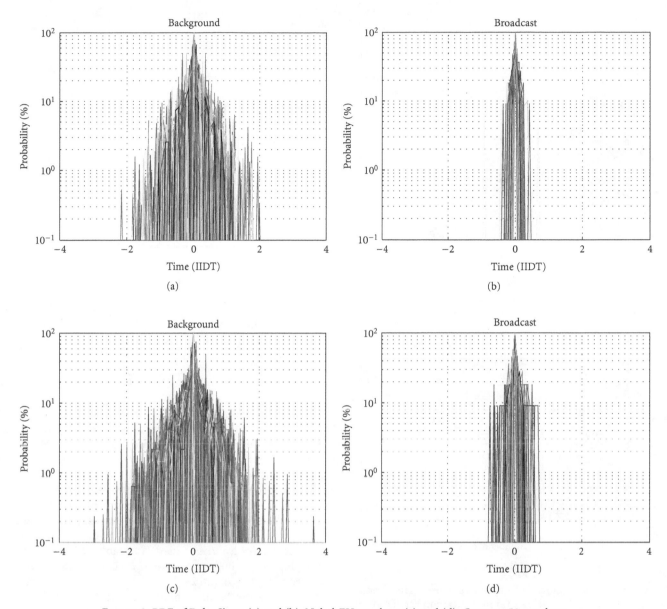

FIGURE 8: PDF of Delay Jitter. (a) and (b): Nobel-EU topology. (c) and (d): Germany50 topology.

specifications, an excess bandwidth of 10% was provisioned for every IPTV multicast tree. The excess bandwidth determines the end-to-end delay. According to Figure 10, an excess bandwidth of 10% yields an end-to-end queueing delay of about 3 seconds on each IPTV multicast tree. The *Application Specific Playback Queue* at each destination node has reconstructed the original bursty IPTV video frames, filtered out the residual network jitter and made all 100 video streams available at each destination IP router in the multicast tree with essentially zero delay jitter and essentially-perfect end-to-end QoS.

6.1. Buffer Sizing in IP Routers.

In this section, we explore the issue of memory requirements in Internet routers. One well-established design rule for buffer sizing in IP networks using TCP flow-control is called the "*classical buffer rule*", also called the "*bandwidth-delay-product*" buffer rule [31]. This design rule states that *each link in each IP router* requires a buffer of $B = O(C \cdot T)$ bits, where C is the link capacity and T is the round-trip time of the flows traversing the link [31]. According to data in [31], a 40 Gbps link handling TCP flows with a round-trip time of 250 millisec requires a buffer size B about five million IP packets per link. Each IP packet may contain up to 1500 bytes (or equivalently 24 fixed-sized cells). Therefore, each link buffer may require up to 7.5 Gigabytes of memory per link. A 16×16 router may require about 120 Gigabytes of high-speed memory. This large buffer size is partially due to the use of the traditional TCP flow-control protocol, which introduces a large jitter into the traffic flows, which in turn necessitates the use of large buffers. The large buffer size is also partially due to the use of sub optimal heuristic schedulers, which introduce a large and potentially unbounded jitter at every router, which in turn necessitates the use of large buffers.

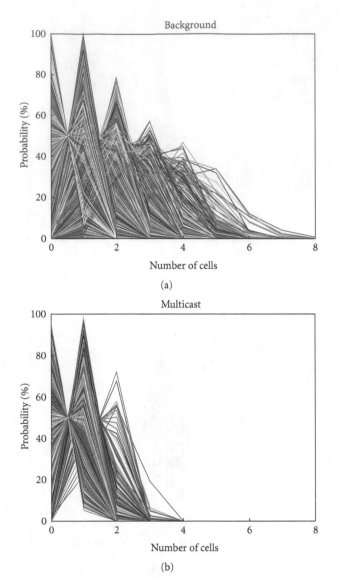

(a)

(b)

FIGURE 9: PDF for number of queued cells per traffic flow per router for Germany50 topology. (a) for background traffic. (b) for multicast traffic.

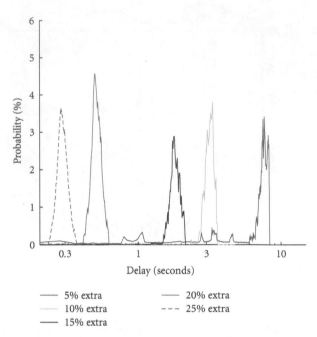

FIGURE 10: Plot of end-to-end delay versus excess bandwidth for multicast traffic.

A *"small buffer rule"* was proposed in [32], where $B = O(C \cdot T/\sqrt{N})$, and where N is the number of long-lived TCP flows traversing the router. With the same parameters reported above, the buffer size B can be reduced to about fifty thousand IP packets [32]. Therefore, each link buffer may require up to 75 Megabytes of memory per link. A 16×16 router may require about 1.2 Gigabytes of high-speed memory.

More recently, [33] proposed a *"tiny buffer rule"* where $B = O(\log W)$, where W is the maximum TCP congestion window size. With the same parameters, [33] suggests that average buffer sizes of between 20–50 IP packets or equivalently about 30,000–75,000 bytes of memory may suffice if 3 important conditions can be met; (a) the jitter of incoming traffic at the source node is sufficiently small, (b) the IP routers introduce a sufficiently small jitter, and (c) 10–15% of the throughput is sacrificed. The paper in [33]

however did not propose a low-jitter scheduling algorithm, which is in itself a major theoretical unsolved problem as Section 3 illustrates. Furthermore, [32, 34] have argued that small buffers may cause significant losses, instability or performance degradation at the application layer.

Our theorems in [10, 11] and our exhaustive simulations indicate that network memory requirements can be several orders of magnitude smaller than those in current IP routers, when a low-jitter scheduling algorithm with a bounded normalized service lead/lag is used, as established in Theorems 1–4. In our IP multicast system, each IP router needs to buffer on average about 2 cells (128 bytes) per flow per router to guarantee 100% throughput and essentially-perfect end-to-end QoS for all provisioned traffic flows, even at 100% network loads. In comparison, existing IP routers using the combination of heuristic schedulers, TCP flow control, and the classic bandwidth-delay-product buffer-sizing rule require buffers of about 5 million IP packets per link at 40 Gbps to achieve high throughput, without providing any rigorous QoS guarantees. The RFSMD algorithm and Theorems 1–4 allow for reductions in buffer sizes by several orders of magnitude compared to the existing IP multicast technology, while simultaneously meeting rigorous QoS constraints.

7. Conclusions

The design of an IPTV multicast system for packet-switched Internet backbone networks has been presented. Three real IP backbone network topologies, the NOBEL-EU European topology, and the GERMANY50 and the NORWAY topologies, were used to illustrate the design. Multiple IPTV multicast tees were provisioned into each network, each carrying 100 IPTV channels. Additional background traffic was added between nodes to essentially fully saturate each network. Every link operates at loads of approximately 99%. A resource reservation algorithm was used to reserve resources for each ITPV multicast tree in the network. A recently proposed *Recursive Fair Stochastic Matrix Decomposition algorithm* was used to compute near-perfect low-jitter transmission schedules for each packet-switched IP router in each multicast tree. The low-jitter schedules remove most of the cell delay jitter associated with the sub optimal dynamic scheduling algorithms used in existing IP routers and minimize the amount of buffering required in the IP routers. Extensive simulations indicate that large-scale IPTV multicasting can be supported. The IPTV traffic is delivered to every destination node with near-minimal delays, near-minimal jitter, zero packet loss rates, and essentially-perfect end-to-end QoS, as confirmed by theory. Our extensive simulations indicate that each IP router typically buffers less than 2 cells (about 128 bytes) of video data per traffic flow per router, several orders of magnitude less buffering than current IP routers require. The multicast technology is also applicable to other multimedia streams over the Internet, including VOIP, Video-on-Demand, Telemedicine, and Telerobotic control over IP. The application of the technology to deliver telerobotic control systems over saturated Internet backbone networks is described in [35].

References

[1] Cisco Systems White Paper, "Approaching the Zettabyte Era," 2008, http://www.cisco.com.

[2] R. Lawler, "Cisco Sees a Zettaflood of IP Traffic-Driven by Video," Contentinople—Networking the Digital Media Industry, 2008, http://www.contentinople.com.

[3] Y. Xiao, X. Du, J. Zhang, F. Hu, and S. Guizani, "Internet protocol television (IPTV): the killer application for the next-generation internet," *IEEE Communications Magazine*, vol. 45, no. 11, pp. 126–134, 2007.

[4] J. M. Boyce, "The US digital television broadcasting transition," *IEEE Signal Processing Magazine*, vol. 26, no. 3, pp. 110–112, 2009.

[5] Cisco Systems White Paper, "Optimizing Video Transport in your IP Triple Play Network," 2006, http://www.cisco.com.

[6] L. Hardesty, "Internet gridlock: video is clogging the internet. How we choose to unclog it will have far-reaching implications," *MIT Technology Review*, 2008.

[7] M. Baard, "NSF Preps New Improved Internet," Wired, August 2005.

[8] BBN Technologies—GENI Project Office, "Global Environment for Network Innovations—GENI System Overview," December 2007.

[9] T. H. Szymanski and D. Gilbert, "Internet multicasting of IPTV with essentially-zero delay jitter," *IEEE Transactions on Broadcasting*, vol. 55, no. 1, pp. 20–30, 2009.

[10] T. H. Szymanski, "A low-jitter guaranteed-rate scheduling algorithm for packet-switched IP routers," *IEEE Transactions on Communications*, vol. 57, no. 11, 2009.

[11] T. H. Szymanski, "Bounds on end-to-end delay and jitter in input-buffered and internally-buffered IP/MPLS networks," in *Proceedings of the IEEE Sarnoff Symposium (SARNOFF '09)*, Princeton, NJ, USA, 2009.

[12] S. Orlowski, R. Wessaly, M. Pioro, and A. Tomaszewski, "SNDlib1.0-survivable network design library," ZIB report ZR-07-15, Networks, October 2009, http://sndlib.zib.de/home.action.

[13] L. Tassiulas and A. Ephremides, "Stability properties of constrained queueing systems and scheduling policies for maximum throughput in multihop radio networks," *IEEE Transactions on Automatic Control*, vol. 27, pp. 1936–1948, 1992.

[14] V. Anantharam, N. McKeown, A. Mekkittikul, and J. Walrand, "Achieving 100% throughput in an input-queued switch," *IEEE Transactions on Communications*, vol. 47, no. 8, pp. 1260–1267, 1999.

[15] N. McKeown, "The iSLIP scheduling algorithm for input-queued switches," *IEEE/ACM Transactions on Networking*, vol. 7, no. 2, pp. 188–201, 1999.

[16] C. E. Koksal, R. G. Gallager, and C. E. Rohrs, "Rate quantization and service quality over single crossbar switches," in *Proceedings of the IEEE Conference on Computer Communications (INFOCOM '04)*, pp. 1962–1973, 2004.

[17] C.-S. Chang, W. J. Chen, and H.-Y. Huang, "On service guarantees for input buffered crossbar switches: a capacity decomposition approach by birkhoff and von neuman," in *Proceedings of the IEEE International Workshop on Quality of Service (iWQoS '99)*, pp. 79–86, 1999.

[18] C.-S. Chang, W.-J. Chen, and H.-Y. Huang, "Birkhoff-von neumann input-buffered crossbar switches for guaranteed-rate services," *IEEE Transactions on Communications*, vol. 49, no. 7, pp. 1145–1147, 2001.

[19] I. Keslassy, M. Kodialam, T. V. Lakshman, and D. Stiliadis, "On guaranteed smooth scheduling for input-queued switches," *IEEE/ACM Transactions on Networking*, vol. 13, no. 6, pp. 1364–1375, 2005.

[20] M. S. Kodialam, T. V. Lakshman, and D. Stilladis, "Scheduling of Guaranteed-bandwidth low-jitter traffic in input-buffered switches," *US patent application no. #20030227901*, 2003.

[21] S. R. Mohanty and L. N. Bhuyan, "Guaranteed smooth switch scheduling with low complexity," in *Proceedings of the IEEE Global Telecommunications Conference (GLOBECOM '05)*, pp. 626–630, 2005.

[22] N. McKeown and B. Prabhakar, "Scheduling multicast cells in an input-queued switch," in *Proceedings of the 15th Annual Joint Conference of the IEEE Computer and Communications Societies (INFOCOM '96)*, vol. 1, pp. 271–278, March 1996.

[23] M. Marsan, A. Bianco, P. Giaccone, E. Leonardi, and F. Neri, "Multicast traffic in input-queued switches: optimal scheduling and maximum throughput," *IEEE/ACM Transactions on Networking*, vol. 11, no. 3, pp. 465–477, 2003.

[24] J. F. Hayes, R. Breault, and M. K. Mehmet-Ali, "Performance analysis of a multicast switch," *IEEE Transactions on Communications*, vol. 39, no. 4, pp. 581–587, 1991.

[25] J. Y. Hui and T. Renner, "Queueing analysis for multicast packet switching," *IEEE Transactions on Communications*, vol. 42, no. 2, pp. 723–731, 1994.

[26] B. Prabhakar, N. McKeown, and R. Ahuja, "Multicast scheduling for input-queued switches," *IEEE Journal on Selected Areas in Communications*, vol. 15, no. 5, pp. 855–866, 1997.

[27] M. Song, W. Zhu, A. Francini, and M. Alam, "Performance analysis of large multicast switches with multicast virtual output queues," *Computer Communications*, vol. 28, no. 2, pp. 189–198, 2005.

[28] S. R. Gulliver and G. Ghinea, "The perceptual and attentive impact of delay and jitter in multimedia delivery," *IEEE Transactions on Broadcasting*, vol. 53, no. 2, pp. 449–458, 2007.

[29] S. Chand and H. Om, "Modeling of buffer storage in video transmission," *IEEE Transactions on Broadcasting*, vol. 53, no. 4, pp. 774–779, 2007.

[30] Y. Bai and M. R. Ito, "Application-aware buffer management: new metrics and techniques," *IEEE Transactions on Broadcasting*, vol. 51, no. 1, pp. 114–121, 2005.

[31] Y. Ganjali and N. McKeown, "Update on buffer sizing in internet routers," *ACM SIGCOMM Computer Communication Review*, vol. 36, no. 5, pp. 67–70, 2006.

[32] G. Vu-Brugier, R. S. Stanojevic, D. J. Leith, and R. N. Shorten, "A Critique of recently proposed buffer sizing strategies," *ACM/SIGCOMM Computer Communication Review*, vol. 37, no. 1, pp. 43–47, 2007.

[33] M. Enachescu, Y. Ganjali, A. Goel, N. McKeown, and T. Roughgarden, "Routers with very small buffers," in *Proceedings of the 25th IEEE International Conference on Computer Communications (INFOCOM '06)*, Barcelona, Spain, April 2006.

[34] A. Dhamdhere and C. Dovrolis, "Open issues in router buffer sizing," vol. 36, no. 1, pp. 87–92.

[35] T. H. Szymanski and D. Gilbert, "Provisioning mission-critical telerobotic control systems in internet backbone networks with essentially-perfect QoS," *IEEE Journal on Selected Areas in Communications*, vol. 28, no. 5, pp. 630–643, 2010.

4

A Survey of Cognitive Radio Access to TV White Spaces

Maziar Nekovee[1,2]

[1] *BT Innovate and Design, Polaris 134, Adastral Park, Martlesham, Suffolk IP5 3RE, UK*
[2] *Centre for Computational Science, University College London, 20 Gordon Street, London WC1H 0AJ, UK*

Correspondence should be addressed to Maziar Nekovee, maziar.nekovee@bt.com

Academic Editor: Fred Daneshgaran

Cognitive radio is being intensively researched as the enabling technology for license-exempt access to the so-called TV White Spaces (TVWS), large portions of spectrum in the UHF/VHF bands which become available on a geographical basis after digital switchover. Both in the US, and more recently, in the UK the regulators have given conditional endorsement to this new mode of access. This paper reviews the state-of-the-art in technology, regulation, and standardisation of cognitive access to TVWS. It examines the spectrum opportunity and commercial use cases associated with this form of secondary access.

1. Introduction

A cognitive radio [1] consists of a cognitive engine (CE), which contains algorithms and toolboxes for radio environment sensing, machine-learning, and reasoning and decision making, and a configurable radio platform, which could be a Software Defined Radio (SDR), that basically does what it is told by the CE. The concept of Cognitive Radio (CR) was first described by Mitola and Maguire [2] as "transforming radio nodes from blind executors of predefined protocols to radio-domain-aware intelligent agents that search out ways to deliver the services that the user wants even if that user does not know how to obtain them". The ideal CR knows everything about the user requirements, the capability of the radio device, the network requirements and the external environment (including the radio environment). It will plan ahead and negotiate for the best part of the spectrum to operate in and at the best power, modulation scheme, and so forth, and manage these resources in real time to satisfy the service and user demands. The ideal CR is currently at the early proof-of-concept stage research, with most of the work taking place in universities.

A much more developed form of the CR technology is cognitive radio for dynamic spectrum access (DSA) [3]. The aim here is to achieve device-centric interference control and dynamic reuse of radio spectrum based on the frequency agility and intelligence offered by cognitive radio technology.

This form of CR technology is currently being intensely researched. However, there is also already significant industry effort towards prototyping, standardisation and commercialisation of the technology. Important industry players with active R&D efforts in cognitive radio technology include Alcatel-Lucent, Ericsson and Motorola from the mobile equipment industry, BT and Orange from network operators, Philips and Samsung from the consumer electronics industry, HP and Dell from the computer industry, and Microsoft and Google from the Internet/software industry. Dynamic spectrum access may take place in several ways: between a licensed primary system and a license-exempt secondary system, for example, secondary spectrum access to digital TV or military spectrum, within the same primary system, for example, micro-macro sharing of licensed spectrum in 3G/LTE femtocells, and finally among two primary systems, for example, real-time leasing and trading of spectrum between two cellular operators.

The first form of dynamic spectrum access is arguably the most disruptive application of the CR technology, as it enables license-exempt users (end-user devices and base stations) to act as spectrum scavengers. They can identify unused portions of licensed spectrum (also called spectrum holes or White Spaces) and make opportunistic use of this spectrum for their connectivity at times and/or locations where they are not used. Allowing the operation of such scavengers promises to greatly increase the efficiency of spectrum usage by preventing exclusively licensed spectrum from being wasted due to low spatial or temporal usage. Mainly for this reason licensed-exempt cognitive access to certain licensed bands is being keenly promoted by the US regulator, the (Federal Communication Commission) FCC [4–7], and more recently also by Ofcom [8–10]. The rationale is to maximise the usage of licensed spectrum through secondary access by cognitive radios and, at the same time, promote rapid introduction of new wireless technologies and services without the need for setting aside any new spectrum for this purpose. Most mobile operators see this from of cognitive access as highly disruptive to their current business model.

In the longer term (3–5 years), we expect that dynamic spectrum access based on cognitive radio will go far beyond opportunistic spectrum access only. As a result of the current trends in spectrum liberalisation, including the availability of licensed spectrum for real-time trading, cognitive devices may be able to access a portfolio of different types of spectrum for their connectivity. This "spectrum portfolio" may include several different type of spectrum: licensed spectrum (e.g., in cellular bands), licensed-exempt spectrum (in the ISM bands), as well as spectrum, that is, acquired in real-time, either through leasing or on a secondary basis. Devices with cognitive functionality will be able to dynamically change their operating spectrum within this portfolio, accessing the best available spectrum on a "just-in-time" basis. This may happen either upon instruction from a base station or autonomously by devices themselves. Depending on the user and network requirements devices may pool together and use several spectrum fragments and vacate some or all of them when they are no longer required or when other more suitable ones become available. These requirements may depend on context, application and location and can include price, Quality of Service (QoS), and energy saving.

To date both in the UK [10] and US [5–7] regulators have committed to licence-exempt cognitive access to the so-called TV White Spaces (TVWS). The TVWS spectrum comprises large portions of the UHF/VHF spectrum that become available on a geographical basis for cognitive access as a result of the switchover from analogue to digital TV. The total capacity associated with TVWS is significant. According to modelling studies commissioned by Ofcom over 50% of locations in the UK are likely to have more that 150 MHz of interleaved spectrum and that even at 90% of locations around 100 MHz of interleaved spectrum might be available for cognitive access [10]. In addition to TVWS, the defence spectrum may provide another significant capacity opportunity for license-exempt cognitive access. For example, around 30% of spectrum below 15 GHz is allocated to Defence in the UK. The UK (Ministry of Defence) MoD had until the late 1990's access to spectrum at no or a low cost. However, following the Cave Audit, the Government has committed to releasing a "significant proportion" of the MOD's spectrum between 2008 and 2010. Results form a 2008 study by PA consulting (commissioned jointly by MoD and Ofcom) suggest that [11] there is significant scope for license-exempt use of the released spectrum using cognitive radio technology, both

on a spatial and a temporal basis. For example, low power cognitive devices could potentially share with radar if the radar sweep can be detected and the transmission of the cognitive device can be timed to avoid interference.

This paper aims to review the state-of-the-art in technology, regulation, and standardisation of cognitive radio access to TVWS. It also examines the spectrum opportunity, potential business applications, and some of the open research challenges associated with this new form of access, drawing lessons and conclusions from recent recent findings in the UK [12, 13], US [14, 15], and elsewhere. The rest of this paper is organised as follows. Section 2 provides a brief overview of cognitive radio access to TV White Spaces. In Section 3 the regulatory status and standardisation efforts are reviewed and some of the outstanding research and technology challenges are discussed. In Section 4 we discuss recent results on quantifying the availability of TVWS spectrum for cognitive access in the UK and the US, and describe some of the prominent candidate use cases of this spectrum. We conclude this paper in Section 5.

2. Cognitive Access to TV White Spaces

2.1. What are TV White Spaces? Broadcast television services operate in licensed channels in the VHF and UHF portions of the radio spectrum. The regulatory rules in most countries prohibit the use of unlicensed devices in TV bands, with the exception of remote control, medical telemetry devices, and wireless microphones. In most developed countries regulators are currently in the process of requiring TV stations to convert from analogue to digital transmission. This Digital Switchover (DSO) was completed in the US in June 2009, and is expected to be completed in the UK by 2012. A similar switchover process is also underway or being planned (or is already completed) in the rest of the EU and many other countries around the world. After Digital Switchover a portion of TV analogue channels become entirely vacant due to the higher spectrum efficiency of digital TV (DTV). These cleared channels will then be reallocated by regulators to other services through auctions.

In addition to cleared spectrum, after the DTV transition there will be typically a number of TV channels in a given geographic area that are not being used by DTV stations, because such stations would not be able to operate without causing interference to cochannel or adjacent channel stations. However, a transmitter operating on such a locally vacant TV channel at a much lower power level would not need a great (physical) separation from cochannel and adjacent channel TV stations to avoid causing interference. Low power devices can therefore operate on vacant channels in locations that could not be used by TV stations due to interference planning. These vacant TV channels are known as TV White Spaces or Interleaved Spectrum in the language of the UK regulator.

2.2. Detection and Incumbent Protection. Secondary operation of cognitive radios in TV bands relies on the ability of cognitive devices to successfully detect TVWS, and is conditioned by regulators on the ability of these devices to avoid harmful interference to licensed users of these bands, which in addition to DTV include also wireless microphones. Both the FCC and Ofcom have considered three methods for ensuring that cognitive devices do not cause harmful interference to incumbent: beacons, geolocation combined with access to a database, and sensing. Currently, the database approach seems to offers the best short-term solution for incumbent detection and interference avoidance. Both in the US and UK regulatory and industry efforts is, therefore, underway to further develop the concepts, algorithms and regulatory framework necessary for this approach.

2.2.1. Beacons. With the beacon method, unlicensed devices only transmit if they receive a control signal (beacon) identifying vacant channels within their service areas. The signal can be received from a TV station, FM broadcast station, or TV band fixed unlicensed transmitter. Without reception of this control signal, no transmissions are permitted. One issue with the control signal method is that it requires a beacon infrastructure to be in place, which needs to be maintained and operated, either by the incumbent or a third party. Furthermore, beacon signals can be lost due to mechanisms similar to the hidden node problem described below.

2.2.2. Geolocation Combined with Database. In this method, a device determines its location and accesses a database to determine the TV channels that are vacant at that location. There are at least three issues associated with this method. There is a need for a new (commercial) entity to build and maintain the database. Devices need to know their location with a prescribed accuracy. For outdoor applications GPS can be used to support these requirements, but in the case of indoor application there are issues with the penetration of GPS deep. Finally, devices need additional connectivity in a different band in order to be able to access the database prior to any transmission in DTV bands. inside buildings.

We note that the latter problems can be addressed in master-slave communication architectures where a master device, for example, an access point or base station, has access to location information and is connected via a wireless or fix link to the Internet. The master node uses its location information to query the geolocation database about TVWS channel availability and based on this information instructs a set of slave devices on the frequencies they can use.

2.2.3. Sensing. Finally, in the sensing method, unlicensed devices autonomously detect the presence of TV signals and only use the channels that are not used by TV broadcaster. Detection of the TV signal can be subject to the hidden node problem, which is depicted in Figure 1. This problem can arise when there is blockage between the unlicensed device and a TV station, but no blockage between the TV station and a TV receiver antenna and no blockage between the unlicensed device and the same TV receiver antenna. In such a case, a cognitive radio may not detect the presence of the TV signal and could start using an occupied channel, causing harmful interference to the TV receiver.

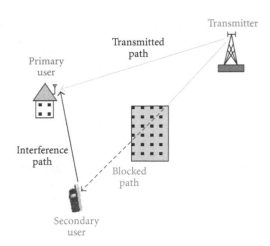

FIGURE 1: The hidden node problem of a sensing-based cognitive radio.

2.3. Regulatory Developments

2.3.1. US. In the US the FCC proposed to allow opportunistic access to TV bands already in 2004 [4]. Prototype cognitive radios operating in this mode were put forward to FCC by Adaptrum, (Institute for Infocomm Research) I2R, Microsoft, Motorola, and Philips in 2008. After extensive tests the FCC adopted in November 2008 a Second Report and Order that establishes rules to allow the operation of cognitive devices in TVWS on a license-exempt basis [5–7]. In summary these rules require cognitive devices to use both spectrum sensing and geolocation. In order to minimise the chance of harmful interference due to the hidden node problem FCC has required that cognitive devices should be able to sense both television signals and wireless microphones down to $-114\,\mathrm{dBm}$. They must also locate their position to within 50 metres and then consult a database that will inform them about available spectrum in that location [5–7].

Mobile devices may transmit in a locally vacant TV channel at up to 100 mW unless they are using a channel adjacent to terrestrial television, in which case their transmission power can only be 40 mW. Fixed devices (base stations or customer premises) may transmit at a locally vacant channel at up to 4 W (EIRP). Devices without geolocation capabilities are also allowed if they are transmitting to a device that has determined its location. In this case, one device would be acting as a master for a network and the other slave devices would operate broadly under its control in terms of the spectrum they would use. Devices that use sensing alone are allowed in principle; however, they must be submitted in advance to the FCC for laboratory and field testing so the FCC can determine whether they are likely to cause harmful interference. The exact process that the FCC will use to determine this has not been specified.

Importantly, the FCC report includes a detailed discussion about whether cognitive access should be licensed, licence-exempt or subject to light licensing. It concludes that the best way to facilitate innovative new applications is via licence-exemption and that licensing would not be practicable for many of the new applications envisaged. It also notes that any licenses would be difficult to define and subject to change (e.g., if television coverage was replanned), so the rights awarded would be rather tenuous.

2.3.2. UK.

In its Digital Dividend Review Statement released in December 2007 the UK regulator, Ofcom, proposed to "allow licence exempt use of interleaved spectrum for cognitive devices" [8]. Furthermore Ofcom stated that "We see significant scope for cognitive equipments using interleaved spectrum to emerge and to benefit from international economics of scale [8]". In a consultation published on 16 February 2009 [9] Ofcom proposed a number of technical parameters for licence-exempt cognitive use of interleaved spectrum which closely follow those suggested by FCC.

Subsequently, in a statement published on July 1 2009 Ofcom proposed to allow sensing alone as well as geolocation for incumbent detection [10]. However, it concludes that in the short term the most important mechanism for spectrum detection will be geolocation. Ofcom is suggesting that further work, possibly leading to a consultation specifically on geolocation, is appropriate. Finally Ofcom states that it "will work with stakeholders to further develop the concepts and algorithms necessary for geolocation and expect to consult further on Geo-location later in 2009" [10]. Following this consultation Ofcom published a discussion paper on geolocation for cognitive access in Novemeber 2009.

2.3.3. Worldwide.

Work on a pan-European specification for cognitive devices is currently taking place within the SE43 working group of (the European Conference of Postal and Telecommunications Administrations) CEPT. An important aim of this group is to define technical and operational requirements for the operation of cognitive radio systems in TV White Spaces in order to ensure the protection of incumbent services/systems and to investigate the amount of spectrum across Europe that is potentially available as White Spaces. Furthermore on a worldwide scale, agenda item 1.19 of the (World Radiocommunications Conference, 2011) WRC-11 will be considering regulatory measures and their relevance, in order to enable the introduction of software defined radio and cognitive radio systems, based on the results of ongoing ITU-R studies.

2.4. Standardisation and Industry Effort.

Industry led research and development on cognitive radio technology has been so far mainly focused in the USA, and is largely driven by the desire of important new players, including Google and Microsoft, to get access to the TVWS spectrum. However, a number of EU-backed and industry-led collaborative projects are currently underway that aim at bringing cognitive radio technology in Europe closer to commercial exploitation. Two major standardisation efforts, which are currently at an advanced stage, are discussed below. It is worth mentioning that in addition to these a number of new standardisation initiatives are underway, which include the IEEE 802.19 and the IEEE 802.11af standards.

2.4.1. The Cognitive Networking Alliance (CogNeA) Standard.

The Cognitive Networking Alliance (CogNea) [16] is an open industry association. The Alliance intends to commercialise low power personal/portable Cognitive Radio platforms by enabling and promoting the rapid adoption, regulation, standardisation and multivendor compliance and interoperability of CRs world wide. Alliance board members include ETRI, HP, Philips, Samsung Electro-Mechanics, Texas Instruments, and more recently BT. The initial geographical focus area is North America. The initial focus radio spectrum is TV White Spaces.

The Alliance intends to promote TVWS spectrum regulations worldwide, and to establish a recognisable CogNeA brand that indicates a device is CogNeA-compliant and can therefore interoperate with other CogNeA-certified devices from various manufacturers. The Alliance also develops specifications for the Common Cognitive Radio Platform (CCRP) which supports multiple applications [17].

The Alliance intends to bring the standard to an international status, in collaboration with an existing Standards Definition Organisation (SDO), to make it globally accepted. The primary target applications for the CogNeA standard are

(i) in-home high definition multimedia networking and distribution solutions that overcome the whole home coverage problems inherent to solutions using ISM bands,

(ii) unlicensed broadband wireless access for communities/neighbourhoods/campuses.

The standard is developing a Common Radio Platform consisting of the Physical Layer (PHY) and the Media Access Layer (MAC). The PHY consists of the Radio Front End, the Baseband, and the Cognitive Entity, which contains a geo-location block, a sensing block and an Internet access and interference map resources. The MAC carries the Communication/Networking protocol, Air access rules, and interface for the higher layers, such as network and application layers.

ECMA International is currently developing a high-speed wireless networking standard for use in the Television White Spaces, based on the contribution from CogNeA. The standard will employ cognitive radio sensing and database technologies to avoid interference with licensed services and other incumbent users in compliance with the FCC regulatory rules. The first draft of the ECMA/CogNeA PHY and MAC standard for operation in TV White Spaces was published in December 2009 [18, 19].

2.4.2. The IEEE 802.22 Standards.

The IEEE 802.22 Working Group [20] has defined an air interface (PHY and MAC) standard based on cognitive radio techniques. The 802.22 standard is being developed for Wireless Regional Area Networks (WRANs). The primary target application of the standard is licensed-exempt broadband wireless access to rural areas in TVWS. The initial geographical focus area is North America. The 802.22 system specifies a fixed point-to-multipoint wireless air interface whereby a base station (BS) manages its own cell and all associated Consumer Premise

Equipments (CPEs). The network architecture including MAC and PHY are derived from IEEE 802.16 WiMAX. The 802.22 PHY layer is designed to support a system which uses vacant TVWS channels to provide wireless communication access over distances of up to 100 Km. The PHY specification is based on Orthogonal Frequency Division Multiple Access (OFDMA) for both the upstream and downstream access.

The IEEE 802.22 standard supports incumbent detection through spectrum sensing (the database approach is optional). The standard specifies inputs and outputs for the sensing function, as well as the performance requirements for the sensing algorithms implemented (e.g., probability of detection, incumbent detection threshold and probability of false alarms). These include energy detector, and cyclostationary and pilot sensing detectors for ATSC DTV signals, and an FFT-based algorithm for detection of wireless microphone signals [21].

The IEEE 802.22 defines a connection oriented and centralised MAC layer. Two important capabilities are introduced in the 802.22 MAC layer to support reliable incumbent detection based on sensing: network-wide quite periods scheduled by each BS during which all transmissions are suspended in order to allow reliable sensing, and channel measurement management to coordinate distributed channel measurement/incumbent detection by CPEs and their reporting to BS.

After an initial accelerated phase, the development of the standard seems to have slowed down during the last year. According to the IEEE 802.22 sources, the standard is currently at the Ballot stage. However, the final completion date for standard is not known yet, and there have been no vendor companies so far to build equipment based on the IEEE 802.22.

3. Research Challenges

3.1. High-Precision Spectrum Sensing. In order to minimise the chance of harmful interference due to the hidden node problem both the FCC and Ofcom require that cognitive devices should be able to sense TV signals at detection margins much lower than that of TV receivers (114 dBm for 6 MHz US channels and −120 dBm for 8 MHz UK channels) [5–7, 10]. Such weak signals are well below thermal noise, and in the presence of noise uncertainty cannot be detected using the energy detection algorithms that are implemented in the current generation of wireless devices [22]. Recent research, however, shows that such sensing levels may be achieved using more sophisticated sensing algorithms that rely on certain features of incumbent signals which are absent in the noise [23].

In the following we briefly discuss some of these "non-blind" sensing techniques. We note that, unlike energy detection, these algorithms are generally not applicable to sensing signals from wireless microphones, most of which use analogue frequency modulation (FM), and refer the reader to [24, 25] for recently proposed algorithms for detection of wireless microphones.

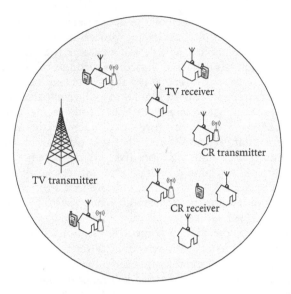

FIGURE 2: In future commercial applications the aggregate power levels of cognitive devices need to be controlled in order to avoid interference to primary receivers.

(i) *Pilot detection.* These sensing algorithms are specific to ATSC signals, which have a DC pilot at a lower band-edge in a known location relative to the signal. Detection is achieved by setting a threshold either on the amplitude or the location of the pilot signal. Detection based on the location of pilot is in particular robust against noise uncertainty, since the position of the pilot can be pinpointed with high accuracy, even if the amplitude is low due to fading [21].

(ii) *Cyclostationary feature detection.* Both the ATSC and DVB-T signals are cyclostationary, that is, the means and correlation sequences of these signals exhibit periodicity. Cyclostationary feature detectors were introduced as a complex two-dimensional signal processing technique for recognition of modulated signals in the presence of noise and interference. Recently they have been proposed by a number of authors [26, 27] for the detection of weak TV signals in the context of spectrum sensing for cognitive radio.

(iii) *Cyclic prefix and autocorrelation detection.* OFDM signals, including DVB-T signals, contain a special sequence called cyclic prefix (CP), where the last D bits of the OFDM symbol is copied to the beginning of the symbol. Cyclic prefix detection is similar to energy detection. However, the test statistics used in the algorithm is the energy contained in the cyclic prefix of each OFDM symbol, instead of the whole symbol [28]. Furthermore, due to the presence of CP the autocorrelation function of DVB-T signals show distinct peaks at nonzero values whose amplitude and position could be used to detect the signal from the noise.

One issue with most of the above sensing algorithms is that they require considerable processing power which may be either not available or not desirable (due to power consumption) in handheld devices. A second problem with high-precision sensing is that the ability of cognitive devices to sense extremely weak TV signals may eliminate the hidden node problem (false negatives) but at the same time it can lead to a situation where a cognitive radio detects TV signals from transmitters that are perhaps hundreds of kilometres away (false positive), thereby removing a considerable portion of usable White Spaces. Very recent studies in the US, for example, indicate that a threshold of -114 dBm reduces the recoverable White Spaces by a factor of 3 [14]. Even worse, initial modelling studies performed at BT [29] show that in some UK locations, a cognitive device with a -114 dBm sensitivity level will identify all DTT channels as occupied, and therefore will have no White Space available for its operation if it relies on naive sensing only!

There has been considerable recent research in cooperative detection algorithms, where sensing measurements performed by multiple devices are combined (using either a soft or a hard decision combining method) in order to achieve higher sensing thresholds than is possible by single devices or to deal with the hidden node problem [30–32]. Interestingly, cooperative sensing was also considered in Ofcom's consultation on cognitive access as a possible approach to the detection problem [9].

One problem of cooperative sensing is that the achievable detection level depends on several factors, including the number of cooperating cognitive devices and their spatial arrangement [30, 31]. Therefore, in general it would be difficult to test and certify the detection capability of such cooperating cognitive devices on an individual basis to check device compliance with regulatory requirements [29]. Furthermore this method requires additional communication overhead since local measurements will be collected at system level in order to make a decision, which is then broadcast to all cognitive radios involved.

Due to the above issues we believe that the most promising application of cooperative sensing will be in master-slave communication scenarios, where a computationally powerful master device (e.g., a WiFi access point or a cellular base station) centrally coordinates and process sensing activities of a set of slave devices in combination and uses the result to refine and geographically extend the results of its own sophisticated sensing algorithms.

3.2. Agile Transmissions and Spectrum Pooling Techniques.

Physical layer transmission techniques that are able to effectively deal with the fragmented nature of TVWS spectrum are a very important component of future cognitive radios. In particular, these techniques must be sufficiently agile to enable unlicensed users to transmit in (locally) available TVWS bands while not interfering with the incumbent users operating at adjacent bands. Moreover, to support throughput-intensive applications, these techniques should be able to achieve high data rates by pooling several (not necessarily contiguous TVWS channels). One technique that seems to meet both these requirements is a variant of orthogonal frequency division multiplexing (OFDM) called *non-contiguous OFDM* (NC-OFDM) [33, 34]. NC-OFDM is capable of deactivating subcarriers across its transmission bandwidth that could potentially interfere with the transmission of other users. Moreover, NC-OFDM can support a high aggregate data rate with the remaining subcarriers, and simultaneously maintain an acceptable level of error robustness. In addition to NC-OFDM several other techniques have been proposed to enable agile waveforming over fragmented spectrum. One prominent example is the use of filterbank multicarrier techniques for such cognitive radio applications [35].

3.3. Multiple Antenna Technologies for Cognitive Radio.

The use of antenna diversity or MIMO antenna architecture can provide a significant increase in the spectral efficiency of wireless systems [36, 37]. However, the use of multiple antennas in cognitive radio networks is underdeveloped. One of the major objectives for cognitive radio is to improve the spectrum utilisation. With the advantages offered by MIMO systems, it is therefore logical to exploit potentials in applying the MIMO antenna architecture to cognitive radio networks. Introducing multiple antenna technologies for cognitive radio (CR) may extend the dimension of CR from the current frequency band and time slot regime even further into spatial domain. A cognitive system using MIMO can significantly improve receiver sensitivity and coverage, hence it may also have impact on the key device parameters such as sensitivity and transmit power in CR, that is, required by regulators.

One issue with the use of MIMO in the context of cognitive access to TVWS is that the typical wavelengths in the UHF bands vary between 0.3–0.6 m. Optimal use of multiple antennas on a single cognitive device, therefore may not be feasible in most applications due to the small footprints involved. However, fixed BWA(Broadband Wireless Access) applications similar to that considered in the IEEE 802.22 that involve large base stations and customer premises may greatly benefit from multiple antenna technologies.

3.4. System-Level Issues.

Almost all research so far has focused on a single cognitive device accessing TVWS spectrum. However, the provision of commercial services based on cognitive radio technologies, for example, mobile broadband or wireless home networks, will inevitably involve situations involving multiple cognitive equipments that may belong to either the same or different service providers. Some open research challenges associated with such service scenarios include the following:

(i) estimation and control of aggregate interference from multiple cognitive devices [38] towards primary users,

(ii) politeness (etiquette) rules that achieve fair and efficient sharing of secondary spectrum among competing cognitive radios [9],

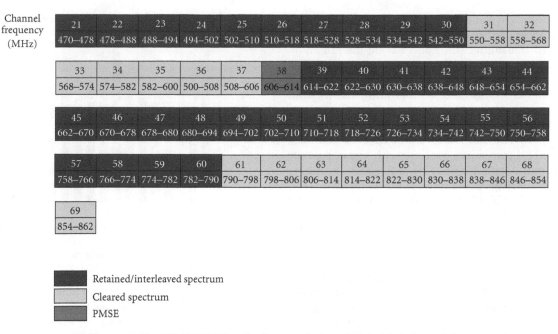

Channel frequency (MHz)											
21	22	23	24	25	26	27	28	29	30	31	32
470–478	478–488	488–494	494–502	502–510	510–518	518–528	528–534	534–542	542–550	550–558	558–568

33	34	35	36	37	38	39	40	41	42	43	44
568–574	574–582	582–600	500–508	508–606	606–614	614–622	622–630	630–638	638–648	648–654	654–662

45	46	47	48	49	50	51	52	53	54	55	56
662–670	670–678	678–680	680–694	694–702	702–710	710–718	718–726	726–734	734–742	742–750	750–758

57	58	59	60	61	62	63	64	65	66	67	68
758–766	766–774	774–782	782–790	790–798	798–806	806–814	814–822	822–830	830–838	838–846	846–854

69
854–862

■ Retained/interleaved spectrum
□ Cleared spectrum
▣ PMSE

FIGURE 3: The UK UHF TV bands after completion of Digital Switchover [9].

(iii) spectrum sensing under aggregate interference conditions,

(iv) quantitative understanding of the scalability of secondary spectrum access networks operating in TVWS spectrum.

4. TVWS Spectrum Availability and Use Cases

4.1. How Much White Spaces Is Available? Figure 3 shows allocation of the UHF spectrum in the UK after the completion of DSO [10]. The 128 MHz of spectrum marked in green (16 bands) is the cleared spectrum which Ofcom plans to license through auctions. The 256 MHz (32 channels) marked in purple is the interleaved spectrum which can be used on a geographical basis for license-exempt access by using cognitive radio technology. Finally the channel marked in pink is licensed by Ofcom for exclusive access for wireless microphones, and so forth, (PMSE).

From the above chart it appears that there is significant capacity available for cognitive access in the UHF bands. However, due to its secondary nature the availability and frequency decomposition of the UHF spectrum for cognitive access is not the same at all locations and depends also on the power levels used by cognitive devices [12, 14]. This is an important feature of license-exempt cognitive access to TV bands which distinguish it from, for example, WiFi access to the ISM bands.

Potential commercial applications of TVWS devices will strongly depend on how the availability of this spectrum varies; both from location to location and as a function of transmit power of cognitive devices. A number of recent studies have investigated various aspect of TVWS spectrum in the US [14, 15]. In the UK we have developed a set of modelling tools that have enabled us to quantify the availability of TVWS spectrum for cognitive access and its variation with location and transmit power.

The first set of these modelling tools [12] makes use of the publicly available maps of DTV coverage in the UK [39] which were generated via computer simulations from the Ofcoms database of location, transmit power, antenna height and transmit frequency of UKs DTV transmitters, and were further validated and improved through direct observations at different locations. It combines these coverage maps with simplified propagation modelling calculations to obtain upper bounds for the vacant TVWS frequencies at any given location as well as a lower-bound estimate for the variations of TVWS spectrum with the transmit power of a cognitive devices.

The computer model for obtaining the upper bounds works as follows [12]. We use the UK National Grid (NG) coordinate system in order to specify the geographical position of any location on the UK map. Given the NG coordinates of a UK location the computer code then maps this location onto the closest grid point on the DTV coverage maps. For a given DTV transmitter this grid point is then evaluated to determine if it falls within the coverage area of that transmitter. If this is the case, then the frequencies associated with the transmitter are tagged as occupied at those locations, otherwise they are tagged as vacant. Repeating this procedure for coverage maps of all DTV transmitters, we then obtain a list of vacant TV frequencies at a given location that can be used by a low-power cognitive devices which is positioned in that location.

In the case of high power cognitive equipments, for example, those considered within the 802.22 standard, the required computations are very intensive. In order to reduce this computational effort, we approximate the actual DTV coverage areas by circular disks which were constructed such that each of them entirely encompassed the coverage area of the associated transmitter while also having the minimum possible surface area. With this simplification, it is then computationally straightforward to calculate from the vacant TV frequencies as a function of both position and transmit power of cognitive devices.

A second modelling tool is currently in its final development stage [40]. The tool makes use of Ofcom's published database of DTV transmitter together with highly accurate terrain data and standard UHF radio propagation models to generate contour maps of the received power for every DTV transmitters in the UK. Combining these contour maps with propagation modelling of cognitive devices, the available TVWS for cognitive access at any given location and for any arbitrary power level is then computed with a spatial resolution of 100 m. The terrain data used in this modelling tool is based on the STRM v2 terrain elevation data. The STRM data set resulted from a collaboration effort between NASA and the US National Geographic Intelligence Agency, as well as the participation of the German and the Italian space agencies, and is at present the most complete high-resolution digital topographic database of Earth.

We have used our first set of modelling tools to investigate the variations in TVWS as a function of the location and transmit power of cognitive radios, and to examine how constraints on adjacent channel emissions of cognitive radios may affects the results. This analysis provides a realistic view on the potential spectrum opportunity associated with cognitive radio access to TVWS in the UK, and also presents the first quantitative study of the availability and frequency composition of TVWS outside the United States. Figure 4 summarises in a bar-chart the availability of TVWS channels for 18 major population centres in England, Wales and Scotland. The total number of channels available at each location is shown as a green bar. These results show that there are considerable variations in the number of TVWS channels as we move from one UK location to another. For any given location, however, a minimum of 12 channels (96 MHz) is accessible to low-power cognitive devices, while the averaged per location capacity is just over 150 MHz.

When a high power cognitive device operates in a vacant TV channel, energy leakage to adjacent channels may cause interference to adjacent frequencies, which may be occupied. Ofcom had raised concerns that operation of low-power cognitive devices on a given channel may also cause adjacent-channel interference for mobile TV receivers that are in close vicinity. Consequently, even in some future use cases, cognitive devices may be constrained not to use vacant channels whose immediate adjacent frequencies are used for mobile TV. The total number of available TVWS after imposing the above adjacent channel constraint are shown as red bars in Figure 4. It can be seen that imposing the constraint greatly reduces the amount of accessible spectrum in most locations considered (on average the available capacity drops to just below 40 MHz/location).

Recent studies on quantifying the availability of TVWS in the United States were reported in [14, 15], and the results are in line with our findings for the UK. In particular a detailed

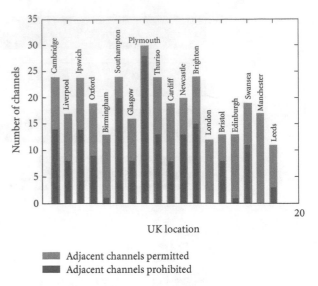

FIGURE 4: Available TVWS capacity for low-power cognitive access in 18 UK locations as obtained from coverage modelling. Results are shown both without (green bars) and with (red bars) considering adjacent channel interference constraint.

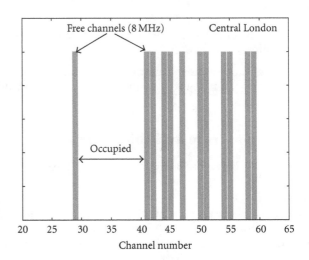

FIGURE 5: TVWS channels available for cognitive access in Central London.

study performed in [14] shows that in the US the main channels of relevance are the lower UHF channels where ~15 (90 MHz) channels per location/per person are available for low power cognitive access. However this number drops significantly (to ~5) when adjacent channels also have to be protected.

In addition to estimating total available TVWS, it is of importance to investigate channel composition of this spectrum. In Figure 5 we show, as an example, channel composition of TVWS in Central London. In this figure vacant channels are shown as blue bars while occupied channels are left black. As can be seen from the figure, the available TVWS channels can be highly non-contiguous. This feature may greatly restrict access to TVWS by most current wireless technologies, as modulation schemes implemented in these technologies often require a contiguous portion of the spectrum. In the case of London although a total of 96 MHz spectrum is in principle available, only 16 MHz can be utilised for contiguous frequency access.

We note that the above results were obtained using a combination of highly realistic DTV coverage maps with a simplified pathloss propagation model, which is adequate when considering low-power cognitive devices. Although our results are in good agreement with other independently obtained modelling results, for example, by Ofcom, we are currently not aware of any actual measurements of TVWS avilability in the UK that could be used to directly validate our modelling results. Furthermore, in order to improve the accuracy of our TVWS estimates for high-power cognitive devices, such as those required in rural broadband applications, we are incorporating standard UHF propagation models such as the ITU-R P.1546-3 (Longley-Rice) model [41] into our calculations.

4.2. Use Cases. In addition to considerable capacity it offers, which is evident from the discussion in the previous section, an important reason why TVWS spectrum has attracted much interest is an exceptionally attractive combination of bandwidth and coverage. Signals in the VHF/UHF TV bands travel much further than both the WiFi and 3G signals and penetrate buildings more readily. This in turn means that these bands can be used for a very wide range of potential new services. In addition to broadband wireless access to undeserved areas, other technologically important applications of TVWS spectrum include the following:

(i) wireless distribution networks for future digital homes and smart energy grids,

(ii) licensed-exempt mobile broadband,

(iii) last mile wireless broadband in urban environments,

(iv) cognitive femtocells/cellular communications in TVWS.

In the following paragraphs we will focus our attention on two future use cases of cognitive access to TVWS, which have recently attracted much attention from both industry and research community.

4.2.1. Future Wireless Home Networks. Fuelled by the quick progress of wireless technologies, broadband adoption, and without the burden of spectrum licences, home wireless networking has become in the last few years a pervasive technology. Between 2004 and 2006, home network adoption boomed across Europe, with growth rates surpassing Asia and North America. France and the UK both trebled the number of households with a home network, putting them slightly ahead of the US Italy and Germany still lagged behind but posted notable growth nonetheless. More than 54% of European households have a computer and a total of 34% are using WiFi routers. The future wireless home will consist not only of PC, laptops and PDAS wirelessly connected to the Internet but also media servers (High Definition TV,

video and audio), access points, computer electronics like wireless cameras and game consoles. Due to sharp decrease in wireless solutions prices and minimum restrictions for access to ISM bands, other domestic applications as well as gas, electricity and water meters will in the future come equipped with radio receivers allowing control, monitoring and easy configuration (the so-called smart grids).

Most of these devices and services support wireless connectivity using one or a number of short-range wireless technologies, such as WiFi (IEEE 802.11), Zigbee (IEEE 802.15.4), and so forth, all operating without the need for a licence in the already congested ISM bands. Home networks of the future operating exclusively in these bands are expected to suffer severe capacity limitations resulting from interference caused by the high device density and limited spectrum availability in the ISM bands. Furthermore, the aggregate interference resulting from these devices is bound to create a high interference burden on the WiFi-based provision of broadband wireless access in homes.

Additional capacity offered by secondary access to TVWS has the potential to solve this capacity limitation problem thereby contributing to increasing takeup of wireless home networking and services, and spurring future technological innovation and revenue generation. In particular, some of the most bandwidth-intensive home networks applications (such as multimedia streaming) can be offloaded to TVWS bands hence freeing up the ISM bands for other consumer applications. Our recent system-wide simulation studies show that [13] due to lower operation frequencies home access points operating in the TVWS UHF frequencies can achieve throughput levels that are either higher or comparable to WiFi access points while using significantly lower transmit power levels (two order of magnitudes in mW) [13]. An additional benefit here is that a significant saving in energy consumption can be achieved in home networking scenarios by switching from the ISM bands to TVWS bands [13]. Furthermore, according to several recent studies [12, 42] the number of available channels for indoor white space transmissions appear to be very significant.

Protection of incumbents in such home networking scenarios can be achieved using a master-slave architecture where functionalities of spectrum detection and/or geolocation and database access and spectrum assignment are all integrated into the home access point [43]. The access point monitors the availability of spectrum in the ISM and TV bands and instruct customer devices which spectrum to use based on their bandwidth and QoS requirements.

4.2.2. Cognitive/TVWS Femtocells. A femtocell is a small base station of 3G/LTE, or WiMAX technology, controlled by the mobile operator and placed inside the home /small office of the customer. Femtocells are useful when a user experiences bad indoor coverage or its application is too capacity-demanding for indoor conditions. The user may be already inside or going inside a building. Femtocells help maintaining a mobile broadband session or to allow it where it previously was not possible. Current generation femtocells use the same frequencies as mobile networks, hence creating

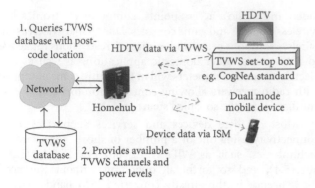

FIGURE 6: Architecture for HDTV distribution using TV White Space spectrum.

a potential source of interference that can be difficult to control since the user femtocell is not controlled by the operator.

Femtocells operating in TVWS would be an alternative to femtocells proprietary technologies that are appearing on the market for dedicated 3G/LTE networks [44]. The main advantage of CR based femtocells compared to traditional femtocells will be reduced or better controlled interference into the operators' network. Another case of great interest to operators is to use CR to backhauling of femtocells (either traditional or CR-based themselves). This allows a mobile operator gain control into the home of the user, should it be outside the DSL coverage or whether the user has another operator delivering broadband to his/her home network.

5. Conclusions

In this paper we surveyed the state-of-the-art in cognitive radio access to TV White Spaces. We showed that a regulatory framework for secondary utilisation of TVWS spectrum is well underway both in the US and UK and important steps in this direction are also being taken within the EU and worldwide. Using result from recent quantitative studies of the TVWS availability in the UK and US we illustrated that cognitive access to these bands provides a very significant spectrum opportunity for a range of indoor and outdoor applications and services. In addition to rural broadband, which is the main focus of the IEEE 802.22 standard, these include wireless home networks, mobile broadband, and TVWS femtocells.

However, effective exploitation of this spectrum for such commercial services requires addressing an array of important technology challenges. One of these, high-precision spectrum sensing, has been the subject of numerous research papers while others, including multiple secondary access, aggregate interference control, and agile modulation techniques, have not yet received the attention we believe they deserve. Furthermore, quantitative techno-economical studies of the commercial feasibility and cost versus benefit associated with use cases of cognitive radio crucial in influencing the takeup of the technology by wireless network and service providers but are currently very limited. Our own research is currently focusing on some of the abovementioned technology and business challenges of cognitive access to TVWS.

Acknowledgments

The author wishes to acknowledge his colleagues at BT, S. Kawade, M. Fitch, X. Gu, K. Briggs, R. MacKenzie, P. Bruce, A. Sago, C. Cheeseman, M. Pine, J. Zhang, N. Edwards, and D. Bryant, for stimulating discussions. He thanks Jonas Kronander from Ericsson AB for reading the manuscript. The author would like to thank the European Union for providing partial funding of this work through the EU FP7 project INFSO-ICT-248303 QUASAR.

References

[1] A. Wyglynski, M. Nekovee, and T. Hou, Eds., *Cognitive Radio Communication and Networks: Principle and Practice*, Academic Press, London, UK, 2010.

[2] J. Mitola III and G. Q. Maguire Jr., "Cognitive radio: making software radios more personal," *IEEE Personal Communications*, vol. 6, no. 4, pp. 13–18, 1999.

[3] M. Nekovee, "Dynamic spectrum access—concepts and future architectures," *BT Technology Journal*, vol. 24, no. 2, pp. 111–116, 2006.

[4] Federal Communications Commission, "Spectrum policy task force," Report of the Spectrum Efficiency Working Group, November 2004, http://www.fcc.gov/sptf/reports.html/.

[5] Federal Communications Commission (FCC), "Second report and order and memorandum. Opinion and order," Tech. Rep. 08-260, November 2008.

[6] Federal Communications Commission (FCC), "Additional spectrum for unlicensed devices below 900 MHz and in the 3 GHz band," ET Docket 02-380, December 2002.

[7] Federal Communications Commission (FCC), "Unlicensed operation in the TV broadcast bands," ET Docket 04-186, May 2004.

[8] Ofcom, "Digital Dividend Review, A statement on our approach towards awarding the digital dividend," December 2007.

[9] "Ofcom Consultation: Digital Dividend," February 2009, http://www.ofcom.org.uk/consult/condocs/cognitive/summary/.

[10] Ofcom, "Statement on Cognitive Access to Interleaved Spectrum," July 2009.

[11] J. Bradford, T. Cook, D. Ramsbottom, and S. Jones, "Optimising usage of spectrum below 15 GHz used for defence in the UK," in *Proceedings of the IET Seminar on Software Defined Radio and Cognitive Radio*, London, UK, September 2008.

[12] M. Nekovee, "Quantifying the availability of TV white spaces for cognitive radio operation in the UK," in *Proceedings of the IEEE International Conference on Communications Workshops (ICC '09)*, Dresden, Germany, June 2009.

[13] S. Kawade and M. Nekovee, "Wireless options for high data-rate indoor users: cognitive access to TV white spaces," in *Proceedings of the IEEE International Symposium on New Frontiers in Dynamic Spectrum Access Networks (DySPAN '10)*, Singapore, April 2010.

[14] M. Mishra and A. Sahai, "How much white space is there?" Tech. Rep., Electrical Engineering and Computer Sciences, University of California at Berkeley, January 2009.

[15] T. X. Brown and D. C. Sicker, "Can cognitive radio support broadband wireless access?" in *Proceedings of the 2nd IEEE International Symposium on New Frontiers in Dynamic Spectrum Access Networks (DySPAN '07)*, pp. 123–132, April 2007.

[16] "CogNeA," http://www.cognea.com/.

[17] K. Challapali, "Philips Research North America (private communication)," FAQ on CogNeA Alliance, K. Kimyacioglu, Philips.

[18] Ecma 392, Ecma International Standard.

[19] J. Wang, M. Sun Song, S. Santhiveeran, et al., "First cognitive PHY/MAC standard for personal/portable devices in TV White Spaces".

[20] "IEEE 802.22," http://www.ieee802.org/22/.

[21] C. Cordeiro, D. Cavalcanti, and S. ShankarA. Wyglynski, M. Nekovee, and T. Hou, "Cognitive radio for broadband wireless access in TV bands: the IEEE 802.22 standards," in *Cognitive Radio Communication and Networking: Principle and Practice*, Academic Press, Boston, Mass, USA, 2009.

[22] A. Sahai and D. Cabric, "Spectrum sensing: fundamental limits and practical challenges," in *Proceedings of the IEEE International Symposium on New Frontiers in Dynamic Spectrum Access Networks (DySPAN '05)*, Baltimore, Md, USA, November 2005.

[23] T. Yücek and H. Arslan, "A survey of spectrum sensing algorithms for cognitive radio applications," *IEEE Communications Surveys and Tutorials*, vol. 11, no. 1, pp. 116–130, 2009.

[24] H.-S. Chen, W. Gao, and D. G. Daut, "Spectrum sensing for wireless microphone signals," in *Proceedings of the 5th Annual IEEE Communications Society Conference on Sensor, Mesh and Ad Hoc Communications and Networks Workshops*, San Francisco, Calif, USA, June 2008.

[25] A. Mossa and A. Jeoti, "Cyclostationary-based spectrum sensing for analog TV and wireless microphone signals," in *Proceedings of the 1st International Conference on Computational Intelligence, Communication Systems and Networks*, pp. 380–385, 2008.

[26] P. D. Sutton, K. E. Nolan, and L. E. Doyle, "Cyclostationary signatures in practical cognitive radio applications," *IEEE Journal on Selected Areas in Communications*, vol. 26, no. 1, pp. 13–24, 2008.

[27] L. P. Goh, Z. Lei, and F. Chini, "DVB detector for cognitive radio," in *Proceedings of the IEEE International Conference on Communications (ICC '07)*, pp. 6460–6465, Glasgow, UK, June 2007.

[28] G. Noh, J. Lee, H. Wang, S. You, and D. Hong, "A new spectrum sensing scheme using cyclic prefix for OFDM-based cognitive radio systems," in *Proceedings of the IEEE Vehicular Technology Conference (VTC '08)*, pp. 1891–1895, May 2008.

[29] "BT Response to Ofcom Consultation on Digital Dividend," Cognitive Access.

[30] A. Ghasemi and E. S. Sousa, "Collaborative spectrum sensing for opportunistic access in fading environments," in *Proceedings of the 1st IEEE International Symposium on New Frontiers in Dynamic Spectrum Access Networks (DySPAN '05)*, pp. 131–136, Baltimore, Md, USA, November 2005.

[31] G. Ganesan and Y. Li, "Cooperative spectrum sensing in cognitive radio, part I: two user networks," *IEEE Transactions on Wireless Communications*, vol. 6, no. 6, pp. 2204–2212, 2007.

[32] Y. Selén and J. Kronander, "Cooperative detection of Programme making special event devices in realistic fading environements," in *Proceedings of the IEEE International Symposium on New Frontiers in Dynamic Spectrum Access Networks (DySPAN '10)*, Singapore, April 2010.

[33] R. Rajbanshi, A. M. Wyglinski, and G. J. Minden, "An efficient implementation of NC-OFDM transceivers for cognitive radios," in *Proceedings of the 1st International Conference on Cognitive Radio Oriented Wireless Networks and Communications (CROWNCOM '06)*, June 2006.

[34] R. Rajbanshi, *OFDMbased cognitive radio for DSA networks*, Ph.D. thesis, University of Kansas, Lawrence, Kan, USA, 2007.

[35] W. Rhee, J. C. Chuang, and L. J. Cimini, "Performance comparison of OFDM and multitone with polyphase filter bank for wireless communications," in *Proceedings of the 48th IEEE Vehicular Technology Conference (VTC '98)*, pp. 768–772, May 1998.

[36] M. Jankiraman, *Space-Time Codes and MIMO Systems*, Artech House, Boston, Mass, USA, 2004.

[37] N. Devroye, P. Mitran, and V. Tarokh, "Limits on communications in a cognitive radio channel," *IEEE Communications Magazine*, vol. 44, no. 6, pp. 44–49, 2006.

[38] N. S. Shankar and C. Cordeiro, "Analysis of aggregated interference at DTV receivers in TV bands," in *Proceedings of the 3rd International Conference on Cognitive Radio Oriented Wireless Networks and Communications (CROWNCOM '08)*, Singapore, May 2008.

[39] "UK FREE.TV," http://www.ukfree.tv/.

[40] K. Briggs, "BT innovate and design," Tech. Rep., July 2009.

[41] P. L. Rice, A. G. Longley, K. A. Norton, and A. P. Barsis, "Transmission loss predictors for tropospheric communication circuits," Tech. Note 101, U S Government Printing Office, Washington, DC, USA, 1965.

[42] E. Obregon and J. Zander, "Short range white space utilization in broadcast systems for indoor environments," in *Proceedings of the IEEE International Symposium on New Frontiers in Dynamic Spectrum Access Networks (DySPAN '10)*, Singapore, April 2010.

[43] M. Nekovee, "Cognitive access to TV White Spaces: spectrum opportunities, commercial applications and remaining technology challanges," in *Proceedings of the IEEE International Symposium on New Frontiers in Dynamic Spectrum Access Networks (DySPAN '10)*, Singapore, April 2010.

[44] D. López-Pérez, A. Valcarce, G. De La Roche, and J. Zhang, "OFDMA femtocells: a roadmap on interference avoidance," *IEEE Communications Magazine*, vol. 47, no. 9, pp. 41–48, 2009.

5

On the QoS of IPTV and Its Effects on Home Networks

Dongyu Qiu

Department of Electrical and Computer Engineering, Concordia University, Montreal, QC, Canada H3G 1M8

Correspondence should be addressed to Dongyu Qiu, dongyu@ece.concordia.ca

Academic Editor: Georgios Gardikis

In Internet Protocol Television (IPTV) systems, Quality-of-Service (QoS) is a critical factor for user satisfaction. In this paper, we first propose a queueing model for IPTV systems and discuss how to ensure the QoS of IPTV. We then use the model to analyze the effects of IPTV traffic on other applications in home networks. We find that TCP congestion control may not work well under this circumstance and propose a new approach to improve the performance of TCP. We also verify our results through *ns*2 simulations.

1. Introduction

In recent years, we have seen a tendency of various services converging to the ubiquitous Internet-Protocol- (IP-) based networks. Besides traditional Internet applications such as web browsing, email, file transferring, and so forth, new applications have been developed to replace old communication networks. For example, Voice over IP (VoIP) can be used as an alternative to traditional telephone network. There are also efforts to provide digital television service over IP networks. IPTV is one of the solutions. In the future, we expect a single network, the IP network, to provide services that have been carried by different networks today.

Transmitting video over IP networks is not a new idea. People have been interested in it since the very early stage of the Internet. However, there are major technical difficulties that prevent transmitting video over IP with satisfactory quality. The IP network is designed to be a best-effort network, which means that it does not provide any QoS guaranty. QoS, on the other hand, is essential to the quality of video. To get good quality, the network has to satisfy certain requirements on bandwidth, end-to-end delay, and jitter, and so forth. Another important issue is scalability. Many systems perform well when the number of users is small. However, when there are thousands of users accessing the service at the same time, which is typical in a broadcasting TV system, it will stress the servers.

With the advances of video encoding and the quick development of communication networks, transmitting video with at least VHS-quality has become possible in recent years. Digital video encoded with MPEG-1 around 1.5 Mbps can provide VHS-quality and MPEG-2 can offer High-Definition TV-quality video around 20 Mbps or higher. The next generation codecs, such as H.264 and VC1, can offer DVD- and HD- quality stream under 10 Mbps. At the same time, Internet access technology has been improved significantly. For example, ADSL can provide upto 8 Mbps download rate and the newest VDSL has up-to 52 Mbps download rate. Cable Modem can provide similar or even higher download bandwidth. With the recent deployment of Fiber to the premises (FTTP), we can expect higher Internet access bandwidth to be provided to home users. Hence, transmitting VHS-quality or even HDTV- quality video over the Internet becomes technically feasible.

In the current Internet, there are basically two solutions to deliver digital television service. The first one is Peer-to-Peer (P2P) video streaming. In [1], a P2P media streaming system called DONet has been proposed. Basically, all P2P video streaming systems work similarly. In such a system, the video is divided into many pieces. When a user obtains a piece, it will serve other peers by uploading this piece. Hence, each user serves as a client and a server at the same time. P2P systems have been proved to have very good scalability [2]. Hence, there is no need for expensive servers and high upload bandwidth to provide P2P video streaming. Due to the low setup cost and excellent scalability, P2P video streaming applications, such as PPLive, PPStream, and sopcast and so forth, have become very popular recently. However, since

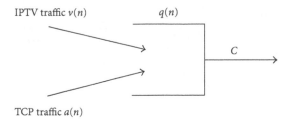

FIGURE 1: The queueing model.

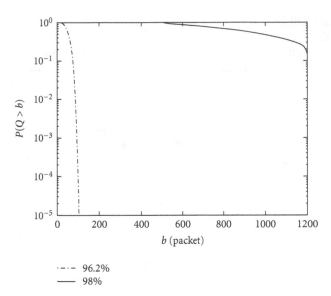

$\cdots$ 96.2%
— 98%

FIGURE 2: The effect of target utilization.

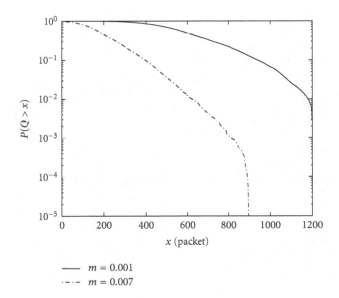

— $m = 0.001$
$\cdots$ $m = 0.007$

FIGURE 3: Queue distribution.

P2P video streaming traffic may cross the whole public Internet, it is very hard to guarantee the QoS in such a system. There is normally little or no QoS management in P2P video streaming. IPTV, on the other hand, takes a different approach to solve the scalability and QoS issues. IPTV has been developed and deployed mainly by large telecommunication providers as a competitive replacement product for digital cable and satellite services. Hence, IPTV systems normally use a closed network infrastructure. In such a system, the IPTV service provider is also the Internet service provider. Since the video streaming traffic is transmitted in a closed network, the QoS management is much easier than that in a P2P system. IPTV uses the multicast technology to solve the scalability issue. When more than one user are watching the same TV channel, the service provider will multicast the video to the users. Hence, only one copy of the video is transmitted and the system has good scalability.

In this paper, we will focus on IPTV systems. The paper is organized as follows. In Section 2, we will propose a queueing model for IPTV systems and discuss how to ensure the QoS of IPTV in such systems. We will also discuss how this will affect other Internet applications in home networks. In Section 3, we will analyze the model and discuss how the system performance can be optimized. Simulation results using *ns2* simulator will be shown in Section 4. Finally, we conclude this paper in Section 5.

2. QoS of IPTV

IPTV is a new technology to delivery digital television service over IP networks. In contrast to the popular P2P video streaming, IPTV systems are normally closed and proprietary. It has been deployed by major telecommunication providers to compete with traditional digital cable service. In an IPTV system, users subscribe to the IPTV service through their Internet service provider. The service provider sometimes also offers VoIP, service as an alternative to traditional telephone service. The combination of IPTV, VoIP, and Internet access is referred to as "Triple-Play" service. IPTV has some significant advantages over digital cable service. For example, it can make the TV viewing experience more interactive and personalized. IPTV also offers Video on Demand (VoD), in which a user can choose movies from a database and play it immediately. However, IPTV also has its own limitations. Since video quality is very

sensitive to packet loss and delay, how to ensure the QoS in a best-effort network like an IP network is a challenge topic.

Internet is a distributed system and there is no centralized control of it. This makes the QoS management extremely hard. The video traffic may travel through some segments of the Internet, where the service provider may have no control at all. In such a scenario, it is very difficult to ensure QoS. Fortunately, in IPTV systems, QoS management is significantly simplified. IPTV is a closed network, in which the service provider not only controls the IPTV system, but also controls the Internet access of the users. In the current Internet, the bottleneck for most connections is normally at the user's Internet access link, which is sometimes called the last mile. In the core of Internet, optical fibers have been deployed to provide tens of Gbps bandwidths and hence are unlikely to be the bottleneck. In an IPTV system, since the service provider also has control of the Internet access links, it can over provision the network to ensure the QoS of IPTV. For example, if the IPTV's bit rate is 3 Mbps, the service provider may over provision the capacity to ensure that the download bandwidth of the user is at least 5 Mbps, thus guaranteeing a minimum QoS level.

However, the simple over provision itself is not enough for IPTV QoS. Besides the IPTV application, there may be many other Internet applications running in the home network. For example, people may watch TV and browse the web at the same time. The traffic from other applications then will compete with the IPTV for the access bandwidth. If the total download rate exceeds the download bandwidth, packets will be dropped and hence it will degrade the video quality of IPTV. The solution to this problem is to give IPTV packets priority over other packets. This mechanism can be implemented in the network layer (e.g., Diffserv [3]) or in the MAC layer (e.g., IEEE802.1p). In either cases, when packets are competing for the output link, packets from IPTV flows will be processed with higher priority. Hence, although there may be other Internet applications, their traffic will not affect the QoS of IPTV. Combined with an appropriate over provision scheme, this mechanism can be used to ensure the QoS of IPTV and it is widely used in current IPTV systems.

Since IPTV traffic is given high priority, other Internet applications have to compete for the residual bandwidth and their performance may be affected. Different with IPTV, where UDP is used to carry the traffic, most other Internet applications such as HTTP, FTP, and SSH, and so forth, use TCP as the transport layer protocol. TCP itself has a built-in congestion control mechanism [4], which means that when TCP detects that the network is congested it will decrease its data rate. This kind of traffic is called elastic traffic and it can adapt to the available bandwidth in the network. Since many advanced video codecs produce variable-bit-rate (VBR) outputs, the available bandwidth for TCP will be time varying. Studying the impact of IPTV traffic on the performance of TCP is an interesting topic. Next, we use a simple queueing model to study it.

As we discussed before, the bottleneck normally happens at the Internet access link. Here, we use a queue to model this link that serves both IPTV and TCP traffics (Figure 1). In this model, C is the link capacity. For example, if the user's download bandwidth is 8 Mbps, then $C = 8$ Mbps. There are both IPTV traffic and TCP traffic on this link. Without loss of generality, we use a discrete time model. $v(n)$ is the data rate of IPTV traffic at time n and $a(n)$ is the data rate of TCP traffic. $q(n)$ is the queue length at time n. In the IPTV system, to ensure the QoS of IPTV, the data rate of IPTV traffic should not exceed the link capacity and hence $v(n) \leq C$. The link capacity available for TCP traffic is then $C - v(n)$, which is normally time varying as we discussed before. The queue length can be expressed as

$$q(n) = [q(n-1) + a(n) + v(n) - C]^+, \qquad (1)$$

where $[x]^+ = x$ if $x \geq 0$ and $[x]^+ = 0$ if $x < 0$.

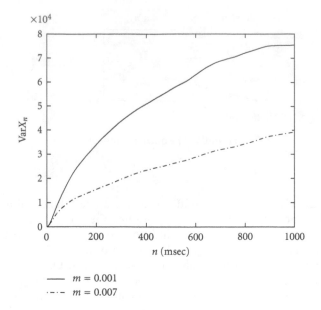

FIGURE 4: $\mathrm{Var}X_n$.

Note that $a(n)$ is the data rate of TCP traffic and hence it can be controlled by TCP. Ideally, we would like to have $a(n) = C - v(n)$ for all time n. If so, the link capacity is fully utilized and the queue length is always 0. However, this is impossible to achieve in real networks due to network delays, estimation errors, and so forth. Next, we discuss how to control $a(n)$ based on information about $v(n)$.

3. Effects of IPTV Traffic on TCP Performance

The objectives of TCP congestion control are high link utilization and small packet loss probability. However, these two objectives are generally conflicting. TCP congestion control always tries to fully utilize the link capacity. In Section 4, we will see that this may cause unnecessary workload to the queue and hence does not work well in practice. Motivated by this, we define $\rho < 1$ to be the target link utilization. Then $u(n) = \rho C - v(n)$ is the residual link capacity that we want TCP traffic to utilize. For the simplicity of analysis, we will first use an explicit-rate control model, in which we assume that we can explicitly set the TCP data rate $a(n)$. Later, we will discuss how the result can be applied to real TCP networks. We also assume that the $a(n)$ is controlled by a linear system, in which

$$\mathrm{a}(n) = L[u(n)]. \qquad (2)$$

A linear feedback control has been found to give good results when we have video traffic as uncontrollable traffic [5], which is exactly what we have in an IPTV system. Let $a(z)$ and $u(z)$ be the Z-transforms of $a(n)$ and $u(n)$, respectively. We have

$$a(z) = H(z)u(z), \qquad (3)$$

where $H(z)$ represents a linear time-invariant system. For example, if $a(n) = u(n-5)$, where 5 is the round trip delay of the TCP connection, then $H(z) = z^{-5}$. This system has been studied in [6] and we list the main results here.

In [6], it has been found that when $H(1) = 1$ the system has some desirable properties. First, the actual utilization of the system will be equal to the target utilization ρ. Secondly, the queue length distribution decays very fast. The tail probability of the queue length can be approximated by

$$\mathbb{P}\{Q > x\} \approx e^{-x^2/2D}, \tag{4}$$

where $D = \sup_n \text{Var}\, X_n$ is a constant and

$$X_n = \sum_{j=-n+1}^{0} \left(a(j) - u(j) - (1-\rho)C \right) \tag{5}$$

is the net input to the queue over a given time period with length n. So, under a given target link utilization, the system performance can be optimized if we can minimize D. Next, we discuss how this can be done in a TCP network.

TCP has been widely used in the current Internet and its congestion control scheme has been shown to work well in many cases. However, it also has some drawbacks. For example, it has no provision for the detection of incipient congestion. When a queue overflows, packets are simply dropped. In past years, many Active Queue Management (AQM) schemes have been proposed [7–9] to improve the performance of TCP. In these schemes, the routers try to detect incipient congestion and mark packets accordingly to control the data rate of TCP flows. In this paper, we choose Random Exponential Marking (REM) [8] as an example to show how our result can be applied to real TCP networks.

In REM, the router maintains a price information, which is calculated based on the TCP data rate and the available bandwidth. The price at time n is given by

$$p(n) = p(n-1) + m(a(n) - u(n)), \tag{6}$$

where $m > 0$ is the step size and is the parameter that we need to choose. Note that here we slightly modified the REM algorithm by replacing the link capacity with the time-varying residual link capacity $u(n)$ to reflect the presence of IPTV traffic. This price information is then sent back to the TCP source through packet marking and TCP will adjust its data rate accordingly. Basically, when the price increases, the data rate will be decreased, and vice verse. This control is normally not linear. However, as an approximation, we can linearize the data rate control around its average value (see [10] for details on how the linearization can be done). Let τ be the round trip delay of the TCP flows. For the simplicity of analysis, we assume that all TCP flows have the same delay. Then the TCP data rate at time n can be expressed as

$$a(n) = -kp(n-\tau), \tag{7}$$

where $k > 0$ is a constant related to the utility function used by TCP. Note that the only approximation we made here is the linearization. The TCP data rate is not reacting instantaneously to the price due to the delay τ. In Z-domain, we then have

$$p(z) = \frac{m}{1-z^{-1}}(a(z) - u(z)),$$
$$a(z) = -kz^{-\tau}p(z). \tag{8}$$

Solving these equations, we have

$$a(z) = \frac{kmz^{-\tau}}{1-z^{-1}+kmz^{-\tau}}u(z), \tag{9}$$

and hence

$$H(z) = \frac{kmz^{-\tau}}{1-z^{-1}+kmz^{-\tau}}. \tag{10}$$

We can easily verify that the system satisfies $H(1) = 1$ and hence has the desirable properties we discussed before. Note that in this system, since k is a constant related to TCP and cannot be changed, we need to choose an appropriate m to optimize the performance. Recall that the system performance is optimized when $D = \sup_n \text{Var}\, X_n$ is minimized. Hence, the problem becomes one of choosing the optimal m such that D is minimized. It is very hard to find a closed-form relation between D and m. However, in a real network, once we obtain the stochastic property of $u(n)$ (which is equivalent to that of $v(n)$, the data rate of IPTV traffic), it is relatively easy to find the optimal m numerically. Next, we show how this can be done through ns2 simulations.

4. Simulation Results

We use the ns2 simulator to simulate the Internet access link of a home network. The link capacity (or the download bandwidth) of the link is $C = 200$ Mbps. Note that the link capacity we use here is higher than that of most home networks due to two reasons. First, different link capacities should give the similar results if we scale all system parameters accordingly [11]. Hence, the absolute value of C is not essential here. Secondly, when C is larger, we can see the performance difference more clearly. The round trip delays of all TCP flows are $\tau = 10$ msec. We use TCP-Reno and the modified REM (see Section 3) as the AQM scheme. All TCP packets have the length of 1000 bytes.

In the first simulation, the link serves 100 TCP flows and there is no IPTV traffic. The REM parameter $m = 0.007$. The target link utilization is set to be 98% and 96.2% respectively. We measure the actual link utilization and find that it is 96.2%, in both cases. Under the same actual link utilization, we compare their queue distributions in Figure 2. We can see that, when the target link utilization is set to 98%, the tail probability is much higher than the other one and hence will have much higher packet loss rate. This tells us that setting a very high target link utilization does not guarantee that the actual link utilization is high and may only cause unnecessary workload.

In the next simulation, we add IPTV traffic into the network. The mean rate of the IPTV traffic is 100 Mbps. The IPTV traffic is generated by using a Gaussian process and is carried by UDP packets. The target link utilization is set to be 96%. The REM parameter m is set to be 0.001 and 0.007, respectively, where $m = 0.001$ is chosen according to the guidelines in [10] and $m = 0.007$ is chosen by our algorithm to minimize D. Our simulation results are shown in Figures 3 and 4. From Figure 3, we can see that, with different REM parameters, the queue distribution can be quite different. In Figure 4, we show the corresponding $\text{Var}\, X_n$. We can see that the smaller the $\text{Var}\, X_n$ (in the case $m = 0.007$), the smaller the queue length. Hence, in a TCP network, minimizing $\text{Var}\, X_n$ will be an effective way to control the loss rate.

5. Conclusion

In this paper, we first discuss how over provisioning and differentiated services can be used to ensure QoS of IPTV. We then use a queueing model to study the effects of IPTV traffic on home networks. Using this model, we analyze the performance of TCP when there is IPTV traffic in the network. Based on the analysis, we give some guidelines on how the system performance can be optimized. We then use REM as an example to show how the results can be applied to real TCP networks. We also verify our results by $ns2$ simulations.

References

[1] X. Zhang, J. Liu, B. Li, and T.-S. P. Yum, "CoolStreaming/DONet: a data-driven overlay network for peer-to-peer live media streaming," in *Proceedings of the Annual Joint Conference of the IEEE Computer and Communications Societies (INFOCOM '05)*, Miami, Fla, USA, March 2005.

[2] D. Qiu and R. Srikant, "Modeling and performance analysis of BitTorrent-like peer-to-peer networks," in *Proceedings of the ACM Conference on Applications, Technologies, Architectures, and Protocols for Computer Communication (SIGCOMM '04)*, pp. 367–377, August 2004.

[3] I. Stoica and H. Zhang, "Providing guaranteed services without per flow management," in *Proceedings of the ACM Conference on Applications, Technologies, Architectures, and Protocols for Computer Communication (SIGCOMM '99)*, pp. 81–94, 1999, http://citeseer.ist.psu.edu/article/stoica99providing.html.

[4] V. Jacobson, "Congestion avoidance and control," in *Proceedings of the ACM Conference on Applications, Technologies, Architectures, and Protocols for Computer Communication (SIGCOMM '88)*, pp. 314–329, 1988.

[5] Y. Zhao, S. Q. Li, and S. Sigarto, "A linear dynamic model for design of stable explicit-rate ABR control schemes," in *Proceedings of the Annual Joint Conference of the IEEE Computer and Communications Societies (INFOCOM '97)*, pp. 283–292, April 1997.

[6] D. Qiu and N. B. Shroff, "Queueing properties of feedback flow control systems," *IEEE/ACM Transactions on Networking*, vol. 13, no. 1, pp. 57–68, 2005.

[7] S. Floyd and V. Jacobson, "Random early detection gateways for congestion avoidance," *IEEE/ACM Transactions on Networking*, vol. 1, no. 4, pp. 397–413, 1993.

[8] S. Athuraliya and S. H. Low, "Optimization Flow Control II: Implementation," Internal report, Melbourne University, 2000.

[9] S. Kunniyur and R. Srikant, "Analysis and design of an adaptive virtual queue (AVQ) algorithm for active queue management," in *Proceedings of the ACM Conference on Applications, Technologies, Architectures, and Protocols for Computer Communication (SIGCOMM '01)*, San Diego, Calif, USA, August 2001.

[10] F. Paganini, J. Doyle, and S. Low, "Scalable laws for stable network congestion control," in *Proceedings of the 40th IEEE Conference on Decision and Control (CDC '01)*, vol. 1, pp. 185–190, December 2001.

[11] P. Tinnakornsrisuphap and A. M. Makowski, "Limit behavior of ECN/RED gateways under a large number of TCP flows," in *Proceedings of the Annual Joint Conference of the IEEE Computer and Communications Societies (INFOCOM '03)*, pp. 873–883, April 2003.

6

Network Performance Evaluation of Abis Interface over DVB-S2 in the GSM over Satellite Network

S. B. Musabekov,[1,2] P. K. Srinivasan,[3] A. S. Durai,[3] and R. R. Ibraimov[4]

[1] *ZTE Investment LLC, Oybek Street 14, Tashkent 100015, Uzbekistan*
[2] *Ahmadabad Earth Station, Space Applications Centre (SAC), Headquarters, 4 Kalidas Road, Dehradun, 248001, India*
[3] *Indian Space Research Organization (ISRO), Ahmedabad, 380015, India*
[4] *Tashkent University of Information Technology (TUIT), 108, Amir Temur Street, Tashkent 100084, Uzbekistan*

Correspondence should be addressed to S. B. Musabekov, smusabekov@yahoo.com

Academic Editor: George Xilouris

This paper deals with establishing a GSM link over Satellite. Abis interface, which is defined between Base Transceiver Station (BTS) and Base Station Controller (BSC), in a GSM network is considered here to be routed over the Satellite. The satellite link enables a quick and cost-effective GSM link in meagerly populated areas. A different scenario comparison was done to understand the impact of Satellite environment on network availability comparing to terrestrial scenario. We have implemented an Abis interface over DVB S2 in NS2 and evaluated the performance over the high delay and loss satellite channel. Network performance was evaluated with respect to Satellite channel delay and DVB S2 encapsulation efficiency under different amount of user traffic and compared with the terrestrial scenario. The results clearly showed an increased amount of SDCCH and TCH channels required in the case of satellite scenario for the same amount of traffic in comparison to conventional terrestrial scenario. We have optimized the parameters based on the simulation results. Link budget estimation considering DVB-S2 platform was done to find satellite bandwidth and cost requirements for different network setups.

1. Introduction

The success story of second-generation (2G) terrestrial mobile systems (GSM) and the relative demise of 2G mobile satellite systems (MSS) such as, Iridium and Globalstar have influenced the future of MSS. These two distinct but interrelated events demonstrate the importance of proper market and business strategies for the success of the future mobile satellite industry. Global System for Mobile communications (GSM) is the most popular means for voice and data communication having more than 2 billion subscribers all over the world. Still 3/4 of the globe is not covered by GSM networks. Despite growing demand for GSM services in rural areas, it is not cost-effective for GSM service providers to cover areas with meager population density. Poor terrestrial infrastructure in remote areas leads to high capital expenditures for establishing new links by means of fiber optic cables or microwave links, leading to an alternate and cost-effective solution like Satellite interface. Proposed work considers DVB-S2 [1] as a physical interface between Earth station and Satellite due to its highly spectrum efficient Modulation and powerful FEC schemes (ModCode). DVB-S2 has two different frames, long (64800 bit) and short (16200 bit) frames. Hence encapsulation efficiency and Network bandwidth utilization should be evaluated for different scenarios.

Presently there are no clear specifications on Abis interface over satellite technology. Still there are many proprietary solutions present at the world market. There is a lack of open standard definition in this area. Issues like change in signaling protocol on Abis interface while routing through Satellite are not addressed. Questions about implications on network availability and integrity while switching to GSM over satellite technology are not discussed elsewhere, which lead to a definition of an open standard architecture for an Abis interface over Satellite. We had proposed in [2] a novel

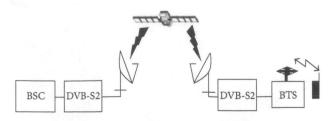

FIGURE 1: Abis interface over Satellite [4].

OSI architecture for Abis over satellite interface but there is a requirement of network performance evaluation, which is attempted in this paper.

We have proposed a new protocol architecture called Abis over IP over DVB-S2 in which the signaling and Transcoding Rate and Adaptation Unit (TRAU) frames are formatted over UDP/IP and RTP/UDP/IP, respectively, and encapsulated in Generic Stream (GS) stream of DVB-S2 over the forward and return link. Simulation is performed using standard network simulator NS-2.33 [3] under delay and different loss scenarios of the Satellite and the results are analyzed.

The following sections are organized as follows. Section 2 provides NS2 network (OSI) model; Section 3 gives the mathematical analysis for the traffic, subscriber density, and BTS capacity requirements for Abis over Satellite and terrestrial Abis. Section 4 describes Simulation Parameters, Results, and Analysis. Section 5 presents link budget estimations for Abis over DVB-S2 platform. Section 6 concludes this paper.

2. Proposed Abis over IP over DVB-S2 Network Performance Evaluation

The system setup for Abis interface over IP over DVB-S2 is shown in Figure 1, where the proposed protocol architecture lies between the BTS and BSC.

Figure 2 shows the proposed signaling protocol architecture for Abis interface over Satellite, and Figure 3 shows framing format. Frames on Abis interface are separated into TRAU frames and Signaling frames. The signaling frames is formatted over UDP/IP and encapsulated into Data Field Length (DFL) of DVB-S2 frame. The traffic in TRAU frames are formatted over RTP/UDP/IP and encapsulated over DVB-S2. Before IP encapsulation timeslot elimination technique may be applied to save bandwidth to considerable amount [5].

In the forward link, that is, from BSC to BTS, these messages describe the link establishment and release information and its acknowledgment to all its BTS [6]. The messages with added UDP and IP header form a multiple transport stream of the DVB-S2 system. The Base Band (BB), FEC and Physical Layer (PL) headers of DVB-S2 frame are added and modulated before given to the RF Satellite channel. The signaling links over the Abis interface are addressed to the different units by Terminal Endpoint Identifiers (TEIs) [7]. UDP header will represent destination port address of LAPD frame. Each of the physical link time slots of E1 [8] is now

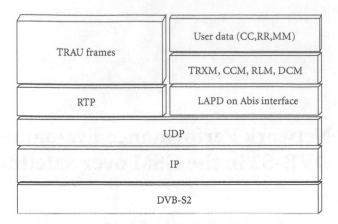

FIGURE 2: Abis interface over Satellite protocol architecture.

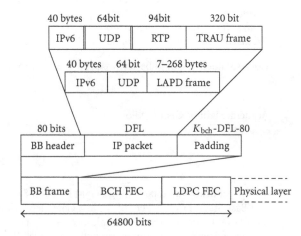

FIGURE 3: Framing format.

distinguished by each stream of the multiplexed GS stream fed to the DVB-S2 system.

TRAU frames [9] which carry voice are encapsulated into Real-Time Protocol (RTP) packets with time stamp of playback to prevent jitter while receiving, then encapsulated into UDP packets. Resulting UDP packets are IP encapsulated and formed Generic stream for the DVB-S2 system. DVB-S2 has inherent bandwidth efficient modulation modes and power efficient coding.

3. Traffic Analyses

This section gives the mathematical analysis for the traffic and subscriber density for the satellite scenario compared with the terrestrial scenario [10]. Each BTS has three sectors (cells). Each cell has one TRX containing one time slot (TS) for BCCH (Broadcasting Control Channel) to broadcast information about serving BTS, SDCCH (Stand Alone Dedicated Control Channel) for signaling during MOC, MTC, and Location Update, FACCH (Fast Associated Control Channel) for transferring measurements results and handover. Other TRX within this cell will have only TCH. If the number of TRX is more than three, then one more SDCCH TS should be added. Traffic refers to the numbers of subscribers the network can support and is described as follows:

$$A = n \times \frac{T}{3600},\qquad(1)$$

where n-Calls are made by a subscriber within an hour, T is Average duration of each call (in seconds), and A is Traffic, in Erlang.

If one call is made by a subscriber within an hour and last 120 seconds, the traffic is calculated as $A = 1 \times 120/3600 = 33$ mErl. For convenience of engineering calculation, the traffic is defined as 25 mErl per subscriber. The SDCCH average process time for MOC, MTC is considered as 3 seconds. Location updating process takes 9 seconds, BHCA (Busy Hour Call Attempts) = 2.

The traffic of SDCCH per subscriber is

$$\frac{3 \times 2 + 9}{3600} = 0.0042 \text{ Erlang.}\qquad(2)$$

For 4 SDCCH and blocking probability of 2%, we can support 1.092 Erlang (from Erlang B table). SDCCH/8 has 8 SDCCH logical channels within one time slot. Hence,

$$\left(\frac{1.092}{0.0042} = 260 \text{ sub}\right) \times 0.025 \text{ Erlang} = 6.5 \text{ Erlang.}\qquad(3)$$

In Erlang B with blocking probability of 2%, 6.5 Erlang needs 12TCH (2TRX). During the establishment and terminating of MOC and MTC, 29 commands and response I frames are transferred between BTS and BSC. Each frame will be delayed by $t \approx 240$ ms while propagating through Satellite. For Satellite communication, SDCCH average process time for MOC and MTC approximately will be 7 seconds due to Satellite delay; location updating process will be 20 seconds. Assuming 2 BHCA, we have the traffic of SDCCH per subscriber as

$$\frac{7 \times 2 + 20}{3600} = 0.0094 \text{ Erlang.}\qquad(4)$$

By 4SDCCH with blocking probability of 2%, we can support 1.092 Erlang (from Erlang B table).

$$\left(\frac{1.092}{0.0094} = 116 \text{ sub}\right) \times 0.025 \text{ Erl} = 2.9 \text{ Erl.}\qquad(5)$$

In Erlang-B with blocking probability of 2%, 2.9 Erlang need 7 TCH (1TRX) channels.

From above calculations, it can be concluded that for Abis over Satellite the same amount of Erlangs on SDCCH channel can support less number of subscribers than in terrestrial communication.

The same amount of subscribers is taken into account for Satellite Abis and terrestrial Abis 200 subscribers. Every time when MS initiates a call, there will be delay during call setup and also during conversation. Since each message signaling and traffic will be delayed while sending over satellite channel, it is considered that after call set-up phase subscriber needs to deliver 40 messages, and message

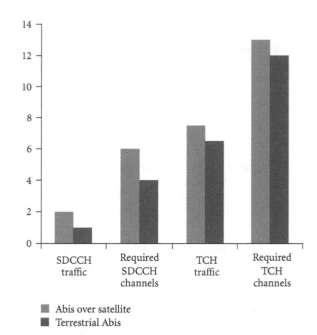

FIGURE 4: Traffic for Abis over Satellite and Terrestrial Abis.

duration is 3 seconds. Hence one conversation time will be $40 * 3 = 120$ seconds. In case of Abis over Satellite, conversation time will increase to 129.6 seconds. Hence mErl per subscriber will increase. Figure 4 shows comparison of Satellite Abis and Terrestrial Abis for the above described scenario. This shows that to support same amount of traffic a number of SDCCH and TCH channels are required in Abis over Satellite scenario. This calculation will give the number of TRX's or TS required for the same amount of the traffic.

4. Simulations

4.1. Simulation Description and Parameters. Simulation of the proposed OSI stack was performed using the NS version 2.33. The LAPD generation was based on the source code found under over which the rest of the OSI stack is incorporated. During simulation, two signaling frames from Um interface are considered Channel request and Connection acknowledgment messages. SABM frame to BSC to establish signaling link between BSC and BTS and sent over UDP/IP and over DVB-S2 frame. Corresponding UA frame will be sent to BTS. When LAPD link is established, Chan_Req message will be forwarded and 27 consecutive command response frames are sent in both directions to simulate call setup scenario. Call is established when connection acknowledgment frame is received. Table 1 shows simulation parameters.

Simulation is done for various scenarios where configuration of BTS varied from 1 TRX to 12 TRX. Each scenario considers different number of users and data rates for Abis interface and Satellite channel. Only CS traffic is considered during simulation over the fixed DVB-S2 frames. Simulation is done to monitor the encapsulation efficiency of Abis interface over IP over DVB-S2 platform.

TABLE 1: Simulation parameters.

Sr. No	Simulation parameter	Value
1	No. of MS/BTS	1–150
2	No. of time slots/BTS	8–168
3	Call duration	120 sec
4	N200	3
5	T200	200 ms–900 ms
6	I-Frame length	7–268 bytes
7	Data rate for one voice channel	16 Kbps
8	DVB-S2 frame	64800/16200 bits
9	DVB-S2 FEC	3/4
10	DVB-S2 DFL	48408/11712 bits
11	Channel delay	250 msec
12	Channel loss Probability	93% Good,7% Bad

4.2. Simulation Results. Three scenarios are considered with different timer $T200$ [11] values of 200 ms and 900 ms and with channel error probability to understand the performance of Abis interface. Figure 5 shows the simulation trace file generated over the NS2 for $T200 = 900$ ms.

Following peace of trace file shows the performance of Abis over Satellite with $T200 = 900$ ms: + enqueue, − dequeue, r - received, 1- BTS, 0- Satellite, 2- BSC. Trace file is depicted in the following sequence.

Frame state – time – from – to – LAPD – byte – via – source – destination - N(S) - N(R) – longitude – latitude – frame

The call set-up time is given by

$$t = N * t' = 30 * 0.334 = 10.02. \tag{6}$$

N: number of command and response I frames, and $t' =$ Satellite delay + processing delay. Typical values obtained from the simulation are $N = 30$, $t' = 33$ msec, which amounts to $t = 10.02$ sec.

Figure 6 shows that for lower timer values, the continuous retransmission may cause link congestion and will delay call set-up time $t = 10.03$ for $T200 = 900$ ms and $t = 10.42$ for T200 = 200 ms.

Hence the optimum value of the T200 retransmission timer has to be setup based on the actual network (satellite + processing) delay experienced.

The call set-up time delay due to lost I frame is given by

$$t = Nl * T200 = 1 * 900 \text{ ms}. \tag{7}$$

Nl: Number of lost I-frame.

The General equation for call set-up time can be written as

$$t = N * t' + Nl * T200. \tag{8}$$

Figure 7 shows the trace generated in NS2 under channel error probability of 7%. From the figure, it can be concluded that continuous retransmission will cause high link congestion, and service availability will be reduced as the TCH call set-up time will not increase dramatically. This

```
+01 0 LAPD 2025- - - - - - - 0 1.0 2.0 −1 0 42.30 −71.10 0.00 −95.00[1 2 U SABME]
−01 0 LAPD 2025 - - - - - - - 0 1.0 2.0 −1 0 42.30 −71.10 0.00 −95.00[1 2 U SABME]
r0.16811 0 LAPD 2025 - - - - - - 0 1.0 2.0 −1 0 42.30 −71.10 0.00 −95.00[1 2 U SABME]
+0.16810 2 LAPD 2025 - - - - - - 0 1.0 2.0 −1 0 0.00 −95.00 30.90 −122.30[1 1 U SABME]
−0.16810 2 LAPD 2025 - - - - - - 0 1.0 2.0 −1 0 0.00 −95.00 30.90 −122.30[1 1 U SABME]
r0.33420 2 LAPD 2025 - - - - - - 0 1.0 2.0 −1 0 0.00 −95.00 30.90 −122.30[1 1 U SABME]
+0.334422 0 LAPD 2025 - - - - - - 0 2.0 1.0 −1 1 30.90 −122.30 0.00 −95.00 [2 1 U UA]
−0.334220 LAPD 2025- - - - - - 0 2.0 1.0 −1 1 30.90 −122.30 0.00 −95.00[2 1 U UA]
-CHAN REQ massage
r0.50022 0 LAPD 2025 - - - - - - 0 2.0 1.0 −1 1 30.90 −122.30 0.00 −95.00[2 1 U UA]
+0.50020 1 LAPD 2025 - - - - - - 0 2.0 1.0 −1 1 0.00 −95.00 42.30 −71.10[1 2 U SABME]
−0.50020 1 LAPD 2025 - - - - - - 0 2.0 1.0 −1 1 0.00 −95.00 42.30 −71.10[1 2 U SABME]
r0.668301 LAPD 2025 - - - - - - 0 2.0 1.0 −1 1 0.00 −95.00 42.30 −71.10[1 2 U UA]- round
trip delay t = 669 ms, T200 > 669 ms
```
```
−9.689 2 0 LAPD 2025 - - - - - - 0 2.0 1.0 −1 15 30.90 −122.30 0.00 −95.00[29 1 S 14 RR]
r9.8551 2 0 LAPD 2025 - - - - - - 0 2.0 1.0 −1 15 30.90 −122.30 0.00 −95.00[29 1 S 14 RR]
+9.8551 0 1 LAPD 2025 - - - - - - 0 2.0 1.0 −1 15 0.00 −95.00 42.30 −71.10[1 30 S 14 RR]
−9.8551 0 1 LAPD 2025 - - - - - - 0 2.0 1.0 −1 15 0.00 −95.00 42.30 −71.10[1 30 S 14 RR]
r10.023201 LAPD 2025 - - - - - - 0 2.0 1.0 −1 15 0.00 −95.00 42.30 −71.10[1 30 S 14
RR] - CON ACK frame received. Time taken to establish a call t = 10.03 seconds.
```

FIGURE 5: Shows the TCH call set-up time for $T200 = 900$ ms.

```
+ 0.0000 1 0 HDLC 28 - - - - - - - 0 1.0 2.0 −1 0 42.30 −71.10 0.00 −95.00[1 2 U SABME]
−0.0000 1 0 HDLC 28 - - - - - - - 0 1.0 2.0 −1 0 42.30 −71.10 0.00 −95.00[1 2 U SABME]
r0.1281 1 0 HDLC 28 - - - - - - - 0 1.0 2.0 −1 0 42.30 −71.10 0.00 −95.00[1 2 U SABME]
+0.1281 0 2 HDLC 28 - - - - - - - 0 1.0 2.0 −1 0 0.00 −95.00 30.90 −122.30[1 1 U SABME]
−0.1281 0 2 HDLC 28 - - - - - - - 0 1.0 2.0 −1 0 0.00 −95.00 30.90 −122.30[1 1 U SABME]
+ 0.2000 1 0 HDLC 28 - - - - - - - 0 1.0 2.0 −1 1 42.30 −71.10 0.00 −95.00[1 2 U SABME]
− 0.2000 1 0 HDLC 28 - - - - - - - 0 1.0 2.0 −1 1 42.30 −71.10 0.00 −95.00[1 2 U SABME]-
T200 = 200 ms timer expired
+ 10.1720 2 0 HDLC 28 - - - - - - - 0 2.0 1.0 −1 45 30.90 −122.30 0.00 −95.00[82 1 S 13 RR]
−10.1720 2 0 HDLC 28 - - - - - - - 0 2.0 1.0 −1 45 30.90 −122.30 0.00 −95.00[82 1 S 13 RR]
r10.2262 0 1 HDLC 28 - - - - - - - 0 2.0 1.0 −1 44 0.00 −95.00 42.30 −71.10[1 83 S 13 RR]
r 10.2981 2 0 HDLC 28 - - - - - - - 0 2.0 1.0 −1 45 30.90 −122.30 0.00 −95.00[82 1 S 13 RR]
+ 10.2981 0 1 HDLC 28 - - - - - - - 0 2.0 1.0 −1 45 0.00 −95.00 42.30 −71.10[1 84 S 13 RR]
−10.2981 0 1 HDLC 28 - - - - - - - 0 2.0 1.0 −1 45 0.00 −95.00 42.30 −71.10[1 84 S 13 RR]
r10.4262 0 1 HDLC 28 - - - - - - - 0 2.0 1.0 −1 45 0.00 −95.00 42.30 −71.10[1 84 S 13 RR]
```

FIGURE 6: TCH call set up time $T200 = 200$ ms.

is because retransmitted I frame will receive response of the first sent I frame. However, under the channel errors, the call set-up time increases due to the actual loss of I frames. Table 2 below gives call set-up time obtained from the simulation under various scenarios.

4.2.1. Comparison of Various Network Scenarios and Network Optimizations. Different scenarios are considered to find optimal network configuration for Abis over DVB-S2 platform Table 3. The number of TRX is varied from 1 to 21. Subsequently, the number of users and data rates on Abis interface and Satellite channel is changed. During simulation FEC 3/4 is considered.

Data rate evaluation is done under different data rate definitions.

(1) *Abis data rate.* Abis data rate corresponds to the data rate after idle time slot elimination. It depends on TRX quantity.

(2) *Useful data rate.* This is the occupied TS of Abis data by one user. This corresponds to one occupied voice channel by each subscriber.

(3) *Satellite data rate.* This is the time interval between consecutive sent DVB-S2 frames. DVB-S2 frame is 16200 bit. For, for example, sending DVB-S2 frame, each 40 ms will give 405 Kbps satellite data rate.

TABLE 2: Call set-up time for different scenarios.

Scenario	Value (seconds)
$T = 900$ ms	10.02
$T = 200$ ms	10.42
$T = 900$ ms + 7% loss	10.92

```
+01 0 LAPD 2025 - - - - - - 0 1.0 2.0 −1 0 42.30 −71.10 0.00 −95.00[1 2 U SABME]
−01 0 LAPD 2025 - - - - - - 0 1.0 2.0 −1 0 42.30 −71.10 0.00 −95.00[1 2 U SABME]
r0.16811 0 LAPD 2025 - - - - - - - 0 1.0 2.0 −1 0 42.30 −71.10 0.00 −95.00[1 2 U SABME]
+0.16810 2 LAPD 2025 - - - - - - - 0 1.0 2.0 −1 0 0.00 −95.00 30.90 −122.30[1 1 U SABME]
−0.16810 2 LAPD 2025 - - - - - - - 0 1.0 2.0 −1 0 0.00 −95.00 30.90 −122.30[1 1 U SABME]
r0.33420 2 LAPD 2025 - - - - - - - 0 1.0 2.0 −1 0 0.00 −95.00 30.90 −122.30[1 1 U SABME]
+0.33422 0 LAPD 2025 - - - - - - - 0 2.0 1.0 −1 1 30.90 −122.30 0.00 −95.00[2 1 U UA]
−0.33422 0 LAPD 2025 - - - - - - - 0 2.0 1.0 −1 1 30.90 −122.30 0.00 −95.00[2 1 U UA]
r0.50022 0 LAPD 2025 - - - - - - - 0 2.0 1.0 −1 1 30.90 −122.30 0.00 −95.00[2 1 U UA]
+0.50020 1 LAPD 2025 - - - - - - - 0 2.0 1.0 −1 1 0.00 −95.00 42.30 −71.10[1 2 U UA]
−0.50020 1 LAPD 2025 - - - - - - - 0 2.0 1.0 −1 1 0.00 −95.00 42.30 −71.10[1 2 U UA]
r0.66830 1 LAPD 2025 - - - - - - - 0 2.0 1.0 −1 1 0.00 −95.00 42.30 −71.10[1 2 U UA]
+9.689 2 0 LAPD 2025 - - - - - - - 0 2.0 1.0 −1 15 30.90 −122.30 0.00 −95.00[29 1 S 14 RR]
−9.689 2 0 LAPD 2025 - - - - - - - 0 2.0 1.0 −41 15 30.90 − 122.30 0.00 −95.00[29 1 S 14 RR] − I
  frame 15 sent
r9.8551 2 0 LAPD 2025 - - - - - - - 0 2.0 1.0 −1 15 30.90 −122.30 0.00 −95.00[29 1 S 14 RR]
+9.8551 0 1 LAPD 2025 - - - - - - - 0 2.0 1.0 −1 15 0.00 −95.00 42.30 −71.10[1 30 S 14 RR]
−9.8551 0 1 LAPD 2025 - - - - - - - 0 2.0 1.0 −1 15 0.00 −95.00 42.30 −71.10[1 30 S 14 RR]
e10.0232 0 1 LAPD 2025 - - - - - - - 0 2.0 1.0 −1 15 0.00 −95.00 42.30 −71.10[1 30 S 14 RR]-
  error
+10.589 2 0 LAPD 2025 - - - - - - - 0 2.0 1.0 −1 15 30.90 −122.30 0.00 −95.00[29 1 S 14 RR]
−10.589 2 0 LAPD 2025 - - - - - - - 0 2.0 1.0 −1 15 30.90 − 122.30 0.00  −95.00[29 1 S 14 RR]-
  T200 = 900 ms expired
r10.7551 2 0 LAPD 2025 - - - - - - - 0 2.0 1.0 −1 15 30.90 −122.30 0.00 −95.00[29 1 S 14 RR]
+10.7551 0 1 LAPD 2025 - - - - - - - 0 2.0 1.0 −1 15 0.00 −95.00 42.30 −71.10[1 30 S 14 RR]
−10.7551 0 1 LAPD 2025 - - - - - - - 0 2.0 1.0 −1 15 0.00 −95.00 42.30 −71.10[1 30 S 14 RR]
r10.9232 0 1 LAPD 2025 - - - - - - - 0 2.0 1.0 −1 15 0.00 −95.00 42.30 −71.10[1 30 S 14 RR]
```

FIGURE 7: TCH call set-up time with channel error probability 7%.

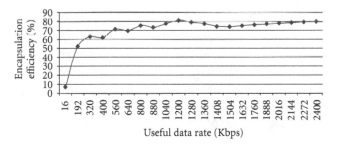

FIGURE 8: Encapsulation efficiency versus useful data rate for DVB-S2 short frames.

From Figure 8, we can observe that configuration of one TRX will have poor encapsulation efficiency. With increasing of Abis data rate encapsulation efficiency improves and varies for different data rates. Figure 9 shows Encapsulation efficiency versus useful data rate for DVB-S2 long frames.

In comparison to DVB-S2 short frames, long frames have almost the same encapsulation efficiency. One disadvantage of DVB-S2 long frames is higher delay.

Figure 10 shows delay versus useful data rate for DVB-S2 short and long frames.

From Figure 10, we can see that in case of one TRX and one occupied TCH delay between transferring DVB-S2 frame will reach 200 ms for long and 50 ms for short frames. Delay between transmissions of DVB-S2 frames will reduce with increase of data rate on Satellite channel and on Abis interface.

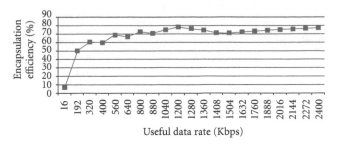

FIGURE 9: Encapsulation efficiency versus useful data rate for DVB-S2 long frames.

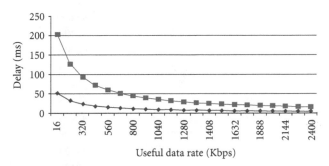

FIGURE 10: Delay versus useful data rate for DVB-S2 short and long frames.

5. Link Budget Estimations for DVB-S2 Platform

Link budget estimations are done considering GSAT-3 (http://www.isro.org/) satellite parameters. DVB-S2 platform has 28 modulation coding (ModCode) modes. Table 4 shows required energy per transmitted symbol E_s/N_0 (dB) is the figure obtained from computer simulations.

From (9), the required E_b/N_o for each ModCode can be calculated

$$\frac{E_b}{N_0} = \frac{E_s}{N_0} - 10 \log(n_{\text{tot}}), \tag{9}$$

where η_{tot} is spectral efficiency.

C/N_0 total can be found from (10).

$$\left(\frac{C}{N_0}\right) = \frac{E_b}{N_0} + 10 \log(R_b) \, (\text{dBHz}). \tag{10}$$

R_b is Information rate (Bits/s).

DVB-S2 platform can support three Roll Off factor modes 0.35, 0.25, and 0.20. During Link Budget estimation, value of 0.25 is considered.

Different scenarios are evaluated with different numbers of BTS and TRX's within BTS. Table 5 shows all three scenarios.

Link Budget Estimations are done considering idle time slot elimination technique.

5.1. Results and Analysis. Table 6 shows obtained results for all DVB-S2 modulation modes with FEC 3/4, for a single BTS connection point-to-point SCPC link.

TABLE 3: Different network parameters during simulation.

Number of TRX	DFL short frame bit	DFL long frame bit	Abis DR Kbps	MS	Useful data rate Kbps	Satellite data rate Kbps
1	11712	48408	320	1	16	400
2	11712	48408	512	12	192	592
3	11712	48408	704	20	320	784
4	11712	48408	896	25	400	976
5	11712	48408	1088	35	560	1168
6	11712	48408	1280	40	640	1360
7	11712	48408	1472	50	800	1552
8	11712	48408	1664	55	880	1744
9	11712	48408	1856	65	1040	1936
10	11712	48408	2048	75	1200	2128
11	11712	48408	2240	80	1280	2320
12	11712	48408	2432	85	1360	2512
13	11712	48408	2624	88	1408	2704
14	11712	48408	2816	94	1504	2896
15	11712	48408	3008	102	1632	3088
16	11712	48408	3200	110	1760	3280
17	11712	48408	3392	118	1888	3472
18	11712	48408	3584	126	2016	3664
19	11712	48408	3776	134	2144	3856
20	11712	48408	3968	142	2272	4048
21	11712	48408	4160	150	2400	4240

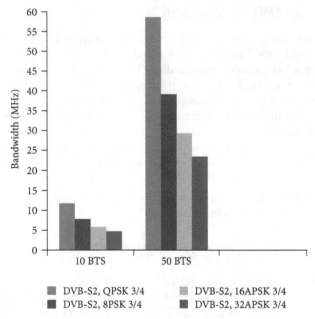

FIGURE 11: Required bandwidth for 10 and 50 BTS.

DVB-S2, QPSK 3/4   DVB-S2, 16APSK 3/4
DVB-S2, 8PSK 3/4   DVB-S2, 32APSK 3/4

TABLE 4: E_s/N_0 performance at Quasi-Error-Free PER $= 10^{-7}$ (AWGN channel).

Mode	Spectral efficiency (η_{tot})	Ideal E_s/N_0 (dB) for FECFRAME length = 64 800 bit
QPSK 3/4	1,487473	4,03
8PSK 3/4	2,228124	7,91
16APSK 3/4	2,966728	10,21
32APSK 3/4	3,703295	12,73

TABLE 5: Number of TRX for each case.

	Single BTS	10 BTS	50 BTS
No of TRX	8,4,1	3	3

Figure 12 illustrates cost of bandwidth per month for single BTS configuration with different number of TRX.

Figure 13 shows a comparison of different scenarios of 10 and 50 BTS configuration with 3 TRX in each BTS.

6. Conclusions

During studies of Abis interface, it was found that one of the weaknesses of this interface is that there is no network layer to serve number of BTSs which are located in different areas within the network and connected via Geostationary Satellite.

Figure 11 gives a comparison between two scenarios considering 10 and 50 BTS for DVB-S2 platform.

The cost of bandwidth on Satellite is taken as 4000 US $ per 1 MHz per month [12]. Since Satellite is distance insensitive, this cost will be constant, in comparison to terrestrial scenario where cost of the 2.048 Mbps E1 channel is distance-dependent.

TABLE 6: Required bandwidth for all modulation modes of DVB-S2 for single BTS configuration.

		SCPC, 8TRX	SCPC, 4TRX	SCPC, TRX
Information Rate	kbps	1664	896	320
Occupied RF bandwidth (QPSK)	KHz	1386,6	746,6	266,6
Occupied RF bandwidth (8PSK)	KHz	924,44	497,77	177,77
Occupied RF bandwidth (16APSK)	KHz	693,33	373,33	133,33
Occupied RF bandwidth (32APSK)	KHz	554,66	298,66	106,66

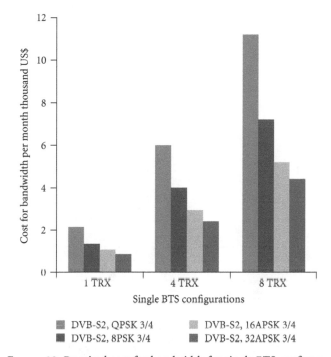

FIGURE 12: Required cost for bandwidth for single BTS configuration.

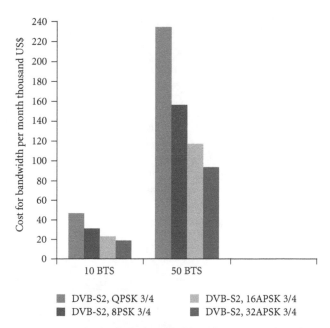

FIGURE 13: Required cost for bandwidth with more number of BTS.

Traffic and subscriber density calculations show that more numbers of SDCCH and TCH channels should be configured to serve the same amount of MS's as in terrestrial scenario.

From the above results, it can be concluded that continuous retransmission of LAPD frames will cause high link congestion which is due to small value of $T200$. Frame loss will delay call set-up time. From simulation, it is observed that round trip delay for DVB-S2 short frames will reach 334 ms. It is suggested to set the number of retransmissions counter N200 to the maximum value in Abis over Satellite to overcome losses on Satellite channel. It is observed that increase of number of TRX and useful data rate will improve encapsulation efficiency, and Satellite resources will be utilized more efficiently while using DVB-S2 platform. It is also observed that DVB-S2 long frames are not suitable because of higher delay between retransmissions. When the number of TRX reaches 10 and the number of MS 75 encapsulation efficiency reaches to 80%, delay between transmitting DVB-S2 short frames will reach 8 ms which is acceptable for Satellite environment.

Simulation results on DVB-S2 encapsulation show that different ModCode modes will give different encapsulation efficiencies. For efficient encapsulation into DVB-S2 frame, appropriate ModCode mode should be chosen; however, the selection of the ModCode is dependent on the channel fades encountered. It is concluded that DVB-S2 will provide several advantages like improved Roll-Off factor, different power and bandwidth efficient modulation modes. For efficient utilization of frequency spectrum parameters such as padding efficiency and overall encapsulation efficiencies should be evaluated.

Present development of 3G and 4G systems in the world market shows that requirement for new services and higher data rates will grow. 3G (WCDMA/UMTS) which offers 2M of data rate per subscriber is a good gateway in the world of Data and Internet. Hence it is important to know how these technologies may be provided in the remote areas efficiently for 24 hours in a day.

Paper addressed only GSM technology. Future work for 3G, 4G technologies should be done.

References

[1] ETSI EN 302 307 version1.1.1, "Digital Video Broadcasting (DVB); Second generation framing structure, channel coding and modulation systems for Broadcasting, Interactive Services, News Gathering and other broadband satellite applications," 2004.

[2] S. B. Musabekov, P. K. Srinivasan, A. S. Durai, and R. R. Ibroimov, "Simulation analysis of abis interface over IP over DVB-S2-RCS in a GSM over satellite network," in *Proceedings of the 4th IEEE/IFIP International Conference in Central Asia on Internet (ICI '08)*, September 2008.

[3] The VINT Project, "The ns Manual (formerly ns Notes and Documentation)," July 2008.

[4] DVB Document A134, "Generic Stream Encapsulation (GSE) Implementation Guidelines," February 2009.

[5] Ses New Skies B.V., "GSM Over Satellite," 2006.

[6] 3GPP TS 08.58 version 8.6.0, "Base Station Controller—Base Transceiver Station (BCS-BTS) Interface Layer 3 Specification," http://www.3gpp.org/.

[7] 3GPP TS 08.56 version 8.0.1, "BSC-BTS Layer 2; Specification," http://www.3gpp.org/.

[8] 3GPP TS 08.54 version 8.0.1, "BSC-BTS Layer 1; Structure of Physical Circuits," http://www.3gpp.org/.

[9] ETSI EN 300 737, "Digital cellular telecommunication systems (Phase2+) In-band control of remote transcoders and rate adaptors for full rate traffic channels," V7.2.1, September 2000.

[10] S. B. Musabekov and R. R. Ibraimov, "NS-2 network performance evaluation of abis interface over DVB-S2 in the GSM over satellite network," in *Proceedings of the 1st Asian Himalayas International Conference on Internet (AH-ICI '09)*, pp. 1–5, 2009.

[11] ETS 300 125, "Integrated Services Digital Network (ISDN);User-network interface data link layer specification; Application of CCITT Recommendations Q.920/I.440 and Q.921/I.441," part-2, subclause 5.9.1, September 1991.

[12] Globecomm, "Optimizing GSM Abis ExtensionsVia Satellite," 2006.

7

A Framework for an IP-Based DVB Transmission Network

Nimbe L. Ewald-Arostegui,[1] Gorry Fairhurst,[1] and Ana Yun-Garcia[2]

[1] School of Engineering, University of Aberdeen, Aberdeen AB24 3UE, UK
[2] Thales Alenia Space, C/Einstein 7, Tres Cantos-Madrid 28760, Spain

Correspondence should be addressed to Nimbe L. Ewald-Arostegui, nimbe@erg.abdn.ac.uk

Academic Editor: Georgios Gardikis

One of the most important challenges for next generation all-IP networks is the convergence and interaction of wireless and wired networks in a smooth and efficient manner. This challenge will need to be faced if broadcast transmission networks are to converge with IP infrastructure. The 2nd generation of DVB standards supports the Generic Stream, allowing the direct transmission of IP-based content using the Generic Stream Encapsulation (GSE), in addition to the native Transport Stream (TS). However, the current signalling framework is based on MPEG-2 Tables that rely upon the TS. This paper examines the feasibility of providing a GSE signalling framework, eliminating the need for the TS. The requirements and potential benefits of this new approach are described. It reviews prospective methods that may be suitable for network discovery and selection and analyses different options for the transport and syntax of this signalling metadata. It is anticipated that the design of a GSE-only signalling system will enable DVB networks to function as a part of the Internet.

1. Introduction

The first generation of DVB standards [1–3] uses a time-division transmission multiplexing method derived directly from the Moving Pictures Expert Group-2 Transport Stream (MPEG-2 TS) standards [4]. The MPEG-2 specifications define the Program Specific Information (PSI), a Table-based signalling system that is multiplexed with the content and allows a receiver to identify MPEG-2 Programs and to demultiplex their Program Elements from the TS. These Tables are segmented in Sections and directly encapsulated into MPEG-2 TS packets, as shown in Figure 1. The Digital Video Broadcasting (DVB) project specified additional types of Table, DVB-Service Information (SI) [5] while the Advanced Television System Committee (ATSC) also defined a set of Tables for the US market [6].

Current signalling metadata relies on this TS packet format [4]. The 2nd generation of DVB systems, DVB-S2/C2/T2 [7–9], preserved this signalling framework utilising MPEG-2 encoded Tables. Some transmission systems use IP-based Service Discovery and Selection (SD&S) procedures to obtain content metadata, for example, acquisition of an Electronic Service Guide (ESG), the network signalling necessary for the initial bootstrapping is sent using MPEG

-2 encoded Tables, for example, in DVB-Handheld (DVB-H) and DVB-Satellite to Handheld (DVB-SH) systems [10, 11].

SD&S is a generic term that has been used to describe various discovery and selection procedures for, mainly, IP-based content metadata. The term Network Discovery and Selection (ND&S) is defined in this paper to describe the discovery and selection of network signalling metadata such as the acquisition of PSI/SI.

Figure 2 illustrates the process of ND&S and SD&S for an example transmission system. ND&S procedures are separated into two logical parts: network discovery starts by acquiring the network bootstrap information from a well-known link stream, followed by selection of the required network service.

First, when a multiplex has been identified at a receiver, the receiver will need to perform a bootstrap of the signalling system, network bootstrapping. The same transmission multiplex may carry bootstrap information for more than one network, if the multiplex supports multiple logical networks. Bootstrap information could also relate to other network services transmitted over other multiplexes, possibly using different transmission technologies. Once the bootstrap has been performed, the receiver has the basic information required to discover the signalling stream—that

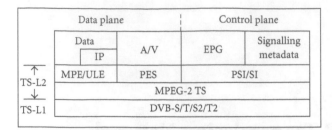

FIGURE 1: Current DVB MPEG-2 TS architecture.

is, the logical flow of signalling information relating to a network service from which it wishes to receive content. The receiver then needs to set a filter that extracts the appropriate signalling from the multiplex selected based on the required network service. The receiver can, then, be used to perform address/service resolution, identifying the required elementary streams or an IP stream that can be used to locate content.

In an all-IP system, the content may be directly accessed, or may be accessed via a content guide such as an ESG. The content guide may be discovered from content bootstrap information provided in a well-known IP stream. More than one network may reference the same content stream as in the case of duplicate multicast content. Similarly, more than one content guide may be active within a network service and the content bootstrap can then be used to select the appropriate content guide. DVB-H and DVB-SH systems follow this two-stage procedure once the PSI/SI information has been extracted.

Current broadcast transmission networks using the TS format can provide platforms for high-speed unidirectional IP transmission, not just for TV-based services. A convergent IP-oriented architecture will ease integration of transmission systems and enable development of multi-network service delivery platforms. The benefits of a DVB IP-based signalling architecture are discussed in Section 3.

The remainder of the paper is divided as follows: a brief description of the current DVB signalling is given in Section 2, GSE suitability, the envisaged IP/GSE signalling framework, and its potential benefits are discussed in Section 3. The requirements of the GSE-only signalling architecture will be identified in Section 4. Then, the different areas that comprise the GSE-only signalling system are analysed, and methods that may address them are discussed in Section 5. Finally, conclusions and future work are stated in Section 6.

2. Current Signalling Framework

In current DVB systems, key-signalling information is sent, in the Programme Association Table (PAT) of PSI, using its well-known 13-bit Packet Identifier (PID) value in the TS packet header. This allows a receiver to readily extract this PID from a received TS multiplex. Figure 3 shows a schematic diagram of this PID acquisition procedure.

In many cases, equipment has hardware support to filter PID values, initially, set to well-known values defined by

the MPEG standard, that is, the fixed PIDs of the PAT, the Conditional Access Table (CAT), and the Transport Stream Descriptor Table (TSDT). Once the PAT has been received and the respective PID of the Network Information Table (NIT) has been extracted (step 1 in Figure 3), the receiver filters this PID, accesses the NIT and re-tunes, if necessary (step 2). Next, the terminal can access the appropriate PAT from where the PIDs of the MPEG-2 Programs' Program Map Table (PMT) can be found (step 3). The receiver can, then, setup filters to receive other PIDs to acquire a full set of relevant signalling information. The receiver can acquire Audio/Video (A/V) Program Elements through their PIDs, which are also advertised in the PMT (step 4). The PID of the Forward Link Signalling (FLS) [12] is also advertised in the PMT.

As shown in Figure 1, alongside these signalling Tables directly encapsulated into TS packets, A/V and data services are adapted to the TS using adaptation protocols such as Packetised Elementary Stream (PES) and Multiprotocol Encapsulation (MPE). If required, data can be placed directly in TS packets using the Unidirectional Lightweight Encapsulation (ULE) [13] protocol.

3. An All-IP Second Generation Transmission Network

The 2nd generation of DVB standards [7–9] foresees the possibility of converged IP-based transmission that supports both broadcast applications and broadband access service by adopting a common IP-based infrastructure. This converged network would bridge the gap between broadcast transmission and traditional networks.

To support a converged approach, the 2nd generation of DVB transmission standards introduced the Generic Stream (GS) in addition to the TS. The GS may be used to carry packets of different sizes, eliminating the TS packet format. The GS is, primarily, expected to be used for network services, where IP packets and other network-layer protocols can be efficiently encapsulated using the Generic Stream Encapsulation, GSE, protocol [14, 15].

GSE provides a network-oriented adaptation layer. Each network layer Protocol Data Unit (PDU) is prefixed by a GSE header, which is shown in Figure 4. GSE supports flexible fragmentation, adapting the encapsulated data to a range of possible physical-layer frame sizes. GSE offers a higher encapsulation efficiency (2%–5% better than the TS counterpart when padding is used for data packets [14]). In addition, GSE is extensible, which allows implementing additional features through its extension headers [16], for example, security, header compression, and timestamps. The base header, present in every encapsulated packet, is 4 Bytes. The additional fields, present only in some packets, are shown shadowed in Figure 4.

While GSE defines the adaptation needed to support data transmission, there is no current specification for a signalling system that could replace the MPEG-2 TS signalling by a system using IP over GSE.

A transition to an IP-based content and signalling will enable common use of IP delivery techniques at the receiver,

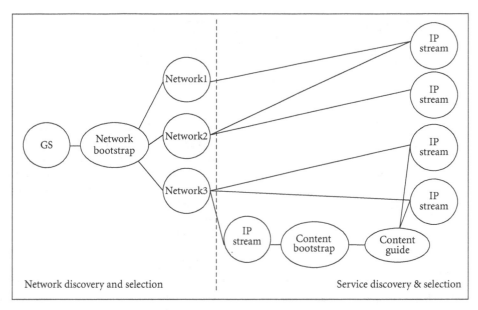

FIGURE 2: ND&S and SD&S procedures.

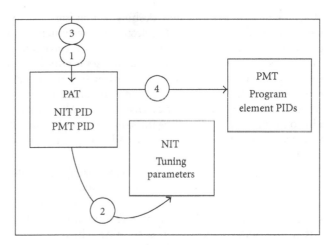

FIGURE 3: Initial acquisition of PIDs.

presenting new opportunities for integrating broadcast content with standard IP applications, and the introduction of value-added services. An IP-based transmission network design also enables the use of data networks (e.g., using wired/wireless Ethernet or mobile platforms) for onward delivery to the TV receiver. An IP-based approach allows reuse of existing techniques and protocol machinery (for configuration, management, accounting, encryption, authentication, etc.). This can support evolution of the services and be used to manage the network and monitor performance.

IP-based transmission products are already available for TV contribution networks and digital satellite news gathering. For example, IP satellite news gathering can significantly benefit from the improved efficiency of DVB-S2 while also utilising standards-based IP-based media codecs.

Broadcast transmission can supplement existing wireless infrastructure where sufficient capacity is not available,

provide a resilient alternate path, or be used to roll out new services. Broadcast networks are especially suited to services that can exploit cost-efficient wide-area delivery using IP multicast.

This paper proposes a framework based on the reference model shown in Figure 5, where we replace TS-L2 (in Figure 1) by the adaptation layer, GS-L2. The signalling metadata is placed at the application layer level, GS-L5, while IP at GS-L3 allows convergence with the Internet. ND&S procedures refer to an IP signalling system associating IP addresses and services with a stream and a specific transmission multiplex. The MPEG-2 TS format is also included to support legacy services.

One simple solution is to encapsulate TS packets in GSE through its TS-Concat extension header [16]. This format allows one or more TS packets to be sent within one GSE packet by combining the group of TS packets with a 4B GSE base header (Figure 4). For a single TS Packet this additional overhead is less than 2%.

Encapsulating the current TS-packed Tables into GSE packets could be an attractive transition method while both TS and GS multiplexes are in use. However, it is likely to constrain the evolution towards an all-IP network and it does not provide an efficient way to transmit PSI/SI Tables. The total overhead would consist of GSE and TS packet headers, and the TS packet padding. For example, if a 30B Table were sent in one TS Packet, the overhead comprised by the TS headers (5B), padding (153B), and the GSE base header (4B) would be 162B, if a Label field (Figure 4) is not used. The impact of overheads on the system efficiency should be considered (preliminary overhead analysis of different encapsulation methods is provided in Section 5.5.2).

However, this is only a partial solution. If signalling were transported using GSE packets instead of TS packets, there would not be a direct equivalent to the PID filters used for TS, that is, GSE does not contain a PID field. Thus, the receiver

S	E	LT	GSE length	Protocol type	Frag ID	Total length	Label	Extension headers
1b	1b	2b	12b	2B	1B	2B	$\frac{3}{6}$B	>= 2B

FIGURE 4: GSE header.

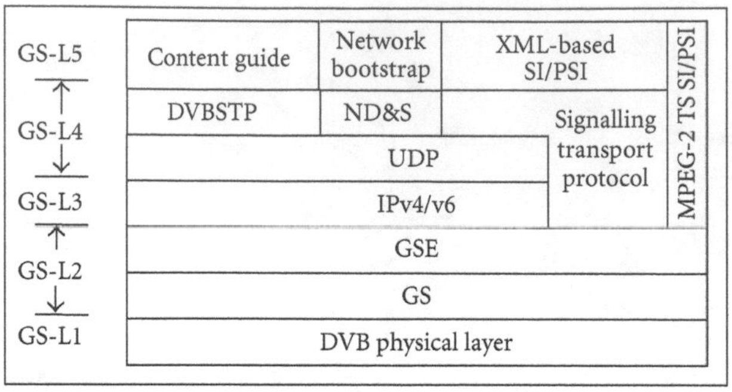

GS-L5	Content guide	Network bootstrap	XML-based SI/PSI	MPEG-2 TS SI/PSI
GS-L4	DVBSTP	ND&S	Signalling transport protocol	
		UDP		
GS-L3	IPv4/v6			
GS-L2	GSE			
	GS			
GS-L1	DVB physical layer			

FIGURE 5: Envisaged DVB IP/GSE signalling framework.

will need to identify which physical-layer frames or GSE packets carry the required network signalling information. Potential procedures to recognise GSE packets conveying signalling are proposed and discussed in this paper.

4. GSE-Only Framework Requirements

This section derives a set of requirements for transition to a GSE-only signalling framework.

4.1. IP Interoperability. The signalling system needs to support the IP protocol stack, as the envisaged system depicted in Figure 5. It must be able to coexist with and provide metadata for IP-based protocols such as the Real-time Transport Protocol (RTP) [17] or the File Delivery over Unidirectional Transport (FLUTE) [18]. As DVB networks become an integral part of the Internet, the use of IP network signalling will allow all-IP delivery of services such as IPTV. Importantly, other supporting functions (including network management and related content) may utilise well-known IP-based tools, which may potentially reduce the cost of development and operation.

4.2. Coexistence with MPEG-2 TS Services. During transition, there is a need to allow the exchange of TS signalling information over a GS transmission network. Various options exist that may enable this transport, including the transmission of MPEG-2 Sections over UDP/IP using GSE encapsulation, or a direct mapping between MPEG-2 SI/PSI and GSE, for example, using the GSE TS-Concat extension [16]. In considering the need for coexistence, the cost of translation and the additional cost (if any) of transmission must be analysed.

4.3. Similar or Higher Efficiency as Current TS Signalling. The overhead arising from the protocols used in the envisaged IP-based signalling framework of Figure 5 must be mitigated.

Although the signalling traffic for typical MPEG-2 TS PSI/SI use-cases typically contributes a small fraction of the total available bandwidth, the performance of the system needs to be evaluated and compared to the efficiency achieved by current MPEG-2 TS SI/PSI systems. Methods must be examined to reduce the additional transmission overhead, such as header compression (e.g., techniques based on Robust Header Compression (ROHC) [19, 20]) or the use of link mechanisms, such as the GSE PDU-Concat extension [16]. This extension allows several IP packets to be delivered to the same destination (GS-L2 address) using a single GSE packet, up to the maximum GSE payload length of 64000B. For example, if ten IP packets were sent in a single GSE packet, this would save 35% of the GS-L2 overhead.

4.4. Signalling Security. When desired, signalling may be secured in an all-IP solution. The security requirements can be different for discovery functions (where all receivers may initially need access during bootstrap), and for individual signalling streams (which may be authorised to specific groups of users). Security of the signalling stream may be provided using a GSE security extension [16]. Alternatively, or in combination, the signalling information may be directly protected by authentication and encryption of the metadata.

4.5. Enabling Service Discovery and Service Description Metadata. The new signalling system should enable a receiver to perform a "network scan" to discover the network and content, equivalent to the current PAT functionality. That is, it would allow a receiver to determine which networks and what content is available by decoding the GS without a priori information. The network discovery methods should identify the multiplex and resolve to a Network Point of Attachment/Medium Access Control (NPA/MAC) address at the GSE level. Supporting a "network scan" will place requirements on the repetition rates of the network signalling stream.

4.6. Providing Easy Identification of Signalling in GSE Streams. A receiver must quickly and efficiently identify the GSE packets carrying network signalling information within the GS. This is needed to provide fast service acquisition and may help in changing to a different service (e.g., to provide fast acquisition of signalling information when zapping between channels). The chosen mechanisms also need to ensure this procedure is not processing intensive at the receiver.

4.7. Quality of Service (QoS) and Timing Reconstruction. The delivery requirements for network signalling need to be considered. It is assumed that packet loss due to link corruption may be disregarded, since in most cases the physical-layer

TABLE 1: Relationships among the proposal requirements and applicability to network/content discovery and selection.

No.	Requirement	Network discovery	Network selection	Service discovery & selection
4.1	IP interoperability		X	X
4.2	Coexistence with MPEG-2 TS services	X	X	X
4.3	Similar, or higher, bandwidth efficiency as current TS signalling	X	X	
4.4	Signalling security		X	
4.5	Enable service discovery and service description metadata		X	X
4.6	Provides easy identification of signalling in GSE streams	X	X	
4.7	QoS and timing reconstruction			X
4.8	Extensible syntax		X	X
4.9	Separation of network and content signalling	X	X	X

waveform will provide a quasi-error-free service using a combination of physical-layer parameters and Forward Error Correction (FEC) coding (e.g., a certain ModCod in DVB-S2). The repetition of signalling also improves robustness and allows fast PSI/SI bootstrap acquisition. The description syntax should allow easily inclusion of QoS descriptors for the network service. A/V timing needs to be synchronised, requiring mechanisms equivalent to the Program Clock Reference/Network Clock Reference (PCR/NCR), for example, using RTP timestamps. The GSE timestamp extension header [16] does not provide the required resolution for synchronisation, since it was designed to support functions with less stringent timing accuracy, such as monitoring and management operations.

4.8. Extensible Syntax. The network signalling metadata syntax should provide a "user-friendly" description to facilitate modification, extension and/or enhancement of the signalling to support new formats and methods from a network/content provider. It should also enable easy addition of new signalling schemes that may be needed to support new applications and new services (requiring new descriptors or Tables).

4.9. Separation of Network and Content Signalling. Network and content signalling should be organised and sent independently from each other, so that a receiver can acquire network signalling faster than that of its content counterpart. This can also permit a receiver to acquire appropriate signalling without the need to parse the entire GS. That is, the identification of GSE packets carrying network signalling should not involve the filtering of all frames at levels GS-L1 or GS-L2. In addition, the method to achieve this separation should be applicable to any DVB standard, allowing sending network signalling with the same technique over any DVB physical frame, making it bearer-agnostic.

4.10. Requirements for ND&S and/or SD&S. Together these requirements may be used to derive a new signalling framework. Requirements 4.2, 4.3, 4.6 and 4.9 involve network discovery procedures, while requirement 4.1 includes network selection and SD&S techniques. For a better

understanding, Table 1 identifies requirements applicable to network discovery, network selection and service discovery and selection.

5. GSE-Only Signalling Framework

This section analyses methods to provide GSE signalling identification and ND&S procedures. The signalling transport protocol and signalling syntax are also studied to identify which may be suitable for a GSE-only signalling framework and may meet the requirements stated in the previous section. Some methods are already used for IP-based signalling of content metadata, however, all current DVB systems use network signalling based on MPEG-2 encoded Tables.

5.1. GSE Signalling Identification. Since there are no PIDs in a GSE-only signalling architecture, the first step towards this framework is to provide ND&S by filtering of signalling information at the GS-L1 or GS-L2 layers, to identify which GSE packets convey signalling information. Procedures for identification of packets carrying signalling metadata are needed to minimise receiver processing. Appropriate techniques can also assist in meeting the requirements for separation of network and content signalling.

A range of techniques is available, as presented in Table 2 and described in detail below. This includes use of fields in the frame header and the allocation of protocol codepoints. Some of these procedures may be jointly used, for example, methods 5.1.4 and 5.1.5. The methods are organised by increasing amounts of information that would need to be parsed by a receiver joining the network. The final solution should preserve flexibility to use different higher layer protocols, introduce security when required, and provide flexibility to optimise the overhead (e.g., use of header compression).

5.1.1. Assignment of a Dedicated Transmission Stream. It is possible to reserve entire transmission frames at the physical-layer for use by a separate signalling stream. This stream could be identified by a physical-layer identifier, for example, a well-known Input Stream Identifier (ISI) value in DVB-

TABLE 2: Candidate methods for identifying GSE packets carrying network signalling.

No.	Candidate method	Filtering level
5.1.1	Assignment of a dedicated transmission stream (e.g., DVB ISI)	GS-L1
5.1.2	Assignment of fields in the transmission frame header	GS-L1
5.1.3	Alignment of signalling transmission to a time-slicing frame	GS-L1
5.1.4	Placement of a GSE packet at a known position within a frame	GS-L2
5.1.5	Assignment of a dedicated GSE Type field value	GS-L2
5.1.6	Assignment of a dedicated Label/NPA or IP address	GS-L2/GS-L3
5.1.7	Assignment of a well-known UDP port	GS-L4

S2/T2. A receiver performing a bootstrap may skip all frames with a different ISI, reducing the receiver information processing load. However, this method could reduce overall system efficiency when the frame size is large. Receivers need to be setup to process more than one ISI, this approach is being tested in some present systems.

5.1.2. Assignment of Fields in the Physical Frame Header. Rather than dedicate a specific channel to signalling, the control information in the physical-layer header may be extended to carry network signalling information. This approach resembles the use of the Fast Information Channel (FIC) in ATSC Mobile Digital Television systems [21]. The FIC channel provides a network bootstrap method that is specified outside the normal frame payload, and hence is independent of the data channel carrying Reed-Solomon (RS) FEC frames, shown in Figure 6. Its data unit is the FIC-Chunk, which provides the binding information between the Mobile/Handheld (M/H) services and the M/H ensembles. A M/H ensemble is a set of consecutive RS frames with the same FEC coding. Information such as the ensemble ID, Tables carried by the ensemble, the number of services carried and the service ID is carried by the FIC-Chunk. This approach is an optimisation of the physical-layer, which may be processed independently of the content. This enables fast tuning and simpler processing at the receiver.

The DVB physical-layer specifications do not provide an equivalent physical-layer signalling channel, although the DVB-S2/T2 frame headers currently have unallocated bits. A single bit in these frames could signal if a GSE packet conveying signalling is present in the frame, otherwise a receiver seeking signalling may ignore the frame. Additional bits could be used, if appropriate and available, to help define the type of signalling, for example, bootstrap or network services signalling. This would require an update to the present DVB transmission standards.

5.1.3. Alignment of Signalling Transmission to a Time-Slicing Frame. Time-slicing is a well-known method used for power-saving in DVB-H and DVB-SH systems. This technique could be applied to signalling to allow a receiver to know which frames may contain signalling information and allow a receiver to skip processing of frames that are known to not contain signalling PDUs. Timeslicing information (i.e., prior knowledge of times when signalling data is to

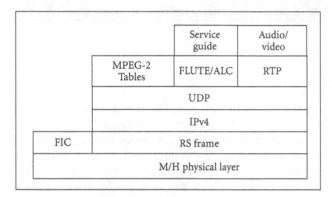

FIGURE 6: Simplified protocol stack for ATSC Mobile DTV.

be sent) would allow a synchronised receiver to disregard a proportion of physical-layer frames. Such an approach may be desirable for mobile applications, and could be extended to all signalling messages in any new system.

5.1.4. Placement of a GSE Packet at a Known Position in a Frame. Transmission frames are typically long compared to the PDUs (signalling or data) that they carry. Processing of a frame that may contain one or more signalling PDUs could be simplified if the signalling information was inserted at a known position within a frame. The flexibility in the fragmentation algorithm of GSE would allow signalling packets to always be placed at the start of the frame payload. Although a receiver would need to inspect all frames, it may then skip any remaining payload after finding the first GSE packet in the S2/T2 frame that does not contain signalling information. This method does not require any change to the present physical-layer or GSE standards.

5.1.5. Allocation of a Dedicated GSE Type Field Value. A receiver needs a simple way to demultiplex GSE signalling packets from data packets. One option is to use the GSE Type field. This may be performed in two ways:

(a) Assign a Well-Known Mandatory Type Field [13, 14]. A mandatory Type field directly precedes the GSE PDU (Figure 4). One mandatory Type is required for each type of signalling information, for example, if IPv4 or IPv6 is used, the version of IP will need to be signalled, or if header

compression is used. GSE-level encryption would prevent visibility of a mandatory Type field prior to decryption.

(b) Assign a Well-Known Optional Type Field. An optional Type field [13] is a separate tag inserted after the GSE base header. In this case, the tag would be used to indicate that the encapsulated PDU carries signalling data. The original Type field would also be present (indicating the version of IP, use of encryption, etc.), so operation would resemble the Router Alert option in the IP header. This is the simplest method, but will add 2B of overhead to the GSE header.

The Internet Assigned Numbers Authority (IANA) assigns Mandatory and Optional Type values. The Institute of Electrical and Electronics Engineers (IEEE) also register EtherTypes that can be used as mandatory Type values.

5.1.6. Allocation of a Dedicated Label/NPA or IP Address. The demultiplexing of signalling from data packets may be aided by using well-known values of other protocol fields. Two methods have been identified at the GSE and IP levels that may assist in this process:

(a) Assignment of a Well-Known Multicast NPA Address. It is attractive to use well-known L2 addresses for bootstrapping, for example, an IANA DVB multicast IP address that maps to a MAC/NPA address [22], but this has limited use for discovery. After bootstrap, a receiver may move to one of several network services, and it may be natural to assign different address to each service. If this method were used to identify signalling, this would prevent suppression of the NPA address/label field in GSE. This suggests there can be no single address binding that applies to all scenarios.

(b) Assignment of a Well-Known IP Address. This method would allow suppression of the NPA/MAC address but requires an IP packet format. Filtering using the IP address is not recommended, since it would preclude the use of link header compression or encryption of the GSE packet payload (since all packets would have to be decompressed and/or decrypted before filtering). The system would also increase complexity when other GSE extensions are present (e.g., timestamps). Well-known IP multicast destination addresses are used in many IP bootstrap procedures, and when present, these would normally result in a mapping to well-known MAC addresses [22].

5.1.7. Assignment of a Well-Known UDP Port. This method requires an IP packet format, as in Section 5.1.6, and deep packet inspection (i.e., parsing of the IP and transport headers). It is not compatible with header compression and with other extension headers. This would not be recommended since the receiver would have to process all packets at GS and IP level to finally filter those conveying signalling at the transport layer level.

5.2. Network Discovery and Selection. This section proposes a two-stage approach which could be used for ND&S, in common with other IP-based systems to provide content discovery and selection. Once the GSE packets carrying signalling metadata are filtered at the GS-L1 or GS-L2 layers, a bootstrap will be performed to select the appropriate network signalling information. The network signalling information can then be used to select the required network service. The procedures below are based on IP satisfying the requirement for IP interoperability when enabling service discovery.

A bootstrap method eliminates the need to manually enter a bootstrap entry point, for example, the need to configure IP/NPA addresses out of band or using device configuration. Instead the device only has to be configured with the logical name for the network to which it is attached.

The format of network bootstrap information could be a Table structure that maps logical names to appropriate discovery entry points, that is, IP addresses where the discovery information can be found. Such a Table may be equivalent to the IP/MAC Notification Table (INT) used by DVB-H systems to signal the availability and location of IP streams. Another format could use a multicast Domain Name Server Service (mDNS SRV) record [23] to specify the network service discovery entry points, similar to the procedure recommended for DVB-IPTV [24]. SRV records convey information about the service, such as the transport protocol used, its priority and the IP address of the server providing the service.

For broadcast networks, the bootstrap could be sent using a well-known IP multicast address. This approach is similar to that for DVB service discovery (*dvbservdsc*) information, that is, *dvbservdsc* information is provided, by default, on the IANA-registered well-known *dvbservdsc* multicast address of 224.0.23.14 for IPv4 and FF0X:0:0:0:0:0:0:12D for IPv6, and on the IANA-registered well-known *dvbservdsc* port 3937 via TCP and UDP [25].

For bidirectional networks, ND&S entry point addresses may be found through the following three options: the Simple Service Discovery Protocol (SSDP) over UDP, SRV records via DNS over UDP or SRV records via DHCP option 15 over UDP. SSDP, defined by Microsoft and Hewlett-Packard, is specified as the Universal Plug and Play (UPnP) discovery protocol [26]. It uses part of the header field format of HTTP1.1. Since it is only partially based on HTTP1.1, it is carried by UDP instead of TCP. A drawback is that SSDP is a proprietary standard. SRV records via DNS or via DHCP option 15 are SD&S procedures (for content metadata) recommended by DVB-IPTV [24] and also used by the Open IPTV Forum (OIPF) framework [27] as well as for the signalling of DVB interactive applications [28]. The methods described for bidirectional networks, are not suited to unidirectional broadcast since they rely on the existence of a return channel. A unidirectional solution applicable to both scenarios, broadcast and interactive, is desirable.

5.3. Signalling Transport Protocol. Selection of a transport protocol for the signalling metadata needs to take into consideration the requirements (similar efficiency than that of TS signalling) and characteristics (high repetition rates) of the metadata.

For unicast scenarios with bidirectional connectivity, HTTP over TCP is a commonly chosen method for unicast content metadata transport since it is used by DVB-IPTV, DVB-H, DVB-SH and OIPF architectures.

A/V data is transmitted over RTP via UDP/IP in DVB-IPTV and DVB-H systems. RTP with an extension header [17] carrying timestamps could be used for synchronisation, as the equivalent to PCR/NCR. Signalling metadata could potentially be sent in a new defined payload format for RTP. RTP can open up a set of media-related services, such as source identification, packet loss measure, jitter control, and reliability techniques. The extension header of RTP may also provide means of performing discovery, although it would also add an overhead of 12 or 16B per Section.

The DVB SD&S Transport Protocol (DVBSTP) [24] over UDP has been specified for reliable multicast SD&S content metadata delivery in architectures compliant with DVB-IPTV [24] and OIPF [27]. It transports eXtensible Markup Language (XML) [29] records and defines the type of payload carried through its Payload ID field (e.g., Content on Demand, Broadcast discovery information). A Compression field indicates the type of compression encoding, if any. A DVBSTP header adds an overhead of at least 12B per Section. The redundancy for network signalling may not be needed when Tables are transmitted at high repetition rates. Since the DVBSTP header provides signalling identification though its Payload ID field, it would allow the receiver to determine whether a signalling stream contains replicated metadata that has been already received or metadata that the receiver does not wish to receive.

The FLUTE [18] protocol has been used for content guide transport over UDP in DVB-H, DVB-SH and ATSC Mobile DTV [21]. FLUTE builds on the Asynchronous Layered Coding (ALC) specification to provide scalable, unidirectional, multicast distribution of objects. ALC/FLUTE was also recommended for the design of a new transport protocol for the delivery of Internet Media Guides (IMGs) by the IETF Multiparty Multimedia Session Control (MMUSIC) group, when seeking to provide a format for content metadata over the Internet [30].

Since the requirements for transport of network signalling metadata differ from those for content metadata, the transport protocols listed above may not be suitable. For example, ALC/FLUTE offers support for FEC-based reliability although this may increase processing overhead and is not required when data is repeated frequently. It also increases transmission cost. DVBSTP adds an overhead of at least 12B and provide reliability (also not required). DVBSTP does provide an indication of the type of XML-record carried through its 1B Payload ID field and the type of compression used through a 3-bit Compression field. These features, together with the ability to determine if content (Table) is encrypted before processing the payload are attractive for a transport protocol. Further work is needed to determine whether the overhead is justified and whether this choice of transport can be efficiently combined with the metadata encoding to optimise overall performance, or whether a new alternate lightweight protocol is preferable.

5.4. Signalling Syntax. This section reviews a set of candidate methods for representing the metadata. It discusses existing SI/PSI, the Session Description Protocol (SDP) [31] and SDP with negotiation capabilities (SDPng) [32], and finally use of XML [29].

5.4.1. Direct Encapsulation of PSI/SI. PSI, SI and FLS syntax has been standardised in MPEG-2 [4, 5, 12] and were outlined in Section 2. Even though this Table-based format is expected to continue for backwards compatibility, it is desirable the transition to a more flexible syntax to allow extensibility and evolution of signalling. Any new method should support MPEG-2 PSI/SI to satisfy the requirement for coexistence.

5.4.2. SDP and SDPng. The IETF MMUSIC group standardised SDP [31] for multimedia session description over IP. SDP defines a format for session description to announce sessions and their parameters to prospective receivers; it does not specify a transport protocol. In bidirectional networks, SDP is commonly transported using the Session Initiation Protocol (SIP), specified in RFC 3261, or the Real Time Streaming Protocol (RTSP), specified in RFC 2326. In a multicast IP network, RFC 2974 specifies how SDP may be transported over the Session Announcement Protocol (SAP) using a set of well-known multicast addresses.

The ESG in DVB-H, the OIPF framework and multicast sessions in ATSC use SDP records. Even though SDP is an IP-level method, it does not provide link-specific information to identify a network service or physical-layer tuning parameters for the transmission multiplex (e.g., frequency, transmission mode, and ISI). Hence, it would need to be extended to be suitable for network signalling.

The IETF started to develop an updated SDP protocol, SDPng. This was intended to address the lack of negotiation capabilities in SDP by providing alternatives for session parameter configurations. That is, an IP host would be able to negotiate session parameters according to its system capabilities. Proposals for SDPng used the XML syntax, Document Type Definitions (DTDs) and Schemas, to allow extensibility. It was one candidate method to convey session parameters for an IMG [30]. However, work on SDPng has not continued since 2003, with no specifications defined, and therefore is not applicable for a GSE-only signalling framework.

5.4.3. XML. The eXtensible Markup Language, XML [29], has been standardised by the Worldwide Web Consortium, W3C. It is now a common syntax for network control information and content metadata. The DVB-IPTV, DVB-H, DVB-SH, OIPF, UPnP and ATSC systems define XML Schemas, while DVB interactive application metadata is defined as XML DTDs [28]. XML Schemas have been developed to make it easier to create and enhance the encoded information and are preferred over DTDs, for example, XML Schemas defined for DVB-IPTV can also be used in the OIPF framework. In contrast to DTDs, XML Schemas provide support for namespaces, can constrain

TABLE 3: Potential methods for a GSE-only signalling framework.

GSE-only signalling framework area	Prospective methods	Section
GSE Signalling Identification	Assignment of a dedicated transmission stream	5.1.1
	Assignment of fields in physical frame header	5.1.2
	Alignment of signalling transmission to a time-slicing frame	5.1.3
	Placement of a GSE packet at a known position in a frame	5.1.4
	Allocation of a dedicated GSE Type field value	5.1.5
	Allocation of a dedicated Label/NPA or IP address	5.1.6
	Assignment of a well-known UDP port	5.1.7
ND&S	Bootstrap Table using well-known multicast addresses	
	SRV record via DNS using well-known multicast addresses	5.2
	SRV record via DHCP option*	
	SSDP	
Transport Protocol	HTTP/TCP*	
	DVBSTP/UDP	
	FLUTE/ALC/UDP	5.3
	RTP/UDP	
	New lightweight transport/UDP	
Syntax	MPEG-2	5.4.1
	XML	5.4.3
	Compressed XML	5.4.3

*This procedure requires bidirectional connectivity.

data based on common data types, and present object oriented features such as type derivation. In addition, XML allows encryption, which could be used to provide signalling security.

A Uniform Resource Name (URN) namespace has been defined for naming resources defined within DVB standards by [25]. DVB specifies XML Schemas and DTDs, namespaces and other types of resource [33]. XML network signalling, in parallel with classical SI/PSI Tables may be used in interactive DVB applications for hybrid broadcast/broadband environments [28].

In a GSE-only signalling framework, metadata syntax could be converted to XML. A simple, but effective method could retain the segmentation of the PSI/SI Tables, since the Section mechanism is an important element of the PSI/SI structure, to allow easy access to parts of the Table. In the XML encoding, the PID may be substituted by the IP destination address and UDP port number, similar to the approach proposed in [34]. This substitution also allows reuse of Tables after the PIDs are mapped to these IP addresses/ports within the PSI/SI.

Since encoding the signalling metadata in XML significantly increases the information rate (due to its inherent verbosity), this will decrease bandwidth efficiency. However, XML data may be readily compressed, for example, two compression algorithms are recommended for DVB-H content metadata: GZIP [35] and BiM [36]. The GZIP format uses the deflate algorithm (RFC 1952). This combines an index (dictionary) approach together with Huffman compression. GZIP is effective on streams with recurring patterns of data, especially when used with large data sets. The ISO MPEG-7 group defined the Binary MPEG format for XML, BiM, as an alternative to text representation. BiM was proposed for TV-Anytime content metadata and afterwards recommended for DVB-IPTV and DVB-H ESG.

BiM compression can reduce the transmission cost up to 60% of the MPEG-2 encoded PSI/SI Tables [34]. However, this adds complexity to the system, since XML Schemas are needed at the receiver to decompress the encoded Sections.

GZIP presents lower complexity than BiM, since no Schemas are needed before decompression at the receiver. This makes it attractive for handheld terminals to minise the processing requirements. However, its compression gain is typically much lower than for BIM; PSI/SI Sections converted into XML and compressed with GZIP can increase the overall volume of data by 30% compared to the original binary encoded size [34]. Section 5.5.2 provides some example comparison of overhead. As in many compression technologies patents need to be considered. Patents have been already registered for a tool for BiM compression.

Other XML compression algorithms are in the process of being developed. One is the Efficient XML Interchange (EXI) by W3C [37]. EXI not only achieves higher compression gains than GZIP, but also presents a lower decoding

TABLE 4: Potential methods to fulfill the GSE-only signalling requirements.

GSE-only signalling requirement	Prospective methods
IP interoperability	Encapsulation of an IP packet as GSE payload.
	Any of the ND&S methods described in Section 5.2.
	Any unidirectional transport protocol.
Separation of network and content signalling	Any methods for GSE signalling identification described in Section 5.1 enabling filtering at GS-L1/L2.
	Transport protocol with a payload type field.
Extensible syntax	XML syntax.
Similar, or higher, bandwidth efficiency to that of current TS signalling	GSE extension headers to indicate compression.
	IP/UDP header compression.
	XML compression.
	New optimised lightweight transport protocol.
Coexistence with MPEG-2 TS services	Encapsulation of TS packet over GSE.
	Encapsulation of TS packet over UDP/IP/GSE.
Signalling security	GSE security extensions.
	Transport protocol with a field to indicate payload encryption.
	XML encryption.
QoS and timing reconstruction	Timestamps in RTP extension header.
	QoS descriptors in XML.
	Signalling repetition rates.
Enable service discovery and service description metadata	Any of the ND&S methods described in Section 5.2.
	XML syntax.
Provides easy identification of signalling in GSE streams	Any methods for GSE signalling identification described in Section 5.1 enabling filtering at GS-L1/L2.

complexity since Schemas are not necessarily needed at the receiver when performing a network scan.

5.5. GSE/IP Signalling System Prospective Methods. Table 3 presents a summary of the prospective methods described in this section. For completeness, it includes methods currently specified for bidirectional links, which are indicated by an asterisk. While techniques may be combined, it is recommended that at least one technique is used at GS-L1 to identify signalling, in order to reduce processing requirements at the receiver.

Table 4 relates these methods to the requirements identified in Section 4. Overall, the processing cost of decoding at the receiver is important when analysing the use of any of the potential methods listed in Tables 3 and 4, in particular those for identification of signalling in GSE streams. We suggest using the extensible syntax XML for network service description metadata. XML encryption and compression would enable signalling security and are expected to result in similar bandwidth efficiency to that of TS, respectively.

5.5.1. Encapsulation. Several network signalling encapsulation options exist for a GSE-only system.

(1) The GSE TS-Concat extension [16] may be used to enable the coexistence with TS services but increases overhead above the current MPEG-2 TS by adding GSE headers. A method is, however, needed to relate the metadata to the IP address.

(2) To reduce overhead, the SI Table may be directly encapsulated as a PDU in the GSE payload. Since a Section should not be larger than 1024B [5], a GSE payload may be able to carry more than one Section. A method is however need to relate the metadata to the IP address.

(3) Network metadata may be encapsulated as UDP datagram's over IP, similar to the current encapsulation performed in DVB-H systems where ESG XML records are sent over FLUTE via UDP/IP. Recent techniques for IP/UDP header compression, such as ROHC [19, 20], may in future further reduce IP overhead.

(4) The PDU-Concat extension [16] can improve system efficiency when transmitting small IP packets by combining several in a single GSE payload, subject to the maximum payload length of 64000B.

5.5.2. Overhead Analysis. This section compares the transmission cost for sending network signalling. The overhead respect to the Table size resulting from the candidate techniques is shown in Table 5. Three Tables sizes were analysed: one comprising a small section of 30B, a second

TABLE 5: Overhead for different combinations of syntax and encapsulation procedure.

| | Overhead (%) | | | | | | | | |
| | $1 \times 30B$ Section | | | $1 \times 1024B$ Section | | | $4 \times 1024B$ Section | | |
DFL (B)	384	3216	7274	384	3216	7274	384	3216	7274
MPEG-2 Section in TS		526			10.1			10.1	
MPEG-2 Section in TS with dedicated ISI	1146	10586	24113	119	213	609	22	63	84
MPEG-2 Section in TS/GSE with TS-Concat		540		11.8		10.5	11.3	10.5	10.1
XML GZIP Section over DVBSTP/UDP/IP/GSE		160		5.8		4.3	5.6	4.5	4.3
XML BiM Section over DVBSTP/UDP/IP/GSE		146		5.2		4.3	4.9	4.2	4.2
XML BiM Section over FLUTE/ ALC/UDP/IP/GSE		146		5.2		4.3	4.9	4.2	4.2
XML GZIP Section over DVBSTP/UDP/IP/GSE with HC		76		3.3		1.8	3.0	2.1	1.9
XML BiM Section over DVBSTP/UDP/IP/GSE with HC		63		2.8		1.8	2.7	2.0	1.8

with a 1024B Section and a final Table comprising four 1024B Sections. The overhead was calculated for a set of DVB-S2/T2 frame sizes (data field lengths, DFL). In DVB-S2, network signalling is expected to be sent using the most robust ModCod supported in the network to reduce the probability of loss and to allow signalling acquisition in all channel conditions. Hence, this will typically result in frames with a small DFL.

The methods were compared to native transmission of MPEG-2 encoded Sections using the TS, as in current DVB signalling. Padding is added to each TS packet, as necessary. Table 5 shows that this padding results in an overhead for a 30B Table that is more than fifty times higher than the corresponding value for the 1024 and 4096B Tables. Section overhead, only considering the TS headers, is 16.6% for the 30B Table and 2.4% for the 1024 and 4096B Tables, but since a whole TS packet needs to be sent, the overhead becomes 526 and 10.1%, respectively, as shown in Table 5.

Section 5.1.1 proposed a method in which the TS packets were sent on a separate stream using a dedicated stream (ISI value). The fixed size of the frame results in a significant overhead given that there is insufficient signalling data to fill the frame. It is assumed that the overall transmission rate allocated to signalling does not result in any empty frames (although the burst-nature of signalling data may be hard to match to a fixed transmission rate).

Encapsulation of TS packets in GSE, as a transition method, is also analysed. GSE TS-Concat is considered for Tables with multiple Sections. As expected, the overhead is higher than that for native TS transmission. This is also higher than the IP-based encapsulation methods.

The next set of methods considers IP-based protocols and XML-translated Sections. Each Section is encapsulated by DVBSTP/UDP/IP or FLUTE/ALC/UDP/IP, where the additional headers contribute 40B. The GSE PDU-Concat extension is used for the Table with four Sections. It is assumed that signalling identification is carried at GS-L1 (e.g., optional GSE Type fields are no considered).

The overhead for the medium and large Tables represents a trade-off with the benefits provided by an IP-based signalling system. Small Tables negatively impact the efficiency of an IP-based signalling framework regardless of the encapsulation technique and frame size, however the overhead is always lower than that of native MPEG-2 TS. This overhead is further reduced when header compression (HC) is considered. Estimates of the compressed size using either GZIP or BiM algorithms are provided. This assumes that BiM compression of the XML-encoded Section results in a reduction of 40% with respect to the size of the MPEG-2 encoded Section [34]. In contrast, applying GZIP to a XML-encoded Section results in an increase of 30% with respect to the size of the MPEG-2 encoded Section [34]. Despite this, using XML with GZIP results in less than half the overhead of the native TS method for the 1024 and 4096B Tables.

DVBSTP and FLUTE resulted in the same overhead. Although, DVBSTP was designed to ease processing of SD&S XML records at the receiver, it results in significant overhead for small PDUs. The 12B of overhead introduced above the UDP layer is seen as an upper bound. This overhead could be reduced further by design of a lightweight transport protocol to replace the DVBSTP header, or by combined optimisation of content-encoding and transport protocol.

The UDP/IP headers are assumed to be compressed to 3B when using a form of header compression, although no method has currently been specified for use with DVB. The use of header compression for signalling should be analysed further given the positive effect on reducing the overhead.

6. Conclusions and Future Work

The convergence of DVB networks with IP infrastructure bridges the gap between broadcast transmission and traditional networks. Current MPEG-2 systems are already used to transmit IP packets, mostly using MPE or ULE, it is expected that future DVB transmission networks adopt an all-IP approach by gradually replacing the TS by the GS. Transition to IP-based content and signalling will enable common use of IP delivery techniques at the receiver, presenting new opportunities for integrating broadcast content with standard IP applications, and the introduction of value-added services.

One major challenge to transitioning broadcast services to the GS is the lack of a GSE-only signalling framework. IP-based procedures for content metadata exist in DVB systems, but current signalling is implemented through MPEG-2 TS Tables. This paper explains the need for a GSE-only signalling framework and formulates a set of requirements, reviews a range of candidate methods, including current IP-based methods and has derived their potential benefits.

The proposed methods can identify GSE packets carrying signalling and replace the role of PIDs. In addition, current IP-based methods may be used as prospective techniques for ND&S procedures and for the signalling syntax. Options were also presented for a signalling transport protocol. Methods for encoding metadata that allow extensibility and easy modification were examined. XML Schemas are strong candidates because of their extensibility characteristics and current common use for content metadata. Indicative performance data is used to compare the anticipated overhead for the various approaches.

This work is intended to guide and inform future standardisation work. As future work, we intend to select the optimal candidate methods and propose a GSE-only signalling architecture. The high-level requirements in terms of signalling for different scenarios, for example, fixed broadcast, interactive, will be also defined, as well as the specification for mapping current SI/PSI/FLS MPEG-2 encoded Tables to their XML-based counterparts.

Acknowledgment

The authors acknowledge the support of the European Space Agency (ESA) Contract 22471/09/NL/AD.

References

[1] ETSI EN 300 421, "Digital Video Broadcasting (DVB); Framing Structure, Channel Coding and Modulation for 11/12—GHz Satellite Services," October 1997.

[2] ETSI EN 300 744, "Digital Video Broadcasting (DVB); framing structure, channel coding and modulation for digital terrestrial television," February 1997.

[3] ETSI EN 300 429, "Digital Video Broadcasting (DVB); framing structure, channel coding and modulation for cable systems," April 1998.

[4] ISO/IEC 13818-1, "Information technology—generic coding of moving pictures and associated audio information: systems," 1995.

[5] ETSI EN 300 468, "Digital Video Broadcasting (DVB)," Specification for Service Information (SI) in DVB systems, February 1998.

[6] ATSC Standard A/65, "Program and System Information Protocol for Terrestrial Broadcast and Cable (PSIP)," December 1997.

[7] ETSI EN 302 307, "Digital Video Broadcasting (DVB); second generation framing structure, channel coding and modulation systems for Broadcasting, Interactive Services, News Gathering and other broadband satellite applications (DVB-S2)," August 2009.

[8] ETSI EN 302 755, "Digital Video Broadcasting (DVB); frame structure channel coding and modulation for a second generation digital terrestrial television broadcasting system (DVB-T2)," September 2009.

[9] ETSI EN 302 769, "Digital Video Broadcasting (DVB); frame structure channel coding and modulation for a second genera-

[10] ETSI TS 102 471, "Digital Video Broadcasting (DVB); IP Datacast over DVB-H: Electronic Service Guide (ESG)," April 2009.

[11] ETSI TS 102 592-2, "Digital Video Broadcasting (DVB); IP Datacast: Electronic Service Guide (ESG) Implementation Guidelines; Part 2: IP Datacast over DVB-SH," January 2010.

[12] ETSI EN 301 790, "Digital Video Broadcasting (DVB); interaction channel for satellite distribution systems," May 2009.

[13] G. Fairhurst and B. Collini-Nocker, "Unidirectional Lightweight Encapsulation (ULE) for Transmission of IP Datagrams over an MPEG-2 Transport Stream (TS)," IETF RFC 4326, December 2005.

[14] J. Cantillo, B. Collini-Nocker, U. De Bie, et al., "GSE: a flexible, yet efficient, encapsulation for IP over DVB-S2 continuous generic streams," International Journal of Satellite Communications and Networking, vol. 26, no. 3, pp. 231–250, 2008.

[15] ETSI TS 102 606 (v1.1.1), "Digital Video Broadcasting (DVB); Generic Stream Encapsulation (GSE) Protocol," October 2007.

[16] G. Fairhurst and B. Collini-Nocker, "Extension Formats for Unidirectional Lightweight Encapsulation (ULE) and the Generic Stream Encapsulation (GSE)," IETF RFC 5163, April 2008.

[17] H. Schulzrinne, S. Casner, R. Frederick, and V. Jacobson, "RTP: A Transport Protocol for Real-Time Applications," RFC 3550, July 2003.

[18] T. Paila, M. Luby, R. Lehtonen, V. Roca, and R. Walsh, "FLUTE—File Delivery over Unidirectional Transport," RFC 3926, October 2004.

[19] L-E. Jonsson, K. Sandlund, G. Pelletier, and P. Kremer, "RObust Header Compression (ROHC): Corrections and Clarifications to RFC 3095," RFC 4815, February 2007.

[20] C. Bormann, "Robust Header Compression (ROHC) over 802 networks," IETF work in progress, July 2009.

[21] ATSC, "A/153: ATSC-Mobile DTV Standard, Part 1-ATSC Mobile Digital Television System," October 2009.

[22] G. Fairhurst and M.-J. Montpetit, "Address Resolution Mechanisms for IP Datagrams over MPEG-2 Networks," IETF RFC 4947, July 2007.

[23] A. Gulbrandsen, P. Vixie, and L. Esibov, "A DNS RR for specifying the location of services (DNS SRV)," RFC 2782, February 2000.

[24] ETSI TS 102 034, "Digital Video Broadcasting (DVB); Transport of MPEG-2 TS Based DVB Services over IP Based Networks," 2007.

[25] A. Adolf and P. MacAvock, "A Uniform Resource Name (URN) Namespace for the Digital Video Broadcasting Project (DVB)," IETF RFC 5328, September 2008.

[26] UPnP Forum, UPnP Device Architecture 1.1, October 2008.

[27] OIPF Functional Architecture [v1.2], March 2008.

[28] ETSI TS 102 809, "Digital Video Broadcasting (DVB); signalling and carriage of interactive applications and services in Hybrid broadcast/broadband environments," January 2010.

[29] World Wide Web Consortium (W3C), "Extensible Markup Language (XML) 1.0 (Fifth Edition)," http://www.w3.org/TR/REC-xml/REC-xml-20081126.xml.

[30] Y. Nomura, R. Walsh, J.-P. Luoma, H. Asaeda, and H. Schulzrinne, "A Framework for the Usage of Internet Media Guides (IMGs)," RFC 4435, April 2006.

[31] M. Handley, V. Jacobson, and C. Perkins, "SDP: Session Description Protocol," RFC 4566, July 2006.

[32] SDPng, http://www.dmn.tzi.org/ietf/mmusic/sdp-ng/index.html.

[33] Repository of DVB Metadata Related Documents, http://www.dvb.org/metadata.

[34] H. Foellscher, "Transmission of media content on IP-based digital broadcast platforms," dissertation, Institute for Communications Technology, Technical University of Braunschweig, July 2007.

[35] P. Deutsh, "GZIP file format specification version 4.3," IETF RFC 1952, May 1996.

[36] ISO/IEC 23001-1 (MPEG-B), "Information Technology—MPEG Systems Technologies—Binary MPEG format for XML".

[37] World Wide Web Consortium (W3C), "Efficient XML Interchange (EXI) Format 1.0," http://www.w3.org/TR/exi/.

8

On the Optimization of the IEEE 802.11 DCF:
A Cross-Layer Perspective

Massimiliano Laddomada[1] and Fabio Mesiti[2]

[1] *Electrical Engineering Department, Texas A&M University-Texarkana, Texarkana, TX 75505, USA*
[2] *DELEN, Politecnico di Torino, 10129 Torino, Italy*

Correspondence should be addressed to Massimiliano Laddomada, mladdomada@tamut.edu

Academic Editor: Petros Nicopolitidis

This paper is focused on the problem of optimizing the aggregate throughput of the distributed coordination function (DCF) employing the basic access mechanism at the data link layer of IEEE 802.11 protocols. We consider general operating conditions accounting for both nonsaturated and saturated traffic in the presence of transmission channel errors, as exemplified by the packet error rate P_e. The main clue of this work stems from the relation that links the aggregate throughput of the network to the packet rate λ of the contending stations. In particular, we show that the aggregate throughput $S(\lambda)$ presents two clearly distinct operating regions that depend on the actual value of the packet rate λ with respect to a critical value λ_c, theoretically derived in this work. The behavior of $S(\lambda)$ paves the way to a cross-layer optimization algorithm, which proved to be effective for maximizing the aggregate throughput in a variety of network operating conditions. A nice consequence of the proposed optimization framework relies on the fact that the aggregate throughput can be predicted quite accurately with a simple, yet effective, closed-form expression. Finally, theoretical and simulation results are presented in order to unveil, as well as verify, the key ideas.

1. Introduction

DCF represents the main access mechanism at the medium access control (MAC) layer [1] of the IEEE 802.11 series of standards, and it is based on carrier sense multiple access with collision avoidance (CSMA/CA).

Many papers, following the seminal work by Bianchi [2], have addressed the problem of modeling, as well as optimizing, the DCF in a variety of traffic load models and transmission channel conditions.

Let us provide a survey of the recent literature related to the problem addressed in this paper. Papers [3–7] model the influence of real channel conditions on the throughput of the DCF operating in saturated traffic conditions. Paper [3] investigates the saturation throughput of IEEE 802.11 in presence of nonideal transmission channel and capture effects.

The behavior of the DCF of IEEE 802.11 WLANs in unsaturated traffic conditions has been analyzed in [8–13], whereby the authors proposed various bidimensional

Markov models for unsaturated traffic conditions, extending the basic bidimensional model proposed by Bianchi [2]. In [14], the authors look at the impact of channel-induced errors and of the received signal-to-noise ratio (SNR) on the achievable throughput in a system with rate adaptation, whereby the transmission rate of the terminal is modified depending on either direct, or indirect measurements of the link quality.

The effect of the contention window size on the performance of the DCF has been investigated in [15–22] upon assuming a variety of transmission scenarios. We invite the interested reader to refer to the works [15–22] and references therein.

In [15], the authors proposed a framework to derive the average size of the contention window that maximizes the network throughput in saturated traffic conditions. Moreover, a distributed algorithm aimed at tuning the backoff algorithm of each contending station was proposed. In [16] (see also [17]), the authors investigated by simulation four schemes to reduce the contention window size of the contending stations in a saturated network. Moreover, the service differentiation mechanism proposed in the IEEE802.11e standard was used to enhance the offered QoS. Paper [18] provided a theoretical framework to optimize the single-user DCF saturated throughput by selecting the transmitted bit rate and payload size as a function of some specific fading channels. However, no packet error constraint was imposed on the transmitted packets. In [19] the authors focused on the optimization of the single-user DCF saturated throughput by varying the PHY layer data rate and the payload size given a packet error rate constraint.

Paper [20] proposed a constant-window backoff scheme in order to guarantee fairness among the contending stations in the investigated network. Comparisons with the binary exponential backoff used in IEEE 802.11 DCF were also given. In [22] the authors proposed a control theoretic approach to adjust the CW of the contending stations based on the average number of consecutive idle slots between two transmissions. Finally, in [21] the authors presented some European projects where cross-layer optimization techniques were under investigation.

As a starting point for the derivations that follow, we adopt the bidimensional model proposed in a companion paper [12] (see also [13]). Briefly, in [12] the authors extended the saturated Bianchi's model by introducing a new idle state, not present in the original Bianchi's model, accounting for the case in which the station queue is empty. The Markov chain of the proposed contention model was solved for obtaining the stationary probabilities, along with the probability τ that a station starts transmitting in a randomly chosen time slot.

Compared to the works proposed in the literature, the novel contributions of this paper can be summarized as follow. Firstly, we investigate the behavior of the aggregate throughput as a function of the traffic load λ of the contending stations, and note that the aggregate throughput $S(\lambda)$ presents two distinct operating regions identified, respectively, by below link capacity (BLC) region and link capacity (LC) region. Derived in closed-form in this work, and identified by S_m throughout the paper, the link capacity of the considered scenario corresponds to the maximum throughput that the network can achieve when the contending stations transmit with a proper set of network parameters. We show that the network operates in the BLC region when the actual value of the packet rate λ is less than a critical value λ_c, theoretically derived in this work.

The second part of this paper is focused on the optimization of the DCF throughput under variable loading conditions. We propose a cross-layer algorithm whose main aim is to allow the network to operate as close as possible to the link capacity S_m. The proposed optimization algorithm relies on a number of insights derived by the behavior of the aggregate throughput $S(\lambda)$ as a function of the traffic load λ, and aims at choosing either an appropriate value of the minimum contention window W_0, or a proper size of the transmitted packets depending on the network operating region. The optimization algorithm is dynamic in that it has to be reiterated in order to follow the variations of the network parameters. Finally, we derive a simple model of

the optimized throughput, which is useful for predicting the aggregate throughput without resorting to simulation.

The rest of the paper is organized as follows. Section 2 briefly presents the Markov model at the very basis of the proposed optimization framework, whereas Section 3 investigates the behavior of the aggregate throughput as a function of the traffic load λ. The proposed optimization algorithm is discussed in Section 4. Section 5 presents simulation results of the proposed technique applied to a sample network scenario, while Section 6 draws the conclusions.

2. Markov Modeling

The bidimensional Markov Process of the contention model proposed in [12], and shown in Figure 1 for completeness, governs the behavior of each contending station through a series of states indexed by the pair (i, k), for all $i \in [0, m]$, $k \in [0, W_i - 1]$, whereby i identifies the backoff stage. On the other hand, the index k, which belongs to the set $[0, W_i - 1]$, identifies the backoff counter. By this setup, the size of the ith contention window is $W_i = 2^i W_0$, for all $i \in [1, m]$, while W_0 is the minimum size of the contention window.

An idle state, identified by I in Figure 1, is introduced in order to account for the scenario in which after a successful transmission there are no packets to be transmitted, as well as for the situation in which the packet queue is empty and the station is waiting for a new packet arrival.

The proposed Markov model accounts for packet errors due to imperfect channel conditions, by defining an equivalent probability of failed transmission, identified by P_{eq}, which considers the need for a new contention due either to packet collisions (P_{col}) or to channel errors (P_e) on the transmitted packets, that is,

$$P_{eq} = P_{col} + P_e - P_e \cdot P_{col}. \tag{1}$$

It is assumed that at each transmission attempt each station encounters a constant and independent probability of failed transmission, independently from the number of retransmissions already suffered.

The Markov Process depicted in Figure 1 is governed by the following transition probabilities ($P_{i,k|j,n}$ is short for $P\{s(t+1) = i, b(t+1) = k \mid s(t) = j, b(t) = n\}$.):

$$P_{i,k|i,k+1} = 1, \quad k \in [0, W_i - 2], \; i \in [0, m],$$

$$P_{0,k|i,0} = \frac{q(1 - P_{eq})}{W_0}, \quad k \in [0, W_0 - 1], \; i \in [0, m],$$

$$P_{i,k|i-1,0} = \frac{P_{eq}}{W_i}, \quad k \in [0, W_i - 1], \; i \in [1, m],$$

$$P_{m,k|m,0} = \frac{P_{eq}}{W_m}, \quad k \in [0, W_m - 1],$$

$$P_{I|i,0} = (1 - q)(1 - P_{eq}), \quad i \in [0, m],$$

$$P_{0,k|I} = \frac{q}{W_0}, \quad k \in [0, W_0 - 1],$$

$$P_{I|I} = 1 - q. \tag{2}$$

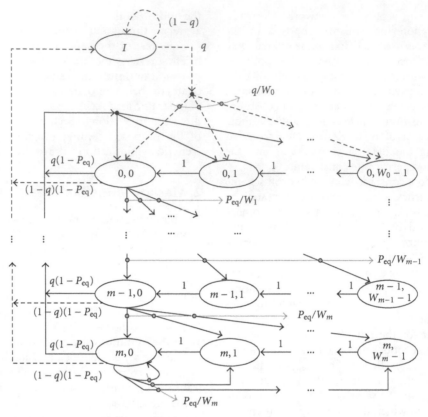

FIGURE 1: Markov chain for the contention model accounting for unsaturated traffic conditions. The model considers m backoff stages. P_{eq} is the probability of failed transmission, accounting for both collisions and channel errors affecting the transmitted packets.

The first equation in (2) states that, at the beginning of each slot time, the backoff time is decremented. The second equation accounts for the fact that after a successful transmission, a new packet transmission starts with backoff stage 0 with probability q, in case there is a new packet in the buffer to be transmitted. Third and fourth equations deal with unsuccessful transmissions and the need to reschedule a new contention stage. The fifth equation deals with the practical situation in which after a successful transmission, the buffer of the station is empty, and as a consequence, the station transits in the idle state I waiting for a new packet arrival. The sixth equation models the situation in which a new packet arrives in the station buffer, and a new backoff procedure is scheduled. Finally, the seventh equation models the situation in which there are no packets to be transmitted and the station is in the idle state.

The stationary distribution of the Markov Model in Figure 1 is employed to compute τ, the probability that a station starts a transmission in a randomly chosen time slot. First of all, observe that a packet transmission takes place when a station goes in one of the states $b_{i,0}$, for all $i \in \{0, m\}$. Therefore, the probability τ can be evaluated by adding up the probabilities $b_{i,0}$ over the set $i \in \{0, \ldots, m\}$. Upon imposing the normalization condition (The probabilities $b_{i,k}$ must add up to 1 for all $k \in \{1, \ldots, W_i - 1\}$, and for all $i \in \{0, m\}$.) on the Markov model in Figure 1, and expressing the probabilities $b_{i,k}$, for all $k \in \{1, \ldots, W_i - 1\}$, as a function

of the probabilities $b_{i,0}$, the probability τ can be rewritten as follows:

$$2\left(1 - 2P_{\text{eq}}\right)q\Big[q\big[(W_0 + 1)\left(1 - 2P_{\text{eq}}\right)$$
$$+ W_0 P_{\text{eq}}\left(1 - \left(2P_{\text{eq}}\right)^m\right)\big] \qquad (3)$$
$$+ 2(1 - q)\left(1 - P_{\text{eq}}\right)\left(1 - 2P_{\text{eq}}\right)\Big]^{-1}.$$

As in Bianchi's work [2], we assume that: (1) the probability τ is constant across all time slots; (2) the probability P_{col} is constant and independent of the number of collisions already suffered.

Given τ, the probability of collision P_{col}, can be defined as follows:

$$P_{\text{col}} = 1 - (1 - \tau)^{N-1}. \qquad (4)$$

Finally, the term q in (3) is the probability of having at least one packet waiting for transmission in the station queue after an average slot duration.

Let us spend few words on the evaluation of q. Upon assuming that the packet interarrival times are exponentially distributed with mean (λ, which is measured in pkt/s, represents the rate at which the packets arrive into the station queue from the upper layers.) $1/\lambda$, the probability q can be well approximated by the following relation in a scenario where the contending stations employ queues of small sizes [9]:

$$q = 1 - e^{-\lambda E[S_{ts}]} \approx \lambda \cdot E[S_{ts}]\Big|_{\lambda \approx 0},$$

$$E[S_{ts}] = (1 - P_t)\sigma + P_t(1 - P_s)T_c \quad (5)$$
$$+ P_t P_s(1 - P_e)T_s + P_t P_s P_e T_e,$$

where $E[S_{ts}]$, the *expected time per slot*, is useful to relate the states of the Markov chain to the actual time spent in each state. As a note aside, notice that $e^{-\lambda E[S_{ts}]}$ in (5) corresponds to the probability that zero packets are received from the upper layers when the packet interarrival times are exponentially distributed.

The other terms involved in $E[S_{ts}]$ are defined as follows [2, 12]: σ is the duration of an empty time slot; P_t is the probability that there is at least one transmission in the considered time slot, with N stations contending for the channel, each transmitting with probability τ; P_s is the conditional probability that a packet transmission occurring on the channel is successful; T_c, T_e, and T_s are, respectively, the average times a channel is sensed busy due to a collision, the transmission time during which the data frame is affected by channel errors, and the average time of successful data frame transmission. These times are defined as follows:

$$T_c = H + E[PL] + ACK_{timeout},$$
$$T_e = H + E[PL] + ACK_{timeout}, \quad (6)$$
$$T_s = H + E[PL] + SIFS + \tau_p + ACK + DIFS + \tau_p,$$

where τ_p is the propagation delay, and H accounts for the PHY and MAC header durations. The other times are noticed in Table 1.

3. Throughput Analysis

The computation of the normalized system throughput relies on the numerical solution of the nonlinear system obtained by jointly solving (1) and (3). The solution of the system, which corresponds to the values of τ and P_{eq}, is used for the computation of the normalized system throughput, that is, the fraction of the time during which the channel is used to successfully transmit payload bits:

$$S = P_t \cdot P_s \cdot \frac{(1 - P_e)E[PL]}{E[S_{ts}]}, \quad (7)$$

whereby $E[PL]$ is the average packet payload length, and $P_t \cdot P_s$ can be rewritten as follows [2]:

$$P_t \cdot P_s = N\tau(1 - \tau)^{N-1}. \quad (8)$$

In order to gain insights on the behavior of the aggregate throughput S, let us investigate the theoretical behavior of (7) as a function of the packet rate λ for two different values of the packet error probability P_e, and minimum contention window $W_0 = 32$, in a scenario with $N = 10$ contending stations transmitting at the bit rate 1 Mbps.

TABLE 1: Typical network parameters.

MAC header	24 bytes	Slot time σ	$20\,\mu s$
PHY header	16 bytes	SIFS	$10\,\mu s$
ACK	14 bytes	DIFS	$50\,\mu s$
τ_p	$1\,\mu s$	EIFS	$300\,\mu s$
W_0	32	ACK timeout	$300\,\mu s$
m	5	CTS timeout	$300\,\mu s$

The two rightmost subplots of Figure 2 show the theoretical behavior of the throughput in (7), as well as simulation results obtained with NS2 by employing the typical MAC layer parameters for IEEE802.11b given in Table 1 [1]. Other parameters are noticed in the label of the figure. Let us spend a few words about the simulation setup in ns-2. In order to account for imperfect channel transmissions, the channel model is implemented using the suggestions proposed in [23], where the outcomes of a binary, equiprobable random variable are used to establish whether each packet is received erroneously. In other words, the random variable is equal to 1 with probability P_e (erroneous transmission), and 0 with probability $1 - P_e$. We notice in passing that the theoretical model developed is independent on the specific propagation channel. The only parameter needed is P_e, which can be appropriately linked to the specific wireless propagation channel upon specifying a threshold of the signal-to-noise ratio allowing perfect reception at the receiver [24].

We adopted the patch NOAH (*NO Ad-Hoc*), available on the authors' website http://icapeople.epfl.ch/ widmer/uwb/ns-2/noah/, for emulating a wireless network in infrastructure mode. The employed traffic model is implemented by generating an exponentially distributed random variable with expected value $1/\lambda$, in accordance to the theoretical model developed in Section 2.

Let us focus on the curves noticed in the two rightmost subplots in Figure 2. Basically, there are two different operating regions of the throughput in (7). As $\lambda \to 0^+$, that is, all the contending stations approach unloaded traffic conditions, the throughput can be approximated as a straight line passing through the point $(S, \lambda) = (0, 0)$:

$$S(\lambda) = N \cdot E[PL] \cdot \lambda. \quad (9)$$

This relation follows from the theoretical throughput noticed in (7) upon approximating the probabilities P_t and P_s in the limit $\lambda \to 0^+$.

Indeed, as $\lambda \to 0^+$, the first relation in (5) yields $q \approx \lambda \cdot E[S_{ts}]$, whereas the probability τ in (3) can be well approximated by $\tau \approx q/(1 - P_{eq})$. Since $P_{col} \to 0$ as $\lambda \to 0^+$ (because $\tau \to 0$), it is $P_{eq} \to P_e$. Furthermore, as $\lambda \to 0^+$, (8) can be approximated by the following relation:

$$P_t \cdot P_s \approx N\tau = N\frac{q}{1 - P_e}. \quad (10)$$

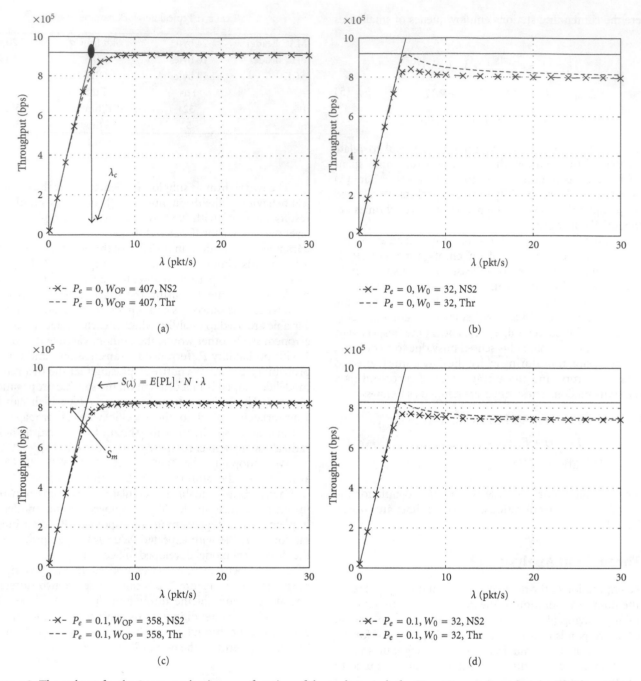

FIGURE 2: Throughput for the 2-way mechanism as a function of the packet rate λ, for $N = 10$, $m = 5$, packet size $E[PL] = 2312$ bytes, and different values of P_e and W_0 as noticed in the respective legends. Continuous straight lines refer to the linear model of the throughput $S(\lambda) = N \cdot E[PL] \cdot \lambda$ derived in (9), while the horizontal line corresponds to S_m noticed in (13). Dashed lines, labeled Thr, refer to the theoretical throughput in (7), while dash-dotted lines labeled NS2 identify the simulation results obtained with ns-2.

Upon substituting (10) in (7), the theoretical throughput can be well approximated as follows:

$$S(\lambda)|_{\lambda \approx 0^+} = \frac{P_t \cdot P_s \cdot (1 - P_e)E[PL]}{E[S_{ts}]}$$

$$\approx NE[PL]\frac{q}{E[S_{ts}]} \approx N \cdot E[PL] \cdot \lambda. \qquad (11)$$

This linear model is depicted in the subplots of Figure 2 overimposed to both theoretical and simulated results. The key observation from this result is that the aggregate throughput produced by N stations approaching unloaded traffic conditions, is only dependent on the number of stations, as well as on the packet size. No other network parameters affect the aggregate throughput in this operating region. Moreover, the results depicted in Figure 2 denote that the derived linear model is valid up to a critical value of

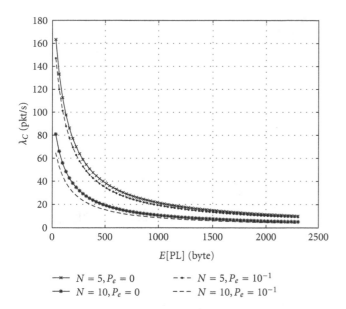

FIGURE 3: Behavior of λ_c in (14) as a function of the packet size $E[PL]$, for two different values of both N and P_e as noticed in the respective legends. Other parameters are as follows: $W_0 = 32$ and $m = 5$.

λ (identified by λ_c throughout the paper), above which the aggregate throughput no longer increases linearly with λ. We

note in passing that, given λ_c, there is no need to simulate the network to obtain the aggregate throughput: it is very well approximated by the theoretical relation derived in (11) for any $\lambda \in [0, \lambda_c]$.

Once again, let us focus on the results shown in the rightmost subplots of Figure 2. The aggregate throughput gets to a maximum at a proper value of λ, above which the effect of the collisions among the stations, as well as the propagation channel, let the throughput reach a horizontal asymptote. The maximum value of $S(\lambda)$ over the whole range of values of λ turns to be quite useful for throughput optimization. Obtained by Bianchi [2] under the hypothesis of saturated network, and considering only collisions among the stations, in our more general model such a maximum can be estimated in two steps. First, rewrite the throughput in (7) as a function of τ by using the relations that define P_t and P_s in terms of the probability τ. Then, equate to zero the derivative of the throughput in (7) with respect to τ, and obtain a solution identified by τ_m. By doing so, the value of τ for which the throughput gets maximized is easily obtained:

$$\tau_m = \frac{\sigma - \sqrt{\sigma[N\sigma - 2(N-1)(\sigma - T_c)]/N}}{(N-1)(\sigma - T_c)}. \tag{12}$$

Finally, evaluate the throughput in (7) on the solution τ_m noticed in (12). Upon following these steps, the maximum throughput takes on the following form

$$S(\tau_m) = S_m$$

$$= \frac{E[PL]}{[T_s - (T_c/(1-P_e)) + (T_e P_e/(1-P_e))] + \left((\sigma - T_c)(1-\tau_m)^N + T_c\right)/N\tau_m(1-\tau_m)^{N-1}(1-P_e)}. \tag{13}$$

The critical value of λ acts as a transition threshold between two operating regions. In the first region, that is, for $\lambda \in [0, \lambda_c]$, the transmissions are affected by relatively small equivalent error probabilities, P_{eq}. In this operating region (In what follows, this operating region will be identified by the acronym BLC, short for Below Link Capacity region.), collisions among stations occur rarely (P_{col} is small) because of the reduced traffic load of the contending stations, and the stations experience good channel quality (P_e is very small). For any $\lambda \leq \lambda_c$, the network is not congested, and the N contending stations are able to transmit data below the link capacity limit denoted by S_m. This is the reason for which the aggregate throughput grows linearly with the traffic load λ.

On the other hand, the aggregate throughput tends to be upperbounded by S_m in (13) for $\lambda \geq \lambda_c$. The reason is simple: the aggregate throughput in this region (In what follows, this operating region will be identified by the acronym LC, short for Link Capacity region.) is affected either by the increasing effect of the collisions among the stations, or by worse channel conditions as exemplified by $P_e \gg 0$. Further insights on this statement can be gained by the

results discussed below in connection with the curves shown in Figure 4.

The critical value of λ can be found as the abscissa where the linear model of the throughput in (9) equates to S_m in (13):

$$\lambda_c = \left[N\left(T_s - \frac{T_c}{1-P_e} + \frac{T_e P_e}{1-P_e} \right) \right.$$
$$\left. + \frac{(\sigma - T_c)(1-\tau_m)^N + T_c}{\tau_m(1-\tau_m)^{N-1}(1-P_e)} \right]^{-1}. \tag{14}$$

The procedure for obtaining λ_c, is clearly highlighted in all the four subplots of Figure 2.

Let us investigate the behavior of the critical value λ_c in (14) against some key network parameters.

Figure 3 shows the behavior of λ_c as a function of the packet size $E[PL]$, for two different values of both N and P_e as noticed in the respective legends. Some observations are in order. λ_c decreases for longer packet sizes $E[PL]$, as well as for increasing number of contending stations, N. The reason relies on the fact that for increasing packet sizes, each

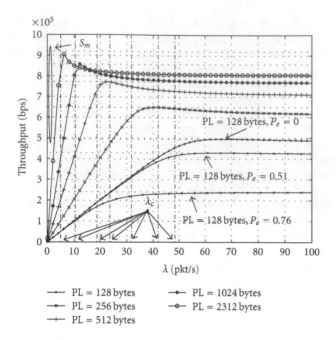

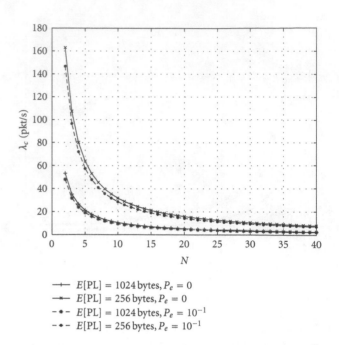

FIGURE 4: Behavior of the aggregate throughput as a function of λ, for five different values of the packet size as noticed in the legend. In each simulated scenario there are $N = 10$ contending stations transmitting at 1 Mbps. Other parameters are as follows: $W_0 = 32$, $P_e = 0$, and $m = 5$. The values of λ_c are noticed on the abscissa, whereas the horizontal lines, labeled by S_m, represent the maximum aggregate throughput (link capacity) evaluated through (13) in each considered scenario. All the thick curves refer to $E[PL] = 128$ bytes, and various packet error probabilities as noticed in the figure.

FIGURE 5: Behavior of λ_c in (14) as a function of the number of contending stations, N, for two different values of both $E[PL]$ and P_e as noticed in the respective legends. Other parameters are as follows: $W_0 = 32$ and $m = 5$.

station occupies the channel longer. Such a behavior is clearly emphasized in Figure 4, where the aggregate throughput for a sample scenario comprising 10 contending stations transmitting with the packet sizes noticed in the legend, is considered. Moreover, given a payload size $E[PL]$, λ_c decreases for increasing packet error probabilities, P_e.

As long as the packet size increases, the aggregate throughput shows an increasing slope in the linear region characterized by traffic loads $\lambda \in [0, \lambda_c]$, as suggested by the theoretical model in (11). Moreover, the value of λ_c tends to decrease because each station tends to occupy the channel longer. The three lower thick curves, labeled by PL $= 128$ bytes, are associated to three different values of packet error probabilities, P_e. Note that the value of λ_c decreases for increasing values of P_e, thus reducing the region characterized by small equivalent error probabilities. As long as $P_e \to 1$, both λ_c and S_m tend to zero, making the aggregate throughput vanishingly small.

Similar considerations may be derived from the behavior of λ_c versus N noticed in Figure 5. Roughly speaking, for fixed values of the packet size, λ_c tends to halve as far as the number of contending stations N doubles. The reason relies on the fact that the probability of collision increases as long as more stations try to contend for the channel.

Figure 6 compares the behaviour of λ_c versus N for the two different data rates 1 and 11 Mbps. From this figure

we can easily note that the values of λ_c corresponding to the high data rate 11 Mbps are roughly three times the ones related to 1 Mbps for each number of contending stations, N, and packet size $E[PL]$ given the increased network capacity available.

4. Throughput Optimization

The considerations deduced in Section 3 are at the very basis of an optimization strategy for maximizing the aggregate throughput of the network depending on the traffic load λ. To this end, we define two optimization strategies: *Contention Window Optimization* and *MAC Payload Size Optimization*. The first strategy is applied when the contending stations operate in the LC region, approaching the link capacity S_m, whereas the second one is used for optimizing the aggregate throughput when the stations operate within the BLC region.

The next two subsections address separately the two optimization strategies, while Section 5 presents the optimization algorithm jointly implementing the two strategies.

4.1. Link Capacity Region: Contention Window Optimization. The first optimization strategy proved to be effective for improving the aggregate throughput in the LC region, that is, for $\lambda > \lambda_c$. The key idea here is to force the contending stations to transmit with a probability τ equal to the one that maximizes the aggregate throughput $S(\lambda)$. In this respect, the probability τ_m in (12) plays a key role.

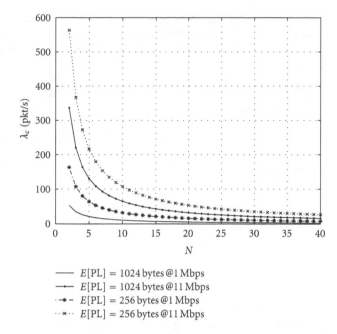

FIGURE 6: Behavior of λ_c in (14) as a function of the packet size $E[PL]$, for two different values of both N and P_e as noticed in the respective legends and for the data rates 1 and 11 Mbps. Other parameters are as follows: $W_0 = 32$ and $m = 5$.

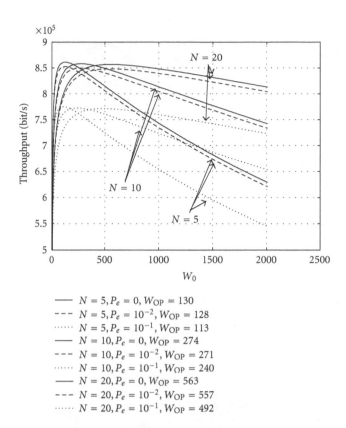

FIGURE 7: Saturation throughput as a function of the minimum contention window size W_0, for three different values of P_e and three values of the number of contending stations N as noticed in the legend. The other parameters are as follows: $m = 5$ and $E[PL] = 1024$ bytes. The optimal contention window size for each set of parameters is shown in the legend. Continuous curves represent the saturation throughput associated to the case $P_e = 0$, the dashed curves refer to the case $P_e = 10^{-2}$, and the dotted curves are related to the case $P_e = 10^{-1}$.

Upon considering saturated conditions, that is, imposing $q \to 1$ in (3), the probability τ can be rewritten as follows:

$$\tau = \frac{2\left(1 - 2P_{eq}\right)}{(W_0 + 1)\left(1 - 2P_{eq}\right) + W_0 P_{eq}\left(1 - \left(2P_{eq}\right)^m\right)} . \quad (15)$$

By substituting $\tau = \tau_m$ in (4), P_{eq} can be rewritten as follows:

$$P_{eq} = 1 - (1 - \tau_m)^{N-1} + P_e - P_e\left[1 - (1 - \tau_m)^{N-1}\right]$$
$$= 1 + (P_e - 1)(1 - \tau_m)^{N-1} = 1 - X(P_e, \tau_m), \quad (16)$$

whereby $X(P_e, \tau_m) = (1 - P_e)(1 - \tau_m)^{N-1}$.

Finally, by equating (15) to τ_m in (12), and solving for W_0, we obtain the optimal minimum contention window size in terms of the key network parameters:

$$W_{OP}$$
$$= \frac{1 - 2\tau_m^{-1} + X(P_e, \tau_m)(4\tau_m^{-1} - 2)}{2X(P_e, \tau_m) - 1 + (1 - X(P_e, \tau_m))\left[1 - 2^m(1 - X(P_e, \tau_m))^m\right]}. \quad (17)$$

This relation yields the value of the minimum contention window W_0 that maximizes the aggregate throughput when the number of contending stations N, the packet error rate over the channel P_e, and the number of backoff stages m, are given. As a note aside, notice that, using W_{OP}, the maximum throughput equates to the link capacity S_m in (13).

Moreover, we notice that for $m = 0$, that is, no exponential backoff is employed, W_{OP} in (17) can be simplified as follows:

$$W_{OP} = \frac{2}{\tau_m} - 1 \quad (18)$$

Considering τ_m as a function of N, and neglecting the multiplicative constant terms, it is simple to notice that τ_m in (12) goes roughly as $1/N$ when $N \gg 1$. Therefore, the optimal contention window W_{OP} grows linearly with the number of contending stations N (when $N \gg 1$) in order to mitigate the effects of the collisions due to an increasing number of contending stations in the network.

In the following, we present simulation results accomplished in NS-2 for validating the theoretical models, as well as the results presented in this section. The adopted MAC layer parameters for IEEE802.11b are summarized in Table 1 [1].

The main simulation results are presented in Figures 2 and 7 in connection to the set of parameters noticed in the respective labels.

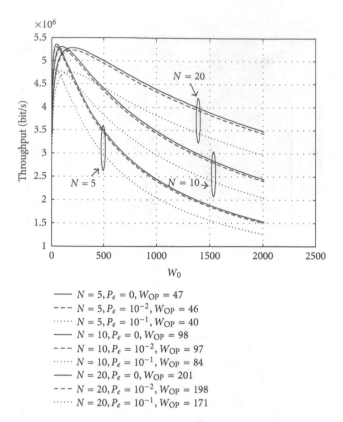

$$N = 5, P_e = 0, W_{\mathrm{OP}} = 47$$
$$N = 5, P_e = 10^{-2}, W_{\mathrm{OP}} = 46$$
$$N = 5, P_e = 10^{-1}, W_{\mathrm{OP}} = 40$$
$$N = 10, P_e = 0, W_{\mathrm{OP}} = 98$$
$$N = 10, P_e = 10^{-2}, W_{\mathrm{OP}} = 97$$
$$N = 10, P_e = 10^{-1}, W_{\mathrm{OP}} = 84$$
$$N = 20, P_e = 0, W_{\mathrm{OP}} = 201$$
$$N = 20, P_e = 10^{-2}, W_{\mathrm{OP}} = 198$$
$$N = 20, P_e = 10^{-1}, W_{\mathrm{OP}} = 171$$

FIGURE 8: Saturation throughput as a function of the minimum contention window size W_0, for data rate 11 Mbps, three different values of P_e and three values of the number of contending stations N as noticed in the legend. The other parameters are as follows: $m = 5$ and $E[\mathrm{PL}] = 1024$ bytes. The optimal contention window size for each set of parameters is shown in the legend. Continuous curves represent the saturation throughput associated to the case $P_e = 0$, the dashed curves refer to the case $P_e = 10^{-2}$, and the dotted curves are related to the case $P_e = 10^{-1}$.

Some observations are in order. Let us focus on the results shown in Figure 2. A quick comparison among the leftmost and the rightmost subplots of Figure 2 reveals that the choice $W_0 = W_{\mathrm{OP}}$ in (17) guarantees improved performance for any $\lambda > \lambda_c$, thus making the aggregate throughput equal S_m. Throughput penalties due to the use of an suboptimal W_0, are in the order of 100 kbps.

Notice also that the value of λ_c is independent from the minimum contention window chosen.

The key observation from the subplots of Figure 2 concerns the fact that the aggregate throughput of the optimized network can be modeled as follows:

$$S(\lambda)|_{W_{\mathrm{OP}}} = \begin{cases} N \cdot E[\mathrm{PL}] \cdot \lambda, & \lambda \le \lambda_c \\ S_m, & \lambda > \lambda_c. \end{cases} \qquad (19)$$

As emphasized by the curves in Figure 2, this model shows a very good agreement with both theoretical and simulation results. Once again, notice that the aggregate throughput may be predicted quite accurately without resorting to simulation.

Let us focus on the results shown in Figure 7, where the saturation throughput is derived as a function of the minimum contention window size W_0. The curves are parameterized with respect to three different values of P_e and N as noticed in the legend. The simulated scenario considers stations transmitting packets of size $E[\mathrm{PL}] = 1024$ bytes. Continuous curves represent the saturation throughput associated to the case $P_e = 0$, the dashed curves refer to the case $P_e = 10^{-2}$, and the dotted curves are related to the case $P_e = 10^{-1}$.

The saturation throughput in each simulated scenario reaches a maximum corresponding to the abscissas $W_0 = W_{\mathrm{OP}}$ predicted by (17) and noticed beside each specific scenario in the legend. Given a predefined number of contending stations, N, we notice that W_{OP} tends to be quite insensitive from the packet error rate P_e, whose main effect corresponds to a reduction of the maximum achievable throughput. This behaviour holds for any given number, N, of contending stations in the network. Moreover, notice that the maximum of the throughput, which settles around the value 8.6×10^5 bps irrespective of N, tends to flatten for an increasing number of contending stations, thus confirming the weak dependence of the maximum of the throughput on the value of the optimal contention window, W_{OP}.

Similar considerations can be drawn from Figure 8 where the higher data rate 11 Mbps has been employed. By contrasting the curves in Figures 7 and 8, it can be easily noted that the optimal minimum contention window sizes W_0 corresponding to 11 Mbps are almost 2.5 times lower than the ones achieved for the lower data rate 1 Mbps.

4.2. Below Link Capacity Region: Payload Size Optimization. The analysis of the aggregate throughput in Section 3 revealed the basic fact that for traffic loads λ less than λ_c, the network is not congested, and each station achieves a throughput roughly equal to $E[\mathrm{PL}] \cdot \lambda$ (the aggregate throughput is thus $S(\lambda) = N \cdot E[\mathrm{PL}] \cdot \lambda$). We note in passing that the throughput does not depend on the minimum contention window W_0 in the LC region. Therefore, given N contending stations, the throughput can only be improved by increasing the payload size $E[\mathrm{PL}]$ when the traffic load satisfies the relation $\lambda \le \lambda_c$.

Before proceeding any further, let us discuss two important issues in connection with the choice of the packet size $E[\mathrm{PL}]$.

As long as the erroneous bits are independently and identically distributed over the received packet (We notice that wireless transceivers make use of interleaving in order to break the correlation due to the frequency selectivity of the transmission channel [24].) the packet error probability P_e can be evaluated as

$$P_e = 1 - [1 - P_e(\mathrm{PLCP})] \cdot [1 - P_e(\mathrm{DATA})], \qquad (20)$$

where,

$$P_e(\mathrm{PLCP}) = 1 - [1 - P_b(\mathrm{BPSK})]^{\mathrm{PHY}h}, \qquad (21)$$

$$P_e(\mathrm{DATA}) = 1 - (1 - P_b)^{\mathrm{MAC}h + E[\mathrm{PL}]}. \qquad (22)$$

```
(1)   do
(2)         Estimation of PER and N
(3)         Evaluate λ_c from (14)
(4)   while (IDLE)
(5)   // Request to Send from Upper Layers:
(6)   if (λ > λ_c)
(7)         // Link Capacity Operating Region:
(8)         The station evaluates W_opt from (17)
(9)   else
(10)        // Below Link Capacity Operating Region:
(11)        compute E[PL]*_1 given λ_c
(12)        compute E[PL]*_2 given P_e
(13)        select E[PL]_opt = min(E[PL]*_1, E[PL]*_2, PL_max)
(14)  end
(15)  send packet
```

ALGORITHM 1: Optimization algorithm accomplished by every contending station.

In the previous relations, MACh and PHYh are, respectively, the sizes (in bits) of the MAC and PLCP (PLCP is short for Physical Layer Convergence Protocol.) headers, and $E[PL]$ is the size of the data payload in bits. Equation (22) accounts for the fact that a packet containing the useful data, is considered erroneous when at least one bit is erroneously received. Relation (20) is obtained by noting that a packet is received erroneously when the errors occur either in the PLCP part of the packet, or in the information data.

We notice that the relations (20) through (22) are valid either with the use of convolutional coding, whereby the bit error rate performance does not depend on the code block size [24], or for protocols that do not employ channel encoding at the physical layer.

From (22) it is quite evident that the higher the payload size, the higher the packet error rate; and viceversa. As a note aside, we notice that this behavior does not hold when concatenated convolutional channel codes [25–27], as well as low-density parity-check codes, are employed as channel codes. Indeed, for these codes the packet error rate depends on the size of the encoded block of data, with longer packets having smaller probability of error compared to shorter packets.

The second issue to be considered during the choice of $E[PL]$ is related to the critical value λ_c, which depends on the packet error probability (P_e defined in (20)), and consequently on the payload size. Given a traffic load λ, any change in $E[PL]$ could affect the network operating region, which might move from the BLC region to the LC region.

Let us discuss a simple scenario in order to reveal this issue. (Where not otherwise specified, we employ the network parameters summarized in Table 1.) Consider a network (identified in the following as scenario A) where $N = 10$ contending stations with traffic load $\lambda = 8$ pkt/s transmit packets of size $E[PL] = 1024$ bytes. Assume that the bit error probability due to the channel conditions is $P_b = 10^{-5}$, which corresponds to a packet error rate $P_e = 8.248 \cdot 10^{-2}$ (from (20)). Upon using the network parameters

summarized in Table 1, the critical load in (14) corresponds to $\lambda_c = 9.61$ pkt/s. Since $\lambda < \lambda_c$, the network is in the BLC operating region. If the stations increase the payload size up to $E[PL] = 2048$ bytes, the packet error rate increases to the value $P_e = 1.546 \cdot 10^{-1}$, with the side effect of decreasing λ_c to 4.71 pkt/s. Therefore, for the given traffic load $\lambda = 8$ pkt/s, the network starts operating into the LC region.

Based on the considerations deduced in the scenario A, the proposed optimization technique aims to optimize the payload size in two consecutive steps. In the first step, we find the size of the payload in such a way that the critical threshold λ_c equals the actual traffic load λ, in order for the network not to operate beyond the BLC region.

The second step verifies whether the packet error rate associated to this payload size, is below a predefined PER-target (identified by PER$_t$), which defines the maximum error level imposed by the application layer. First of all, given an estimated bit error probability at the physical layer, solve (22) for $E[PL]$. Then, solve (20) for $1 - P_e(\text{DATA})$, and substitute the relation in place of $1 - P_e(\text{DATA})$. Considering $P_e = \text{PER}_t$, the following maximum payload size follows:

$$E[PL]^{\max}\big|_{\text{PER}_t} = \left\lceil \frac{\ln(1 - \text{PER}_t/1 - P_e(\text{PLCP}))}{\ln(1 - P_b)} - \text{MAC}h \right\rceil, \tag{23}$$

whereby $\lceil \cdot \rceil$ is the ceil of the enclosed number.

Let us consider again the scenario A discussed previously with the application of this algorithm. Consider 10 stations transmitting packets of size $E[PL] = 1024$ bytes at the traffic load $\lambda = 5$ pkt/s. Assume that the bit error rate imposed by the specific channel conditions is $P_b = 10^{-5}$, yielding $P_e = 8.248 \cdot 10^{-2}$ and $\lambda_c = 9.6$ pkt/s. Moreover, assume a target PER equal to (This is the maximum PER specified in the IEEE 802.11b standard [1], guaranteed at the receiver when the received power reaches the receiver sensitivity.) $\text{PER}_t = 8 \cdot 10^{-2}$.

Since $\lambda < \lambda_c$, after the first step, the algorithm selects the optimal size $E[PL]^*_1 = 1938$ bytes, which moves the working point near the link capacity and leads to the actual packet error rate $P_e = 1.47 \cdot 10^{-1}$. Since the constraint $P_e \leq \text{PER}_t$ is not satisfied, the proposed method estimates the size $E[PL]$ in order to attain the PER$_t$ constraint. The packet size becomes eventually $E[PL]^*_2 = 991$ bytes (from (23)), yielding a packet error rate $P_e \simeq 8 \cdot 10^{-2}$ and a $\lambda^*_c = 9.92$ pkt/s, thus leaving the working point in the BLC region.

Finally, the optimal payload size is

$$E[PL] = \min\left\{E[PL]^*_1, E[PL]^*_2, \text{PL}_{\max}\right\} = E[PL]^*_2, \tag{24}$$

where $\text{PL}_{\max} = 2312$ bytes is the maximum packet size imposed by the standard [1].

Simulation results of a sample network employing the algorithm described above, are presented in the next section, along with a sample code fragment summarizing the key steps of the optimization technique.

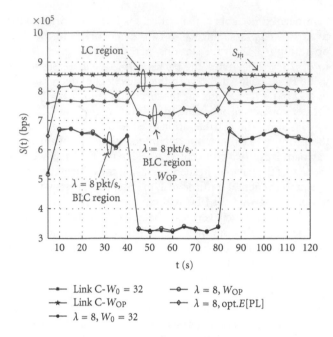

FIGURE 9: Aggregate throughput of a network with a maximum number of stations equal to 10, transmitting at the fixed bit rate 1 Mbps. Curve S_m represents the maximum link capacity evaluated through (13). The other network parameters are described in the paper. Curves labeled *LC region* refer to a scenario whereby the contending stations transmit with packet rate $\lambda = 10^3$ pkt/s. In all the scenarios investigated in the figure, during the time intervals $[0,40]$ s and $[80,120]$ s ten stations contend for the channel, while in the time interval $[40,80]$ s only 5 stations are active. Curves labeled ($\lambda = 8$ pkt/s, BLC region) refer to a scenario whereby the contending stations operate in the BLC region. In this situation, the optimization of the contention window does not improve the aggregate throughput and the two curves are superimposed. In the BLC region, the aggregate throughput can be improved by varying the transmission packet size as emphasized by the curve labeled ($\lambda = 8$ pkt/s, BLC region, W_{OP}).

5. Simulation Results

In this section, we present simulation results for a network of $N = 10$ contending stations, employing the optimization strategies described in Section 4.

The basic steps of the proposed optimization algorithm are summarized in Algorithm 1. Let us spend a few words about the implementation of the proposed algorithm in a WLAN setting employing the infrastructure mode, where an Access Point (AP) monitors the transmissions of N contending stations.

The evaluation of the critical value λ_c in (14) requires the estimation of three key parameters of the network: the number of contending stations N, the packet error rate P_e, and the value of the optimal τ_m, which depends on N. Each station can estimate the number of contending stations by resorting to one of the algorithms proposed in [28–30]. On the other hand, the packet error probability P_e, may be evaluated through (20), once the bit error probability P_b at the physical layer is estimated. We recall that P_b can

be estimated by employing proper training sequences at the physical layer of the wireless receiver [24].

Finally, the value of the optimal W_{OP} can be evaluated by each station with the parameters N and P_e. A similar reasoning applies for the estimation of the optimal packet size.

We have realized a C++ simulator implementing all the basic directives of the IEEE 802.11b protocol with the 2-way handshaking mechanism, namely exponential backoff, waiting times, post-backoff, and so on. In our simulator, the optimization algorithm is dynamically executed for any specified scenario. For the sake of analyzing the effects of the optimization, the instantaneous network throughput is evaluated over the whole simulation. The aggregate throughputs obtained in the investigated scenarios are shown in Figure 9.

In the first scenario, we considered a congested network in which 10 stations transmit packet of fixed size 1028 bytes at the packet load $\lambda = 1000$ pkt/s and bit rate 1 Mbps. Other parameters are $W_0 = 32$, and $m = 5$, whereas the channel conditions are assumed to be ideal. As shown in Figure 9 (curve labeled LC region with asterisk-marked points), the aggregate throughput is about 7.6×10^5 bps. After 40 s, 5 out of the 10 stations turn their traffic off. Between 40 s and 80 s, the aggregate throughput increases to about 8.2×10^5 bps because of the reduced effect of the collisions among the contending stations. After 80 s, the 5 stations turn on again and the aggregate throughput decreases to 7.6×10^5 bps.

Consider again the same scenario over a time interval of 120s, whereby the contending stations adopt the optimal contention window. Upon using (17), the optimal contention window is $W_{OP}^{0-40} = 275$ when 10 stations transmit over the network, and $W_{OP}^{40-80} = 130$ during the interval in which only 5 stations contend for the channel.

The aggregate throughput in the optimized scenario is about 8.6×10^5 bps, as noticed by the star-marked curve in the same figure. We notice that the optimized throughput is quite constant over the whole simulation independently on the number of contending stations in the network, approaching the theoretical maximum throughput $S_m = 8.6 \times 10^5$ bps obtained from (13). Moreover, notice that the two curves S_m related to both $N = 5$ and 10 are almost superimposed.

Consider another scenario differing from the previous one in that the contending stations operate in the BLC region. As above, 10 stations contend for the channel in the time intervals $[0,40]$ s and $[80,120]$ s, while during the time interval $[40,80]$ s 5 out of the 10 stations turn off. The traffic load is $\lambda = 8$ pkt/s, and the packet interarrival times are exponentially distributed.

Let us focus on the aggregate throughput depicted in Figure 9. The curves related to the scenario at hand are identified by the labels $\lambda = 8$ pkt/s. As a result of the application of the proposed algorithm to the choice of the packet size, we obtain $E[PL]_{opt}^{0-40} = 1383$ bytes for the case when 10 stations are transmitting, and $E[PL]_{opt}^{40-80} = 2312$ bytes in the other scenario with 5 active stations.

Simulation results show that the proposed algorithm guarantees improved throughput performance on the order of 160 kbps when 10 stations are active, and about 400 kbps when only 5 stations contend for the channel. We notice in passing that, despite the optimization, the aggregate throughput could not reach the maximum S_m because of the low traffic load. Indeed, the capacity link S_m could be achieved by using a packet size longer than either the one imposed by the standard [1], and the value obtained from (23).

For the sake to verify that the optimization of the minimum contention window does not affect the aggregate throughput in the BLC region, Figure 9 also shows the aggregate throughput obtained by simulation using a minimum contention window equal to W_{OP}. Notice that the related curve is superimposed to the one related to the scenario in which the contending stations employ the minimum contention window $W_0 = 32$ suggested by the standard [1].

6. Conclusions

This paper proposed an optimization framework for maximizing the throughput of the distributed coordination function (DCF) basic access mechanism at the data link layer of IEEE 802.11 protocols. Based on the theoretical derivations, as well as on simulation results, a simple model of the optimized DCF throughput has been derived. Such a model turns to be quite useful for predicting the aggregate throughput of the DCF in a variety of network conditions.

For throughput modeling, we considered general operating conditions accounting for both nonsaturated and saturated traffic in the presence of transmission channel errors identified by the packet error rate P_e. Simulation results closely matched the theoretical derivations, confirming the effectiveness of both the proposed DCF model and the cross-layer optimization algorithm.

References

[1] P802.11, "IEEE Standard for Wireless LAN Medium Access Control (MAC) and Physical Layer (PHY) Specifications," November 1997.

[2] G. Bianchi, "Performance analysis of the IEEE 802.11 distributed coordination function," *IEEE Journal on Selected Areas in Communications*, vol. 18, no. 3, pp. 535–547, 2000.

[3] F. Daneshgaran, M. Laddomada, F. Mesiti, M. Mondin, and M. Zanolo, "Saturation throughput analysis of IEEE 802.11 in the presence of non ideal transmission channel and capture effects," *IEEE Transactions on Communications*, vol. 56, no. 7, pp. 1178–1188, 2008.

[4] Q. Ni, T. Li, T. Turletti, and Y. Xiao, "Saturation throughput analysis of error-prone 802.11 wireless networks," *Wireless Communications and Mobile Computing*, vol. 5, no. 8, pp. 945–956, 2005.

[5] P. Chatzimisios, A. C. Boucouvalas, and V. Vitsas, "Influence of channel BER on IEEE 802.11 DCF," *Electronics Letters*, vol. 39, no. 23, pp. 1687–1689, 2003.

[6] Y. Zheng, K. Lu, D. Wu, and Y. Fang, "Performance analysis of IEEE 802.11 DCF in imperfect channels," *IEEE Transactions on Vehicular Technology*, vol. 55, no. 5, pp. 1648–1656, 2006.

[7] H. C. Lee, "Impact of bit errors on the DCF throughput in wireless LAN over ricean fading channels," in *Proceedings of the International Conference on Digital Telecommunications (ICDT '06)*, p. 37, August 2006.

[8] Y. S. Liaw, A. Dadej, and A. Jayasuriya, "Performance analysis of IEEE 802.11 DCF under limited load," in *Proceedings of the Asia-Pacific Conference on Communications*, vol. 1, pp. 759–763, October 2005.

[9] D. Malone, K. Duffy, and D. Leith, "Modeling the 802.11 distributed coordination function in nonsaturated heterogeneous conditions," *IEEE/ACM Transactions on Networking*, vol. 15, no. 1, pp. 159–172, 2007.

[10] F. Daneshgaran, M. Laddomada, F. Mesiti, and M. Mondin, "On the linear behaviour of the throughput of IEEE 802.11 DCF in non-saturated conditions," *IEEE Communications Letters*, vol. 11, no. 11, pp. 856–858, 2007.

[11] G. R. Cantieni, Q. Ni, C. Barakat, and T. Turletti, "Performance analysis under finite load and improvements for multirate 802.11," *Computer Communications*, vol. 28, no. 10, pp. 1095–1109, 2005.

[12] F. Daneshgaran, M. Laddomada, F. Mesiti, and M. Mondin, "Unsaturated throughput analysis of IEEE 802.11 in presence of non ideal transmission channel and capture effects," *IEEE Transactions on Wireless Communications*, vol. 7, no. 4, pp. 1276–1286, 2008.

[13] F. Daneshgaran, M. Laddomada, F. Mesiti, and M. Mondin, "A model of the IEEE 802.11 DCF in presence of non ideal transmission channel and capture effects," in *Proceedings of the 50th Annual IEEE Global Telecommunications Conference (GLOBECOM '07)*, pp. 5112–5116, Washington, DC, USA, November 2007.

[14] D. Qiao, S. Choi, and K. G. Shin, "Goodput analysis and link adaptation for IEEE 802.11 a wireless LANs," *IEEE Transactions on Mobile Computing*, vol. 1, no. 4, pp. 278–292, 2002.

[15] F. Calì, M. Conti, and E. Gregori, "Dynamic tuning of the IEEE 802.11 protocol to achieve a theoretical throughput limit," *IEEE/ACM Transactions on Networking*, vol. 8, no. 6, pp. 785–799, 2000.

[16] A. Khalaj, N. Yazdani, and M. Rahgozar, "The effect of decreasing CW size on performance in IEEE 802.11 DCF," in *Proceedings of the 13th IEEE International Conference on Networks Jointly Held with the 7th IEEE Malaysia International Conference on Communications (ICCN '05)*, pp. 521–525, November 2005.

[17] A. Khalaj, N. Yazdani, and M. Rahgozar, "Effect of the contention window size on performance and fairness of the IEEE 802.11 standard," *Wireless Personal Communications*, vol. 43, no. 4, pp. 1267–1278, 2007.

[18] S. Choudhury and J. D. Gibson, "Payload length and rate adaptation for multimedia communications in wireless LANs," *IEEE Journal on Selected Areas in Communications*, vol. 25, no. 4, pp. 796–807, 2007.

[19] S. Choudhury and J. D. Gibson, "Throughput optimization for wireless LANs in the presence of packet error rate constraints," *IEEE Communications Letters*, vol. 12, no. 1, pp. 11–13, 2008.

[20] H. Anouar and C. Bonnet, "Optimal constant-window backoff scheme for IEEE 802.11 DCF in single-hop wireless networks under finite load conditions," *Wireless Personal Communications*, vol. 43, no. 4, pp. 1583–1602, 2007.

[21] C. Verikoukis, L. Alonso, and T. Giamalis, "Cross-layer optimization for wireless systems: a european research key

challenge," *IEEE Communications Magazine*, vol. 43, no. 7, pp. 1–3, 2005.

[22] Q. Xia and M. Hamdi, "Contention window adjustment for IEEE 802.11 WLANs: a control-theoretic approach," in *Proceedings of the IEEE International Conference on Communications (ICC '06)*, pp. 3923–3928, June 2006.

[23] X. Wu, "Simulate 802.11b channel within NS-2," April 2004, http://www.comp.nus.edu.sg/~wuxiucha/research/reactive/publication/Simulate80211ChannelWithNS2.pdf.

[24] J. G. Proakis, *Digital Communications*, McGraw Hill, New York, NY, USA, 4th edition, 2001.

[25] F. Daneshgaran and M. Laddomada, "Optimized prunable single-cycle interleavers for turbo codes," *IEEE Transactions on Communications*, vol. 52, no. 6, pp. 899–909, 2004.

[26] F. Daneshgaran and M. Laddomada, "Reduced complexity interleaver growth algorithm for turbo codes," *IEEE Transactions on Wireless Communications*, vol. 4, no. 3, pp. 954–964, 2005.

[27] F. Daneshgaran, M. Laddomada, and M. Mondin, "Interleaver design for serially concatenated convolutional codes: theory and application," *IEEE Transactions on Information Theory*, vol. 50, no. 6, pp. 1177–1188, 2004.

[28] A. L. Toledo, T. Vercauteren, and X. Wang, "Adaptive optimization of IEEE 802.11 DCF based on Bayesian estimation of the number of competing terminals," *IEEE Transactions on Mobile Computing*, vol. 5, no. 9, pp. 1283–1296, 2006.

[29] G. Bianchi and I. Tinnirello, "Kalman filter estimation of the number of competing terminals in an IEEE 802.11 network," in *Proceedings of the 22nd Annual Joint Conference on the IEEE Computer and Communications Societies (INFOCOM '03)*, pp. 844–852, March-April 2003.

[30] J.-S. Kim, E. Serpedin, and D.-R. Shin, "Improved particle filtering-based estimation of the number of competing stations in IEEE 802.11 networks," *IEEE Signal Processing Letters*, vol. 15, pp. 87–90, 2008.

9

Collaborative Spectrum Sensing Optimisation Algorithms for Cognitive Radio Networks

Kamran Arshad, Muhammad Ali Imran, and Klaus Moessner

Centre for Communication Systems Research, University of Surrey, Guildford GU2 7XH, UK

Correspondence should be addressed to Kamran Arshad, k.arshad@surrey.ac.uk

Academic Editor: Massimiliano Laddomada

The main challenge for a cognitive radio is to detect the existence of primary users reliably in order to minimise the interference to licensed communications. Hence, spectrum sensing is a most important requirement of a cognitive radio. However, due to the channel uncertainties, local observations are not reliable and collaboration among users is required. Selection of fusion rule at a common receiver has a direct impact on the overall spectrum sensing performance. In this paper, optimisation of collaborative spectrum sensing in terms of optimum decision fusion is studied for hard and soft decision combining. It is concluded that for optimum fusion, the fusion centre must incorporate signal-to-noise ratio values of cognitive users and the channel conditions. A genetic algorithm-based weighted optimisation strategy is presented for the case of soft decision combining. Numerical results show that the proposed optimised collaborative spectrum sensing schemes give better spectrum sensing performance.

1. Introduction

As numbers of wireless devices, innovative services, and number of mobile users continue to grow, more and more spectrum resources will be needed to guarantee desired Quality of Service. Mobile users want high-quality calls, streaming videos, and high-speed downloads, placing more and more stress on the limited radio spectrum available to the network operators. The radio spectrum spans around 300 billion frequencies; however, only a tiny fraction of frequencies can be used for commercial or personal radio communications; fundamental physical limits apply [1]. In the current spectrum regulatory framework, most frequency bands are exclusively allocated to the privileged users, often called Primary User (PU), which have all the rights to use the allocated bands. This approach protects PU's from any intersystem interference, but on the other hand, it yields highly inefficient use of the spectrum.

Measurements conducted by the Office of Communications (Ofcom) in UK and the Spectrum Policy Task Force (SPTF) in USA indicate that many chunks of the licensed spectrum are not used or only partially used, for significant periods of time [2, 3]. Spectrum occupancy measurements undertaken by Ofcom in Central London, at Heathrow airport and in some rural areas of the country, clearly show that there are significant portions of the radio spectrum which are not fully utilised in various geographical areas of the United Kingdom [4]. Similarly, in New York city maximum spectrum occupancy is reported as only 13.1% and downtown of Washington D.C. indicated spectrum occupancy of less than 35% of the radio spectrum below 3 GHz [5]. These studies clearly suggest that currently spectrum scarcity is mainly due to the inefficient use of spectrum rather than the physical shortage of spectrum. Particularly in UK, Olympic Games 2012 put extra pressure on Ofcom to plan the efficient use of radio spectrum to satisfy over 10 million spectators, around 15,000 participants and about 20,000 media personnel in the UK who will beam live pictures and commentary all around the world. Moreover, emerging as well as some existing operators are faced with the difficult task to gain access to the radio spectrum to operate their services [6]. In addition, access to a block of spectrum is very expensive as seen when the five operators were licensed for the 3rd generation mobile systems in the UK at a cost of around £22.5 billion [7]. More recently (early 2009), the FCC spectrum auction in USA raised a record $19.9 billion dollars [8].

Cognitive Radio (CR) is widely regarded as the technology which will increase spectrum utilisation significantly in the next generation wireless communication systems by implementing opportunistic spectrum sharing. Spectrum sensing is one of the most critical functionalities in a cognitive radio network; it allows the unauthorised users, called Secondary Users (SUs), to detect unused portions of the spectrum called "spectrum holes" and opportunistically utilise these spectrum holes without causing harmful interference to the PU. The main goal of spectrum sensing is to obtain awareness about the spectrum usage and the existence of the PU in a certain geographical area at a particular period of time. In order to evaluate the performance of spectrum sensing, two metrics are of great interest: probability of detection and the probability of false alarm. Probability of detection, P_d, determines the level of interference-protection provided to the PU while probability of false alarm, P_f, indicates percentage of spectrum holes falsely declared as occupied [9]. In the context of opportunistic spectrum access, P_d must be higher than some predefined threshold while P_f should be lower than some desired criteria or as minimum as possible.

To enhance the performance of spectrum sensing, many techniques are available in the literature, and a brief survey has been recently published in [10]. In practice, CRs usually have no or limited knowledge about the primary signals; hence the optimal spectrum sensing technique is energy detection [11]. An energy detection approach for spectrum sensing at an individual CR has been assumed in this paper because of its simplicity, ease of implementation, and low computational complexity [9]. Moreover, the aim of this paper is to characterise gains achieved by collaboration of users without going into the details of complex local spectrum sensing schemes. The more sophisticated techniques like match filter detection or cyclostationary feature detection can be used for signal classification if more a priori knowledge about the structure of the primary signal is available [10]. However, performance of the energy detector is susceptible to noise power uncertainty [12]. Nevertheless, it has been shown that Collaborative Spectrum Sensing (CSS) is capable of delivering the desired detection performance under noise uncertainty for a large number of users [9]. However, energy detectors do not work efficiently for detecting spread spectrum signals [10]; spread spectrum signals are out of the scope of this paper.

1.1. Prior Work. The spectrum scarcity and spectrum under-utilisation problem has stimulated a number of exciting activities in the technical, economic, and regulatory domains in searching for better spectrum management policies and techniques, for example, FCC opened up some analogue TV bands for unlicensed access [13]. However, spectrum sharing with PU must be done in a controlled way so that the PU operation in the particular frequency band is not disturbed. Furthermore, the IEEE standard 802.22 for unlicensed access to the TV bands is in its final stages of development

[14]. Recently, Ofcom released Digital Dividend Review Statement (DDRS) which shows a radical shift in spectrum sharing policy in the UK and Ofcom is proposing to "allow license exempt use of interleaved spectrum for cognitive devices" [15]. Also, the European Commission (EU) paid much attention on dynamic spectrum management and the CR theme, and sponsored many FP5, FP6, and FP7 projects such as DRIVE [16], OverDRIVE [17], WINNER [18], E2R I/II [19], ORACLE [20], E3 [21], and "Radio Access and Spectrum" (RAS) cluster [22] tackling this issue. Similarly, several other projects outside Europe including the Defense Advanced Research Project Agency (DARPA)'s Next Generation program [23] and National Science Foundation program "NeTS-ProWiN" [24] show a significant momentum to shift spectrum access policy.

The cognition capability of a CR can make opportunistic spectrum access possible which can be implemented either by knowledge management mechanisms or by spectrum sensing functionality. A mobile network operator, for example, can equip the terminals with management mechanisms to select the most appropriate radio access technology of its heterogenous infrastructure [25, 26]. Concentrating on spectrum sensing, observations of a single CR are not always trustworthy because a CR may have good line of sight with the primary receiver but may not be able to see the primary transmitter due to shadowing or fading, known as "hidden node" problem. Collaboration has been proposed as a solution to the problems that arise due to such uncertainties in the channel. It has been shown many times in the literature that spectrum sensing performance can be greatly improved by CSS when a number of SUs share their sensing information; fusion of this information leads to a final decision about the existence of the PU. For an overview of recent advances in CSS, the reader can refer to [9, 27–32]. Existence of a large number of cognitive users creating multiple CRN's is highly probable in the future communication systems. However, the CSS mechanisms generate a large amount of traffic overhead since each SU needs to transmit its own decision; therefore collaboration of users needs to be refined and optimised [9].

Various techniques for the optimisation of CSS in terms of fusion rule [29], number of users [33], and thresholds [34] have been proposed. It has been argued in the literature that fusion schemes strongly impact on the spectrum sensing performance including probabilities of detection and false alarm [29]. In CSS, a CR can transmit either its local observations (soft decision) or a 1-bit decision (hard decision) to a common receiver, often called fusion centre. When hard decisions are combined at the fusion centre, the K-out-of-N fusion rule is normally used [33]. In the literature, there are some studies on the optimisation of the K-out-of-N rule to minimise total decision error probability [29] and to maximise the SUs throughput [35]; however, those algorithms were designed for a specific scenario of TV bands sharing in an AWGN channel. A fusion rule based on selected information for spectrum sensing is considered in [36], in which only users that have sufficient information send their 1-bit decision to the fusion centre and the fusion centre employs best fusion rule based on the received information.

A new fusion rule including "No decision" information from the cooperative nodes was proposed in [28].

The optimum fusion rule for combining soft decisions is Chair-Varshney rule which is based on log-likelihood ratio test [37]. Various other techniques for combining soft decisions are presented in [38]. However, most of the prior research work focuses on the case when SUs are far away from the primary transmitter and hence the same path loss or Signal-to-Noise Ratio (SNR) was assumed for all collaborating SUs [9, 29, 33]. The effects of different SNRs on detection performance are studied under AWGN channel conditions in [39]. Moreover, previous research highlighted CSS techniques which combine data from the CR nodes with equal weights and with perfect reporting channels [9, 40, 41], which is clearly not the case in realistic scenarios and might lead to misleading interpretation of results. The reporting channel for an ith user is defined as the channel between ith user and the fusion centre. Performance of CSS with noisy reporting channels was considered for the case of hard decision fusion in [31].

Collaborative spectrum sensing schemes with weighted user contributions have been recently proposed in [42, 43]. In [42] average signal power at an SU was exploited to assign weights to different collaborating cognitive nodes. In [43] a linear optimal strategy for CSS was presented and optimal weights for each SU in an AWGN channel were derived analytically. However, the shortcomings of existing literature in weighted CSS are in the fact that perfect reporting channels have been assumed instead of more realistic fading channels.

1.2. Major Contributions. In this paper, the optimisation of CSS is documented and optimum decision fusion is evaluated for hard and soft decision fusion at the fusion centre. Main contributions of this paper are summarised as follows.

(i) Hard decision fusion is attractive because of lower communication overhead over the reporting channels. In this paper, the problem of hard decision fusion at the fusion centre is addressed and answers this simple question: for optimal fusion does the fusion centre only need 1-bit decision? Different scenarios are considered with users close to the primary transmitter have the different SNR values. It is concluded that in order to achieve optimum spectrum sensing performance, the fusion centre must have SNR information for each CR and channel conditions along with their 1-bit decisions.

(ii) Maximum diversity in CSS is achieved when all collaborating users experience identical and independent fading or shadowing effects, which is not possible in reality if users are too close to each other. Multipath fading can be assumed to be independent from one user to another but shadowing is normally correlated over large distances. Thus, secondary users in close vicinity of each other make similar measurements and this limits the collaboration gains.

In this paper, correlated log-normal shadowing is considered among collaborative users and it is shown that correlated shadowing has direct impact on the optimal fusion rule at the fusion centre.

(iii) Genetic Algorithm- (GA-) based weighted collaborative spectrum sensing strategy is proposed in this paper to combat the effects of channel and enhance spectrum sensing performance. The proposed optimum spectrum sensing framework is based on a model that is realistic and also takes into account both channels, that is, channel between PU and SUs as well as the reporting channels. It is shown in this paper that imperfect reporting channel and different SU SNR values have direct impact on the performance of CSS. Secondary users transmit their soft decisions to the fusion centre and a global decision is made at the fusion centre which is based on a weighted combination of the local test statistics from individual SUs. The weight of each SU is indicative of its contribution to the final decision making. For example, if an SU has a high SNR signal and also has a good reporting channel (higher reporting channel gain), then it is assigned a larger contributing weight. The optimum CSS problem is formulated as a nonlinear optimisation problem in this paper. For a given probability of false alarm and channel conditions, optimal weights are chosen in such a way that it maximises global probability of detection at the fusion centre. With a realistic fading channel it is hard to derive an analytical expression for the optimum weights and hence a GA-based solution is proposed.

1.3. Organisation of the Paper. The remainder of this paper is organised as follows. In Section 2 the system model is briefly introduced and the use cases are defined. Section 3 discusses local spectrum sensing under channel fading conditions and its limitations. Section 4 briefly explains CSS and decision fusion techniques for both HDC and SDC, considered in this paper. Section 5 proposes a framework for optimisation of fusion rules for HDC. In order to achieve optimum spectrum sensing performance, GA is used to calculate the weights for each collaborative user in Section 6. Finally Section 7 concludes the paper.

2. System Model for Cognitive Radio Network

Consider a cognitive radio network, with M cognitive users (indexed by $i \in \{1, 2, \ldots, M\}$), and a fusion centre to sense a portion of the spectrum of bandwidth "W" in order to detect the existence of the PU, as shown in Figure 1. Assume that each CR is equipped with an energy detector and is able to perform local spectrum sensing independently. Each CR makes its own observation based on the received signal, that is, noise only or signal plus noise. Hence, the spectrum sensing problem can be considered as a binary hypothesis testing problem with two possible hypothesis $\mathcal{H}_0$ and $\mathcal{H}_1$ defined as [38]

$$x_i(t) = \begin{cases} n_i(t), & \mathcal{H}_0, \\ h_i s(t) + n_i(t), & \mathcal{H}_1, \end{cases} \quad (1)$$

where $s(t)$ is the PU signal and is assumed to be an identical and independent random process (i.i.d.) with zero mean and variance σ_s^2. For the ith SU, the receiver noise is modelled as $n_i(t)$ which is also assumed to be an i.i.d. random process with zero mean and variance σ_n^2 and h_i is the complex gain of the channel between the PU and the ith SU. Further, it is assumed that $s(t)$ and $n_i(t)$ are independent of each other. The power transmitted by the PU is received at the SU and the ratio of received power to the power of noise at the SU is defined as the SNR at the SU energy detector. The received SNR at the ith SU can be more precisely defined as

$$\gamma_i \triangleq \frac{\mathrm{E}\left[|h_i|^2\right]\sigma_s^2}{\sigma_n^2}. \quad (2)$$

System model and use cases for considered scenarios are shown in Figure 1. Two use cases are assumed in this paper. Use Case 1 refers to the case when PU transmitter is far away from the CRN and hence same SNR can be assumed for all SUs. In use Case 2, the PU is not far away from the M SUs and each user has a different value of SNR depending on its distance from the PU and its channel conditions.

3. Local Spectrum Sensing

The performance of a given spectrum sensing scheme is fundamentally limited by the radio propagation channel. Typically, the effects of a radio channel can be divided into three main parts: path loss, small-scale fading, and large-scale fading (shadowing) [44]. Path loss effects are incorporated in the received SNR at a cognitive radio terminal. Small-scale fading causes rapid, random variations in the signal strength at the CR receiver and is modelled by Rayleigh fading in this paper. Shadowing is the slow variation of received signal power as the cognitive radio moves in and out of the shadow of large structures like mountains, buildings, and so forth. Shadowing is often modelled as a log-normal distributed random process that varies around a local mean given by the path loss and with the standard deviation σ_{dB} which depends on the environment [45].

3.1. AWGN Channel. In energy detection-based spectrum sensing, the received radio frequency energy in the considered channel or frequency band W is measured over a time interval T to determine whether the PU signal $s(t)$ is present. Assume that the time bandwidth product is always an integer and is denoted by $N = TW$. Test statistic u_i calculated by an ith user is given as

$$u_i = \sum_{k=1}^{N} \left| x_i\left(\frac{k}{W}\right) \right|^2. \quad (3)$$

u_i is compared with a predefined threshold λ_i to get the local decision:

$$u_i \underset{\mathcal{H}_0}{\overset{\mathcal{H}_1}{\gtrless}} \lambda_i. \quad (4)$$

The binary decision is given by D_i; $D_i = 1$ when $u_i > \lambda_i$ and 0 otherwise. u_i is the sum of squares of N Gaussian random variables and it is well known that the sum of squares of Gaussian variables follows a chi-square distribution [46]. Thus u_i follows a central chi-square distribution with $2N$ degrees of freedom under hypothesis $\mathcal{H}_0$ and a noncentral chi-square distribution with $2N$ degrees of freedom and non-centrality parameter of $2N\gamma_i$ under hypothesis $\mathcal{H}_1$. Therefore, the probability density function (pdf) of random variable U_i under the two hypotheses can be written as

$$f_{U_i}(u) = \begin{cases} \dfrac{u^{N-1} e^{-u/2}}{2^N \Gamma(N)}, & \mathcal{H}_0, \\ \dfrac{1}{2}\left(\dfrac{u}{2N\gamma_i}\right)^{(N-1)/2} e^{-(u+2N\gamma_i)/2} I_{N-1}\left(\sqrt{2Nu\gamma_i}\right), & \mathcal{H}_1, \end{cases} \quad (5)$$

where $\Gamma(\cdot)$ is the gamma function and $I_{N-1}(\cdot)$ is the modified Bessel function of the first kind. For an ith user probability of false alarm, $\mathrm{Pr}(\mathcal{H}_1 \mid \mathcal{H}_0)$, and detection, $\mathrm{Pr}(\mathcal{H}_1 \mid \mathcal{H}_1)$ can be derived from (5) and is given as

$$P_f^i = \mathrm{Pr}\{U_i > \lambda_i \mid \mathcal{H}_0\} = \frac{\Gamma(N, \lambda_i/2)}{\Gamma(N)}, \quad (6)$$

$$P_d^i = \mathrm{Pr}\{U_i > \lambda_i \mid \mathcal{H}_1\} = Q_N\left(\sqrt{2N\gamma_i}, \sqrt{\lambda_i}\right), \quad (7)$$

where $\Gamma(a, x)$ is incomplete gamma function and $Q_N(a, b)$ is the generalised Marcum Q-function. Detailed derivations of P_f^i and P_d^i are given in Appendices A and B.

For the purpose of simplifying (5) an approximate model for energy detection-based spectrum sensing observations can be built. It has been shown in [47] that the approximated model converges faster and has lower approximation error when N is asymptotically large. So when N tends towards infinity (practically when $N \geq 10$ [46]), the chi-square distribution defined in (5) converges to a normal distribution, that is,

$$U_i \sim \begin{cases} \mathcal{N}\left(N\sigma_i^2, 2N\sigma_i^4\right), & \mathcal{H}_0, \\ \mathcal{N}\left((N+\gamma_i)\sigma_i^2, 2(N+2\gamma_i)\sigma_i^4\right), & \mathcal{H}_1. \end{cases} \quad (8)$$

Similarly, P_f^i and P_d^i defined in (6) and (7) can be approximated as

$$P_f^i = Q\left(\frac{\lambda_i - \mathbb{E}[U_i \mid \mathcal{H}_0]}{\sqrt{\mathrm{Var}[U_i \mid \mathcal{H}_0]}}\right) = Q\left(\frac{\lambda_i - N\sigma_i^2}{\sqrt{2N}\sigma_i^2}\right),$$

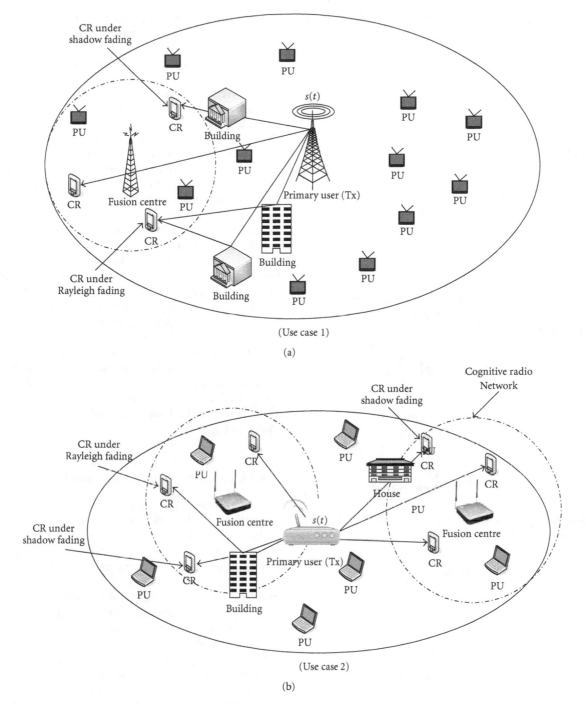

(Use case 1)

(a)

(Use case 2)

(b)

FIGURE 1: Use cases considered in paper.

$$P_d^i = Q\left(\frac{\lambda_i - \mathbb{E}[U_i \mid \mathcal{H}_0]}{\sqrt{\mathrm{Var}[U_i \mid \mathcal{H}_0]}}\right) = Q\left(\frac{\lambda_i - (N + \gamma_i)\sigma_i^2}{\sqrt{2(N + 2\gamma_i)\sigma_i^2}}\right), \quad (9)$$

where $\mathbb{E}[\cdot]$ and $\mathrm{Var}\,g[\cdot]$ denote expectation and variance operations, respectively.

3.2. Spectrum Sensing in Fading Channels. When the SU is in a fading channel, the channel gain h_i for an ith user is varying due to the fading and P_d^i becomes conditional probability dependent on instantaneous SNR γ_i. As expected, P_f^i is

independent of γ_i and remains static. Average probability of detection can be obtained by averaging instantaneous P_d^i over fading statistics, where the pdf of received SNR is $f_\gamma(x)$:

$$P_{d,\mathrm{fading}}^i = \int_\gamma P_d^i(x) f_\gamma(x) dx. \quad (10)$$

When the channel is Rayleigh faded, then γ_i is exponentially distributed with $\overline{\gamma}_i$ as its mean value. Similarly when channel is shadow faded, then γ_i is log-normally distributed with mean $\overline{\gamma}_i$ and characterised by dB-spread of shadowing σ_{dB} [38]. Hence,

$$f_{\gamma_i}(x)$$

$$= \begin{cases} \dfrac{1}{x}\exp\left(-\dfrac{x}{\overline{\gamma}_i}\right); & \text{Rayleigh Fading,} \\[3mm] \dfrac{\xi}{x\sigma_{dB}\sqrt{(2\pi)}}\exp\left(-\dfrac{10\log_{10}(x)-\mu_{x_{dB}}}{2\sigma_{dB}^2}\right); & \text{Shadow Fading,} \end{cases}$$

(11)

where $\xi = 10/\ln(10)$ and $\mu_{x_{dB}}$ is the mean of $x_{dB} = 10\log(x)$. The conversion from linear mean to the log mean (in dB) can be derived as [45]

$$\mu_{x_{dB}} = 10\log_{10}(\overline{\gamma}_i) - \frac{\sigma_{dB}^2}{2\xi}.$$

(12)

Substituting (7) and (11) in (10), for Rayleigh fading channel average probability of detection for the ith user can be calculated by [38]

$$P_{d,rayl}^i = \int_\gamma \frac{1}{x} Q_N\left(\sqrt{2Nx},\sqrt{\lambda_i}\right)\exp\left(-\frac{x}{\overline{\gamma}_i}\right)dx$$

$$= e^{-\lambda_i/2}\sum_{n=0}^{N-2}\frac{1}{n!}\left(\frac{\lambda_i}{2}\right)^N + \left(\frac{1+\overline{\gamma}_i}{\overline{\gamma}_i}\right)^{N-1}$$

(13)

$$\times\left[e^{-\lambda_i/2(1+\overline{\gamma}_i)} - e^{-\lambda_i/2}\sum_{n=0}^{N-2}\frac{1}{n!}\frac{\lambda_i\overline{\gamma}_i}{2(1+\overline{\gamma}_i)}\right].$$

For shadow fading, close form solution of (10) is not known and a numerical solution is required:

$$P_{d,shadow}^i = \int_\gamma Q_N\left(\sqrt{2Nx},\sqrt{\lambda_i}\right)\frac{1}{x\sigma_{dB}\sqrt{2\pi}}$$

$$\times\exp\left(-\frac{10\log(x)-\mu_{x_{dB}}}{2\sigma_{dB}^2}\right)dx$$

$$= \frac{1}{\sigma_{dB}\sqrt{2\pi}}\sum_{x=x_0}^{x_f} Q_N\left(\sqrt{2Nx},\sqrt{\lambda_i}\right)$$

$$\times\exp\left(-\frac{10\log(x)-\mu_{x_{dB}}}{2\sigma_{dB}^2}\right)\frac{\Delta x}{x},$$

(14)

where Δx and x_f are chosen as to minimise numerical approximation error.

3.3. Numerical Evidence. The performance of local spectrum sensing is evaluated using theoretical results as well as Monte Carlo simulations by plotting complementary Receiver Operating Characteristics (ROC) curves (plot of $P_m = 1 - P_d$ versus P_f). In Monte Carlo simulations, probability of false alarm and miss detection is calculated by comparing sensing observations with a predefined threshold,

and results are obtained by simulations over $1,000,000$ noise realisations. It is assumed that N is an integer value and set to be 5.

Figure 2 shows the ROC curves for local spectrum sensing in AWGN, Rayleigh fading, and Shadowing for different values of σ_{dB}. Spectrum sensing results for AWGN channel are provided for comparison and simulation results are validated by comparing with analytical results. It is clear from Figure 2 that both Rayleigh and shadow fading degrades the performance of spectrum sensing. For example, in Rayleigh fading channel, in order to achieve $P_m < 10^{-1}$ where $P_m = 1 - P_d$, we need $P_f > 0.4$ which results in poor spectrum utilisation and vice versa. Similarly, it can be seen from Figure 2 that local spectrum sensing is more difficult in shadow fading and with increase in shadowing (or σ_{dB}) detector performance further degrades.

Another important metric to characterise spectrum sensing performance is the minimum detected SNR. This metric is defined as the lowest SNR that a sensing algorithm is able to detect with reliability of P_f and P_d for a given PU signal, propagation conditions and observation time. Figure 3 plots the minimum detectable SNR by a CR under different channel conditions for a targeted $P_f = 10^{-1}$. It is clear from Figure 3 that shadowing affects detector performance more than Rayleigh fading. In order to achieve $P_f = 10^{-1}$ in given scenario, the required SNR is around 10 dB while for the lower values of $\overline{\gamma}$ this is not possible as shown in Figure 3.

4. Collaborative Spectrum Sensing

Section 3 shows that local spectrum sensing has some limitations and it is hard to detect signals of low SNR for desired performance. Among many other challenges (e.g., see [48]) one of the most important challenges for the implementation of CRN is the hidden node problem, when a CR is shadowed or in a deep fade [41]. To address these problems multiple CRs can collaborate with each other in order to make a global decision about the existence of the PU. It has been shown by previous research that CSS can improve detection performance in the fading channels; for example, see [9] and references therein. In CSS, every SU performs its own spectrum sensing measurements and can also make a local decision on whether the PU is present or absent. All of the SUs forward their soft (local measurement) or hard (1-bit) decision to a common receiver, often called fusion centre or a band manager. Fusion centre may be centralised or distributed; in centralised CSS all the SUs send their decisions to the fusion centre, which may be an Access Point (AP) in wireless LAN or a CR base station in a cellular system, while, in distributed CSS, all the SUs may behave as a fusion centre and receive sensing information from the neighboring nodes. In both cases, fusion centre fuse collected decisions and make a final decision to declare the presence (or otherwise) of primary users in observed frequency band. The results presented in [40, 49] show that SDC outperforms HDC in terms of probability of miss detection. While HDC outperforms SDC when the

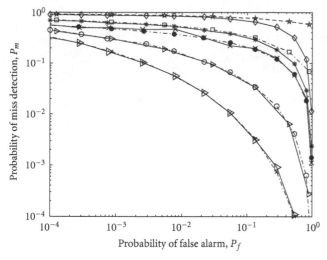

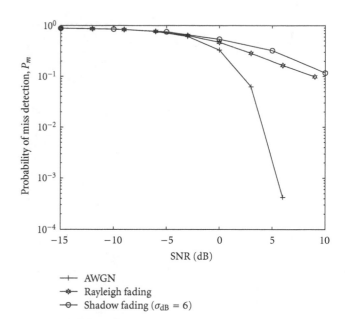

FIGURE 2: Receiver operating characteristics for local spectrum sensing in Rayleigh and Shadow Fading channels with γ = 5 dB, N = 5.

FIGURE 3: Probability of miss detection versus minimum detected SNR in shadow fading for $P_f = 10^{-1}$, $\gamma_{dB} = 5$, $N = 5$.

number of collaborative users is large [41] and further HDC needs a low-bandwidth control channel. In CSS, sharing information within CRN and combining result from various measurements is a challenging task, which is the main scope of this paper.

4.1. Hard Decision Combining. In HDC, fusion centre collects binary decisions from the individual SUs, identifies the available spectrum, and then broadcasts this information to the other SUs. The optimal decision fusion is based on Neyman-Pearson criterion by comparing Likelihood Ratio with the threshold vector as

$$\frac{f(\mathbf{D} \mid \mathcal{H}_1)}{f(\mathbf{D} \mid \mathcal{H}_0)} \overset{\mathcal{H}_1}{\underset{\mathcal{H}_0}{\gtrless}} \underline{\lambda}, \qquad (15)$$

where $\mathbf{D} = [D_1, D_2, \dots, D_M]^T$ denotes binary decisions from M SUs and $D_i \in \{0, 1\}$, $\underline{\lambda}$ is the optimal threshold vector and $f(\mathbf{D} \mid \mathcal{H}_0)$, and $f(\mathbf{D} \mid \mathcal{H}_1)$ represents the probability density functions of $\mathbf{D}$ under hypothesis $\mathcal{H}_0$ and $\mathcal{H}_1$, respectively. Mathematical analysis using Neyman-Pearson criterion is mathematically untractable especially if the local measurements are correlated and hence sub optimal solutions are always preferable [50].

There are many other ways to combine or fuse hard decisions based on counting rules; most commonly used in the literature are *OR, AND* and in general *K*-out-of-*M* fusion rule [36, 42, 51]. In *AND* all CRs should declare $\mathcal{H}_1$ in order to make a global decision that PU is present while in *OR* rule, fusion centre declares $\mathcal{H}_1$ if any of the received decision is $\mathcal{H}_1$. At the fusion centre, all D_i's are fused together according to the following fusion rule [9]:

$$y_c = \begin{cases} \sum_{i=1}^{M} D_i \geq K, & \mathcal{H}_1, \\ \sum_{i=1}^{M} D_i \leq K, & \mathcal{H}_0. \end{cases} \qquad (16)$$

It can be seen from (16) that the *OR* corresponds to the case when $K = 1$ while for *AND* rule $K = M$.

It has been reported that for many cases of practical interest, the *OR* fusion rule delivers better performance [9]. In order to demonstrate improvement in spectrum sensing performance by collaboration of SUs *OR* fusion rule is used at the fusion centre in this section. Figures 4 and 5 show ROC curves for use Case 1 (as shown in Figure 1) with different number of CRs under i.i.d. log-normal shadowing with $\bar{\gamma}_1 = \bar{\gamma}_2 = \cdots = \bar{\gamma}_i = 5$ dB and $N = 5$. In these results, AWGN curves for single users are shown for comparison. As seen in Figures 4 and 5 CSS mitigates the effects of shadow fading effectively. It can also be seen in Figure 4 that by incorporating more and more users performance even better than in the AWGN scenario can be achieved. This stems from the fact that with more number of SUs there are more chances that a single user has its instantaneous SNR above average.

As stated in Section 3 another important parameter to analyse performance of a detection algorithm is minimum

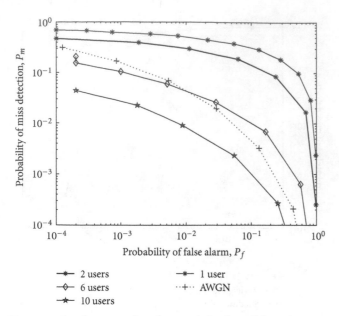

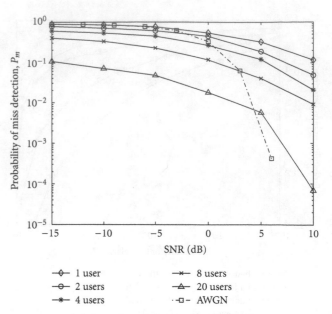

FIGURE 4: Receiver operating characteristics for collaborative spectrum sensing under shadow fading, $\sigma_{dB} = 6$, $N = 5$.

FIGURE 6: Probability of miss detection versus minimum detected SNR in shadow fading, $P_f = 10^{-1}$, $\sigma_{dB} = 6$, $\gamma = 5$ dB, $N = 5$.

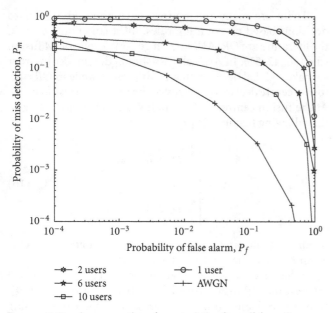

FIGURE 5: Receiver operating characteristics for collaborative spectrum sensing under shadowing, $\sigma_{dB} = 10$, $N = 5$.

detected SNR. A good detection scheme must be able to detect signals of low SNR, and in Section 3 it has been shown that shadowing affects detected SNR by a user. Figure 6 shows that by incorporating a large number of users it is possible to achieve the desired performance even at low SNR levels. By comparing Figures 3 and 6 it can be seen that under shadow fading ($\sigma_{dB} = 6$) and for desired performance, for example, $P_f = 10^{-1}$ and $P_d = 10^{-1}$ local sensing requires received signal of at least 10 dB while collaboration of 20 users can detect signal of SNR as low as -15 dB.

4.2. Soft Decision Combining.
In order to simplify the analysis with fusion of soft decisions, it has been assumed that the value of N is large. With this assumption the summary statistics at local secondary nodes $\mathbf{U}$ (as defined in (8)) can be considered, which is transmitted to the fusion centre through the reporting channels. In this paper realistic noisy reporting channels with variable channel gains are considered. A system model is shown in Figure 13.

4.2.1. Equal Gain Combining.
Statistics of local observations for an ith SU after passing through the channel of gain g_i and noise $n_i \sim \mathcal{N}(0, \delta_i^2)$ is

$$
y_i \sim \begin{cases} \mathcal{N}\left(Ng_i\sigma_i^2, 2Ng_i^2\sigma_i^4 + \delta_i^2\right), & \mathcal{H}_0, \\[2mm] \mathcal{N}\left(\left(N + \overline{\gamma}_i\right)g_i\sigma_i^2, 2\left(N + 2\overline{\gamma}_i\right)g_i^2\sigma_i^4 + \delta_i^2\right), & \mathcal{H}_1, \end{cases} \tag{17}
$$

where δ_i^2 is the noise variance of the ith reporting channel. For the soft decision fusion scheme, fusion centre decides between $\mathcal{H}_0$ and $\mathcal{H}_1$ by comparing sum of individual observations y_c with a global threshold λ_c:

$$
y_c = \sum_{i=1}^{M} y_i \underset{\mathcal{H}_0}{\overset{\mathcal{H}_1}{\gtrless}} \lambda_c. \tag{18}
$$

4.2.2. Weighted Combining.
In weighted combining, global test statistics is calculated at the fusion centre by assigning weights w_i to the received observation from an ith user y_i by

$$
y_c = \sum_{i=1}^{M} w_i \cdot y_i = \mathbf{w}^T \mathbf{y}, \tag{19}
$$

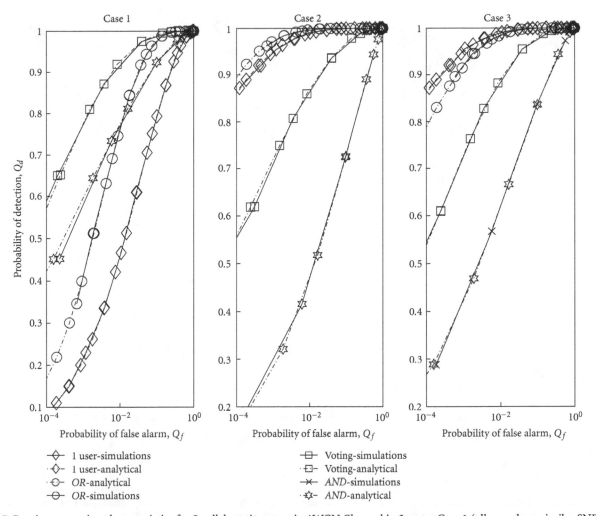

FIGURE 7: Receiver operating characteristics for 5 collaborating users in AWGN Channel in 3 cases: Case 1 (all users have similar SNR), Case 2 (half of the users have high SNR), and Case 3 (only one user has high SNR).

where $\mathbf{w} = [w_1, w_2, \ldots, w_M]^T \in \mathbb{R}^{M \times 1}$ and the received decision vector at the fusion centre is defined as $\mathbf{y} = [y_1, y_2, \ldots, y_M]^T \in \mathbb{R}^{M \times 1}$. Weight vector $\mathbf{w}$ at the fusion centre satisfies $\sum_{i=1}^{M} w_i = 1$. From (17) and (19) the distribution of y_c is given as

$$y_c$$
$$\sim \begin{cases} \mathcal{N}\left(\sum_{i=1}^{M} N g_i \sigma_i^2 w_i, \sum_{i=1}^{M} \left(2 N g_i^2 \sigma_i^4 w_i^2 + \delta_i^2 w_i^2 \right) \right); & \mathcal{H}_0 \\ \\ \mathcal{N}\left(\sum_{i=1}^{M} \left(\left(N + \overline{\gamma}_i \right) g_i \sigma_i^2 w_i \right), \right. \\ \\ \left. \sum_{i=1}^{M} \left(2 \left(N + 2\overline{\gamma}_i \right) g_i^2 \sigma_i^4 w_i^2 + \delta_i^2 w_i^2 \right) \right); & \mathcal{H}_1. \end{cases}$$
$$(20)$$

Assume $\mathbf{h} = [h_1, h_2, \ldots, h_M]^T \in \mathbb{R}^{M \times 1}$, $\mathbf{g} = [g_1, g_2, \ldots, g_M]^T \in \mathbb{R}^{M \times 1}$, $\boldsymbol{\gamma} = [\gamma_1, \gamma_2, \ldots, \gamma_M]^T \in \mathbb{R}^{M \times 1}$, $\boldsymbol{\sigma} =$

$[\sigma_1^2, \sigma_2^2, \ldots, \sigma_M^2]^T \in \mathbb{R}^{M \times 1}$, and $\boldsymbol{\delta} = [\delta_1^2, \delta_2^2, \ldots, \delta_M^2]^T \in \mathbb{R}^{M \times 1}$. Furthermore, defined matrices $\boldsymbol{\Sigma}$, $\boldsymbol{\Delta}$, $\boldsymbol{\Gamma}$, and $\mathbf{G}$ that all belong to $\mathbb{R}^{M \times M}$ represent the diagonal matrices formed by placing the vectors $\boldsymbol{\sigma}$, $\boldsymbol{\delta}$, $\overline{\boldsymbol{\gamma}}$, and $\mathbf{g}$ on the diagonal, respectively. The statistics of y_c under $\mathcal{H}_0$ and $\mathcal{H}_1$ can be written as

$$\mathrm{E}[y_c \mid \mathcal{H}_0] = N \mathbf{g}^T \boldsymbol{\Sigma} \mathbf{w},$$

$$\mathrm{Var}[y_c \mid \mathcal{H}_0] = \mathbf{w}^T \left[2 N \mathbf{G}^2 \boldsymbol{\Sigma}^2 + \boldsymbol{\Delta} \right] \mathbf{w},$$

$$\mathrm{E}[y_c \mid \mathcal{H}_1] = \mathbf{g}^T ((N\mathbf{I} + \boldsymbol{\Gamma}) \odot \boldsymbol{\sigma}) \mathbf{w}, \qquad (21)$$

$$\mathrm{Var}[y_c \mid \mathcal{H}_1] = \mathbf{w}^T \left[2(N\mathbf{I} + 2\boldsymbol{\Gamma}) \mathbf{G}^2 \boldsymbol{\Sigma}^2 + \boldsymbol{\Delta} \right] \mathbf{w}.$$

To make a decision on the presence of a primary transmitter, the global decision statistic y_c as defined in (21) is compared with a threshold λ_c. Global probability of false

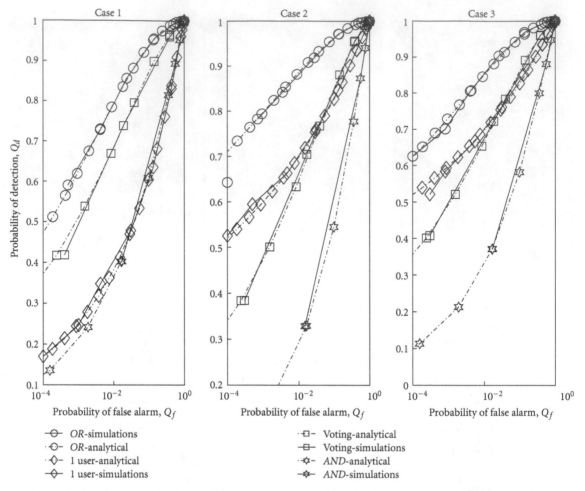

FIGURE 8: Receiver operating characteristics for 5 collaborating users in Rayleigh fading Channel in 3 cases: Case 1 (all users have similar SNR), Case 2 (half of the users have high SNR), and Case 3 (only one user has high SNR).

alarm and detection at the fusion centre, as denoted by Q_f and Q_d, are given as

$$Q_f = Q\left(\frac{\lambda_c - N\mathbf{g}^T\boldsymbol{\Sigma}\mathbf{w}}{\sqrt{\mathbf{w}^T\left[2N\mathbf{G}^2\boldsymbol{\Sigma}^2 + \boldsymbol{\Delta}\right]\mathbf{w}}}\right),$$

$$Q_d = Q\left(\frac{\lambda_c - \mathbf{g}^T((N\mathbf{I} + \boldsymbol{\Gamma}) \odot \boldsymbol{\sigma})\mathbf{w}}{\sqrt{\mathbf{w}^T\left[2(N\mathbf{I} + 2\boldsymbol{\Gamma})\mathbf{G}^2\boldsymbol{\Sigma}^2 + \boldsymbol{\Delta}\right]\mathbf{w}}}\right),$$

(22)

where $Q(\cdot)$ is the tail probability of the normalised Gaussian distribution.

5. Optimised User Collaboration Scheme for HDC

Section 4.1 shows that collaboration of SUs improves spectrum sensing performance by utilising space diversity of users. In this section, the problem of hard decision fusion at the fusion centre is considered in the presence of i.i.d. and spatially correlated shadowing. In the past, emphasis was given to collaborative spectrum sensing when all users

have same received SNR; however, in this section, a scenario where users have different γ_i with AWGN and log-normal shadowing is considered. Three different cases in use Case 2 are considered here which represents three different scenarios depending on the location of PU and SUs. Case 1 refers to a scenario in which all the SUs are relatively close to each other and hence having similar values of SNR. Case 2 depicts the situation when half of the collaborating users have high SNR values while in Case 3 only one use has a high SNR value as compared to other collaborating SUs.

Different decision fusion schemes at the fusion centre including *OR*, *AND*, *Voting*, and *1-user* cases are considered. In *Voting*-based decision fusion scheme all SUs vote and fusion centre declare an opportunity if the majority of the collaborative SUs declare an opportunity. In *1-user* case although fusion centre receives information from all users, it uses only one user information in order to make a global decision.

5.1. Independent and Identically Distributed Shadowing

5.1.1. Mathematical Formulation. The global probability of detection Q_d and probability of false alarm Q_f at the fusion

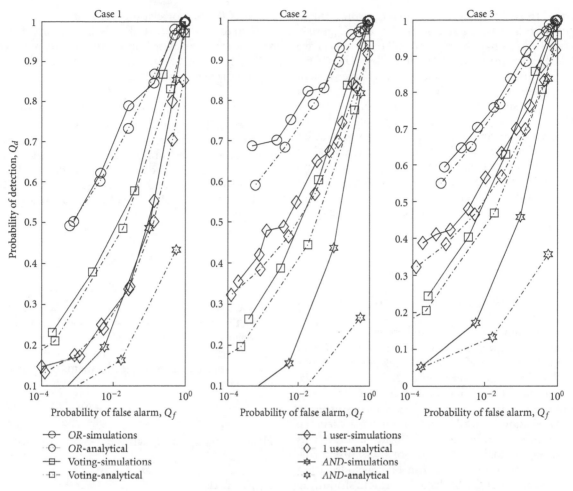

FIGURE 9: Receiver operating characteristics for 5 collaborating users in shadow fading ($\sigma_{dB} = 6$) in 3 cases: Case 1 (all users have similar SNR), Case 2 (half of the users have high SNR), and Case 3 (only one user has high SNR).

centre can be expressed as a function of the probability of detection (or false alarm) of each SU, obtaining the joint probability of M independent events as

$$Q_d = R(\mathbf{D}) \prod_{S_0} \left(1 - P_d^i\right) \prod_{S_1} P_d^i,$$

$$Q_f = R(\mathbf{D}) \prod_{S_0} \left(1 - P_f^i\right) \prod_{S_1} P_f^i. \tag{23}$$

S represents the set of all secondary users with $\mathcal{S} = \mathcal{S}_0 \cup \mathcal{S}_1$ where $\mathcal{S}_0$ is the group of SUs that has decided that PU signal is absent while $\mathcal{S}_1$ is the group of SUs that has decided that PU signal is absent and $R(\mathbf{D})$ is the decision fusion rule at the fusion centre. Value of $R(\mathbf{D})$ depends on what type of fusion rule is used at the fusion centre. So for the given formulation, K-out-of-M rule can be formulated as

$$R(\mathbf{D}) = \begin{cases} 1 \ (\text{PU present}) & \text{if } \sum_{i=1}^{M} D_i \geq K, \\ \\ 0 \ (\text{PU absent}) & \text{if } \sum_{i=1}^{M} D_i < K. \end{cases} \tag{24}$$

For the fusion rules considered in this section, K is given as

$$K = \begin{cases} 1, & \text{OR}, \\ M, & \text{AND}, \\ \left\lceil \dfrac{M}{2} \right\rceil, & \text{Voting}, \end{cases} \tag{25}$$

where $\lceil \cdot \rceil$ is the ceil function.

For 1-user rule,

$$R(\mathbf{D}) = \begin{cases} 1, & \text{if } D_i = 1, \\ 0, & \text{otherwise}, \end{cases} \tag{26}$$

where the ith user is chosen as

$$i = \arg\max_j \left\{ \gamma_j \right\}. \tag{27}$$

5.1.2. Simulation Results. Figure 7 shows collaborative spectrum sensing performance when 5 SUs collaborate with each other and make collaborative decision; analytical results validating the simulation results are shown. When all users have similar γ_i (Case 1) in AWGN channel, then the optimal decision fusion rule is *Voting* rule as evident from Figure 7. When half of the users have high γ_i and half of the users have low γ_i (Case 2), then the optimal decision rule is *OR*. Case 3 refers to the situation when only one user has higher γ_i than others; in this case the collaborative spectrum sensing works even worse than a single node. From these results it can be concluded that it is not necessary that collaboration of users always improves spectrum sensing performance and in order to derive an optimum performance individual γ_i should be considered. Without knowing γ_i the performance is always suboptimal; so in the proposed scenario it is suggested that users estimate local γ_i and send this information along with their 1-bit decision. Local SNR can be estimated by using a test statistics defined in (5) as

$$\hat{\gamma}_i = \frac{1}{Z}\sum_{i=1}^{Z} u_i - X, \qquad (28)$$

where $\hat{\gamma}$ is estimated SNR, Z is the number of test statistics, and X is $\mathrm{E}(u_i \mid \mathcal{H}_0)$.

In Rayleigh fading and shadowing, collaborative spectrum sensing is an ideal solution because diversity gain achieved by collaboration effectively cancels the deleterious effects of fading. Figures 8 and 9 show detection performance under Rayleigh fading and shadowing with the three cases considered in this section. Value of dB-spread is assumed to be 6 dB for the shadowing while other parameters remain the same. As can be seen from these results, in all three cases spectrum sensing performance is superior if *OR* fusion rule is used at the fusion centre. So it can be concluded from simulation results that under Rayleigh fading and shadowing with i.i.d. measurements most optimal fusion rule is *OR* rule and collaboration of users is required. Further, with the increase of shadowing, sensing performance of two user collaboration with highest γ_i is better than collaboration of all users. It can be concluded that even in fading or shadowing it is important for the fusion centre to know the SNR values of the users to make a decision about which fusion rule gives better performance.

5.2. Spatially Correlated Shadowing.

Up to this point, it is assumed that all collaborating cognitive users have identical and independent shadowing. However, usually there is a degree of spatial correlation associated with log-normal shadowing [52] and assumption of identically and independent (i.i.d.) shadowing is not always true. In this section, the impact of spatially correlated shadowing on decision fusion when users have different SNR is studied under different channel conditions. It is concluded that correlation has a direct impact on the optimum decision fusion rule at the fusion centre.

It is logical to think that spatially correlated shadowing would degrade the performance of CSS because such users are likely to experience similar observations thereby countering collaborative gains. In this paper correlated shadowing is modelled using the exponential correlation model [52]:

$$r(d) = e^{-ad}, \qquad (29)$$

where $r(d)$ is the correlation matrix, d is the distance between two secondary users, and a is a constant depending on the environment. Based on measurements reported in [52], $a \approx 0.12/\mathrm{m}$ for urban environment and $a \approx 0.002/\mathrm{m}$ for suburban environment.

5.2.1. Mathematical Formulation.

Assume that γ_i is the received SNR at the ith SU on a logarithmic scale. Hence under shadow fading γ_i has a Gaussian distribution with variance of σ_{dB}^2 and a mean value of μ_γ (in dB). The value of μ_γ is determined by the distance dependent path loss. Under two hypotheses $\mathcal{H}_0$ and $\mathcal{H}_1$ the distribution of γ_i for M SUs under spatially correlated shadowing can be expressed as

$$\boldsymbol{\gamma}_{\mathrm{dB}} \sim \begin{cases} \mathcal{N}\left(0 \times \mathbf{u}_M, \sigma_{\mathrm{dB}}^2 \boldsymbol{\Xi}\right), & \mathcal{H}_0, \\ \mathcal{N}\left(\boldsymbol{\mu}_\gamma, \sigma_{\mathrm{dB}}^2 \boldsymbol{\Xi}\right), & \mathcal{H}_1, \end{cases} \qquad (30)$$

where $\boldsymbol{\gamma}_{\mathrm{dB}} = [\gamma_1, \gamma_2, \ldots, \gamma_M]^T$, $\mathbf{u}_M$ is an $M \times 1$ vector of all ones, and $\boldsymbol{\Xi}$ is the normalised covariance matrix of $\boldsymbol{\gamma}_{\mathrm{dB}}$. Using the exponential correlation model defined in (29), the covariance matrix $\boldsymbol{\Xi}$ is an $M \times M$ matrix. Assuming that all SUs are uniformly distributed in a 1-dimensional plane within a total distance of κ, the elements of covariance matrix are given as

$$\Xi_{i,j} = e^{(-a\kappa/(M-1))|i-j|}. \qquad (31)$$

Hence, the covariance matrix $\boldsymbol{\Xi}$ can be expressed as

$$\boldsymbol{\Xi} = \begin{bmatrix} 1 & \mathcal{A} & \mathcal{B} & \cdots & e^{-a\kappa} \\ \mathcal{A} & 1 & \mathcal{A} & \cdots & e^{-a\kappa|M-2|/(M-1)} \\ \vdots & \vdots & \vdots & \cdots & \vdots \\ e^{-a\kappa} & \mathcal{B} & e^{-3a\kappa/(M-1)} & \cdots & 1 \end{bmatrix}, \qquad (32)$$

where $\mathcal{A}$ denotes $e^{-a\kappa/(M-1)}$ and $\mathcal{B}$ denotes $e^{-2a\kappa/(M-1)}$.

The probability density function of γ_i can be expressed for the M collaborative SUs having correlated shadow fading as

$$f\left(\boldsymbol{\gamma}_{\mathrm{dB}}\right) = \frac{1}{\sqrt{2\pi}\sigma_{\mathrm{dB}}^2}\boldsymbol{\Xi}^{-1}\exp\left\{-\frac{\left(\boldsymbol{\gamma}_{\mathrm{dB}} - \mu_\gamma\right)^2}{2\sigma_{\mathrm{dB}}^2}\boldsymbol{\Xi}^{-1}\right\}. \qquad (33)$$

From (32) it is clear that $\boldsymbol{\Xi}$ is a diagonal constant matrix or Toeplitz matrix, and its inverse may be expressed as [53]

$$\boldsymbol{\Xi}^{-1} = \frac{1}{1 - e^{2a\kappa/(M-1)}}\begin{bmatrix} 1 & -\mathcal{A} & 0 & \cdots & 0 \\ -\mathcal{A} & 1 + e^{-2a\kappa/(M-1)} & -\mathcal{A} & \cdots & 0 \\ \vdots & \vdots & \vdots & \cdots & \vdots \\ 0 & 0 & \cdots & -\mathcal{A} & 1 \end{bmatrix}, \qquad (34)$$

where $\mathcal{A}$ denotes $e^{-a\kappa/(M-1)}$.

5.2.2. Simulation Results.

It is shown in this section that spatial correlation among users directly impacts the decision fusion at the fusion centre. Figures 10, 11, and 12 show ROC

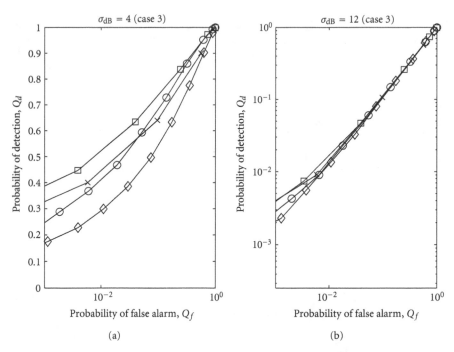

FIGURE 10: Receiver operating characteristics for 5 collaborating users in spatially correlated shadowing fading (Case 1: all users have similar SNR).

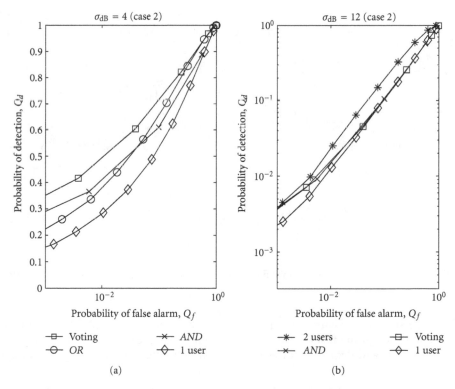

FIGURE 11: Receiver operating characteristics for 5 collaborating users in spatially correlated shadowing fading (Case 2: half of the users have high SNR).

curves of 5 collaborating users under spatially correlated shadowing with dB-spread of 4 dB and 12 dB for the three cases defined in Section 5.1. In case of correlated shadowing with lower values of σ_{dB}, the *Voting* fusion rule outperforms *OR* fusion rule and performance of *AND* fusion rule is better than *OR*. This is due to the fact that all secondary users are close to each other and have similar values of γ_i; hence user observations are similar to each other. However, sensing performance in heavily shadowed environment (e.g., when $\sigma_{dB} = 12$) for all fusion schemes is almost similar in all

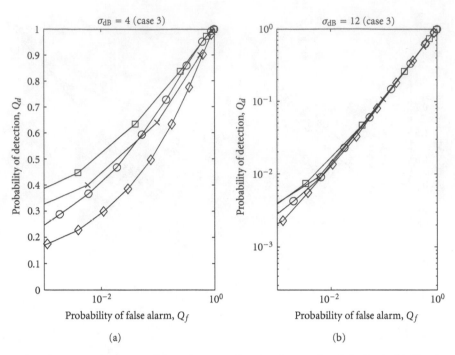

FIGURE 12: Receiver operating characteristics for 5 collaborating users in spatially correlated shadowing fading (Case 3: only one user has high SNR).

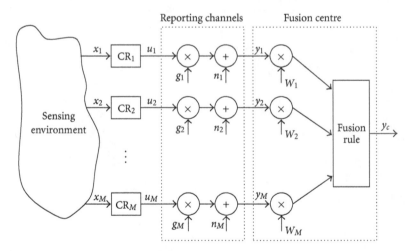

FIGURE 13: Schematic diagram of weighted collaboration at fusion centre for soft decision combining with imperfect reporting channels.

three cases. Hence, it can be seen from Figures 10, 11, and 12 that for optimal decision fusion at the fusion centre, it is important to consider the effects and degree of correlation among users.

6. Optimised User Collaboration Scheme for SDC

In this section, goal is to optimise CSS when collaborating SUs send their soft decisions to the fusion centre by maximising the global probability of detection (or alternatively minimising global probability of miss detection) for a given value of probability of false alarm and channel conditions.

Referring to Section 4.2 for the framework of soft decision combing at the fusion centre, global probability of detection can be written in terms of global probability of false alarm (using (22)):

$$
Q_d = Q\left(\frac{\sqrt{\mathbf{w}^T\left[2N\mathbf{G}^2\mathbf{\Sigma}^2 + \mathbf{\Delta}\right]\mathbf{w}}\, Q^{-1}\left(Q_f\right)}{\sqrt{\mathbf{w}^T\left[2(N\mathbf{I} + 2\mathbf{\Gamma})\mathbf{G}^2\mathbf{\Sigma}^2 + \mathbf{\Delta}\right]\mathbf{w}}} \right.
$$

$$
\left. + \frac{N\mathbf{g}^T\mathbf{\Sigma}\mathbf{w} - \mathbf{g}^T((N\mathbf{I} + \mathbf{\Gamma}) \odot \boldsymbol{\sigma})\mathbf{w}}{\sqrt{\mathbf{w}^T\left[2(N\mathbf{I} + 2\mathbf{\Gamma})\mathbf{G}^2\mathbf{\Sigma}^2 + \mathbf{\Delta}\right]\mathbf{w}}} \right). \tag{35}
$$

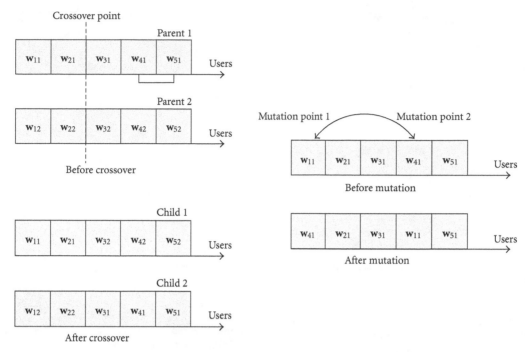

FIGURE 14: Crossover and mutation operations in genetic algorithm.

Maximising Q_d, as defined in (35), is equivalent to minimise $\varphi(\mathbf{w})$ as $Q(x)$ is a decreasing function of x, where $\varphi(\mathbf{w})$ is given by

$$
\begin{aligned}
\varphi(\mathbf{w}) &= \frac{\sqrt{\mathbf{w}^T\left[2N\mathbf{G}^2\mathbf{\Sigma}^2 + \mathbf{\Delta}\right]\mathbf{w}}\,Q^{-1}\left(Q_f\right)}{\sqrt{\mathbf{w}^T\left[2(N\mathbf{I} + 2\mathbf{\Gamma})\mathbf{G}^2\mathbf{\Sigma}^2 + \mathbf{\Delta}\right]\mathbf{w}}} \\
&\quad + \frac{N\mathbf{g}^T\mathbf{\Sigma}\mathbf{w} - \mathbf{g}^T((N\mathbf{I} + \mathbf{\Gamma}) \odot \boldsymbol{\sigma})\mathbf{w}}{\sqrt{\mathbf{w}^T\left[2(N\mathbf{I} + 2\mathbf{\Gamma})\mathbf{G}^2\mathbf{\Sigma}^2 + \mathbf{\Delta}\right]\mathbf{w}}} \qquad (36) \\
&= \frac{\sqrt{\mathbf{w}^T\left[2N\mathbf{G}^2\mathbf{\Sigma}^2 + \mathbf{\Delta}\right]\mathbf{w}}\,Q^{-1}\left(Q_f\right) - \mathbf{\Gamma}\mathbf{g}^T\mathbf{\Sigma}\mathbf{w}}{\sqrt{\mathbf{w}^T\left[2(N\mathbf{I} + 2\mathbf{\Gamma})\mathbf{G}^2\mathbf{\Sigma}^2 + \mathbf{\Delta}\right]\mathbf{w}}}.
\end{aligned}
$$

Similarly for fading channels, the average probability of detection can be obtained by averaging Q_d over fading statistics as described in Section 3.2. Now the optimisation problem can be formulated as

$$
\text{minimise} \quad \varphi(\mathbf{w})
$$

$$
\text{s.t.} \quad \sum_{i=1}^{M} w_i = 1, \quad w_i \geq 0, \quad \forall i \in \{1, 2, 3, \dots, M\}.
$$

$$(37)$$

6.1. GA-Based Weighted Collaborative Spectrum Sensing. This section describes the design of a GA-based weighted CSS framework for the case of SDC at the fusion centre. In this work, GA is used as a solution approach to minimise $\varphi(\mathbf{w})$ as defined in (36) for a given value of Q_f. The GA has been

proposed as a computational analogy of adaptive systems by Holland [54]. They are modelled based on the principles of natural evolution and selection and is briefly described in this section. An initial population is first generated and then the fitness of each chromosome in the initial population is evaluated using a predefined fitness function. A loop is initiated to simulate the generations and in each generation, chromosomes are selected probabilistically according to their fitness. The genes of the selected individuals will mutate and crossover to produce offsprings to maintain the population size. The GA continues to iterate until the convergence is achieved or until it exceeds the maximum number of generations.

6.1.1. Seeding. The algorithm starts by randomly generating an initial population of possible solutions. Here, the initial population is the randomly generated values of weights satisfying the constraints as described in (37). Seeding is a process of setting the initial population to some initial configuration. If the initial population is seeded properly, the performance of GA can be greatly enhanced. Since GA works by probabilistically mutating and combining, the convergence of algorithm can be achieved quickly if the population is initially preset to a good solution.

6.1.2. Fitness Function. A fitness function plays a central role in GA. It evaluates fitness of each chromosome and forces the algorithm to search for optimal solutions and is the only link between actual problem and the GA. A fitness function ranks chromosomes in a given population; so individuals having better fitness values have higher chances of survival and reproduction in the next generation. In this paper,

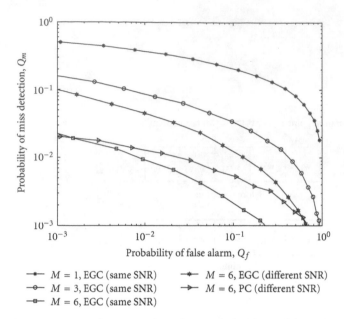

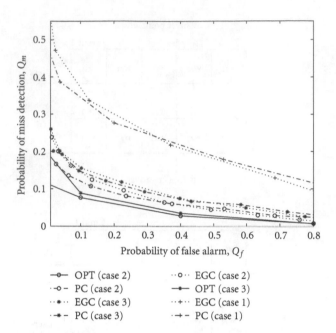

FIGURE 15: Receiver operating characteristics for collaborative spectrum sensing with perfect reporting channel, $N = 10$.

FIGURE 17: Receiver operating characteristics for collaborative spectrum sensing for 6 users in Rayleigh fading channel with imperfect reporting channels, $N = 10$ (Case 1: All users have good reporting channel, Case 2: All users have bad reporting channel, and Case 3: Two of the users have good reporting channel).

6.1.3. Selection.
Once the chromosomes in a given population have been evaluated according to their fitness values, the one with the better fitness will be selected, and the others will be eliminated. There are many different strategies available in the literature to implement selection algorithm [56]. The simplest and the most widely used selection scheme, the roulette wheel selection, is used in simulations [55].

6.1.4. Elitism.
The number of chromosomes in a population with the best-scaled fitness value guaranteed to survive in the next generation and represented by Elitism is called Elite children. Proper value of Elite children is important in the fast convergence of GA.

6.1.5. Crossover and Mutation.
Crossover process in GA combines two individuals (parents) and produces entirely new chromosomes (children). The main idea behind crossover operation is that the children may be better than both of the parents if they take the best attributes from each parent. Generally, crossover occurs during evolution according to a specified probability and is typically in the range of 80% to 90%. Although a number of crossover techniques are available in the literature, the simplest crossover technique, called single-point crossover [56], is used in this study.

Mutation is another genetic operation which alters one or more genes in a chromosome from its original state. This introduces new genetic material in the population. With the new gene, GA may be able to arrive at a better solution than previously possible. Mutation also occurs during the evolution process by some prespecified probability and this value is normally small as compared to the crossover

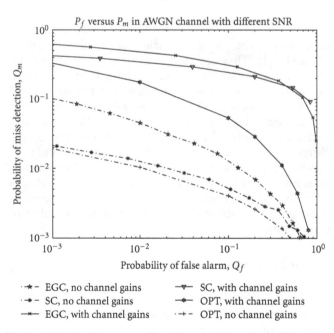

FIGURE 16: Receiver operating characteristics for collaborative spectrum sensing for 6 users in AWGN channel with im-perfect reporting channels, $N = 10$.

$\varphi(\mathbf{w})$ is used as a fitness function to evaluate the fitness of individuals. After calculating the fitness of each individual, all fitness values are scaled in a range that is suitable for the selection algorithm. The selection algorithm uses these scaled fitness values to choose the parents of the next generation. The range of scaled values affects the performance of GA, and in this paper the scaling method described by Goldberg [55] is used.

TABLE 1: GA parameter configuration.

TABLE 1: GA parameter configuration.

Parameter	Value
Population Size	100
Number of Generations	40
Elitism	2%
Mutation Probability	2%
Crossover Probability	80%
Initialisation Method	Random
Crossover operation	Single point
Selection Method	Roulette wheel

probability. In the classical mutation process, one or more pairs of genes are selected randomly and swapped to produce new offsprings. Figure 14 illustrates the process of crossover and mutation for the case of 5 collaborating users.

6.1.6. Termination. Termination is the criteria by which GA decides whether to continue or stop searching for better solutions. There are many possibilities to terminate GA including generation number, evolution time, and population convergence, and so forth and in this work generation number criterion is used for terminating the GA. Based on a number of test experiments, the best suited GA parameter configuration was set up for the optimisation problem and parameters are listed in Table 1.

6.2. Numerical Result and Discussions. In this section, proposed GA-based weighted CSS scheme for SDC is simulated and compared with existing weighting schemes proposed in [42], that is, Equal Gain Combining (EGC) and Proportional Combining (PC). EGC is the weighting scheme in which all the collaborating SUs have equal weights and in PC the fusion centre assigns proportional weight to SUs according to their SNR values. Numerical results are obtained from simulations for use Case 2 over $1,000,000$ noise realisations for the given set of noise variances. Noise variance of all collaborating users for the primary channel (i.e., channel between primary transmitter and secondary users) is assumed to be $\sigma^2 = 1$ and noise variance of the reporting channels is assumed to be $\delta^2 = 1\,\text{dB}$. Value of N is assumed to be 10 in all simulations.

Figure 15 shows the probability of miss detection Q_m against probability of false alarm Q_f with different number of collaborating users and their corresponding SNR values. A perfect reporting channel is assumed here and the channel between SUs and PU is considered to be AWGN channel. Figure 15 shows clearly that with an increase in the number of collaborating users sensing performance improves if all SUs have same SNR. However, when the cognitive users have different mean SNR values, then the sensing performance degrades with equal gain combining. Proportional weights assigned to different users according to their SNR values improve sensing performance as compared to equal gain combining approach. From the results it is concluded that

users SNRs have a direct impact on the spectrum sensing performance.

Figure 16 plots the Q_m versus Q_f for the case when cognitive users have different SNRs and the reporting channel is not perfect; that is, practical AWGN channels exist between SUs and the fusion centre with different channel gains defined as $\mathbf{g} = [0.32, 0.2, 0.2, 0.1, 0.3, 0.15]^T$. The value of channel gain is dependent on the location of the fusion centre and the SU and is varying over time. It can be seen from Figure 16 that reporting channel gains degrade the performance of spectrum sensing. Without channel gains, PC performs better than EGC, but, in the presence of reporting channel, PC does not perform much better than EGC. This is mainly because of the fact that in the presence of imperfect reporting channel, optimum weights of cognitive users are not only dependant on SNR values but also depend on reporting channel conditions. Under such conditions an analytical expression for the probability of detection is derived and optimum weights are calculated using GA. The result shows that the proposed GA-based optimal weights, denoted as "OPT," yield superior spectrum sensing performance in both cases, that is, with and without reporting channel gain.

In order to evaluate the performance of proposed optimised collaborative spectrum sensing framework, performance of GA-based optimisation algorithm is tested in fading channel. Three different cases were considered: Case 1 refers to the case in which all the SUs have good reporting channel, Case 2 is the case in which all the collaborating cognitive users have bad reporting channel, while in Case 3 two of the collaborating users have strong channel, while others have bad reporting channel. As seen from Figure 17 spectrum sensing performance is the worst for Case 1 and the best for Case 3; however, in all of the three cases, the performance of the proposed optimised thresholds outperforms the other solutions.

7. Conclusions

Spectrum is a scarce resource and it has been a major focus of research over the last several decades. Cognitive radio technology, which is a one of the promising approaches to utilise radio spectrum efficiently, has become an attractive option. Deployment of cognitive radio networks mainly depends on the ability of cognitive devices to detect licensed or primary users accurately and hence minimise interference to the licensed users. Spectrum sensing has been identified as a key functionality of a cognitive radio. However, as observations of a single cognitive radio are not always trustworthy, so collaboration of cognitive users is normally required to improve licensed users detection performance. In this paper, optimisation algorithms for both hard decision and soft decision combining are presented for collaborative spectrum sensing. It is well known that fusion strategy at the fusion centre has direct impact on the overall performance of collaborative spectrum sensing. We consider optimisation of both hard and soft decision fusion and develop algorithms to optimise spectrum sensing performance. It is concluded that in order to derive an optimum fusion rule, the fusion centre must know the collaborating users estimated SNR values, channel conditions, as well as their 1-bit decision for the case of hard decision fusion. We also proposed a genetic algorithm-based optimisation of weighted collaborative spectrum sensing in which weights are assigned to the information provided by the users to improve CSS in terms of ROC. The optimum weight vector is obtained by maximising the global probability of detection at the fusion centre. Simulation results show that the proposed strategies improve spectrum sensing performance in terms of global probability of miss detection. However, proposed schemes require knowledge about SNR of all users, channel conditions, reporting channel gains, and so forth which need larger bandwidths. Our future research will consider efficient protocols and techniques to optimise bandwidth utilisation for the cases presented in this paper.

Appendices

A. Derivation of Probability of False Alarm for Energy Detector

The probability distribution function of a chi-square random variable X with $2N$ degrees of freedom is given by

$$f_X(x) = \frac{x^{N-1}e^{-x/2}}{2^N\Gamma(N)}, \tag{A.1}$$

where $\Gamma(\cdot)$ is gamma function and is defined as

$$\Gamma(u) = \int_0^\infty a^{u-1}e^{-t}dt. \tag{A.2}$$

Now for a given threshold λ the probability of false alarm under hypothesis $\mathcal{H}_0$ (as defined in (1)) can be computed as

$$P_f = \text{Prob}\{X > \lambda \mid \mathcal{H}_0\}$$

$$= \int_\lambda^\infty f_X(x)dx \tag{A.3}$$

$$= \int_\lambda^\infty \frac{x^{N-1}e^{-x/2}}{2^N\Gamma(N)}dx.$$

Let $x = 2u$; so,

$$P_f = \frac{1}{2^N\Gamma(N)} \int_{\lambda/2}^\infty 2^{N-1}u^{N-1}e^{-u}2\,du$$

$$= \frac{1}{\Gamma(N)} \int_{\lambda/2}^\infty u^{N-1}e^{-u}du. \tag{A.4}$$

From the definition of incomplete gamma function $\Gamma(s,x) = \int_x^\infty t^{s-1}e^{-t}dt$,

$$P_f = \frac{\Gamma(N,\lambda/2)}{\Gamma(N)}. \tag{A.5}$$

B. Derivation of Probability of Detection for Energy Detector

Probability density function of noncentral chi-square random variable x with $2N$ degrees of freedom and noncentrality parameter of $2N\gamma$ is given by

$$f_X(x) = \frac{1}{2}\left(\frac{x}{2N\gamma}\right)^{(N-1)/2} \exp\left(-\frac{x+2N\gamma}{2}\right)I_{N-1}\left(\sqrt{2N\gamma x}\right). \tag{B.1}$$

So for the threshold λ, probability of detection, that is, probability that $X > \lambda$ under $\mathcal{H}_1$, is given as

$$P_d = \text{Prob}\{X > \lambda \mid \mathcal{H}_1\}$$

$$= \int_\lambda^\infty f_X(x)dx$$

$$= \int_\lambda^\infty \frac{1}{2}\left(\frac{x}{2N\gamma}\right)^{(N-1)/2} \exp\left(-\frac{x+2N\gamma}{2}\right)I_{N-1}\left(\sqrt{2N\gamma x}\right)dx. \tag{B.2}$$

Assume $x = z^2$; then,

$$P_d = \int_{\sqrt{\lambda}}^\infty \frac{1}{2}\left(\frac{z^2}{2N\gamma}\right)^{(N-1)/2}$$

$$\times \exp\left[-\frac{z^2+2N\gamma}{2}\right]I_{N-1}\left(z\sqrt{2N\gamma}\right)2z\,dz$$

$$= \int_{\sqrt{\lambda}}^\infty \frac{1}{(2N\gamma)^{(N-1)/2}}z \cdot z^{N-1} \tag{B.3}$$

$$\times \exp\left[-\frac{z^2+\left(\sqrt{2N\gamma}\right)^2}{2}\right]I_{N-1}\left(z\sqrt{2N\gamma}\right)dz.$$

Using definition of generalised Marcum Q-function,

$$Q_m(\alpha,\beta) = \frac{1}{\alpha^{m-1}}\int_\beta^\alpha x^m \exp\left[-\frac{x^2+\alpha^2}{2}\right]I_{m-1}\left(\sqrt{\alpha x}\right)dx. \tag{B.4}$$

P_d can be expressed in terms of generalised Marcum Q-function, with $m = N$, $x = z$, $\alpha = \sqrt{2N\gamma}$, and $\beta = \sqrt{\lambda}$, as

$$P_d = Q_N\left(\sqrt{2N\gamma},\sqrt{\lambda}\right). \tag{B.5}$$

Acknowledgments

This work was performed in the project E3 which has received research funding from the EU FP7 framework. This paper reflects only the authors views and the community is not liable for any use that may be made of the information contained therein. The contributions of colleagues from the E3 consortium are hereby acknowledged.

References

[1] "International Telecommunication Union: Radio Regulations Revised," 1994.

[2] "Technology Research Programme: Research and Development at Ofcom 2004/05," October, p.37, 2005, http://www.ofcom.org.uk/research/technology/overview/techrandd200405/.

[3] "Federal Communications Commission: Spectrum policy task force report," November 2002, http://fjallfoss.fcc.gov/.

[4] A. Shukla, "Cognitive radio technology—a study for Ofcom," Tech. Rep. 830000143, QinetiQ Ltd, Hampshire, UK, 2006.

[5] M. McHenry, E. Livsics, T. Nguyen, and N. Majumdar, "XG dynamic spectrum sharing field test results," in *Proceedings of the 2nd IEEE International Symposium on New Frontiers in Dynamic Spectrum Access Networks*, pp. 676–684, May 2007.

[6] Spectrum Management Advisory Group (SMAG), "Position Paper on UMTS," March 2009, http://www.ofcom.org.uk/static/archive/ra/smag/papers/umts.htm.

[7] P. Leaves, *Dynamic spectrum allocation between cellular and broadcast systems*, Ph.D. dissertation, University of Surrey, 2004.

[8] "FCC Auctions March 2008," July 2009, http://wireless.fcc.gov/.

[9] A. Ghasemi and E. S. Sousa, "Opportunistic spectrum access in fading channels through collaborative sensing," *IEEE Journal of Communications*, vol. 2, no. 2, pp. 71–81, 2007.

[10] T. Yücek and H. Arslan, "A survey of spectrum sensing algorithms for cognitive radio applications," *IEEE Communications Surveys and Tutorials*, vol. 11, no. 1, pp. 116–130, 2009.

[11] H. Urkowitz, "Energy detection of unknown deterministic signals," *IEEE Proceedings*, vol. 55, no. 4, pp. 523–531, 1967.

[12] A. Sonnenschein and P. M. Fishman, "Radiometric detection of spread-spectrum signals in noise of uncertain power," *IEEE Transactions on Aerospace and Electronic Systems*, vol. 28, no. 3, pp. 654–660, 1992.

[13] Federal Communications Commission, "Notice of Proposed Rule Making, in the matter of unlicensed operaion in TV broadcast bands," May 2004, http://www.fcc.gov/.

[14] IEEE802.22, "Working Group on Wireless Regional Area Networks (WRAN)," Tech. Rep., IEEE, New York, NY, USA, 2009.

[15] Ofcom, "Digital Divident Review, A statement and our approach to awarding the digital divident," December 2007, http://www.ofcom.org.uk/consult/condocs/ddr/.

[16] DRIVE Project Web Site, March 2009, http://www.ist-drive.org/index2.html.

[17] Over-DRiVE Project Web Site, March 2009, http://www.ist-overdrive.org/.

[18] WINNER Project Web Site, March 2009, https://www.ist-winner.org.

[19] E2R II Project Web Site, March 2009, E2R II Project.

[20] ORACLE Project Web Site, March 2009, http://www.ist-oracle.org/.

[21] E3 Project Web Site, March 2009, https://ict-e3.eu/.

[22] Radio Access & Spectrum Cluster Web Site, March 2009, http://www.newcom-project.eu:8080/Plone/ras.

[23] DARPA neXt Generation (XG) Communications Working Group, March 2009, http://www.ir.bbn.com/projects/xmac/working-group/index.html.

[24] National Science Foundation, "Networking Technology and Systems (NeTS) Program Solicitation," March 2009, http://www.nsf.gov/pubs/2005/nsf05505/nsf05505.htm.

[25] P. Demestichas, A. Katidiotis, K. A. Tsagkaris, E. F. Adamopoulou, and K. P. Demestichas, "Enhancing channel estimation in cognitive radio systems by means of Bayesian networks," *Wireless Personal Communications*, vol. 49, no. 1, pp. 87–105, 2008.

[26] P. Demestichas, "Enhanced network selections in a cognitive wireless B3G world," *Annals of Telecommunications*, vol. 64, no. 7-8, pp. 483–501, 2009.

[27] Z. Xueqiang, C. U. I. Li, C. Juan, W. U. Qihui, and W. Jinlong, "Cooperative spectrum sensing in cognitive radio systems," in *Proceedings of the 1st International Congress on Image and Signal Processing (CISP '08)*, pp. 262–266, June 2008.

[28] W. Wang, W. Zou, Z. Zhou, H. Zhang, and Y. Ye, "Decision fusion of cooperative spectrum sensing for cognitive radio under bandwidth constraints," in *Proceedings of the 3rd International Conference on Convergence and Hybrid Information Technology (ICCIT '08)*, pp. 733–736, December 2008.

[29] W. Zhang, R. K. Mallik, and K. Ben Letaief, "Cooperative spectrum sensing optimization in cognitive radio networks," in *Proceedings of IEEE International Conference on Communications (ICC '08)*, pp. 3411–3415, cn, June 2008.

[30] X. Chen, Z. s. Bie, and W. l. Wu, "Detection efficiency of cooperative spectrum sensing in cognitive radio network," *Journal of China Universities of Posts and Telecommunications*, vol. 15, no. 3, pp. 1–7, 2008.

[31] T. Aysal, S. Kandeepan, and R. Piesiewicz, "Cooperative spectrum sensing over imperfect channels," in *Proceedings of IEEE Globecom Workshops (GLOBECOM '08)*, pp. 1–5, December 2008.

[32] K. Arshad and K. Moessner, "Collaborative spectrum sensing for cognitive radio," in *Proceedings of IEEE International Conference on Communications Workshops (ICC '09)*, pp. 1–5, June 2009.

[33] E. Peh, Y. C. Liang, E. Peh, and Y. C. Liang, "Optimization for cooperative sensing in cognitive radio networks," in *Proceedings of IEEE Wireless Communications and Networking Conference (WCNC '07)*, pp. 27–32, April 2007.

[34] D. J. Kadhim, S. Gong, W. Liu, and W. Cheng, "Optimization of Cooperation sensing spectrum performance," in *Proceedings of WRI International Conference on Communications and Mobile Computing (CMC '09)*, pp. 78–82, cn, February 2009.

[35] E. Peh, Y.-C. Liang, and Y. L. Guan, "Optimization of cooperative sensing in cognitive radio networks: a sensing-throughput tradeoff view," in *Proceedings of IEEE International Conference on Communications*, June 2009.

[36] C. Sun, W. Zhang, and K. Letaief, "Cluster-based cooperative spectrum sensing in cognitive radio systems," in *Proceedings of IEEE International Conference on Communications (ICC '07)*, pp. 2511–2515, June 2007.

[37] Z. Chair and P. K. Varshney, "Optimal data fusion in multiple sensor detection systems," *IEEE Transactions on Aerospace and Electronic Systems*, vol. 22, no. 1, pp. 98–101, 1986.

[38] F. F. Digham, M. S. Alouini, and M. K. Simon, "On the energy detection of unknown signals over fading channels," *IEEE Transactions on Communications*, vol. 55, no. 1, pp. 21–24, 2007.

[39] W. Wang, L. Zhang, W. Zou, and Z. Zhou, "On the distributed cooperative spectrum sensing for cognitive radio," in *Proceedings of International Symposium on Communications and Information Technologies (ISCIT '07)*, pp. 1496–1501, November 2007.

[40] E. Visotsky, S. Kuffher, and R. Peterson, "On collaborative detection of TV transmissions in support of dynamic spectrum sharing," in *Proceedings of the 1st IEEE International Symposium on New Frontiers in Dynamic Spectrum Access Networks (DySPAN '05)*, pp. 338–345, December 2005.

[41] S. M. Mishra, A. Sahai, and R. W. Brodersen, "Cooperative sensing among cognitive radios," in *Proceedings of IEEE International Conference on Communications (ICC '06)*, pp. 1658–1663, August 2006.

[42] F. E. Visser, G. J. M. Janssen, and P. Pawełczak, "Multinode spectrum sensing based on energy detection for dynamic spectrum access," in *Proceedings of the 67th IEEE Vehicular Technology Conference (VTC '08)*, pp. 1394–1398, June 2008.

[43] Z. Quan, S. Cui, and A. Sayed, "Optimal linear cooperation for spectrum sensing in cognitive radio networks," *IEEE Journal on Selected Topics in Signal Processing*, vol. 2, no. 1, pp. 28–40, 2008.

[44] S. Haykin, "Cognitive radio: brain-empowered wireless communications," *IEEE Journal on Selected Areas in Communications*, vol. 23, no. 2, pp. 201–220, 2005.

[45] A. Goldsmith, *Wireless Communications*, Cambridge University Press, New York, NY, USA, 2005.

[46] P. K. Varshney, *Distributed Detection and Data Fusion*, Springer, Secaucus, NJ, USA, 1996.

[47] R. F. Mills and G. E. Prescott, "A comparison of various radiometer detection models," *IEEE Transactions on Aerospace and Electronic Systems*, vol. 32, no. 1, pp. 467–473, 1996.

[48] I. Akyildiz, W.-Y. Lee, M. C. Vuran, and S. Mohanty, "A survey on spectrum management in cognitive radio networks," *IEEE Communications Magazine*, vol. 46, no. 4, pp. 40–48, 2008.

[49] T. Weiss, J. Hillenbrand, and F. Jondral, "A diversity approach for the detection of idle resources in spectrum pooling systems," in *Proceedings of the 48th International Scientific Colloquium*, pp. 37–38, September 2003.

[50] C. Da Silva, B. Choi, and K. Kim, "Distributed spectrum sensing for cognitive radio systems," in *Proceedings of the Information Theory and Applications Workshop (ITA '07)*, pp. 120–123, March 2007.

[51] A. K. Kattepur, A. T. Hoang, Y.-C. Liang, and M. J. Er, "Data and decision fusion for distributed spectrum sensing in cognitive radio networks," in *Proceedings of the 6th International Conference on Information, Communications and Signal Processing (ICICS '07)*, pp. 1–5, December 2007.

[52] M. Gudmundson, "Correlation model for shadow fading in mobile radio systems," *Electronics Letters*, vol. 27, no. 23, pp. 2145–2146, 1991.

[53] R. A. Horn and C. R. Johnson, *Matrix Analysis*, Cambridge University Press, Cambridge, UK, 1985.

[54] J. H. Holland, *Adaptation in Natural and Artificial Systems: An Introductory Analysis with Applications to Biology, Control, and Artificial Intelligence*, MIT Press, Cambridge, Mass, USA, 1992.

[55] D. E. Goldberg, *Genetic Algorithms in Search, Optimization and Machine Learning*, Addison-Wesley Longman, Boston, Mass, USA, 1989.

[56] M. Gen and R. Cheng, *Genetic Algorithms and Engineering Design*, Wiley, New York, NY, USA, 1997.

10

Cross-Layer Optimization of DVB-T2 System for Mobile Services

Lukasz Kondrad,[1] **Vinod Kumar Malamal Vadakital,**[1] **Imed Bouazizi,**[2] **Miika Tupala,**[3] **and Moncef Gabbouj**[1]

[1] *Department of Signal Processing, Tampere University of Technology, 33720 Tampere, Finland*
[2] *Nokia Research Center, 33720 Tampere, Finland*
[3] *Nokia, 24100 Salo, Finland*

Correspondence should be addressed to Lukasz Kondrad, lukasz.kondrad@tut.fi

Academic Editor: Georgios Gardikis

Mobile broadcast services have experienced a strong boost in recent years through the standardization of several mobile broadcast systems such as DVB-H, ATSC-M/H, DMB-T/H, and CMMB. However, steady need for higher quality services is projected to surpass the capabilities of the existing mobile broadcast systems. Consequently, work on new generations of mobile broadcast technology is starting under the umbrella of different industry consortia, such as DVB. In this paper, we address the question of how DVB-T2 transmission can be optimized for improved mobile broadcast reception. We investigate cross-layer optimization techniques with a focus on the transport of scalable video (SVC) streams over DVB-T2 Physical Layer Pipes (PLP). Throughout the paper, we propose different optimization options and verify their utility.

1. Introduction

The success of the DVB family of standards over the last decade and the constant development of new technologies resulted in the creation of a second generation of DVB standards that is expected to bring significant improvements in performance and to cater for the evolving market needs for higher bandwidth. One of the standards is DVB-T2 [1], a new digital terrestrial TV standard, which is an upgrade for the widely used DVB-T system. The initial tests show that the new standard brings more than 40% bit-rate improvement compared to DVB-T [2].

The second generation of DVB standards also benefits from the latest state of the art coding technologies. The Scalable Video Coding (SVC) standard [3] was developed as an extension of the H.264 Advanced Video Coding (H.264/AVC) [3] codec. The new standard is advantageous especially as an alternative to the simulcast distribution mode, where the same service is broadcasted simultaneously to multiple receivers with different capabilities. Instead of sending two or more independent streams to serve user groups of different quality requirements as in simulcast, an SVC encoded bit-stream, consisting of one base layer and one or more enhancements layers, may be transmitted to address the needs of those user groups. The enhancement layers improve the video in temporal, spatial, and/or quality domain. DVB recognized the potential of the SVC standard and adopted it as one of the video codecs used for DVB broadcast services [4].

In addition to the efficient simultaneous serving of heterogeneous terminals, building DVB services that make use of SVC may bring additional benefits. Among others benefits, deployment of SVC will enable providing conditional access to particular video quality levels, ensure graceful degradation using unequal error protection for higher reliability of the base layer that acts as a fallback alternative, as well as the introduction of new backwards-compatible services [5].

The recent DVB-T2 standard, on the other hand, provides a good baseline for the future development of a new mobile broadcast system. The new system would be able to reuse the infrastructure and components that would be available for DVB-T2. At the same time, it would benefit from the significantly increased channel capacity to achieve high quality mobile multimedia services.

When targeting mobile devices, different challenges, such as power consumption limitations and mobility-incurred transmission errors, need to be addressed. Handheld mobile terminals operate on a limited power. Therefore, power optimization becomes an important issue to be considered, when designing algorithms for handheld mobile devices. The DVB-T2 standard allows for data transmission in bursts in one T2 frame. However, when H.264/SVC is transmitted not all receivers are interested in the enhancement layers. To solve the problem, a novel signalling method and a data scheduler for H.264/SVC are proposed. Due to the proposed solution a portable receiver would be able to receive only the relevant data and consequently switch off the receiver for longer periods of time and hence save battery life.

Another challenge arises from the high-bit error rates that a mobile transmission channel is subject to. The DVB-T2 standard was already developed with portable receivers as one of the target user groups. Time interleaving, subslicing, and Forward Error Correction (FEC) are tools that constitute part of the DVB-T2 standard.

This basic support for mobile terminals may be tailored further to optimize mobile reception. As an example, service specific error robustness is enabled by the DVB-T2 standard. Each service may be configured to use a different Forward Error Correction (FEC) code rate, thus resulting in different protection levels. Unfortunately, this differentiation is only possible at service level, but not among the components of the same service. The same drawbacks apply to the time slicing approach that is specified in DVB-T2.

Finally, bandwidth is a crucial resource which should be used efficiently when transmitting to mobile devices. DVB-T2 comes with many possible ways of IP data encapsulation and transmission. Each method brings different overheads. Therefore, it is important to know when and how to choose a particular encapsulation method. This paper discusses the data overhead problem and provides a conceptual solution. Furthermore, an optimal cross-layer scheduling method for IP transmission over DVB-T2 is also proposed. This cross layer optimization takes into consideration the dependencies of data parts within a H.264/SVC coded bit-stream for unequal error protection.

The rest of this paper is organized as follows. Background information about the DVB-T2 broadcast system is presented in Section 2. The Scalable Video Coding standard is described in Section 3. In Section 4, we address the power consumption issues in mobile broadcast. An approach for minimizing power consumption during reception of SVC over DVB-T2 is presented. Subsequently, the challenges of the mobile channel and the increased error rates are examined in Section 5. Further optimizations to the DVB-T2 system are presented in Section 6. The paper is concluded in Section 7.

2. DVB-T2

Digital television is steadily gaining a large interest from users all over the world, and in order to satisfy growing demands DVB organization decided to design a new physical layer for digital terrestrial broadcast television. The main goals of the new standard were to achieve more bit-rate compared to the first generation DVB-T standard, targeting HDTV services, improve single frequency networks (SFN), provide service specific robustness, and target services for fixed and portable receivers. As a result of the work carried inside the DVB organization the DVB-T2 specification was released in June 2008.

2.1. Physical Layer. The DVB-T2 standard specifies mainly the physical layer structure and defines the construction of the over-the-air signal which is produced at the T2 modulator. Figure 1 depicts the high level architecture of the DVB-T2 system.

The DVB-T2 physical layer data channel is divided into logical entities called the physical layer pipe (PLP). Each PLP carries one logical data stream. An example of such a logical data stream would be an audio-visual multimedia stream along with the associated signalling information. The PLP architecture is designed to be flexible so that arbitrary adjustments to robustness and capacity can be easily done. Data within a PLP is organized in the form of baseband (BB) frames and within a PLP the content formatting of BB frames remains the same.

PLPs are further organized as slices in a time-frequency frame structure, and this structure is shown in Figure 2. Data that is common to all PLPs is carried in a "common PLP", located at the beginning of each T2 frame. PSI/SI tables carrying, for example, EPG information for the whole multiplex is an example of such common data.

The input preprocessor module though not a part of the DVB-T2 system may be included to work as a service splitter, scheduler, or demultiplexer for Transport Streams (TS) to prepare data to be carried over T2.

The preprocessor module is not defined as a part of the T2 system. However, functionally, it could perform tasks such as service splitting, scheduling or transport stream (TS) demultiplexing and preparing the incoming data for T2 processing.

The input processing module is responsible for constructing a BB frame. It operates individually on the contents of each PLP. The input data from the preprocessor module is first sliced into data fields. A data field can include an optional padding or in-band signalling data. A BB header is included at the start of each data field. The data field along with the BB header form a BB frame. The FEC code rate applied on the BB frame dictates the payload size of a BB frame. A BB frame can be classified into one of two frame size categories: short and long. A short BB frame has data length varying from 3072 to 13152 bits and a long BB frame has data length varying from 32208 to 53840 bits. The structure of a BB frame is depicted in Figure 3.

FEC coding is handled by the bit interleaving, coding and modulation unit. It uses chain codes. The outer code is a Bose-Chaudhuri-Hocquenghem (BCH) [6] code while the inner code is Low Density Parity Check (LDPC) [7]. The FEC parity bits are appended at the end of the BB frame to create the FEC frame. A short FEC frame is 16200 bits in size and

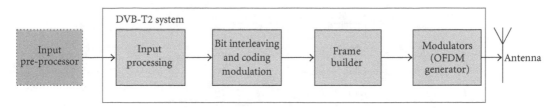

FIGURE 1: High level architecture of DVB-T2 system.

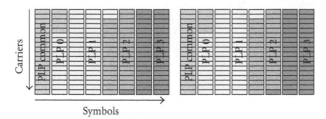

FIGURE 2: Different PLP's occupying different slices of individual modulation, code rate, and time interleaving.

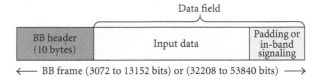

FIGURE 3: BB frame structure.

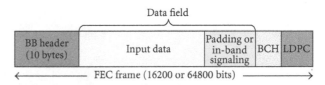

FIGURE 4: FEC frame structure.

a long FEC frame is 64800 bits in size. The structure of an FEC frame is shown in Figure 4. The FEC code construction is followed by bit interleaving, followed by mapping of the interleaved bits to constellation symbols.

The next block in the DVB-T2 system is the frame builder block, which is responsible for creating superframes. Each super frame is 64 seconds long. The super frames are further subdivided into T2 frames. A T2 frame consists of one P1 preamble symbol followed by one or more P2 preamble symbols. Data symbols obtained from the bit interleaving, coding and modulation module are appended after the P2 symbols. The preamble symbols are explained in detail the next paragraph. The T2 frames are further divided into OFDM symbols. These OFDM symbols are then passed on to the OFDM generator module. The structural composition of a super frame is shown in Figure 5.

Two types of signalling symbols are used in DVB-T2. They are (a) P1 symbols and (b) P2 symbols. P1 signalling symbols are used to indicate the transmission type and the basic transmission parameters. The content of P2 signalling symbols can be further subclassified as L1 presignalling and the L1 postsignalling. The L1 presignalling enables the reception and decoding of the L1 postsignalling, which in turn conveys the parameters needed by the receiver to access the physical layer pipes. The L1 postsignalling can be further subclassified into two parts: configurable and dynamic, and these may be followed by an optional extension field. CRC and padding ends the L1 post signalling field. The structure is depicted in Figure 6. Configurable parameters cannot change during the transmission of a super-frame while dynamic parameters can be changed within one super-frame.

DVB-T2 demodulator module receives one, or more, RF signals and outputs one service stream and one signalling stream. Based on the information in the signalling stream the client can choose which service to receive. Then a decoder module depending on the received service stream and signalling stream outputs the decoded data to a user.

2.2. IP over DVB-T2. DVB-T2 provides two main encapsulation protocols, the MPEG-2 TS [8] packetization, which has been the classical encapsulation scheme for DVB services, and the Generic Stream Encapsulation (GSE) [9], which was designed to provide appropriate encapsulation for IP traffic.

The standard ways to carry IP datagrams over MPEG2-TS are Multiprotocol Encapsulation (MPE) [10] and Unidirectional Lightweight Encapsulation (ULE) [11]. However, their design was constrained by the fact that DVB protocol suite used MPEG2-TS at the link layer. MPEG-2 TS is a legacy technology optimized for media broadcasting and not for IP services. Furthermore, the MPEG2 TS MPE/ULE encapsulation of IP datagrams adds additional overheads to the transmitted data, thus reducing the efficiency of the utilization of the channel bandwidth.

An alternative to MPEG2 TS is GSE which was design mainly to carry IP content. GSE is able to provide efficient IP datagrams encapsulation over variable length link layer packets, which are then directly scheduled on the physical layer BB fames. Using GSE to transport IP datagrams reduces the overhead by a factor of 2 to 3 times when compared to MPEG-TS transmission

3. Scalable Video Coding (SVC)

Scalable Video Coding (SVC) concept has been widely investigated in academia and industry for the last 20 years. Almost every video coding standards, such as H.262 [12], H.263 [13], and MPEG-4 [14], supports some degree of scalability. However, before H.264/SVC standard, scalable video coding was always linked to increased complexity and a drop

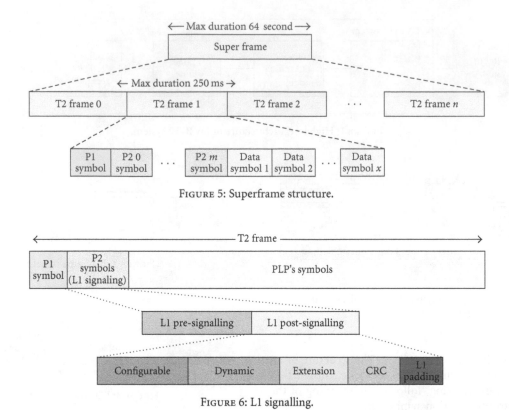

FIGURE 5: Superframe structure.

FIGURE 6: L1 signalling.

in coding efficiency when compared to nonscalable video coding. Hence, SVC was rarely used and it was preferred to deploy simulcast, which provides similar functionalities as an SVC bit-stream by transmission of two or more single layer streams at the same time. Though simulcast causes a significant increase in the resulting total bit rate, there is no increase in the complexity.

The new H.264/SVC standard is an extension of H.264/AVC standard. It enables temporal, spatial, and quality scalability in a video bit-stream. However, in contrary to the previous implementations of scalability, H.264/SVC is characterized by good coding efficiency and moderate complexity, and hence it can be seen as a superior alternative to the simulcast. Moreover, simulations [15] show better savings in bandwidth when using H.264/SVC in comparison to simulcast.

The idea behind SVC is that the encoder produces a single bit-stream containing different representations of the same content with different characteristics. An SVC decoder can then decode a subset of the bit-stream that is most suitable for the use case and the decoder capabilities. A scalable bit stream consists of a base layer and one or more enhancement layers. The removal of enhancement layers leads to a decoded video sequence with reduced frame rate, picture resolution, or picture fidelity. The base layer is an H.264/AVC bit-stream which ensures backwards compatibility to existing receivers. Through the use of SVC we can provide spatial resolution, bit rate, and/or even power adaptation. Additionally, by exploiting the intrinsic media data importance (e.g., based on the SVC layer to which those media units belong) higher error and loss resilience may be achieved. As a result, the enhanced service consumers (those consuming the base and enhancement layers) may then benefit from graceful degradation in the case of packet losses or transmission errors which was proven in [16].

When temporal scalability is used, frames from higher layers can be discarded, which results in a lower frame rate, but does not introduce any distortion during play out of the video. This results from the fact that hierarchical bipredictive frames are used. Other modes of scalability that SVC supports are spatial scalability and quality scalability. In the case of spatial scalability, the encoded bit-stream contains substreams that represent the same content at different spatial resolutions. Spatial resolution is a major motivation behind the introduction of SVC to mobile TV services. It addresses a heterogeneous receiver population, where terminals have different display capabilities (e.g., QVGA and VGA displays). Coding efficiency in spatial scalability is achieved by exploiting interlayer dependencies while maintaining low complexity through a single loop decoder requirement. Quality scalability enables the achievement of different operation points each yielding a different video quality. Coarse Granular Scalability (CGS) [17] is a form of quality scalability that makes use of the same tools available for the spatial scalability. Medium Granular Scalability (MGS) [17] achieves different quality encodings by splitting or refining the transform coefficients.

For detailed information about architecture, system, and transport interface for SVC, the reader is referred to the Special Issue on Scalable Video Coding in IEEE Transactions on Circuits and Systems for Video Technology [18].

4. Power Consumption

Handheld mobile terminals operate on a limited power. Therefore, power optimization becomes an important issue to be considered when designing transmission technologies for handheld mobile devices. One solution to optimize power consumption for data transmission to handheld devices is Time Division Multiplexing (TDM). The idea is to send data in bursts so that a receiver can switch off when data is not transmitted, thus saving power. In DVB-T2 the concept of TDM is introduced by subslicing PLPs data within one T2 frame or by time interleaving. PLP may not appear in every T2 frame of the superframe, and this is signalled by a frame interleaving parameter. However, the interval between successive frames is fixed and can not change within one super frame. Therefore, time slicing is not as flexible as in the case of DVB-H [19]. Furthermore, since in the DVB-T2 system, data is transmitted over fully transparent PLP, in order for a receiver to decode, it first needs to parse the signalling information associated with the data and then parse the proper PLP. The type of data in the PLP in a given T2 frame is unknown to the receiver, until data is parsed by upper layers.

If Scalable Video Coding (SVC) transmission is used, receivers with lower capabilities, interested only in the base layer data, are also forced to receive other enhancement layers transmitted on dedicated PLPs. Only when the data is parsed by upper layers, the receiver may discard irrelevant data which belongs to the enhancement layers. The lack of information about the type of data that is delivered in the PLP leads to high penalty of processing power on power constrained terminals.

The problem could be solved by signalling the type of data contained in each T2 frame for each specific PLP. This information would then be used by receiver to skip data of PLPs in a frame that does not contain the required information. This solution would also allow the use of a single PLP for the whole service, including all related SVC layers, while avoiding the penalty on power constrained receivers. DVB-T2 allows dynamic signalling. Therefore, this additional information may be included in L1 signalling carried in each T2 frame. The signalling information may change in every T2 frame, and it would indicate the data type carried by PLP symbols in a T2 frame.

A comparative example of how data is currently transmitted (without specifying methods of scheduling input data to BB frame) and how it may be transmitted if scheduling is applied is shown in Figures 7 and 8, respectively.

The scheduler or data preprocessor assigns the data from different SVC layers to different T2 frames. As an example, data from the base layer as well as the audio streams could be mapped to odd T2 frames, while the data of the enhancement layer could be mapped to even T2 frames. The L1 signalling that is included in each T2 frame would carry an indication of the frame with the highest importance.

Due to the data type information carried in PLP symbols in any given T2 frame, the receiver could discard the frame if it is not needed, without any further processing. Additionally, if a delta time concept is used, as in DVB-H, the receiver would be able to know the time to the next T2 frame that comprises the needed data, thus enabling more power saving through longer switch-off time.

As an example, the well-known City sequence, encoded using SVC and where the base layer has a resolution of QVGA at 15 fps and the enhancement layer has a resolution of VGA at 30 fps, gives a base layer to enhancement layer bit-rate ratio of 1 to 3 [20], which is necessary to maintain similar video quality levels at base and enhancement layers. Accordingly, the usage of the proposed scheduling method at the transmitter yields savings of 75% of the on-time for receivers that are only interested in consuming the base layer stream.

The drawback of transmitting all SVC layers over one PLP is that modulations and physical layer FEC code rates are the same for all SVC layers. Therefore, unequal error protection (UEP) scheme for different layers may be implemented only on upper layers, which might be not as strong as a differentiation of robustness by using different modulations and FEC codes on physical layer.

An alternative solution would be to deliver different layers of SVC bit-stream on separate PLPs. As a result service component specific robustness could be applied by using different coding and modulation setting for each PLP. Moreover, needed data could be extracted by a receiver by parsing only the required PLP. However, complexity issue should be considered for this use case. As a receiver would need to reserve resource for each PLP separately it would require more processing power, memory, and energy which could minimize battery lifetime. Moreover, additional circuitry essential for the simultaneous reception of multiple PLPs could increase the cost of the receiver in comparison to one PLP model. Finally, this solution would imply that receivers interested in higher quality/resolution are able to receive multiple data PLPs simultaneously, which is currently not required by the DVB-T2 specification.

5. Mobile Transmission Channel

A mobile transmission channel is highly error prone. Many contributions have been made in the literature to address the issue of robustness against packet loss in mobile data transmission over a fading channel. One of the main techniques to cope with the problem is Forward Error Correction (FEC). FEC is a technique where the transmitter adds redundancy, known as repair symbols, to the transmitted data, enabling the receiver to recover the transmitted data, even if there were transmission errors. No feedback channel is needed to recover the lost data in this technique, which makes it well suited for broadcast transmission.

Besides FEC, DVB-T2 standard introduced other tools to cope with channel errors, interleaving of T2 frames over time and subslicing of PLP data inside one T2 frame. The purpose of time interleaving is to protect a transmission against burst errors. subslicing has two consequences. First, it divides the data into slices that are transmitted in different parts of a T2 frame, which gives tolerance to short burst errors and to some extent also against slow fading. On the other hand,

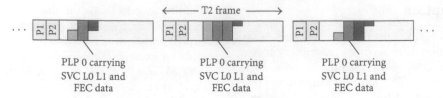

FIGURE 7: Transmission of data over one PLP.

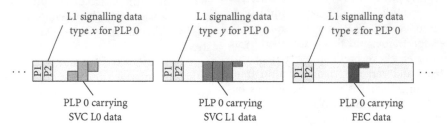

FIGURE 8: Transmission of scheduled data over one PLP with additional L1 signalling.

increasing the number of sub-slices increases the number of used OFDM symbols. This gives extra time diversity which is important in mobile channels.

To fully understand how and what benefits these tools bring when a mobile channel is considered, simulations of DVB-T2 physical layers were performed. The simulation description and the results obtained are presented in the next subsection. Subsequently, in Section 5.2 the improvement which could be introduced at the link layer is discussed.

5.1. Physical Layer. To study the suitability of the DVB-T2 standard for mobile and handheld reception and to find the relevant parameter combinations a set of simulation was performed. The simulation analyzed how time interleaving, subslicing, and FEC cope with channel errors. For the simulation a DVB-T2 physical layer model implemented in Matlab was utilized. The model uses ideal synchronization with ideal channel estimation and an ideal demapper benefiting from error-free a priori information for the rotated constellations. The model was verified by comparing the performance to the results presented in the DVB-T2 Implementation Guidelines [21].

The simulations were carried for transmission of twelve identical PLPs with 1 Mbit/s service bit rate which cover mobile broadcasting scenario. For simulation, the maximum length T2 frames (250 ms) comprising the short 16200 bits long FEC frames were used. The modulation parameters were set to 16 QAM, 8 k FFT size, and 1/4 guard interval. Moreover, P1 (not-boosted) pilot pattern and constellation rotation were used. As a transmission channel, the TU6 80 Hz model was employed. All the error calculations were performed by averaging the individual error rates to minimize variations due to dynamic channel.

In Figure 9, results for different time interleaving and subslicing settings are presented. It can be clearly seen that by increasing the interleaving length and number of sub-slices the performance of the system can be improved.

TABLE 1: Average on-time.

$N_{subslices}$	Avg. on-time [%]	Avg. on-time per frame [ms]
1	8.0	20.0
2	8.5	21.2
3	8.9	22.3
5	9.8	24.5
9	11.6	29.0
270	92.4	230.0

The highest possible number of sub-slices, 270, is greater than the number of OFDM symbols in a T2 frame, which effectively means continuous transmission. This "full sub-slicing" scenario always gives a better performance compared to the single sub-slice case. It is also understandable that increasing the time interleaving length does not significantly improve the performance with full subslicing because most of the time diversity is already there even with the shortest interleaver. Additionally, in Figure 10, subslicing without time interleaving comparison is presented.

The performance of different FEC code rates with different time interleaving is presented in Figure 11. The results clearly show that DVB-T2 is well equipped with tools which can improve the mobile broadcasting. However, it is important to properly choose the parameters. The use of subslicing should be carefully considered due to power consumption. A high number of sub-slices means longer on-the-air transmission. In Table 1, the average on-time number of sub-slices is presented. It can be seen that, for example, using nine sub-slices results in 45% increase in on-time compared to one sub-slice, consequently leading to higher power consumption by a mobile receiver. One possibility to achieve good time diversity and low power consumption is to use the full subslicing scheme, and transmit the PLPs in T2 frames periodically with some interval. In the T2 specification, this is enabled by the frame interval parameter.

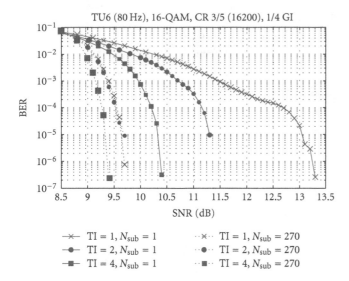

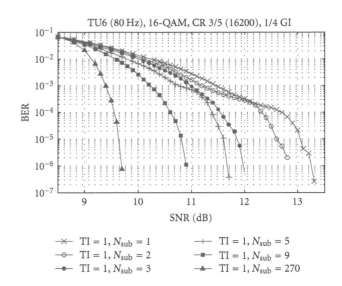

FIGURE 9: TU6 80 Hz: time interleaving and subslicing comparison.

FIGURE 10: TU6 80 Hz: subslicing comparison.

Moreover, for real-time services the total interleaving length is limited by the required channel zapping time, which plays an important role in the user experience [22]. Furthermore, stronger FEC code rate consumes more bandwidth. It is known that time-interleaving as well as error correction can be performed also by upper layers and thus brings more flexibility to the system. In [23] authors show that Upper Layer FEC (UL-FEC) may bring improvement in DVB-S2, which uses similar physical layer FEC codes to DVB-T2. The UL-FEC is discussed in the next subsection.

5.2. Link Layer (BB-FEC (Base Band—FEC)). DVB-T2 standard uses FEC codes at the physical layer by introducing the FEC-FRAME concept described in Section 2. Accordingly, it may be said that transmission errors after physical layer decoding are reflected at the BB frame level. Moreover, it may be assumed that if the combined BCH/LDPC FEC decoding fails, then the whole BB frame is marked as lost. However, the corrupted data from the BB frame may be recovered if any UL-FEC method was applied on the transmitted data.

There are many UL-FEC methods tailored for different types of content delivery and different receiver groups. As an example, if a file needs to be delivered to a set-top box then Application Layer FEC (AL-FEC) which employs Raptor Code [24] may be used. On the other hand, if a streaming content needs to be delivered to portable/handset receivers then MPE-FEC [19], MPE-IFEC [25], or Link Layer FEC (LL-FEC) may be applied.

MPE-FEC scheme was shown to bring benefits for mobile transmission in DVB-H standard [26]. Similarly, a LL-FEC could be applied in DVB-T2 to combat errors caused by the mobile fading channel. However, data in DVB-T2 may be transmitted by using MPE/TS, ULE/TS or by using GSE. When MPE/TS is used for data transmission, the MPE-FEC technology used in DVB-H may be used. If IP data is transmitted over ULE/TS or GSE then a new method for constructing LL-FEC along with a new method

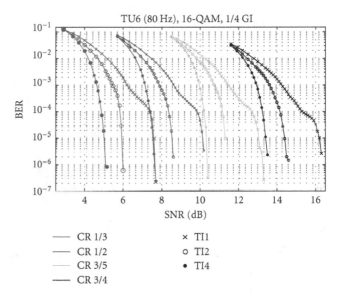

FIGURE 11: TU6 80 Hz: Code rate and time interleaving comparison.

of signalling is needed. To avoid diversification of FEC correction methods depending on the data transmission technology used, this paper proposes to shift the MPE-FEC paradigm to lower layer, that is, BB frame layer which is called BB-FEC.

In BB-FEC, the FEC source block is created from data in k BB frames. The number of rows, where each row is one byte, is equal to the data field size of the BB which corresponds to the data of a BB frame, excluding the BB header, BCH, and LDPC repair bits. This means that the payload of a BB frame (without FEC repair bits) gets mapped to a FEC source symbol. Next, FEC encoding is performed rowwise to generate the repair symbols. The resulting repair symbols are put to a new columnwise BB frames where exactly one column of repair symbol is put in one BB frame. The FEC table construction is presented in Figure 12.

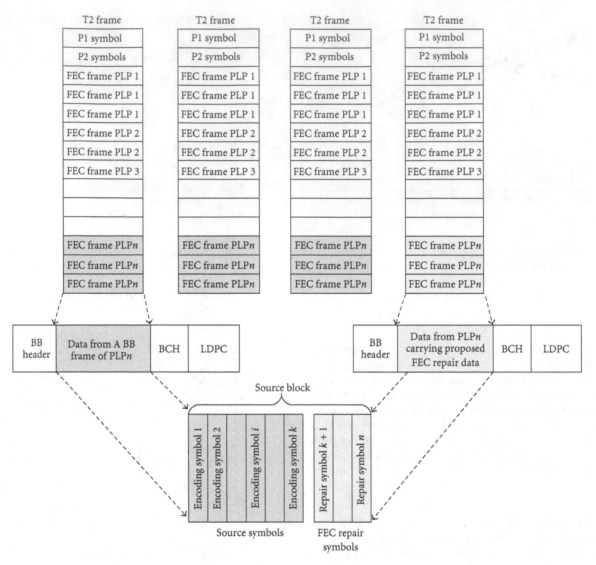

FIGURE 12: Example of a construction of a link layer FEC table.

The advantage of BB-FEC over MPE-FEC is that due to the mapping of one column to exactly one FEC frame the fragmentation of errors between many columns is avoided.

Additionally, if transmission of scalable service presented in Section 4 is considered, BB-FEC can be employed to enable unequal error protection. Two separate source blocks, as depicted on Figure 12, can be constructed one containing a BB frame with a base layer data and one containing a BB frame with enhancement layers. Next, in each of the source blocks different FEC code rates can be applied, and thus unequal error protection can be achieved.

Deciding which specific FEC code, for example, Reed-Solomon [27], Raptor, LDPC or other, to use in BB-FEC requires further studies. Moreover, it is important to specify the proper technique of decoding as it was shown in [28]. Therefore, the BB-FEC is presented here only as a concept and will be investigated in future work.

6. Further Optimization

In the previous sections it was shown that using FEC correction, and by proper data scheduling, efficiency in transmission can be achieved. However, it is also important to save the bandwidth where possible and use expensive resources efficiently. The data throughput is maximized by reducing overhead without losing functionality or by minimizing padding by proper data scheduling. In this section we show how IP/UDP header may be compressed which leads to a gain in the bandwidth.

6.1. Header Compression. Channel bandwidth is a scarce resource which should be utilized in the most efficient way. When source data is prepared for transmission each layer adds its own header to help properly decode the received data. Parts of the header data may be redundant depending on the transmission scenario. These protocol overheads can

TABLE 2: UDP header.

Bits Offset	0–15	16–31
0	Source Port	Destination Port
32	Length	Checksum

TABLE 3: IPv6 header.

Bits Offset	0–7	8–15	16–23	24–31
0	Version	Traffic Class	Flow Label	
32		Payload Length	Next Header	Hop Limit
64		Source Address		
96				
128				
160				
192		Destination Address		
224				
256				
288				

be minimized, without sacrificing functionality, by tailoring the headers to the bearer needs, which consequently would lead to network throughput improvement.

Data is transmitted over the Internet using protocols which allow routing over a path with multiple hops. Thus, protocol headers are important to ensure reliable interchange of data over a communication channel with multiple hops. However, in hop-to-hop case where only one link exists, such as DVB-T2, many of the header fields, which are used in traditional Internet, serve no useful purpose and are redundant.

In DVB system the overhead of transmitted data usually comprises 8 bytes of UDP header, presented in Table 2, 40 bytes of IP header, presented in Table 3, and 7 to 10 bytes of GSE header, 2 bytes of MPE header and 4 bytes of CRC, or 4 bytes of ULE header and 4 bytes of CRC check. If MPE or ULE is used as an IP carrier then, additionally, 4 bytes of TS header for every 184 bytes of data is added. If the average protocol data unit (PDU), for example RTP packet, size is assumed to be 1000 bytes, the overhead is 55 or 58 bytes when GSE is used, 88 bytes when MPE over TS is used, and 84 bytes when ULE over TS is used. Choosing GSE instead of MPE over TS may already bring a 35 to 37% overhead reduction with similar error performance. However, in all of the cases the largest part of the overhead is IP/UDP header which is 48 bytes for each data packet irrespective of its size. IP/UDP data header information is hardly used for point-to-point broadcast transmission. The information transmitted by IP header may be extracted from lower layer or from out of the band signalling. The large part of the IP header and UDP header fields are constant and repeated from packet to packet.

There are many header compression schemes [29] which are adopted by various standardization bodies including 3GPP [30] and 3GPP2 [31]. However, these technologies assume an existence of the return channel which excludes their use in DVB-T2 broadcast scenario. Therefore, a new scheme dedicated to DVB-T2 should be created.

The fields of the IPv6 header such as Traffic Class, Flow Label, Next Header, Hop Limit, and Source Address are static for each packet and could be transmitted out of band. The functionality of the remaining three fields, Version, Payload Length, and Destination Address, could be shifted to lower layers. If this is done, then the whole IP header would be redundant and could be deleted. Similar to IPv6 header, in UDP header, source port field value could be transmitted out of band and the length value extracted from lower layers. In Table 4, a possible gain, when IP/UDP header deletion is used, is presented.

From Table 4 it can be seen that the size of the transmitted PDU should be as large as possible. Moreover, if the overhead is taken as a criterion then GSE should be used as the encapsulation method. By properly choosing the average packet size (APS) as well as the used encapsulation method the gain can be significant, from 41% when the APS is 100 bytes and MPE is used to 3.98% when the APS is 1400 and GSE is used. Further, if IP/UDP header is compressed the overhead goes below 1%. If two extreme cases are compared the data throughput difference is about 40%.

6.2. IP Encapsulation. Transmission errors after physical layer decoding are seen at the BB frame level. It is assumed that if the combined BCH/LDPC FEC decoding fails, then the whole BB frame is marked as lost. To minimize the effects of a BB frame loss, a scheduling algorithm for optimized mapping of service data to the data field of the BB frames is now presented. The scheduler constitutes a part of the preprocessor in the DVB-T2 transmission chain. One scheduler is allocated for each PLP in order to operate on the data packets of that PLP.

In [32], we proposed a scheduling algorithm that avoids fragmentation of the IP packets containing media data of higher importance. By avoiding fragmentation of important media units, improved error resilience is achieved. Additionally, restricted time interleaving is applied to IP packets that contain media units of a higher importance access unit. Time interleaving spreads the media units of an access unit across multiple T2 frames. Consequently, losses which are typically of a bursty nature would most likely not affect the complete access unit. As an example, an intradecoder refresh IDR picture that consists of several slices would ultimately be mapped into several BB frames that are spread over multiple T2 frames. Transmission errors may corrupt a set of consecutive BB frames depending on the burst length. Due to the time interleaving, the impact of loss of a set of consecutive BB frames would less likely result in significant loss to the random access points.

As mentioned earlier, the time interleaving is restricted to limit the required initial buffering time and to keep the channel switch time within an acceptable range. The number of T2 frames that are used for the time interleaving of the random access point and the related group of pictures is restricted to 1 to 1.5 seconds. With a typical T2 frame duration of 250 ms, the total number of T2 frames used for time interleaving a group of pictures is then 4 to 6 T2 frames.

TABLE 4: Transmission overheads.

Average Packet Size [bytes]	Uncompressed IP/UDP headers			Compressed IP/UDP headers		
	MPE [%]	ULE [%]	GSE [%]	MPE [%]	ULE [%]	GSE [%]
100	41,52	38.65	36,71	21,26	15.97	12,28
200	28,06	25.93	22,48	14,53	11.50	6,54
400	17,53	16.14	12,66	9,30	7.62	3,38
600	13,29	12.28	8,81	7,41	6.25	2,28
800	11,01	10.21	6,76	6,43	5.55	1,72
1000	9,58	8.93	5,48	5,84	5.12	1,38
1200	8,61	8.05	4,61	5,44	4.84	1,15
1400	7,89	7.41	3,98	5,15	4.63	0,99

TABLE 5: PSNR and Packet error rate (crew).

BB frame error rate [%]	Generic		Proposed Scheduling Algorithm	
	Packet error rate [%]	PSNR [dB]	Packet error rate [%]	PSNR [dB]
7.33	9.12	28.72	9.03	29.19
3.32	4.42	32.48	4.43	32.74
1.80	2.22	34.93	2.14	35.63
1.55	2.03	35.26	2.01	35.66
0.00	0.00	39.85	0.00	39.85

The size of the data field in a BB frame for a specific service depends on the selected modulation scheme and the physical layer FEC code rate. Upon determining the size of the payload of a BB frame, the number of BB frames needed to transmit the set of pictures of the video stream can be calculated based on the total size of the media units to be transmitted. The number, M, of BB frames allocated for the service in each T2 frame can be dynamically determined according to the following equation:

$$M = \frac{S}{(PS \times N)},$$ (1)

where PS is a payload size of the BB frame allocated for the service, N is number of T2 frames, S is a total size of media units over the duration of N T2 frames.

After determining the BB frame allocation over the set of T2 frames, the scheduling algorithm proceeds by mapping media data packets to BB frames. The target thereby is manifold. First, the mapping algorithm avoids fragmentation of important media units over more than one BB frame. Secondly, it aims at providing maximum error resilience through time interleaving. Finally, the algorithm aims at increasing bandwidth usage efficiency by avoiding total fragmentation overhead and padding operations.

The problem discussed above is equivalent to the bin packing problem (packing objects of different sizes and weights/importance into bins of equal sizes) [33] and is an NP-hard problem. A heuristic solution to keep the complexity within a still manageable range while achieving a close to optimal solution is followed. The algorithm is described below.

(1) Arrange media packets in descending order of importance.

(2) Start from higher importance media packets (e.g., those containing base layer IDR pictures) and assign them to maximally distant BB frames.

(3) For the rest of the media packets, order media packets according to their size in decreasing order.

(4) Loop through the set of media packets and

   (a) assign packet to the best fitting BB frame (the BB frame that leaves the least free space after adding the media packet);

   (b) if no fitting BB frame is found queue the media packet at the tail of the set of media packets;

   (c) stop if no media packet can be mapped to available free space;

   (d) end Loop.

(5) Fragment the left-over media packets starting from the first BB frame.

The proposed scheduling algorithm is wellsuited for handling scalable media such as an SVC media stream. The scheduler complexity is limited to the handling of the RTP packet header and the RTP payload format. Given that the set of media encoding options in a broadcast scenario is limited, this additional functionality would not significantly increase the complexity of the scheduler.

Now, a comparison of the scheduling method described above and the generic approach without scheduling is presented.

TABLE 6: PSNR and Packet error rate (crowd).

BB frame error rate [%]	Generic		Proposed Scheduling Algorithm	
	Packet error rate [%]	PSNR [dB]	Packet error rate [%]	PSNR [dB]
7.33	8.81	23.81	8.67	24.04
3.32	4.48	26.15	4.45	26.00
1.80	2.23	27.48	2.18	27.99
1.55	2.07	27.95	2.04	28.09
0.00	0.00	30.88	0.00	30.88

TABLE 7: Number of erroneous packets (crew).

BB frame error rate [%]	Generic			Proposed Scheduling Algorithm			
	I	P	B	I	P	B	
7.33	169	1034	236	139	913	373	Error packets
	72	419	91	0	246	342	Error packets due to fragmentation
3.32	88	481	129	54	470	175	Error packets
	43	229	67	0	154	174	Error packets due to fragmentation
1.80	38	255	58	36	204	97	Error packets
	13	94	20	0	27	95	Error packets due to fragmentation
1.55	33	219	68	21	184	112	Error packets
	16	92	32	0	39	101	Error packets due to fragmentation

For the simulations, the crew and crowd sequences, with a resolution of 1280 × 720 and 600 and 500 frames, respectively, were used. The sequences were encoded using the main profile of H.264/AVC. To create a simple temporal scalability structure, every second picture was encoded as a nonreference B picture. This meant that a base layer with 15 fps and an enhancement layer with 30 fps were created. The encoding parameters were set as follows. Bitrate ~8 Mbits/s, an IDR picture was inserted once every 30 pictures and the maximum slice size was set to 1300 bytes.

To conduct the simulations, an Input preprocessor (IPP) was implemented. The physical layer transmission over a DVB-T2 bearer was simulated to generate BB frame error patterns that were used for evaluating the optimization approaches. Four different error patterns, containing 1.55%, 1.80%, 3.32%, and 7.33% lost BB frames respectively, were used throughout the simulations. Based on the bit-error patterns, a BB frame was marked as lost if the BCH/LDPC decoding process fails to recover from the bit errors at that BB frame.

Each NAL unit of the encoded sequence is packetized as a GSE packet, where an additional 67 bytes header is added to correspond to the GSE/IP/UDP/RTP headers. The subsequent scheduling is performed by the scheduler submodule of the IPP module, which operates on sets of packets that belong to a single group of pictures (GoP).

At the receiver side, the resulting errors at the BB frames were mapped on the data packets, where the loss of one or more data fragments of a data packet would result in discarding of the whole packet as it would be useless for the media decoder. Next, the lost NAL units were discarded from the error-free sequence, and erroneous bit-stream was decoded using H.264/AVC decoder with motion vector copy error concealment method.

The following configurations of the scheduler have been analyzed in the simulations.

(1) A generic approach without scheduling. The scheduler based on data field length of BB frame fragments the packets as they come and adds new GSE header and CRC check to fragmented packet.

(2) A cross-layer approach where the scheduler uses information from the physical layer (data filed length of a BB frame) and application layer (priority of the packet). Based on that information an algorithm, described in this subsection, was examined.

In Tables 5 and 6 PSNR values and packet loss rates are depicted for each of the tested configuration for crew and crowd sequences, respectively. It can be seen that thanks to the proposed cross layer scheduling approach, the packet loss rate can be reduced and consequently around 0.5 dB PSNR gain was achieved.

The gain in PSNR is achieved not only by packet loss reduction but also due to spreading errors through less important packets. In Tables 7 and 8, the number of erroneous packets as well as the number of erroneous packets as a result of the fragmentation process are presented.

The results show that due to scheduling none of the packets belonging to I frames is lost because of fragmentation. Additionally, due to the time interleaving applied to the I packets, a reduced number of these packets are affected by errors. Moreover, it is shown that the proposed scheduling method move most of the errors to the packets belonging to the less important B frames.

In Figures 13 and 14, PSNR plots for the first 120 frames of both sequences crew and crowd, after transmission over the channel with highest BB frame error rate, are presented.

TABLE 8: Number of erroneous packets (crowd).

BB frame error rate [%]	Generic			Proposed Scheduling Algorithm			
	I	P	B	I	P	B	
7.33	142	801	210	137	707	291	Error packets
	57	321	82	0	183	287	Error packets due to fragmentation
3.32	93	427	66	75	368	140	Error packets
	47	204	32	0	165	121	Error packets due to fragmentation
1.80	27	226	39	33	161	91	Error packets
	10	85	13	0	26	81	Error packets due to fragmentation
1.55	31	201	39	34	141	92	Error packets
	14	88	18	0	17	90	Error packets due to fragmentation

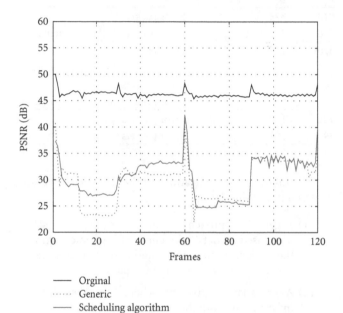

- Orginal
- Generic
- Scheduling algorithm

FIGURE 13: PSNR of crew sequence for the first 120 frames.

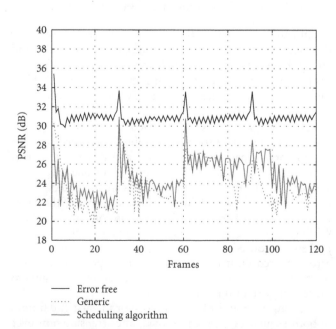

- Error free
- Generic
- Scheduling algorithm

FIGURE 14: PSNR of crowd sequence for the first 120 frames.

It can be seen that due to the spread of errors among packets rapid quality change can be avoided, as for example, in the first 30 frames of the crew sequence. Additionally, it can be observed that on both plots almost all I frames (30th, 60th, 90th, and 120th frames) have higher PSNR value when scheduling algorithm is used. Consequently, it should lead to less prediction errors which would be visible during playback of the decoded video. Even scheduling algorithm may sometimes show a weaker performance than that of the generic transmission, for example, it can be seen on Figure 13, frames 60 to 90, that the overall results proved that due to the scheduling algorithm the errors are moved to the less important data packets which lead to unequal error resilience of the transmitted stream. Finally, it should be noted that the 0.5 dB gain on average achieved by scheduling algorithm does not fully reflect the subjective gain which may be achieved by a viewer.

7. Conclusions

This paper discussed the use of DVB-T2 system as a bearer for mobile data using H.264/SVC. Three important challenges for mobile transmission: power consumption, transmission errors, and data throughput were discussed. A scheduling method exploiting H.264/SVC bit-stream characteristics so as to reduce power consumption was proposed. Due to the grouping of each scalable layer into separate transmission data bursts, a receiver with lower capabilities would be able to reduce power consumption by receiving only relevant data. Furthermore, a bursty transmission introduces further time interleaving on application layer data and consequently makes the transmitted data more robust to errors. Since DVB-T2 was developed with portable receivers as one of the target user groups, it comes with dedicated tools to cope with an error-prone mobile transmission channel. The performance of these tools was investigated, and the results showed that they can bring significant gain. To bring additional flexibility to the DVB-T2 transmission system, a BB-FEC concept was proposed. The introduction of BB-FEC enables unequal error protection on transmitted data even if one PLP is used for service transmission. Finally, when mobile channels are considered, bandwidth is a scare resource which has to be utilized optimally. Three popular encapsulation methods were compared from an overhead perspective, and IP/UDP overhead compression was discussed. A novel packet scheduling method, which uses the bandwidth efficiently and provide unequal error resilience for transmitted packet, was described and supported by simulation results.

Acknowledgment

This work was partially supported by Nokia and the Academy of Finland, Project No. 129657 (Finish Centre of Excellence program 2006–2011).

References

[1] ETSI EN 302 755 V 1.1.1, "Digital Video Broadcasting (DVB): frame structure channel coding and modulation for a second generation digital terrestrial television broadcasting system (DVB-T2)," Draft, July 2008.

[2] "DVB-T2—the HDTV generation of terrestrial DTV," DVB-TM-3997, March 2008.

[3] ITU-T Recommendation, H.264, "Advance Video Coding for generic audiovisual services," November 2007.

[4] ETSI TS 102 005 V1.4.1, "Digital Video Broadcasting (DVB); specification for the use of Video and Audio Coding in DVB services delivered directly over IP protocols," Working Draft.

[5] T. Schierl, C. Hellge, S. Mirta, K. Grüneberg, and T. Wiegand, "Using H.264/AVC-based scalable video coding (SVC) for real time streaming in wireless IP networks," in Proceedings of the IEEE International Symposium on Circuits and Systems (ISCAS '07), pp. 3455–3458, May 2007.

[6] R. C. Bose and D. K. Ray-Chaudhuri, "On a class of error correcting binary group codes," Information and Control, vol. 3, no. 1, pp. 68–79, 1960.

[7] R. G. Gallager, "Low-density parity-check codes," IRE Transactions on Information Theory, vol. 8, no. 1, pp. 21–28, 1962.

[8] ISO/IEC IS 13818-1, "Information technology—generic coding of moving pictures and associated audio information: systems".

[9] ETSI TS 102 606 V1.1.1, "Digital Video Broadcasting (DVB); Generic Stream Encapsulation (GSE) Protocol," October 2007.

[10] ETSI EN 301 192 V 1.4.2, "Digital Video Broadcasting (DVB); DVB specification for data broadcasting," April 2008.

[11] IETF RFC 4326, G. Fairhurst, and B. Collini-Nocker, "Unidirectional Lightweight Encapsulation (ULE) for Transmission of IP Datagrams over an MPEG-2 Transport Stream (TS)," December 2005.

[12] ISO/IEC IS 13818-2, "Information Technology—generic coding of moving pictures and associated audio information: video".

[13] ITU-T Recommendation, "H.263: Video Coding for Low Bit Rate Communication," 1998.

[14] ISO/IEC IS 14496-2, "Information Technology—Coding of Audio-Visual Objects—Part 2: Visual," 1998.

[15] M. Wien, H. Schwarz, and T. Oelbaum, "Performance analysis of SVC," IEEE Transactions on Circuits and Systems for Video Technology, vol. 17, no. 9, pp. 1194–1203, 2007.

[16] C. Hellge, T. Schierl, and T. Wiegand, "Mobile TV using scalable video coding and layer-aware forward error correction," in Proceedings of the IEEE International Conference on Multimedia and Expo (ICME '08), pp. 1177–1180, 2008.

[17] H. Schwarz, D. Marpe, and T. Wiegand, "Overview of the scalable video coding extension of the H.264/AVC standard,"

IEEE Transactions on Circuits and Systems for Video Technology, vol. 17, no. 9, pp. 1103–1120, 2007.

[18] "Special issue on scalable video coding-standardization and beyond," IEEE Transactions on Circuits and Systems for Video Technology, vol. 17, no. 9, pp. 1097–1269, 2007.

[19] ETSI EN 302 304 V 1.1.1, "Digital Video Broadcasting (DVB); Transmission System for Handheld Terminals (DVB-H)," November 2004.

[20] L. Kondrad, I. Bouazizi, and M. Gabbouj, "Media aware FEC for scalable video coding transmission," in Proceedings of the IEEE Symposium on Computers and Communications, pp. 7–12, Sousse, Tunisia, July 2009.

[21] ETSI TR 102 831 V1.1, "Implementation guidelines for a second generation digital terrestrial television broadcasting system (DVB-T2)," February 2009.

[22] M. Rezaei, M. M. Hannuksela, and M. Gabbouj, "Tune-in time reduction in video streaming over DVB-H," IEEE Transactions on Broadcasting, vol. 53, no. 1, part 2, pp. 320–328, 2007, special issue on Mobile Multimedia Broadcasting.

[23] J. Lei, M. A. Vazquez Castro, F. Vieira, and T. Stockhammer, "Application of link layer FEC to DVB-S2 for railway scenarios," in Proceedings of the 10th International Workshop on Signal Processing for Space Communications (SPSC '08), October 2008.

[24] A. Shokrollahi, "Raptor codes," IEEE Transactions on Information Theory, vol. 52, no. 6, pp. 2551–2567, 2006.

[25] DVB BlueBook A131, "Digital Video Broadcasting (DVB); MPE-IFEC," November 2008.

[26] V. K. M. Vadakital, M. Hannuksela, H. Pekkonen, and M. Gabbouj, "On datacasting of H.264/AVC over DVB-H," in Proceedings of the 7th IEEE Workshop on Multimedia Signal Processing (MMSP '05), p. 4, Shanghai, China, October-November 2005.

[27] L. Rizzo, "Effective erasure codes for reliable computer communication protocols," ACM Computer Communication Review, vol. 27, pp. 24–36, 1997.

[28] J. Paavola, H. Himmanen, T. Jokela, J. Poikonen, and V. Ipatov, "The performance analysis of MPE-FEC decoding methods at the DVB-H link layer for efficient IP packet retrieval," IEEE Transactions on Broadcasting, vol. 53, no. 1, pp. 263–275, 2007.

[29] ITEF RFC 1144 and V. Jacobson, "Compressing TCP/IP Headers for Low-Speed Serial Links," February 1990.

[30] http://www.3gpp.org/.

[31] http://www.3gpp2.org/.

[32] L. Kondrad, I. Bouazizi, V. K. M. Vadakital, M. M. Hannuksela, and M. Gabbouj, "Cross-layer optimized transmission of H.264/SVC streams over DVB-T2 broadcast system," in Proceedings of the IEEE International Symposium on Broadband Multimedia Systems and Broadcasting (BMSB '09), pp. 1–5, May 2009.

[33] S. Martello and P. Toth, "A mixture of dynamic programming and branch-and-bound for the subset-sum problem," Management Science, vol. 30, no. 6, pp. 765–771, 1984.

11

Resource Allocation with MAC Layer Node Cooperation in Cognitive Radio Networks

Andreas Merentitis and Dionysia Triantafyllopoulou

Department of Informatics and Telecommunications, University of Athens, Panepistimiopolis, Ilissia, 15784 Athens, Greece

Correspondence should be addressed to Dionysia Triantafyllopoulou, siarina@di.uoa.gr

Academic Editor: Hamid Sadjadpour

An algorithm for cooperative Dynamic Spectrum Access in Cognitive Radio networks is presented. The proposed algorithm utilizes Medium Access Control layer mechanisms for message exchange between secondary nodes that operate in license exempt spectrum bands, in order to achieve interference mitigation. A fuzzy logic reasoner is utilized in order to take into account the effect of the coexistence of a large number of users in the interference as well as to cope for uncertainties in the message exchange, caused by the nodes' mobility and the large delays in the updating of the necessary information. The proposed algorithm is applied in Filter Bank Multicarrier, as well as Orthogonal Frequency Division Multiplexing systems, and its performance is evaluated through extensive simulations that cover a wide range of typical scenarios. Experimental results indicate improved behaviour compared to previous schemes, especially in the case of uncertainties that cause underestimation of the interference levels.

1. Introduction

The proliferation of mobile devices, coupled with the ever-increasing demand for higher data rates' support, constitutes static frequency allocation schemes suboptimal, as they frequently result in spectrum underutilization. Cognitive Radios (CRs) supporting Opportunistic Spectrum Access (OSA) [1] emerged as a new paradigm that offers an effective solution to the problem of spectrum scarcity. However, the increased variance in spectrum availability combined with the end users' diverse characteristics and Quality of Service (QoS) requirements poses a number of challenges that need to be addressed.

More specifically, for Cognitive Radio systems operating in licensed spectrum bands with coexistence of both primary and secondary users, the operations of spectrum sensing, defined as the identification of the spectrum bands that are available for transmission, and spectrum mobility, that is, the vacation of the wireless channel when a primary user is detected, are of key importance. On the other hand, Cognitive Radio systems operating in license exempt spectrum bands, where different operators coexist, require efficient spectrum decision and spectrum sharing algorithms as well as power control mechanisms for interference mitigation. For example, if all users transmit at the maximum valid power level, then every user is causing significant interference to all the others, a fact that can result in reduced total utility from the network perspective and, finally, poor QoS for the end users.

In this scope, algorithms that employ cooperative spectrum sharing in order to maximize the overall system performance are required. These algorithms need to be *distributed*, in order to be applied efficiently in ad hoc networks operating in unlicensed spectrum bands where synchronization is necessary only for users of the same operator. Such algorithms should also be able to employ *efficient message exchange* schemes in order to maximize the overall system utility (therefore, the related systems are classified as cooperative CR systems); however, uncertainties in message exchange should also be considered. Furthermore, they should be able to *converge* to an optimal solution within a finite number of iterations to be applicable to real systems.

In order to address some of the previous challenges, the authors in [2] propose a price-based iterative water-filling algorithm which allows users to converge to the Nash Equilibrium. This algorithm can be implemented in a distributed manner with CRs negotiating their best transmission powers and spectrum. In [3], a Dynamic Open Spectrum Sharing Medium Access Control (MAC) protocol for wireless ad hoc networks is proposed. This protocol performs real-time dynamic spectrum allocation by allowing nodes to adaptively select an arbitrary spectrum for the incipient communication subject to spectrum availability. In [4], a distributed approach to spectrum allocation that starts from the previous spectrum assignment and performs a limited number of computations to adapt to recent topology changes is considered. According to the proposed local bargaining approach, the users affected by a mobility event self-organize into bargaining groups and adapt their spectrum assignment to approximate a new optimal conflict-free assignment. The authors in [5] propose a graph-theoretic model for efficient and fair access in open spectrum systems. Three policy-driven utility functions that combine efficient spectrum utilization and fairness are described, and a vertex labeling mechanism is used to build both centralized and distributed approximation algorithms. In [6], a group-based coordination scheme, and distributed group setup and maintenance algorithms where users select coordination channels adaptively are proposed. In [7], an algorithm that allows for transmission power and transmission frequencies to be chosen simultaneously by Cognitive Radios competing to communicate over a frequency spectrum is proposed. Finally, in [8], an algorithm in which each user selects a single channel along with its transmission power by taking into account information concerning the interference caused to other users in the network is introduced.

In this paper, an algorithm based on the spectrum sharing scheme of [8] for distributed interference compensation in Cognitive Radios that operate in license exempt spectrum bands is proposed. The proposed algorithm refines the utility function used in [8] to improve the system scalability in the case of a large number of user pairs and to take into account uncertainties that may be the result of user mobility and large delays in the update of the interference prices. More specifically, a fuzzy logic reasoner is utilized in order to take into account the effect of a large number of users and the related interference as well as to cope for uncertainties in the message exchange process. The performance of the proposed algorithm is evaluated through simulations. In this direction, the overall utility value of the algorithm is compared to the utility of a simple "always select the maximum valid power" policy. The proposed algorithm is also applied in both Filter Bank Multicarrier (FBMC) and Orthogonal Frequency Division Multiplexing (OFDM) systems in order to show its flexibility and capability of transparently exploiting an improved Physical layer, without any further modifications. Moreover, comparison with the distributed algorithm of [8] is used to validate the improvement in terms of the overall utility level under uncertainties that cause 25% underestimation of the interference. Finally, in order to quantify the improvement

using conventional network metrics and to show the relation between a higher overall utility value and parameters that directly affect the user experience, comparison with the algorithm of [8] in terms of Signal-to-Interference-plus-Noise Ratio (SINR) is also performed. Experimental results indicate that SINR is consistently improved with the use of the proposed algorithm.

The rest of the paper is organized as follows. Section 2 describes in detail the proposed algorithm. Fuzzy Inference for defining the algorithm parameters is outlined in Section 3. In Section 4, the performance of the proposed algorithm is evaluated through simulations. Finally, Section 5 contains conclusions and plans for future work.

2. Algorithm Outline

The main idea of the proposed algorithm is that users exchange information concerning their interference levels, using explicit MAC layer message exchange mechanisms. A transmitter sets its power level by considering not only its own SINR information, but also the negative impact in utility for other users caused from the greater interference that will come as a side effect of the increase in transmission power of that particular user. This functions as a counter-motive that prevents users from always increasing their transmission power towards the maximum valid level.

Assuming a system with a total of L user pairs in a spectrum band with K available channels, the SINR of the ith user pair, $i \in \{1, 2, \ldots, L\}$ in the kth channel, $k \in \{1, 2, \ldots, K\}$, is given by the following equation [8]:

$$\gamma_i\left(p_i^k\right) = \frac{p_i^k \cdot h_{ii}}{n_0 + \sum_{j \neq i} p_j^k \cdot h_{ji}}, \qquad (1)$$

where p_i^k is the transmission power for user i on channel k, h_{ii} is the link gain between the ith receiver and the ith transmitter, $n_0 = 10^{-2}$ is the noise level, p_j^k, $j \in \{1, 2, \ldots, L\}$, $j \neq i$, is the transmission power for all other users on channel k, and h_{ji} is the link gain between the ith receiver and the jth transmitter. It should be noted that $h_{ij} \neq h_{ji}$, since the first expresses the gain between the ith transmitter and the jth receiver and the latter expresses the gain between the jth transmitter and the ith receiver.

In the general case, the carrier frequency of a signal is varied; therefore the magnitude of the change in amplitude will also vary. The coherence bandwidth measures the separation in frequency after which two signals will experience uncorrelated fading. More specifically, in the case of frequency-selective fading, the coherence bandwidth of the channel is smaller than the bandwidth of the signal. Thus, different frequency components of the signal experience decorrelated fading. On the other hand, in the case of flat fading, the coherence bandwidth of the channel is larger than the bandwidth of the signal. Therefore, all frequency components of the signal will experience the same magnitude of fading. In the following analysis, a flat-faded channel without shadowing effects is assumed. For a flat-faded channel, there are no delay spread and no frequency selectivity, as mentioned previously. Thus, a single coefficient is used for channel attenuation. Since the described channel is static, that is, the coefficient is fixed, the only attenuation present is the path loss. Therefore, in this particular case, h is strictly the channel attenuation or channel gain. In this paper, the environment is assumed to cause average-to-high loss (path loss exponent equals three, a value typical for indoor urban environments), thus the channel gain is $h_{ji} = d_{ji}^{-3}$, where d is the distance between the jth transmitter and the ith receiver.

In order to model the impact on utility for user i caused by the transmission of all other users, the notion of interference price is adopted from [8]. Interference price is defined as

$$\pi_i^k = \frac{\partial u_i\left(\gamma_i\left(p_i^k\right)\right)}{\partial\left(\sum_{j \neq i} p_j^k \cdot h_{ji}\right)}, \tag{2}$$

where $u_i(\gamma_i(p_i^k)) = \theta_i \log(\gamma_i(p_i^k))$ is the logarithmic utility function and θ_i is a user-dependent parameter. As shown, the interference price expresses the marginal utility degradation due to a marginal increase in sustained interference. Interference prices are exchanged between the users in a completely asynchronous fashion, while every user is able to update its own price and power level at different times. Each user selects an appropriate transmission power level in order to maximize the difference between the increase in its own utility minus the utility degradation for others, caused by the increased interference as expressed by the interference price. Specifically, the mathematical formula that [8] attempts to maximize is

$$u_i\left(\gamma_i\left(p_i^k\right)\right) - p_i^k \sum_{j \neq i} \pi_j^k \cdot h_{ji}. \tag{3}$$

The first part of this equation is closely related to the Shannon capacity for user i (the constant term is excluded in order to have a form that can be proved to converge in all cases [8]). Increasing that part is directly related to an increase in the maximum bit rate. However, since the transmission of every user is considered as noise by the other users, the second term expresses the utility loss of the other users if user i increases its transmission power level.

The algorithm is comprised by the following steps.

(1) *Initialization*: For every user $i \in \{1, 2, \ldots, L\}$ transmitting in channel k, select a valid transmission power level p_i^k and a positive value for the interference price π_i^k.

(2) *Power Update*: For every user i at a time interval $t_{ai} \in T_i$, where T_i is a set of positive time instances in which the user i will update its transmission power level and $t_{a1} \neq t_{a2} \neq \cdots \neq t_{ai}$, set p_i^k to maximize (3).

(3) *Interference Price Update*: For every user i at a time interval $t_{bi} \in T_i'$, where T_i' is a set of positive time instances in which the user i will update its interference price and $t_{b1} \neq t_{b2} \neq \cdots \neq t_{bi}$, calculate and announce the updated interference price π_i^k and notify the other users for the updated value.

Steps (2) and (3) are repeated asynchronously for all users until the algorithm reaches its final steady state. In order to perform the power update of step (2), users select p_i^k from the set TP of the allowable transmission power levels, so that the surplus of (3) is maximized. Provided that the allowable power levels are equidistant values with each one being derived from its previous by adding a constant increment, then it can be proved that the algorithm converges, as long as the increment is sufficiently small. Moreover, if the problem is partitioned so that there is a single available spectrum area, or the algorithm is executed only for subgroups selecting the same spectrum area M, then it converges to a global maximum under arbitrary asynchronous updates [8].

In order to execute the algorithm, every user in the network needs to know its own SINR value and channel gain as well as the channel gains and the interference prices announced by other users. The SINR and the channel gain between a user pair can be calculated at the receiver and forwarded back to the transmitter. The channel gains between users can be calculated if receivers periodically broadcast a beacon [9] (h_{ii} message between Receiver i and Transmitter i in Figure 1). This information can also be provided on demand through a specially defined message sent from the receiver. Thus, in case the transmitter requires channel gain information before the reception of the next scheduled beacon, it can request this information from the receiver who will respond with the relative measurements. Finally, interference price values can be also conveyed in the same manner (message π_{ij} from Receiver i to Transmitter j in Figure 1). Every user announces a single interference price, therefore the delay that is introduced by the algorithm scales linearly with the number of users. This also implies that, given the fact that the updates are distributed in an asynchronous manner, the complexity of the algorithm is polynomial to the number of users and available power levels (that depend on the size of the increment in the Power Update step).

In the original version of the algorithm of [8], an underestimation of the interference prices is likely to occur in some cases. This can be caused by problems in message exchange, for example, due to users' mobility or increased update time intervals for the interference prices, considering that updates are asynchronous for all users. The effect of this underestimation is the convergence of the algorithm to a nonoptimal solution. Moreover, as the number of user pairs increases, the highest allowable transmission power level is more likely to be chosen, since the previous problems escalate. This is not desirable, since it will often result in increased interference to a potentially large number of neighboring users, especially in the case that the interference is underestimated for the reasons mentioned above.

Therefore, in this work, a coefficient "α" is introduced in order to improve the scalability of the algorithm in case a large number of users are sharing the same spectrum band and to cope with uncertainties, such as large update intervals and problems in the message exchange mechanism. In both cases, there is a danger that the impact of the interference on other users due to the increase in transmission power

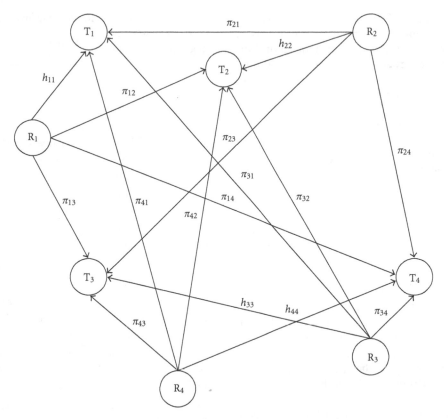

FIGURE 1: An example network topology with four transmitter-receiver pairs.

will be underestimated as explained above. Thus, factor α needs to avert this scenario by increasing the weight of the second term of (3), which expresses the utility loss other users will experience from a transmission power increase. In such cases, it will compensate for the underestimation of interference, by increasing the value of the second term and, therefore, it can result in a system that approximates the case of "perfect" message exchange (without long delays, reduced message range, etc. that reduce the second term in (3)).

If coefficient α is included as a weight multiplied with the subtracted interference term, then the following equation is derived, that is the objective to be maximized:

$$u_i\left(\gamma_i\left(p_i^k\right)\right) - a \cdot p_i^k \sum_{j \neq i} \pi_j^k \cdot h_{ji}. \quad (4)$$

In a "real" protocol implementation, parameters such as the storage requirements and scalability of the message exchange mechanism should be addressed. Moreover, the overhead and delays introduced by message exchange should be taken into consideration together with parameters such as timeliness and path optimality (for increased reliability in message transmission). However, the performance of the original version of the algorithm in [8] was shown not to degrade sharply in case the message exchange is imperfect (e.g., if the nodes can only exchange messages with their closest neighbors up to a specific range, or if some messages are lost). This characteristic is the outcome of the fact that,

in the case of imperfect message exchange, the algorithm gracefully degrades towards the "worst case" scenario of unregulated transmission with the maximum allowable power level, as the value of the subtracted term is gradually underestimated in (3). The term "graceful degradation" refers to that fact that when a certain number of messages are lost, the performance of the system does not drop sharply towards the worst case. This characteristic is greatly desirable for systems that operate in faulty or unreliable environments (e.g., [10]). In this work, the previous property is further improved with the introduction of coefficient α that provides the capability to handle uncertainties.

3. Fuzzy Inference

Fuzzy logic is well suited for the purpose of defining the value of factor α since it can address vague and unclear requirements efficiently and the system can be easily fine-tuned to exhibit the desirable behavior. Fuzzy logic is based on fuzzy set theory, in which every object has a grade of membership in various sets. Inputs are mapped to membership functions or sets (fuzzification process). Knowledge of a restricted domain is captured in the form of linguistic rules. Relationships between two goals are defined using fuzzy inclusion and noninclusion between the support and hindering sets of the corresponding goals [11]. As a last step, the required output is defuzzified (to numerical) from the "THEN" part of the rules in order to produce the consequent.

An important advantage of fuzzy logic is that it can be applied transparently in combination with other well-known decision methods, such as multiobjective genetic algorithms [12] and game theoretic approaches [13]. Moreover, proper definition of the linguistic rules can be used to reduce signaling overhead by avoiding the ping-pong phenomenon, that is, when decisions or selections are made and the input variables are not constant but temporarily present regressive behavior. Network-related decision making and resource allocation based on fuzzy logic approaches have been proposed in various works, such as [14], with promising results.

For the previous reasons, but mainly due to its effectiveness in dealing with uncertainties and vague requirements, fuzzy logic was selected for defining the value of coefficient α, that is, the weight of the subtracted interference-related term in (4). Specifically, α is defined as:

$$\alpha = \frac{1}{\beta} \cdot \text{IW} + \gamma, \qquad (5)$$

Where IW is the Interference Weight derived after defuzzification. IW takes values in the range ($\beta_{\min}$–$\beta_{\max}$) in order to provide adequate resolution capabilities for the fuzzy reasoner, also according to the specific ranges of the membership functions. Parameter β has the value of $\beta_{\max}$, while γ equals 1. This implies that α cannot be greater than two, meaning that the underestimation of the interference is not expected to be greater than 100%. Beyond that point, message exchange is not considered very reliable and the algorithm degrades towards the "always transmit with the maximum power" case (although a portion of the underestimation is still alleviated). On the other hand, if uncertainties are very low, the first term of the sum is converging to zero and the value of the equation is approximately equal to that of the original algorithm. For all other cases the first term is a nonzero value in the (0,1) interval that compensates for a typical underestimation of the interference due to imperfect message exchange.

The fuzzy reasoner used for deriving α is of type "Mamdani", because it is intuitive, well suited for human input, flexible, and widely accepted. It receives three inputs (number of users, mobility level, and update time interval for the interference prices) and generates one output (the Interference Weight). The input membership functions are triangular (selected mainly for simplicity in calculations) and three membership functions per input variable are defined, therefore the number of fuzzy rules is $3^3 = 27$.

The membership functions for the output variable "Interference Weight" are five and the output value is set in the range (0–500), in order to achieve a greater degree of resolution and flexibility for the output of the fuzzy reasoner. The membership functions mf1–mf5 are given the labels "very low", "low", "moderate", "high" and "very high", respectively, in Table 1.

As can be seen, the number of users is selected to be the dominant factor, which has the greatest effect in the final outcome. This is a result of the fact that if the number of users is large, even a small increase in the transmission power of a user has the potential to cause increased interference

TABLE 1: Rules of the fuzzy reasoner.

Rule number	Users	Update interval	Mobility level	Consequent
1	Low	Low	Low	Very low
2	Low	Low	Moderate	Very low
3	Low	Low	High	Low
4	Low	Moderate	Low	Low
5	Low	Moderate	Moderate	Low
6	Low	Moderate	High	Low
7	Low	High	Low	Low
8	Low	High	Moderate	Low
9	Low	High	High	Moderate
10	Moderate	Low	Low	Low
11	Moderate	Low	Moderate	Low
12	Moderate	Low	High	Moderate
13	Moderate	Moderate	Low	Moderate
14	Moderate	Moderate	Moderate	Moderate
15	Moderate	Moderate	High	High
16	Moderate	High	Low	Moderate
17	Moderate	High	Moderate	High
18	Moderate	High	High	High
19	High	Low	Low	Moderate
20	High	Low	Moderate	High
21	High	Low	High	High
22	High	Moderate	Low	High
23	High	Moderate	Moderate	High
24	High	Moderate	High	Very high
25	High	High	Low	High
26	High	High	Moderate	Very high
27	High	High	High	Very high

and reduce the QoS to a large number of users if its effect is underestimated due to uncertainties in message exchange. The update time interval and the mobility level have similar weights but different behaviors. The first has a uniform effect over the entire valid range of update times; while the latter starts to affect the outcome only after a relatively high level, but after which it increases sharply, as only after a relatively high level of mobility is reached, users are likely to underestimate the interference they will cause to others (due to problems in message exchange, etc.).

The Defuzzification method used for generating the final crisp value is "Centroid", also known as "Center of Gravity (COG)". This method determines the center of the area below the combined membership function; therefore the final output u_{COG} is given from (6), where u_i are the centers of the membership functions $\mu_F(u)$:

$$u_{\text{COG}} = \frac{\sum_1^{27} u_i \cdot \mu_F(u_i) du}{\sum_1^{27} \mu_F(u_i) du}. \qquad (6)$$

The defuzzification method takes into account the area as a whole, counting overlapping regions only once.

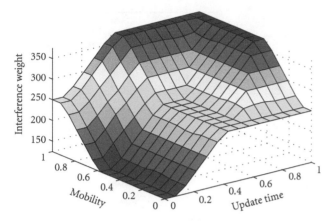

FIGURE 2: Interference weight as a function of the update interval and the mobility level.

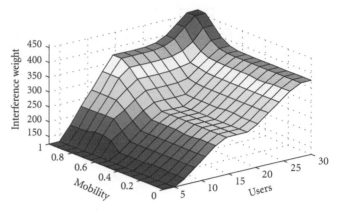

FIGURE 4: Interference weight as a function of the mobility level and the number of users.

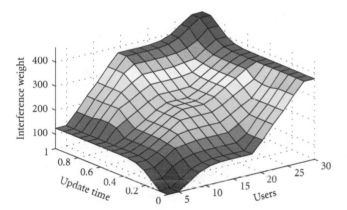

FIGURE 3: Interference weight as a function of the update interval and the number of users.

The three-dimensional (3D) representation of the Interference Weight (crisp value in the range (0–500)) as a function of the interference price update time interval and the mobility level is presented in Figure 2.

The coefficient increases with the update time interval as it is more likely that transmitters do not have the updated interference price information for other users. The increase is approximately uniform for the entire valid update time range. On the other hand, the coefficient also increases as the level of mobility increases. However, in this case the increase is not uniform but begins after a relatively high mobility level is reached and then rises quickly. The exhibited behavior is the outcome of the fuzzy rules defined in Table 1.

The 3D representation of the Interference Weight derived from the specified rule base and defuzzification method as a function of the interference price update time interval (defined as up to 100 seconds but normalized in the (0–1) range) and the number of users (up to 20 user pairs) is presented in Figure 3.

For the update time interval, the behavior is similar to that in the previous case. On the other hand, the coefficient also increases with the number of users. The increase is rather sharp (as determined by the rules in Table 1) and the value of the coefficient is rising quickly even for a relatively small

number of users. This is necessary because, as mentioned previously, when the number of user pairs is large, even a small increase in interference has the potential to affect many users and significantly decrease the overall utility of the network.

The 3D representation of the Interference Weight as a function of the number of users and the mobility level, depicted in Figure 4, is presenting for both parameters the behavior explained above. The overall form of the figure resembles the previous; however the mobility level is starting to affect the outcome only after a threshold is crossed, as expected according to the selected set of fuzzy rules.

The overall methodology for the derivation of the optimal transmission power of every user pair is depicted in Figure 5. Initially, the number of user pairs is defined, together with the mobility level and the update time interval for the interference prices. As a next step, fuzzification of the values takes place in order to prepare them for elaboration in a fuzzy logic context. Following the fuzzification process, fuzzy reasoning based on a set of predefined rules (Table 1) is applied. These rules describe the desired behaviour of the system and define the impact of the input parameters (number of users, mobility level, and update time interval) in the value of the Interference Weight. After fuzzy reasoning is completed, the result is defuzzified to numerical, giving the crisp value of the Interference Weight. The topology characteristics are used to initialize the simulator and every user selects a valid initial value for the transmission power level p_i^k and the interference price π_i^k. Finally, the users proceed to update their transmission power levels and interference prices asynchronously in order to maximize (4). The process is completed when the system reaches a steady point in which no user is requesting to modify its transmission level.

4. Performance Evaluation

The performance of the proposed algorithm is evaluated through extensive MATLAB simulations. In this direction, the overall utility value of the algorithm is initially compared to the utility of a simple "always select the maximum

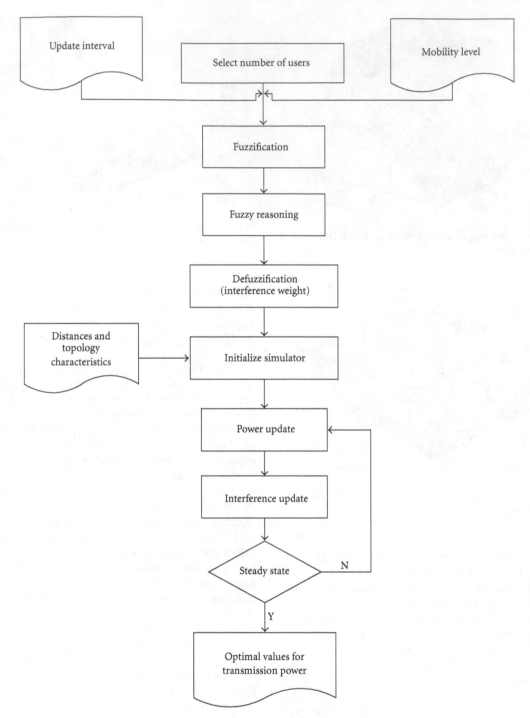

FIGURE 5: Overall methodology for deriving the transmission power levels.

valid power" policy as well as the utility of the original algorithm. The proposed algorithm is also applied in both FBMC and OFDM systems in order to validate its flexibility and capability of transparently exploiting an improved Physical layer, without any further modifications. Moreover, a scenario of long update time intervals in which some of the messages are delayed causing other nodes to not have the latest interference price information is considered, in order to study the performance of both algorithms in a specific case of nonideal message exchange. Finally, in order

to quantify the improvement using conventional network metrics and to show the relation between a higher overall utility value and parameters that directly affect the user experience, comparison with the algorithm of [8] in terms of SINR is also performed.

As explained previously, users set their power level so as to maximize (4). The total "useful" utility for the network is the sum of the utilities for every user pair. The distance between users that constitute a pair is a random number in the (1–20) meters range, while the distance between users

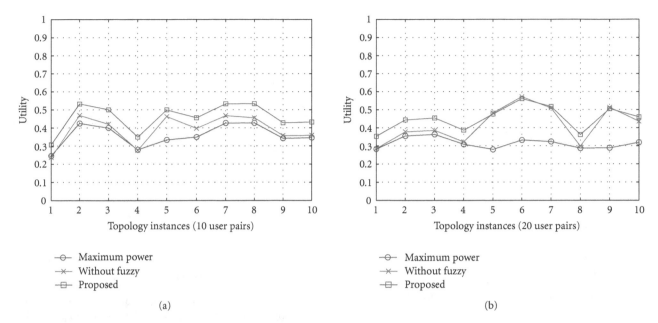

FIGURE 6: Utility values for the proposed algorithm, the always transmit with the maximum valid power scenario and the original algorithm without coefficient α for (a) 10 and (b) 20 user pairs.

that are not a pair is a random value in the [5, 50] meters range. This is a more common and more practically significant scenario than using entirely random values, (e.g., it is often encountered in a conference room as well as an airport or train station, where coworkers are initiating a point-to-point ad hoc communication). The value of β in (5) is set to 500, since the Interference Weight takes values in the range (0–500), in order to provide adequate resolution capabilities. For all cases we assume the presence of uncertainties due to imperfect message exchange (one in every four messages is lost) that cause 25% underestimation of the interference. If such uncertainties are not present, then the algorithm behaves similarly to the algorithm of [8]. In the presence of uncertainties, parameter α compensates for the underestimation of interference and helps the system converge near its optimal point, as described in the previous sections.

The improvement in the total utility of the network if the proposed algorithm is utilized over the scenario in which every user transmits using the maximum allowable power level as well as over the original version of the algorithm that does not include the coefficient α, is depicted in Figure 6. The vertical axis depicts the achieved useful utility while the horizontal axis represents the corresponding topology instance. The considerable range over which the distance values are selected, coupled with the randomness of the relative positions between nodes and the presence of uncertainties that cause underestimation of the interference in ways that are not necessarily uniform (e.g., only some messages may be delayed), causes the final value of the utility function to vary significantly between different experiments both for the original and the proposed algorithm. Thus, the final utility of each topology instance is the average utility of ten experiments for the same instance. Finally, in order to study the effect of the number of users on the system, a scenario of 10 user pairs and 20 user pairs was simulated.

The utility for the scenario in which the users transmit always using the maximum power level defines the lower bound for the behaviour of the system. The proposed algorithm outperforms the original one, for the majority of times, with a more significant improvement for the lower utility values. This property is very important since it can improve the Bit Error Rate (BER) and raise QoS from poor to acceptable levels. Furthermore; the proposed algorithm always outperforms the always maximum power scenario, while the original algorithm in some cases results in similar performance. The reason for this is that the existence of the coefficient α in the proposed algorithm does not allow the system to reach the worst case of completely unregulated transmission since it always compensates for at least a portion of the underestimated interference. Another interesting point is that as the number of users increases, the average utility of the system decreases although extreme values are not affected significantly. This is justified by the fact that the interference exhibits a cumulative behavior that affects all other user pairs, therefore reducing the average utility. However, extreme values are mainly the outcome of the topology and the relative distance of the user pairs, thus, are less sensitive to the number of users.

The next step is to compare the results of the proposed algorithm using OFDM and FBMC systems. However, a short outline of the FBMC technique is required. According to the principle of transmission based on filter banks, the transmitter incorporates a Synthesis Filter Bank (SFB) while the receiver incorporates an Analysis Filter Bank (AFB). In the structure, the Fast Fourier Transform (FFT) is present as in OFDM [15]. It is however augmented, to complete a filter bank, by the Polyphase Network (PPN) which is comprised of a set of digital filters, whose coefficients globally form the impulse response of the so-called prototype low-pass filter. FBMC systems have somewhat increased hardware

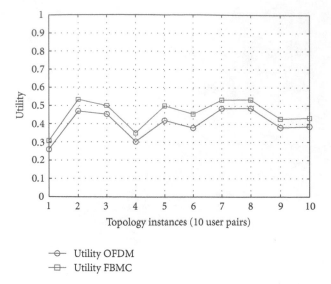

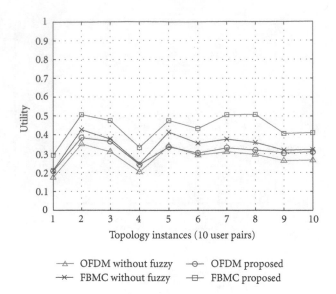

FIGURE 7: Utility function for the proposed algorithm with FBMC and OFDM.

FIGURE 8: Utility values for the original and the proposed algorithm with both FBMC and OFDM, under the assumption of long message delays (10 user pairs).

complexity compared to the classical OFDM approach but compensate for this with a number of advantages. Among others, they do not require guard time and cycle prefix, while the use of Offset QAM (OQAM) implies that the full capacity of the transmission bandwidth is achieved. The improvement in the total utility of a network consisting of ten user pairs if the proposed algorithm is used with FBMC over OFDM is depicted in Figure 7.

This improvement stems from the fact that FBMC uses lower transmission power for the same bandwidth compared to OFDM [16] and therefore causes reduced interference. The proposed algorithm is able to transparently exploit this improvement and translate it in increased utility values.

To evaluate the resilience of the algorithm in the presence of long update time intervals we perform simulations with the assumption that some of the messages are delayed and, consequently, other nodes do not have the latest interference price information that has been announced. Thus, the definition of "long update times" that we consider in this work is to be at least equal to twice the average update time (so that other nodes have updated the announced interference price in this interval). Since it is already established that transmitting with the maximum power is the lower bound of performance for both the original and the proposed algorithm, in this scenario, we evaluate the behaviour of the original and the proposed algorithm with both FBMC and OFDM in order to study the effect of increased delays on each of these cases.

The first point that is noteworthy is the fact that the improved Physical layer of FBMC in this scenario provides a significant advantage that even surpasses the advantage offered by the proposed algorithm. Therefore, using FBMC with the original algorithm is better for this case than using OFDM with the proposed algorithm. The best option is to use the proposed algorithm with FBMC, combining the advantage of improved Physical layer capabilities

and improved upper-layer functions. Regarding the latter point, the proposed algorithm consistently outperforms the original one when both use the same Physical layer (FBMC) under the assumption of long delays. Furthermore, if we juxtapose Figure 8 with Figure 6 we can derive some additional conclusions. Specifically, although the average utility values are reduced for all algorithms, the proposed algorithm is not affected as much as the original from the increased delays, thus the property of "graceful degradation" is indeed enhanced. Since real systems usually have to cope with nonideal conditions, this property is highly desirable.

Finally, it is very important to quantify the performance improvement in terms of conventional network metrics to show the relation between a higher overall utility value and parameters that directly affect the user experience. Since the main comparison is between the original algorithm and the proposed one, their behaviour in terms of SINR is compared in Figure 9. SINR is chosen as the most appropriate metric for comparison as it reflects directly on the QoS and the final user experience and can also be compared without considering external parameters, such as modulation and coding schemes that will impact for example the final BER of the system. The two graphs are following a similar pattern but the proposed algorithm consistently outperforms the original when the interference is underestimated, as it compensates for the interference underestimation and raises SINR to acceptable levels, especially for the lower values.

Regarding the overall simulation time and scalability properties of the algorithm, for all cases, the number of iterations for convergence is comparable to the number of user pairs. More specifically, for 10–30 user pairs usually less than thirty and up to fifty iterations are required for reaching the final steady state. Furthermore, the average execution time on a Core2 Quad Q9400 CPU operating at 2.66 GHz is less than two minutes for up to 20 user pairs and approximately five minutes for up to 30 user pairs.

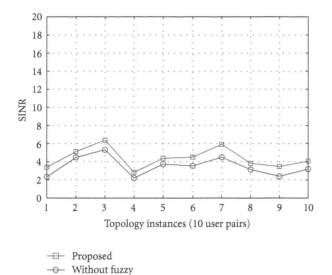

Proposed
Without fuzzy

FIGURE 9: SINR for the original and the proposed algorithm under 25% underestimation of interference.

5. Conclusion

In this paper, an improved algorithm, based on the algorithm of [8], was presented for cooperative DSA in unlicensed bands, utilizing MAC layer mechanisms for message exchange (interference prices) between the secondary nodes in order to achieve interference mitigation. The main improvement in this work compared to [8] is the introduction of a coefficient α that is serving as the weight of the interference term, increasing its impact in cases of imperfect message exchange, long update time intervals for interference prices, as well as increased number of users. In such cases, the interference that is caused to other user pairs by an increase in the transmission power of a user is often underestimated, resulting in a convergence of the algorithm to a nonoptimal solution. In the presence of such uncertainties, if this underestimation is compensated by a properly defined weight parameter, the system approximates its optimal behavior as in the case of "perfect" message exchange.

The value of the weight parameter was derived from a fuzzy logic reasoner. Fuzzy logic was selected because it is particularly effective in dealing with uncertainties and vague requirements. Moreover, the outcome of the proposed algorithm has been compared to the original algorithm in terms of the overall utility level (defined as the sum of the user utilities) under uncertainties that cause 25% underestimation of interference. Furthermore, comparison was also made between the proposed algorithm in FBMC and OFDM systems. In this case, using FBMC increased the achieved utility. The improvement stems from the fact that FBMC uses lower transmission power for the same bandwidth compared to OFDM and therefore causes reduced interference. Additionally, a scenario of long update time intervals in which some of the messages are delayed causing other nodes to not have the latest interference price information was considered, and the performance of both algorithms in a case of nonideal message exchange was evaluated. Results indicate that the algorithm consistently outperforms previous schemes in terms of SINR under uncertainties and can transparently exploit the improved Physical layer offered by FBMC.

Acknowledgments

This work was performed in Project PHYDYAS which has received research funding from the Community's Seventh Framework program. This paper reflects only the authors' views and the Community is not liable for any use that may be made of the information contained therein. The contributions of colleagues from PHYDYAS consortium are hereby acknowledged.

References

[1] P. Pawelczak, S. Pollin, H.-S. W. So, A. Bahai, R. Prasad, and R. Hekmat, "Quality of service assessment of opportunistic spectrum access: a medium access control approach," *IEEE Wireless Communications*, vol. 15, no. 5, pp. 20–29, 2008.

[2] F. Wang, M. Krunz, and S. Cui, "Price-based spectrum management in cognitive radio networks," in *Proceedings of the 2nd International Conference on Cognitive Radio Oriented Wireless Networks and Communications (CrownCom '07)*, pp. 70–78, August 2007.

[3] L. Ma, X. Han, and C.-C. Shen, "Dynamic open spectrum sharing MAC protocol for wireless ad hoc networks," in *Proceedings of the 1st IEEE International Symposium on New Frontiers in Dynamic Spectrum Access Networks (DySPAN '05)*, pp. 203–213, November 2005.

[4] L. Cao and H. Zheng, "Distributed spectrum allocation via local bargaining," in *Proceedings of the 2nd Annual IEEE Communications Society Conference on Sensor and Ad Hoc Communications and Networks (SECON '05)*, pp. 475–486, September 2005.

[5] C. Peng, H. Zheng, and B. Y. Zhao, "Utilization and fairness in spectrum assignment for opportunistic spectrum access," *Mobile Networks and Applications*, vol. 11, no. 4, pp. 555–576, 2006.

[6] J. Zhao, H. Zheng, and G.-H. Yang, "Distributed coordination in dynamic spectrum allocation networks," in *Proceedings of the 1st IEEE International Symposium on New Frontiers in Dynamic Spectrum Access Networks (DySPAN '05)*, pp. 259–268, November 2005.

[7] M. Bloem, T. Alpcan, and T. Basar, "A stackelberg game for power control and channel allocation in cognitive radio networks," in *Proceedings of the 2nd International Conference on Performance Evaluation Methodologies and Tools*, Nantes, France, October 2007.

[8] J. Huang, R. A. Berry, and M. L. Honig, "Spectrum sharing with distributed interference compensation," in *Proceedings of the 1st IEEE International Symposium on New Frontiers in Dynamic Spectrum Access Networks (DySPAN '05)*, pp. 88–93, November 2005.

[9] J. Huang, R. A. Berry, and M. L. Honig, "Distributed interference compensation for wireless networks," *IEEE Journal on Selected Areas in Communications*, vol. 24, no. 5, pp. 1074–1084, 2006.

[10] O. A. Rawashdeh, "Towards decentralized management of graceful degradation in distributed embedded systems," in

Proceedings of IEEE Dependable Systems and Networks Conference (DSN '08), Anchorage, Alaska, USA, June 2008.

[11] C. Carlsson and R. Fullér, "Fuzzy multiple criteria decision making: recent developments," *Fuzzy Sets and Systems*, vol. 78, no. 2, pp. 139–153, 1996.

[12] S. Buljore, M. Muck, P. Martigne, et al., "Introduction to IEEE P1900.4 activities," *IEICE Transactions on Communications*, vol. E91-B, no. 1, pp. 2–9, 2008.

[13] W. Wei and M.-J. Wang, "Fuzzy-MOGA-based traffic signal control at intersection," in *Proceedings of the International Conference on Machine Learning and Cybernetics*, vol. 1, pp. 639–644, November 2003.

[14] A. Merentitis, E. Patouni, N. Alonistioti, and M. Doubrava, "To reconfigure or not to reconfigure: cognitive mechanisms for mobile devices decision making," in *Proceeding of the 68th IEEE Vehicular Technology Conference (VTC '08)*, pp. 1–5, September 2008.

[15] H. Zhang, D. Le Ruyet, and M. Terre, "Spectral efficiency comparison between OFDM/OQAM- and OFDM-based CR networks," *Wireless Communications and Mobile Computing*, vol. 9, no. 11, pp. 1487–1501, 2009.

[16] D. S. Waldhauser, L. G. Baltar, and J. A. Nossek, "Filter bank based multicarrier systems," in *Proceedings of Techniken, Algorithmen und Konzepte für Zukünftige COFDM Systeme (TakeOFDM '08)*, 2008.

12

Multimodal Indexing of Multilingual News Video

Hiranmay Ghosh,[1] Sunil Kumar Kopparapu,[2] Tanushyam Chattopadhyay,[3] Ashish Khare,[1] Sujal Subhash Wattamwar,[1] Amarendra Gorai,[1] and Meghna Pandharipande[2]

[1] *TCS Innovation Labs Delhi, TCS Towers, 249 D&E Udyog Vihar Phase IV, Gurgaon 122015, India*
[2] *TCS Innovation Labs Mumbai, Yantra Park, Pokhran Road no. 2, Thane West 400601, India*
[3] *TCS Innovation Labs Kolkata, Plot A2, M2-N2 Sector 5, Block GP, Salt Lake Electronics Complex, Kolkata 700091, India*

Correspondence should be addressed to Hiranmay Ghosh, hiranmay.ghosh@tcs.com

Academic Editor: Ling Shao

The problems associated with automatic analysis of news telecasts are more severe in a country like India, where there are many national and regional language channels, besides English. In this paper, we present a framework for multimodal analysis of multilingual news telecasts, which can be augmented with tools and techniques for specific news analytics tasks. Further, we focus on a set of techniques for automatic indexing of the news stories based on keywords spotted in speech as well as on the visuals of contemporary and domain interest. English keywords are derived from RSS feed and converted to Indian language equivalents for detection in speech and on ticker texts. Restricting the keyword list to a manageable number results in drastic improvement in indexing performance. We present illustrative examples and detailed experimental results to substantiate our claim.

1. Introduction

Analysis of public newscast by domestic as well as foreign TV channels for tracking news, national and international views and public opinion is of paramount importance for media analysts in several domains, such as journalism, brand monitoring, law enforcement and internal security. The channels representing different countries, political groups, religious conglomerations, and business interests present different perspectives and viewpoints of the same event. Round the clock monitoring of hundreds of news channels requires unaffordable manpower. Moreover, the news stories of interest may be confined to a narrow slice of the total telecast time and they are often repeated several times on the news channels. Thus, round-the-clock monitoring of the channels is not only a wasteful exercise but is also prone to error because of distractions caused while viewing extraneous telecast and consequent loss of attention. This motivates a system that can automatically analyze, classify, cluster and index the news-stories of interest. In this paper we present a set of visual and audio processing techniques that helps us in achieving this goal.

While there has been significant research in multimodal analysis of news-video for their automated indexing and classification, the commercial applications are yet to mature. Commercial products like BBN Broadcast monitoring system (http://www.bbn.com/products_and_services/bbn_broadcast_monitoring_system/) and Nexidia rich media solution (http://www.nexidia.com/solutions/rich_media) offer speech analytics-based solution for news video indexing and retrieval. None of these solutions can differentiate between news programs from other TV programs and additionally cannot filter out commercials. They index the complete audio-stream and cannot define the story boundaries. Our work is motivated towards creation of a usable solution that uses multimodal cues to achieve a more effective news video analytics service. We put special emphasis on Indian broadcasts, which are primarily in English, Hindi (Indian national language), and several other regional languages.

We present a framework for multimodal analysis of multilingual news telecasts, which can be augmented with tools and techniques for specific news analytics tasks, namely delimiting programs, commercial removal, story boundary detection and indexing of news stories. While there has been significant research in tools for each of the tasks, an overall framework for news telecast analysis has not yet been proposed in literature. Moreover, automated analysis of Indian language telecasts raises some unique challenges. Unlike most of the channels in the western world, Indian channels do not broadcast "closed captioned text", which could be gainfully employed to index the broadcast stream. Thus, we need to rely completely on audio-visual processing of the broadcast channels. Our basic approach is to index the news stories with relevant keywords discovered in speech and in form of "ticker text" on the visuals. While there are several speech processing and OCR techniques, we face significant challenges in using them for processing Indian telecasts. The major impediments are (a) low resolution (768×576) of the visual frames and (b) significant noise introduced in the analog cable transmission channels, which are still prevalent in India. We have introduced several preprocessing and postprocessing stages to audio and visual processing algorithms to overcome these difficulties. Moreover, the speech and optical character recognition (OCR) technologies for different Indian languages (including Indian English) are under various stages of development under the umbrella of TDIL project [1–5] and are far from a state of maturity. All these factors lead to difficulties in creating a reliable transcript of the spoken or the visual text. We have improved the robustness of the system by restricting the audio-visual processing tasks to discover a small set of keywords of domain interest. These keywords are derived from Really Simple Syndication (RSS) feeds pertaining to the domain of interest. Moreover, these keywords are continuously updated as new feeds arrive and thus, they relate to news stories of contemporary interest. This alleviates the problem of long turn-around time associated with manual updates of the dictionaries, which may fail to keep pace with a fast changing global scenario. We create a multilingual keyword list in English and Indian languages to enable keyword spotting in different TV channels, both in spoken and visual forms. The multilingual keyword list helps us to automatically map the spotted keywords in different Indian languages to their English (or any other language) equivalents for uniform indexing across multiple channels.

The rest of the paper is organized as follows. We review the state-of-the-art in news video analysis in Section 2. Section 3 provides the system overview. Section 4 describes the techniques adopted by us for keyword extraction from speech and visuals from multilingual channels in details. Section 5 provides an experimental evaluation of the system. Finally, Section 6 concludes the paper and provides direction for future work.

2. Related Work

We provide an overview of research in news video analytics in this section to put our work in context. There has been much research interest in automatic interpretation, indexing and retrieval of audio and video data. Semantic analysis of multimedia data is a complex problem and has been attempted with moderate success in closed domains, such as sports, surveillance and news. This section is by no means a comprehensive review on audio and video analytic techniques that has evolved over the past decade, as we concentrate on automated analysis of broadcast video.

Automated analysis, classification and indexing of news video contents have drawn the attention of many researchers in recent times. A video comprising visual and audio components leads to two complementary approaches for automated video analysis. Eickeler and Mueller [6] and Smith et al. [7] propose classification of the scenes into a few content classes based on visual features. A motion feature vector has been computed from the differences in the successive frames and HMM's have been used to characterize the content classes. In contrast, Gauvain et al. [8] proposes an audio-based approach, where the speech in multiple languages has been transcribed and the constituent words and phrases have been used to index the contents of a broadcast stream. Later work attempts to merge the two streams of research and proposes multimodal analysis, which is reviewed later in this section.

A typical news program on a TV channel is characterized by unique jingles at the beginning and the end of the newscast, which provide a convenient means to delimit the newscast from other programs [9]. Moreover, a news program has several advertisement breaks, which need to be removed for efficient news indexing. Several methods have been proposed for TV Commercial (We have used "commercial" and "advertisement" interchangeably in this paper.) detection. One simple approach is to detect the logos of the TV channels [10], which are generally absent during the commercials, but this might not hold good for many contemporary channels. Sadlier et al. [11] describes a method for identifying the ad breaks using "black" frames that generally precedes and succeeds the advertisements. The black frames are identified by analyzing the image intensity of the frames and audio intensity at those time-points. While American and European channels generally use black frames for separation of commercials and programs, it is not so for other geographical regions, including India [12]. Moreover, the heuristics used to ignore the extraneous black frames appearing at arbitrary places within programs are difficult to generalize. Hua et al. [13] have used the distinctive audio-visual properties of the commercials to train an SVM based classifier to classify video shots into commercial and noncommercial categories. The performance of such classifiers can be enhanced with application of the principle of temporal coherence [12]. Six basic visual features and five basic audio features derived context-based features have been used in [13] to classify the shots using SVM and further postprocessing.

The time-points in a streamed video can be indexed with a set of keywords, which provide the semantics of the video-segment around the time-point. Most of the American and European channels accompanied with closed caption text, which are transcripts of the speech, are aligned with the video time-line and provides a convenient mechanism for indexing a video. Where closed captioned text is not available, speech recognition technology needs to be used.

There are two distinct approaches to the problem. In phoneme-based approach [14], the sequence of phonemes constituting the speech is extracted from the audio track and is stored as metadata in sync with the video. During retrieval, a keyword is converted to a phoneme string and this phoneme string is searched for in the video metadata [15]. In contrast, [16] proposes a speaker independent continuous speech recognition engine that can create a transcript of the audio track and align it with the video. In this approach the retrieval is based on the keywords in text domain. The difference is primarily in the way the speech data is transcribed and archived. In the phoneme-based storage, there is no language dictionary used and the speech data is represented by a continuous string of phonemes. While in the later case a pronunciation dictionary is used to convert short phoneme sequences into known dictionary words and the actual phoneme sequence is not retained. Phone level approach is generally more error-prone than word-based approaches because the phoneme recognition accuracies are very poor, typically 40–50%. Moreover, word-based approach provides more robust information retrieval results [17] because in the word-based storage, a speech signal is tagged by at least 3 best (often referred to as n-best) phonemes (instead of only one phoneme) at each instance and the word dictionary is used to resolve which sequence of phonemes to use to be able to correlate the speech with a word in the dictionary. Additional sources of information that can be used for news video indexing constitute output from Optical Character Recognition (OCR) on the visual text, face recognizer and speaker identification [18].

Once the advertisement breaks are removed from a news-program, the latter needs to be broken down into individual news stories for further processing. Chua et al. [19] provide a survey of the different methods used based on the experience of TRECVID 2003, which defined news story segmentation as an evaluation task. One of the approaches involve analysis of speech [20, 21], namely, end-of-sentence identification and text tiling technique [22] which involves computing lexical similarity scores across a set of sentence and has been used earlier for story identification in text passages. Purely text-based approach generally yields low accuracy, motivating use of audio-visual features. Identification of anchor shots [23], cue phrases, prosody, and blank frames in different combinations are used together with certain heuristics regarding news production grammar in this approach. A third approach uses machine learning approach where an SVM or a Maximum Entropy classifier classifies a candidate story boundary point based on multimodal data, namely, audio, visual, and text data surrounding the point. While, some of these approaches use a large number of low-level media features, for example, face, motion, and audio classes, some others [24] proposes abstracting low level features to mid-level to accommodate multimodal features without significant increase in dimensionality. In this approach, a shot is preclassified to semantic categories, such as anchor, people, speech, sports, and so forth, which are then combined with a statistical model such as HMM [25]. The classification of shots also helps in segmenting the corpus into subdomains, resulting in more accurate models and hence, improved story-boundary detection. Besacier et al. [26] report use of long pause, shot boundary, audio change (speaker change, speech to music transition, etc.), jingle detection, commercial detection and ASR output for story boundary detection. TRECVID prescribes use of F1 Score [27], the harmonic mean of precision and recall, as a measure of the accuracy. An accuracy of F1 = 0.75 for multimodal story boundary detection has been reported in [22].

Further work on news video analysis extends to conceptual classification of stories. Early work on the subject [23] achieves binary classification shots to a few predefined semantic categories, like "indoors" versus "outdoor", "nature" versus "man-made", and so forth. This was done by extracting the visual features of the key-frames and using a SVM classifier. Higher level inferences could be drawn by observing co-occurrence of some of these semantic levels, for example, occurrence of "sky", "water", "sand", and "people" on a video frame implied a "beach scene". Later work has found that the performance of concept detection is significantly improved by use of multimodal data, namely audio-visual features and ASR transcripts [24]. A generic approach for multimodal concept detection that combines outputs of multiple unimodal classifiers by ensemble fusion has been found to perform better than early fusion approach that aggregates multimodal features into a single classifier. Colace et al. [28] introduced a probabilistic framework for combining multimodal features for classifying the video shots in a few predefined categories using Bayesian Networks. The advantage of Bayesian classifiers over binary classifiers is that the former not only classifies the shots but also ranks the classification. While judicious combination of multimodal improves the performance of concept detection, it has also been observed that use of query-independent weights to combine multiple features performs worst than text alone. Thus, the above approaches for shot classification could not scale beyond a few predefined conceptual categories. This prompts use of external knowledge to select appropriate feature-weights for specific query classes [18]. Harit et al. [29] provide a new approach to use an ontology that can be used to reason with media properties of concepts and to dynamically derive a Bayesian Network for scene classification in a query context. Topic clustering, or clustering news-videos at different times and from different sources is another area of interest. An interesting open question has been the use of audio-visual features in conjunction with text obtained from automatic speech recognition in discovering novel topics [24]. Another interesting research direction is to investigate video topic detection in absence of Automatic Speech Recognition (ASR) data as in the case of "foreign" language news video [24].

3. Framework for Telecast News Analysis

We envisage a system where a large number of TV broadcast channels are to be monitored by a limited number of human monitor. The channels are in English, Hindi (National language of India), and a few other Indian regional

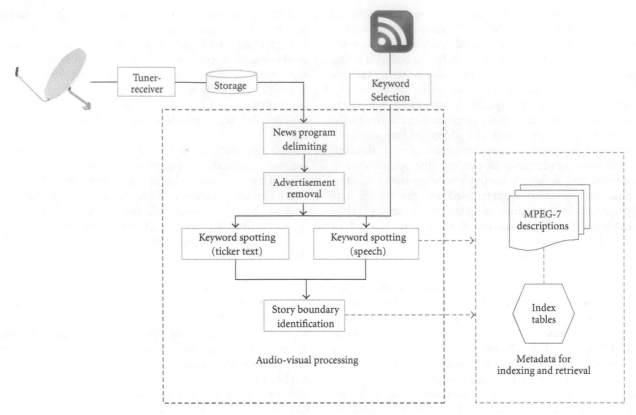

FIGURE 1: System architecture.

languages. Many of the channels are news channels but some are entertainment channels, which have specific time-slots for news. The contents of the news channels contain weather reports, talk shows, interviews and other such programs besides news. The programs are interspersed with commercial breaks. The present work focuses on indexing news and related programs only.

Figure 1 depicts the system architecture. At the first step of processing, the broadcast streams are captured from Direct to House (DTH) systems and are decoded. They are initially dumped on the disk in chunks of manageable size. These dumps are first preprocessed to identify the news programs. While the time-slots for news on the different channels are known, the accurate boundaries of the programs are identified with the unique jingles that characterize the different programs on a TV channel [9]. The next processing step is to filter out the commercial breaks. Since the black frame-based method does not work for most of the Indian channels, we propose to use a supervised training method [13] for this purpose. At the end of this stage, we get delimited news programs devoid of any commercial breaks.

The semantics of the news contents are generally characterized by a set of keywords (or key phrases) which occur either in the narration of the newscaster or in the ticker text [30] that appears on the screen. The next stage of processing involves indexing the video stream with these extracted keywords. Many American and European channels broadcast transcript of the speech as closed captioned text, which can be used for convenient indexing of the news stream. Since there is no closed captioning available with Indian news channels, we use image and speech processing techniques to detect keywords from both visual and spoken audio track. The video is decomposed into constituent shots, which are then classified into different semantic categories [7, 28], for example, field-shots, news-anchor, interview, and so forth—this classification information is used in the later stages of processing. We create an MPEG-7 compliant content description of the news video in terms of its temporal structure (sequence of shots), their semantic classes and the keywords associated with each shot. An index table of keywords is also created and linked to the content description of the video. The next step in processing is to detect the story boundaries. We propose to use multi-modal cues, visual, audio, ASR output, and OCR data, to identify the story boundaries. We select some of the methods described in [19]. Late fusion method is preferred because of lower dimensionality of features in the supervised training methods and better accuracy [24]. Once the story boundaries are known, analysis of keywords spotted in the story leads to their semantic classification.

In rest of this paper, we deal with the specific problem of indexing the multilingual Indian newscasts with keywords identified in the visuals (ticker text) and in the audio (speech) and improving the indexing performance of news stories with multimodal cues.

4. Keyword-Based Indexing of News Videos

This stage involves indexing of a news video stream with a set of useful keywords and key-phrases (We will use the "keywords" and "key-phrases" interchangeably further in this section.). Since closed captioned text is not available with Indian telecasts, we need to rely on speech processing to extract the keywords. Creating a complete transcript of the speech as in [8] is not possible for Indian language telecasts because of limitations in the speech recognition technology. A pragmatic and more robust alternative is to spot a finite set of contemporary keywords of interest in different Indian languages in the broadcast audio stream. The keywords are extracted from a contemporary RSS feed [31]. We complement this approach with spotting the important keywords in the ticker text that is superimposed on the visuals on a TV channel. While OCR technologies for many Indian languages used for ticker text analysis are also not sufficiently robust, extraction of keywords from both audio and visual channels simultaneously, significantly enhances the robustness of the indexing process.

4.1. Creation of a Keyword File. RSS feeds, made available and maintained by websites of the broadcasting channels or by purely web-based news portals, captures the contemporary news in a semistructured XML format. They contain links to the full-text news stories in English. We select the common and proper nouns in the RSS feed text and the associated stories as the keywords. These proper nouns (typically names of people and places) are identified by a named entity detection module [32] while the common nouns can be identified using frequency count. A significant advantage of obtaining a keyword list from the RSS feeds is the currency of the keywords because of dynamic updates of the RSS feeds. Moreover, the RSS feeds are generally classified into several categories, for example, "business-news" and "international", and it is possible to select the news in one or a few categories that pertains to analyst's domain of interest. Restricting the keyword list to a small number helps in improving the accuracy of the system, especially for keyword spotting in speech.

The English keywords so derived, form a set of concepts, which need to be identified in both speech and visual forms from different Indian language telecasts. While there are some RSS feeds in Hindi and other Indian Languages (For instance, see http://www.voanews.com/bangla/rss.cfm (Bangla), http://feeds.feedburner.com/oneindia-thatstelugu-all (Telugu) and http://feeds.feedburner.com/oneindia-thatshindi-all (Hindi).), aligning the keywords from independent RSS feeds proves to be difficult. We derive the equivalent keywords in Indian languages from the English keywords, each of which is either a proper or a common noun. We use a word level English-to-Indian language dictionary to find the equivalent common noun keywords in an Indian language. We use a pronunciation lexicon (A lexicon is an association of words and their phonetic transcription. It is a special kind of dictionary that maps a word to all the possible phonemic representations of the word.) for transliterating proper names in a semi-automatic matter as suggested in [15]. It is to be noted that (a) the

```
<RULE NAME="KeyWord">
  <L PROPNAME="keyword">

    <CONCEPT NAME= "Afghanistan">
        <ENG KEY= "Afghanistan">Afghanistan</ENG>
        <BEN KEY= "Afganistan"> আফগানিs ান </ BEN>
        <HIN KEY= "Afganistan">अफगानिस्तान </ HIN>
        <TEL KEY= "Afganistan" > అఫ్గానిస్తన </ TEL>

    </CONCEPT>

    <CONCEPT NAME= "Rajshekhar">
        <ENG KEY= "Rajshekhar">Rajshekhar</ENG>
        <BEN KEY= "Rajshekhar">বাজশেখব</BEN>
        <HIN KEY= "Rajshekhar">राजशेखर </HIN>
        <TEL KEY= "Rajshekhar"> రాజశేఖర్ </TEL>

    </CONCEPT>

    <CONCEPT NAME= "Terrorist">
        <ENG KEY= "Terrorist">Terrorist </ENG>
        <BEN KEY= "Santrasbaadi"> সন্ত্রাসবাদী </BEN>
        <HIN KEY= "Atankabaadi">आतंकबादी </HIN>
        <TEL KEY= "Atankavaadi"> అతన్కవాది </TEL>

    </CONCEPT>
  </L>
</RULE NAME>
```

FIGURE 2: Keyword list structure.

translation of the keyword in English is possible only when the keyword is present in the dictionary else it is transliterated and (b) transliteration of nouns in Indian languages are phonetic and hence there are no transliteration problems that are more visible in a nonphonetic language like English.

Finally, the keywords in English and their Indian language equivalents and their pronunciation keys are stored as a multilingual dynamic keyword list structure in XML format. This becomes an active keyword list for the news video channels and is used for both keyword spotting in speech and OCR. We show a few sample entries from a multilingual keyword list file in Figure 2. The first two entries represent proper nouns, the name of a place (Afghanistan) and a person (Rajashekar), respectively. The third entry (terrorist) corresponds to a common noun. In Figure 2 every concept is expressed in three major Indian languages, Bangla, Hindi, and Telugu, besides English. We use ISO 639-3 codes (See http://www.sil.org/iso639-3/.) to represent the languages. KEY entries represent pronunciation keys and are used for keyword spotting in speech. The words in Indian languages are encoded in Unicode (UTF-8) and are used as dictionary entries for correcting OCR mistakes. Each concept is associated with a NAME in English, which is returned when a keyword (speech or ticker text) in any of the languages is spotted either in speech or ticker-text, thus resulting in a built-in machine translation.

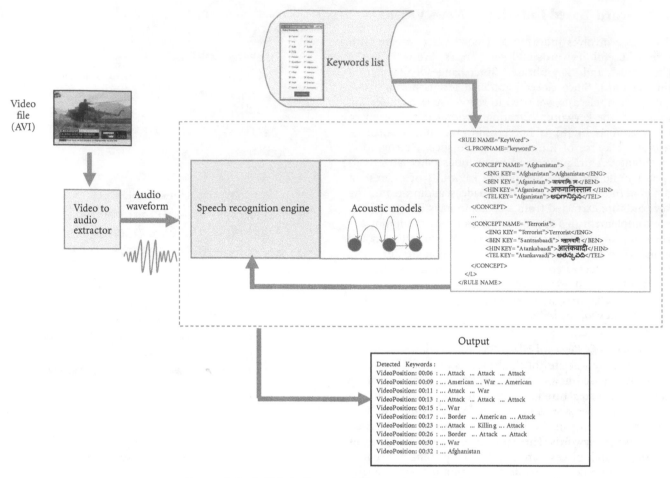

FIGURE 3: Typical block diagram of a keyword spotting system.

4.2. Keyword Spotting and Extraction from Broadcast News.
Audio keyword spotting system essentially enables identification of words or phrases of interest in an audio broadcast or in the audio track of a video broadcast. Almost all the audio keyword spotting systems take the acoustic speech signal (a time sequence, $x(t)$) as input and use a set of (N) keywords or key phrases ($\{K_i\}_{i=1}^{N}$), as reference to spot the occurrences of these keywords in the broadcast [33]. A speech recognition engine ($S : x(t) \rightarrow x(s); x(s)$ is a string sequence $\{s_k\}_{k=1}^{N}$), which is generally speaker independent and large vocabulary, is employed and is ideally supported by the list of keywords that need to be spotted (if $x(s) \in \{K_i\}_{i=1}^{N}$; then S, the speech recognition engine, is deemed to have spotted a keyword). Internally, the speech recognition engine has a built in pronunciation lexicon which is used to associate the words in the keyword list with the recognized phonemic string from the acoustic audio.

A typical functional keyword spotting system is shown in Figure 3. The block diagram shows as a first step the audio track extraction from a video broadcast. The keyword list is the list of keywords or phrases that the system is supposed to identify and locate in the audio stream. Typically this human readable keyword list is converted into a speech grammar file (FSG (finite state grammar) and CFG (context free grammar) are typically grammar used in speech recognition

literature.). The speech recognition engine (in Figure 3) makes use of the acoustic models and the speech grammar file to ear mark all possible occurrences of the keywords in the acoustic stream. The output is typically the recognized or spotted words and the time instance at which that particular keyword occurred.

An audio KWS system for broadcast news has been proposed in [34]. The authors suggest the use of utterance verification (using dynamic time warping), out-of-vocabulary rejection, audio classification, and noise reduction to enhance the keyword spotting performance. They experimented on Korean news based on 50 keywords. More recent works include searching multilingual audiovisual documents using the International Phonetic Alphabet (IPA) [35] and transcription of Greek broadcast news using the HMM toolkit (HTK) [36]. We propose a multichannel, multilingual audio KWS system which can be used as a first step in broadcast news clustering.

In a multi channel, multilingual news broadcast scenario the first step towards coarse clustering of broadcast news can be achieved through audio KWS. As mentioned in earlier section broadcast news typically deals with people (including organizations and groups) and places; this makes broadcast news very rich in proper names which have to be spotted in audio. Notice that these words to be spotted

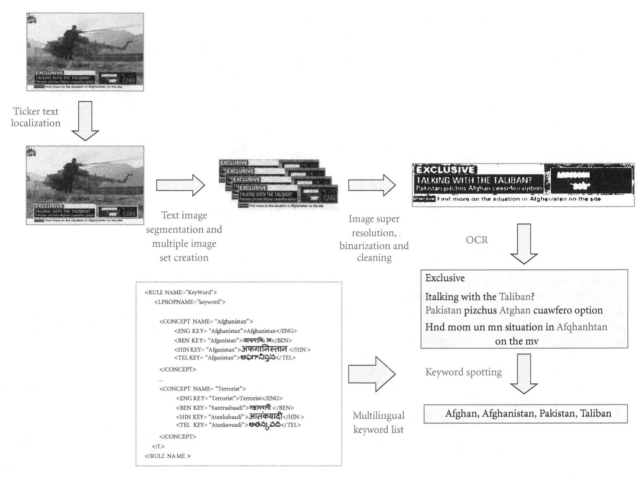

FIGURE 4: Keyword extraction from ticker text.

are largely language independent, the language independence comes because most of the Indian proper names are pronounced similarly in different Indian languages, implying that the same set of keywords or grammar files can be used irrespective of language of broadcast. In some sense we do not need to (a) identify the language being broadcast and (b) maintain a separate keyword list for different language channels. However, there is a need for a pronunciation dictionary for proper names. Creating a pronunciation lexicon of proper names is time consuming unlike a conventional pronunciation dictionary containing commonly used words. Laxminarayana and Kopparapu [15] have developed a framework that allows a fast method of creating a pronunciation lexicon, specifically for Indian proper names, which are generally phonetic unlike in other languages, by constructing a cost function and identifying a basis set using a cost minimization approach.

4.3. Keyword Extraction from News Ticker Text. News Ticker refers to a small screen space dedicated to presenting headlines or some important news. It usually covers a small area of the total video frame image (approximately 10–15%). Most of the news channels use two-band tickers, each having a special purpose. For instance, the upper band is generally used to display regular text pertaining to the story which is currently on air whereas "Breaking News" or the scrolling ticker on the lower band relates to different stories or displays unimportant local news, business stocks quotes, weather bulletin, and so forth. Knowledge about the production rule of specific TV channel or program is necessary to segregate the different types of ticker texts. We attempt to identify the desired keywords specified in the multilingual keyword list in the upper band, which relates to the current news story in different Indian channels.

Figure 4 depicts an overview of the steps required for keyword spotting in the ticker text. As the first step, we detect the ticker text present in the news video frame. This step is known as text localization. We identify the groups of video frames where ticker text is available and mark the boundaries of the text (highlighted by yellow colored boxes in the figure). The knowledge about the production rules of a channel helps us selecting the ticker text segments relevant to the current news story. In the next step, we extract these image segments from the identified groups of frames. Further, we identify the image segments containing the same text and combine the information in these images to obtain a high-resolution image using image super-resolution technique. We binarize this image and apply touching character segmentation as an image cleaning step.

These techniques help improve the recognition rate of OCR. Finally, the text images are processed by OCR software and desired keywords are identified from the resultant text using the multilingual keyword list. The following subsections give detailed explanation of these steps.

4.3.1. Text Localization in News Video Frames. The text recognition in a video sequence involves detection of the text regions in a frame, recognizing the textual content and tracking the ticker news video in successive frames. Homogeneous color and sharp edges are the key features of texts in an image or video sequence. Peng and Xiao [37] have proposed color-based clustering accompanied with sharp edge features for detection of text regions. Sun et al. [38] propose a text extraction by color clustering and connected component analysis followed by text recognition using a novel stroke verification algorithm to build a binary text line image after removing the noncharacter strokes. A multi-scale wavelet-based texture feature followed by SVM classifier is used for text detection in image and video frames [39]. An automatic detection, localization and tracking of text regions in MPEG videos are proposed in [40]. The text detection is based on wavelet transform and modified k-means classifier. Retrieval of sports video databases using SIFT feature-based trademark matching is proposed by [41]. The SIFT based approach is suitable for offline processing in video database but is not a feasible option in real time MPEG video streaming.

The classifier-based approaches have a limitation that if the test data pattern varies from the data used in learning, robustness of the system gets reduced. In the proposed method we have used the hybrid approach where we localize the candidate text regions initially using the compressed domain data processing and process the region of interest in pixel domain to mark the text region. This approach has a benefit over other in two aspects namely robustness and time complexity.

Our proposed methodology is based on the following assumptions.

(1) Text regions have significant contrast with background color.

(2) News ticker text is horizontally aligned.

(3) The components representing texts region has strong vertical edges.

As stated above we have used compressed domain features and time domain features to localize the text regions. The steps involved are as follows.

(1) Computation of Text Regions Using Compressed Domain Features. In order to determine the text regions in the compressed domain, we first compute the horizontal and vertical energies at the sub block (4×4) level and mark the subblocks as text or nontext assuming that the text regions generally possess high vertical and horizontal energies. To mark the high energy regions we first divide the entire video frame into small blocks each of size 4×4 pixels.

Next, we apply integer transformation on each of the blocks. We have selected Integer transformation in place of DCT to avoid the problem of rounding off and complexity of floating point operation. We compute the horizontal energy of the subblock by summing the absolute amplitudes of the horizontal harmonics (C_{U0}) and the vertical energy of the subblock by summing the absolute amplitudes of the vertical harmonics (C_{0V}). Then we compute the average horizontal text energy (E_{Avg_Hor}) and the average vertical text energy (E_{Avg_Ver}) for each row of subblocks. Lastly we mark candidate rows if both (E_{Avg_Hor}) and (E_{Avg_Ver}) exceed threshold value α, where α is calculated as $\mu_E + a\sigma_E$ where "a" is empirically selected by analyzing the mean and standard deviation of energy values observed over a large number of Indian broadcast channels.

(2) Filter Out the Low Contrast Components in Pixel Domain. Human eye is more sensitive in high-contrast regions compared to the low-contrast regions. Therefore, it is reasonable to assume that the ticker-text regions in a video are created with significant contrast with background colour. This assumption is found to be valid in most of the Indian channels. At the next step of processing, we remove all low-contrast components from the candidate text regions identified in the previous step. Finally, the candidate text segments are binarized using Otsu's method [42].

(3) Morphological Closing. The text components sometimes get disjointed depending on the foreground and background contrast and the video quality. Moreover, non textual regions appear as noise in the candidate text regions. A morphological closing operation is applied with rectangular structural elements with dimension of 3×5 to eliminate the noise and indentify continuous text segments.

(4) Confirmation of the Text Regions. Initially we run a connected component analysis for all pixels after morphological closing to split the candidate pixels into n number of connected components. Then we eliminate all the connected components which do not satisfy shape features like size and compactness (Compactness is defined as the number of pixel per unit area.).

Then we compute the mode for x and y coordinates of top left and bottom right coordinates of the remaining components. We compute the threshold as the mode of the difference between the median and the position of all the pixels.

The components, for which the difference of its position and the median of all the positions are less than the threshold, are selected as the candidate texts. We have used Euclidean distance as a distance measure.

(5) Confirmation of the Text Regions Using Temporal Information. At this stage, the text segments have been largely identified. But, some spurious segments are still there. We use heuristics to remove spurious segments. Human vision psychology suggests that eyes cannot detect any event within 1/10th of a second. Understanding of video content requires

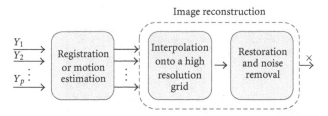

FIGURE 5: Stages of image super resolution.

Transcription	śivō rakṣatu gīrvāṇabhāṣārasāsvādatatparān
Bengālī	শিবো রক্ষতু গীর্বাণভাষারসাস্বাদতৎপরান্
Devanāgarī	शिवो रक्षतु गीर्वाणभाषारसास्वादतत्परान्
Gujarātī	શિવો રક્ષતુ ગીર્વાણભાષારસાસ્વાદતત્પરાન્
Gurmukhī	ਸ਼ਿਵੇ ਰਕਸ਼ਤੁ ਗੀਰ੍ਵਾਣਭਾਸ਼ਾਰਸਾਸ੍ਵਾਦਤਤ੍ਪਰਾਨ੍
Oṛiyā	ଶିବୋ ରକ୍ଷତୁ ଗୀର୍ବାଣଭାଷାରସାସ୍ବାଦତତ୍ପରାନ୍
Tamiḷ	ஷிவோ ரக்ஷது கீர்வாணபாஷாரஸாஸ்வாததத்பராந்
Teḷugu	శివో రక్షతు గీర్వాణభాషారసాస్వాదతత్పరాన్
Kannada	ಶಿವೋ ರಕ್ಷತು ಗೀರ್ವಾಣಭಾಷಾರಸಾಸ್ವಾದತತ್ಪರಾನ್
Malayāḷam	ശിവോ രക്ഷതു ഗീർവാണഭാഷാരസാസ്വാദതത്പരാൻ
Grantha	ꢴꢶꢮꣀ ꢬꢒ꣄ꢲꢡꢸ ꢔꢷꢬ꣄ꢮꢵꢠꢨꢵꢰꢵꢬꢱꢵꢱ꣄ꢮꢵꢣꢡꢡ꣄ꢦꢬꢵꢥ꣄

FIGURE 6: Samples of a few major Indian scripts (Source: http://www.myscribeweb.com/Phrase_sanskrit.png.).

at least 1/3rd of a second, that is, 10 frames in a video with frame-rate of 30 FPS. Thus, any information on video meant for human comprehension must persist for this minimum duration. It is also observed that the noise detected as text does not generally persist for significant duration of time. Thus, we eliminate any detected text regions that persists for less than 10 frames. At the end of this phase, we get a set of groups of frames (GoF) containing ticker text. The information together with the coordinates of the bounding boxes for the ticker text are recorded at the end of this stage of processing.

4.3.2. Image Super Resolution and Image Cleaning.

The GoF containing ticker text regions cannot be directly used with OCR software because the size of the text is still too small and lacks clarity. Moreover, the characters in the running text are often connected and need to be separated from each other for reliable OCR output.

To accomplish this task we interpolate these images to a higher resolution by using Image Super Resolution (SR) techniques [43, 44] and subsequently perform touching character segmentation as image cleaning process in order to address these problems. The processing steps are given below.

(1) Image Super Resolution (SR). Figure 5 shows different stages of a multiframe image SR system to produce an image with a higher resolution (X) from a set of images $(Y_1, Y_2, \ldots, Y_p)$ with lower resolution. We have used SR technique presented in [45], where information from a set of multiple low resolution images is used to create a higher resolution image. Hence it becomes extremely important to find images with the same ticker text. We perform pixel subtraction of both the images in a single pass. We now count the number of nonblack pixels by using intensity scheme $(R, G, B) < (25, 25, 25)$. We then normalize this count by dividing it by total number of pixels and record this value. If this value exceeds statistically determined threshold "β", we declare the images as nonidentical otherwise we place both the images in the same set. As shown in Figure 5, multiple low resolution images are fed to an image registration module which employs frequency domain approach and estimates the planar motion which is described as function of three parameters: horizontal shift (Δx), vertical shift (Δy), and the planar rotation angle (Φ). In Image Reconstruction stage, the samples of the different low-resolution images are first expressed in the coordinate frame of the reference image. Then, based on these known samples, the image

values are interpolated on a regular high-resolution grid. For this purpose bicubic interpolation is used because of its low computational complexity and good results.

(2) Touching Character Segmentation. We binarize the high-resolution image by Otsu's method [42] containing ticker text. We generally find some of the text characters touching each other in the binarized image because of noise that can adversely affect the performance of the OCR. Hence, we follow up this step with segmentation of touching characters for improved character recognition.

For Touching Character Segmentation, we initially find the average character width for all the characters in the region of interest (ROI) by $\mu_{WC} = (1/n) \sum_{i=1}^{n} WC_i$ where "n" is the number of characters in the ROI and "WC_i" is the character width of the ith component. We then compute the threshold for character length and the components with a width greater than that threshold are marked as candidate touching characters. The threshold for character length is computed as $(T_{WC} = \mu_{WC} + 3 * \sigma_{WC})$. We have used $(3 * \sigma_{WC})$ to ensure higher recall. For our purpose threshold is nearly 64. Then we split them into number of possible touches. The number of touches in a candidate component is computed as the ceiling value of the ratio between actual width and the threshold value, that is, $n_i = [WC_i/T_{WC}] + 1$. In some Indian languages (like Bangla and Hindi), the characters in a word are connected by a unique line called *Shirorekha*, also called the "head line". Touching character segmentation for such languages is preceded by the removal of *shirorekha*, which makes character segmentation more efficient.

4.3.3. OCR and Dictionary-Based Correction.

The higher quality image obtained as a result of last stage of processing is processed with OCR software to create a transcript of the ticker text in the native language of the channel. The transcript is generally error-prone and we use the multilingual keyword list in conjunction with an approximate string matching algorithm for robust recognition of the desired keywords in the transcript. There are telecasts in English, Hindi (the national language), and several regional languages in India. Many of the languages use their own

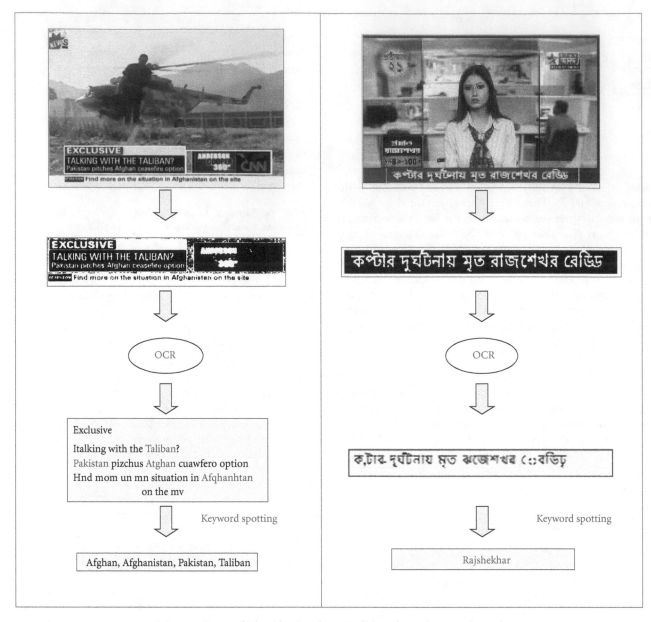

FIGURE 7: Keyword Identification from English and Bangla news channel.

scripts. Samples of a few major Indian scripts are shown in Figure 6.

The development of OCR in many of these Indian languages is more complex than English and other European languages. Unlike these languages, where the number of characters to be recognized is less than 100, Indian languages have several hundreds of distinct characters. Nonuniformity in spacing of characters and connection of the characters in a word by *Shirorekha* in some of the languages are other issues. There has been significant progress in OCR research in several Indian languages. For example, in Hasnat et al. [46], Lehal [1], and Jawahar et al. [2], word accuracy over 90% has been attained. Still, many of the Indian languages lack a robust OCR and are not amenable to reliable machine processing. For selecting a suitable OCR to work with

English and Indian languages, we looked for the highly ranked OCRs identified at The Fourth Annual Test of OCR Accuracy [47] conducted by Information Science Research Institute (ISRI (http://www.isri.unlv.edu/ISRI/)). Tesseract [48] (More information on Tesseract and download packages are available at http://code.google.com/p/tesseract-ocr/.), an open source OCR, finds a special mention because of its reported high-accuracy range (95.31% to 97.53%) for the magazine, newsletter, and business letter test-sets. Besides English, Tesseract can be trained with a customized set of training data and can be used for regional Indian languages. Adaptation of Tesseract for Bangla has been reported in [46]. Thus, we find Tesseract to be a suitable OCR for creating transcripts of English and Indian language ticker text images extracted from the news videos.

TABLE 1: Results for keyword spotting in speech with master keyword list.

Story id	Instances of keywords present	Keywords found		Retrieval performance		
		True positives	False Positives	Recall (%)	Precision (%)	F-measure (%)
[1]	[2]	[3]	[4]	[5]	[6]	[7]
				$[3]/[2] * 100$	$[3]/([3] + [4]) * 100$	$2 * [5] * [6]/([5] + [6])$
English Channels						
E001	12	2	5	16.67	28.57	21.05
E002	40	10	6	25.00	62.50	35.71
E003	13	2	3	15.38	40.00	22.22
E004	67	8	12	11.94	40.00	18.39
E005	91	6	7	6.59	46.15	11.54
E006	51	7	8	13.73	46.67	21.21
E007	7	1	3	14.29	25.00	18.18
E008	7	1	3	14.29	25.00	18.18
E009	29	10	6	34.48	62.50	44.44
Overall (English)	*317*	*47*	*53*	*14.83*	*47.00*	*22.54*
Bangla Channels						
B001	7	1	0	14.29	100.00	25.00
B002	14	2	5	14.29	28.57	19.05
B003	13	2	1	15.38	66.67	25.00
B004	13	1	7	7.69	12.50	9.52
B005	29	2	7	6.90	22.22	10.53
Overall (Bangla)	*76*	*8*	*20*	*10.53*	*28.57*	*15.38*
Overall	**393**	**55**	**73**	**13.99**	**42.97**	**21.11**

TABLE 2: Results for keyword spotting in speech with constrained keyword list.

Story id	Instances of keywords present	Keywords found		Retrieval Performance		
		True positives	False Positives	Recall (%)	Precision (%)	F-measure (%)
[1]	[2]	[3]	[4]	[5]	[6]	[7]
				$[3]/[2] * 100$	$[3]/([3] + [4]) * 100$	$2 * [5] * [6]/([5] + [6])$
English Channels						
E001	12	5	4	41.67	55.56	47.62
E002	40	15	3	37.50	83.33	51.72
E003	13	4	1	30.77	80.00	44.44
E004	67	17	6	25.37	73.91	37.78
E005	91	14	8	15.38	63.64	24.78
E006	51	12	5	23.53	70.59	35.29
E007	7	1	0	14.29	100.00	25.00
E008	7	1	0	14.29	100.00	25.00
E009	29	12	4	41.38	75.00	53.33
Overall (English)	*317*	*81*	*31*	*25.55*	*72.32*	*37.76*
Bangla Channels						
B001	7	3	0	42.86	100.00	60.00
B002	14	3	1	21.43	75.00	33.33
B003	13	4	1	30.77	80.00	44.44
B004	13	1	2	7.69	33.33	12.50
B005	29	8	3	27.59	72.73	40.00
Overall (Bangla)	*76*	*19*	*7*	*25.00*	*73.08*	*37.25*
Overall	**393**	**100**	**38**	**25.45**	**72.46**	**37.66**

TABLE 3: Results for keyword spotting in ticker text with master keyword list.

Story id	No. of distinct ticker texts	Total instances of keywords present	Keywords found			
			On raw frame	On localized text region	After image super-resolution	After dictionary based correction
[1]	[2]	[3]	[4]	[5]	[6]	[7]
English Channels						
E001	5	41	17	19	24	29
E002	4	26	8	9	16	20
E003	4	23	9	10	13	16
E004	6	40	18	19	25	31
E005	4	31	10	13	17	22
E006	7	46	21	23	28	34
E007	4	21	8	9	12	17
E008	1	1	1	1	1	1
E009	5	19	9	9	11	14
Subtotal—English	40	248	101	112	147	184
Retrieval performance—English (%)			*40.73*	*45.16*	*59.27*	*74.19*
Bangla Channels						
B001	3	7	0	0	2	4
B002	3	7	1	1	2	4
B003	5	9	3	3	6	7
B004	3	6	1	1	2	3
B005	5	11	4	4	5	7
Subtotal—Bangla	19	40	9	9	17	25
Retrieval performance—Bangla (%)			*22.5*	*22.5*	*42.5*	*62.5*
Overall retrieval performance (%)			**38.19**	**42.01**	**56.94**	**72.57**

Despite preprocessing of the text images and high accuracy of Tesseract, the output of the OCR phase contains some errors because of poor quality of the original TV transmission. While it is difficult to improve the OCR accuracy, reliable identification of a finite set of keywords is possible with a dictionary-based correction mechanism. We calculate a weighted Levenshtein distance [49] between every word in the transcripts with the words in corresponding language in the multilingual keyword list and recognize the word if the distance is less than a certain threshold "β". The weights in computing the Levenshtein distance is based on visual similarity of the characters in an alphabet, for example, comparison of "l" (small L) and "1" (numeric one) has a lower weight than two other characters, say "a" and "b". We also put a higher weight for the first and the last letters in a word, considering that OCR has a lower error-rate for them because of the spatial separation (on one side) of these characters. Figure 7 shows examples of transcription and keyword identification from news channels in English and Bangla. We map the Bangla keywords to their English (or any other language) equivalents for indexing using the multilingual keyword file.

5. Experimental Results and Illustrative Examples

We have tested the performance of keyword-based indexing with a number of news stories recorded from different Indian channels in English and in Bangla, which is one of the major Indian languages. The news stories chosen pertained to two themes of national controversy, one involving the comments from a popular cricketer and the other involving a visa-related scam. These stories had been recorded over two consecutive dates. Each of the stories is between 20 seconds and 4 minutes in duration. RSS feeds from "Headlines India" (http://www.headlinesindia.com/) on the same dates have been used to create a master keyword-file with 137 English keywords and their Bangla equivalents. In order to test the improvement in accuracy with restricted domain-specific keyword set, we created a keyword file collected from "India news" category, to which the two stories belonged to. This restricted keyword-file contained 16 English keywords and their Bangla equivalents. The restricted keyword set formed was a subset of the master keyword set.

Sections 5.1 and 5.2 present performance of audio and visual keyword extraction, respectively. Section 5.3 present

TABLE 4: Results for keyword spotting in ticker text with constrained keyword list.

Story id	No. of distinct ticker texts	Total instances of keywords present	Keywords found			
			On raw frame	On localized text region	After image super-resolution	After dictionary-based correction
[1]	[2]	[3]	[4]	[5]	[6]	[7]
English Channels						
E001	5	36	15	17	22	27
E002	4	23	6	7	14	18
E003	4	23	9	10	13	16
E004	6	35	17	19	24	28
E005	4	31	10	13	17	22
E006	7	39	19	21	25	31
E007	4	18	7	8	11	16
E008	1	1	1	1	1	1
E009	5	16	7	7	9	12
Subtotal—English	40	222	91	103	136	171
Retrieval performance—English (%)			*40.99*	*46.40*	*61.26*	*77.03*
Bangla Channels						
B001	3	6	0	0	2	4
B002	3	6	1	1	2	4
B003	5	7	3	3	5	6
B004	3	4	1	1	2	3
B005	5	11	4	4	5	7
Subtotal—Bangla	19	34	9	9	16	24
Retrieval performance—Bangla (%)			*26.47*	*26.47*	*47.06*	*70.59*
Overall retrieval performance (%)			**39.06**	**43.75**	**59.38**	**76.17**

the overall indexing performance on combining audio and visual cues. Section 5.4 presents a few illustrative examples that explain the results.

5.1. Keyword Spotting in Speech.

Table 1 presents the results for keyword spotting in speech in the same set of news-stories observed with the master list of keywords. Column [2] represents the number of instances when any of the keywords occurred in the speech. We call keyword spotting to be successful, when a keyword is correctly identified in the time neighborhood (within a +/− 15 ms window) of the actual utterance. Column [3] indicates the number of such keywords for each news story. Column [4] indicates when a keyword is mistakenly identified, though it was actually not uttered at that point of time. We compute the retrieval performances recall, precision and F-measure (Harmonic mean of precision and recall) in columns [5]–[7].

We note that the overall retrieval performance is quite poor, more so for Bangla. It is not surprising because we have used a Microsoft speech engine that is trained for American English. The English channels experimented with were *Indian* channels and the accent of the narrators were quite distinct. We performed the same experiments with the constrained set of keywords. Table 2 presents the results in detail. We note that both recall and precision has significantly improved with the constrained set of keywords, which were primarily proper nouns. The retrieval performance for

Bangla is now comparable to that of English. This justifies the use of a dynamically created keyword list for keyword spotting, which is a key contribution in this paper. We note that the precision is quite high (72%), implying that the false positives are low. However, the recall is still pretty low (25%). We will show how we have exploited redundancy to achieve a reliable indexing despite poor recall at this stage.

5.2. Keyword Spotting in Ticker Text.

Table 3 depicts a summary of results for ticker text extraction from the English and Bangla Channels tested with master keyword list. Each of the news stories is identified by a unique id in column [1]. Column [2] presents the number of distinct ticker text frames detected in the story. Column [3] indicates the total instances of keywords built from the master keyword list actually present in the ticker text accompanying the story. Columns [4]–[6] show the number of keywords correctly detected when the full-frame, the localized text region and the super-resolution image (of localized text region) are subjected to OCR. Column [7] depicts the number of keywords correctly identified after dictionary-based correction is applied over the OCR result from the super-resolution image of localized text region. We note that the overall accuracy of keyword detection progressively increases from 38.2% to 72.6% through these stages of processing. In Table 3, retrieval performance refers to the recall value. We have observed very few false positives

TABLE 5: Indexing performance for audio, visual and combined channels.

	Audio			Visual			Combined		
Story id	No. of distinct keywords	Keywords correctly identified	Indexing Performance IP_a (%)	No. of distinct keywords	Keywords correctly identified	Indexing Performance IP_v (%)	No. of distinct keywords	Keywords correctly identified	Indexing Performance IP_o (%)
[1]	[2]	[3]	[4]	[5]	[6]	[7]	[8]	[9]	[10]
	$|K_a|$	$|K_a|$	[3]/[2] ∗ 100	$|K_v|$	$|k_v|$	[6]/[5] ∗ 100	$|K_o|$	$|K_o|$	[9]/[8] ∗ 100
English channels									
E001	8	5	62.50	13	9	69.23	13	11	84.62
E002	10	7	70.00	9	7	77.78	14	12	85.71
E003	7	5	71.43	10	8	80.00	11	9	81.82
E004	12	9	75.00	13	10	76.92	17	15	88.24
E005	21	12	57.14	11	8	72.73	21	18	85.71
E006	13	9	69.23	15	11	73.33	16	14	87.50
E007	5	2	40.00	10	9	90.00	14	13	92.86
E008	5	2	40.00	1	1	100.00	5	3	60.00
E009	12	9	75.00	9	9	100.00	15	14	93.33
Overall (English)	93	60	64.52	91	72	79.12	126	109	86.51
Bangla channels									
B001	3	2	66.67	4	2	50.00	5	5	100.00
B002	5	4	80.00	4	2	50.00	9	7	77.78
B003	7	4	57.14	6	5	83.33	9	8	88.89
B004	6	3	50.00	3	3	100.00	7	5	71.43
B005	9	6	66.67	5	4	80.00	10	8	80.00
Overall (Bangla)	30	19	63.33	22	16	72.73	40	33	82.50
Overall	**123**	**79**	**64.23**	**113**	**88**	**77.88**	**166**	**143**	**86.14**

(<1%), that is, a keyword mistakenly identified though it is actually not there in the text, and hence we do not present precision in the table. We also observe that the average accuracy for detecting Bangla text with OCR is significantly poor compared to that of the English text, which can be attributed to the OCR performance and quality of visuals, but there is significant improvement after dictionary-based correction.

Similar to audio keyword spotting we performed the same experiments with the constrained set of keywords. Table 4 presents the results in details. We found that by using constrained keywords list the results at every stage have improved, though not as significantly as in the case of speech.

5.3. Improving Indexing Performance by Exploiting Redundancy. While, we have presented the retrieval performance for audio and visual keyword recognition task in the previous sections, the goal of the system is to index the news-stories with appropriate keywords. We define the indexing performance of the system as

$$IP = \frac{|k|}{|K|} \times 100, \qquad (1)$$

where k is the set of distinct keywords correctly identified (and used for indexing the story) and K is the set of distinct keywords present in the story.

The indexing performance is improved by exploiting redundancy in occurrence of keywords in audio-visual forms. In particular, we exploit two forms of redundancy.

(a) The same keywords are uttered several times in a story or appear several times on ticker text. A keyword missed out in one instance is often detected in another instance providing better indexing performance

(b) The same keyword may appear in both audio and visual forms. A keyword often missed in the speech is often detected in visuals and vice-versa. This adds to indexing performance too.

Let K_a and K_v denote the set of distinct keywords actually occurring in the speech and the visuals, respectively, in a news story. Then, $K_o = K_a \cup K_v$ represents the set of keywords appearing in the news-story. Similarly, let k_a and k_v represent the set of distinct keywords detected in the speech and visuals respectively. Then, $k_o = k_a \cup k_v$ represents the set of keywords detected in the news-story. The audio, visual, and overall indexing performance (IP_a, IP_v, and IP_o, resp.)

Stage	Image	OCR output	Keywords spotted
English news story (E004)			
Full frame (binarized)		The comment that star ED the controver Y …galnxn l:nursh¤•1o:Sa•:Mn Tendulkar has man bowled J al uc ua breaking Snlumn Khurmumd: Smzmn 'fuvwdulknr "('|[sAE*g5 Mw; Ima bcwlnd Thuckumy on thm Hamm N; gw :§::;.·:, ?::~r gx: eé §§§ §¤§¥1s§ ¥	Tendulkar(1)
After text localization		Salman Knumhaco: Sachin Tendulkar has man bowled Bal Tbuckuav	Salman Sachin Tendulkar Bal (4)
After image cleaning and super resolution		Salman Knurshaadz Sachin Tendulkar nas clean howled Bal Thackeray	Salman Sachin Tendulkar Bal Thackeray (5)
After dictionary based correction	----	----	Salman Khursheed Sachin TendulkarBal Thackeray (6)
Bangla news story (B004)			
Full frame (binarized)		ৈড য় \\\ ড়ুট্সছ়ু ঢ়ু-:ঢ়ৗ জিঢ়্যৗঢ়্যা ঢ়ুড়ু--র ।.!ঢ়ুন়ূ ৈড়ড় ছ়ু-ছ়ু */ ড়ী ৈড়ড়ীর়ঁড়ী 6ঁ ।ৱৈড় -ৈড়. ৱ ।চৗ।ৱৱৱৗৱৱ।ৱ।।।ৱ, চ়ানূ -ঁ ৈড়ৗ ঁ ঢ়ুঢ়ুড়ি।ৱ। ।ম়ুড়ী ।ম়ুঢ়ুৈড় 44সিউড়িয় 2 ন়ুস়র বূ়্ুতে ভ়ূ।ামূ-ল-সিপিৈ সমঘ়র্ ঙী! 'শ়ৃঢি ঢ়ুখ়ুঢ়ু কেলেলেল-ৈগঙ্গা ঢ়ুঢ়ু	None (0)
After text localization		সিউ়ড়িয় 2 ন়সুর বূ়্ুতে ত়ু।ামূ-ল-সিপিৈ ম সংঘর্ন	সিপিৈ ম (1)
After image cleaning and super resolution	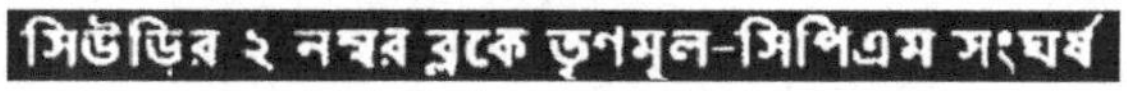	সিউ়ড়ির 2 ন়সর- বূ়্ুেক ভূণসুল-সিপিৈ ম সংঘর্ন	সিপিৈ ম ভূণসুল (2)
After dictionary based correction	----	----	সিপিৈ ম ভূণসুল সংঘর্ষ (3)

Figure 8: OCR outputs at different stages of English and Bangla ticker text processing.

can be measured as

$$\text{IP}_a = \frac{|k_a|}{|k_a|} \times 100, \qquad \text{IP}_v = \frac{|k_v|}{|k_v|} \times 100,$$

$$\text{IP}_o = \frac{|k_o|}{|k_o|} \times 100 \equiv \frac{|k_a \cup k_v|}{|k_a \cup k_v|} \times 100. \qquad (2)$$

Table 5 depicts the indexing performance of the audio, the visual and the overall system, with the constrained keyword list. Note that the indexing performances of audio and visual channels, both English and Bangla, are significantly higher than the respective recall values. This is because of the redundancy of occurrence of keywords

[1]	Keyword spotted in ticker text [2]	Keywords spotted in speech [3]	Combined keyword list [4]
English news story (E002)			
	Thackeray Sachin Sena Salman sports politics Milkha (7)	Kiran More* Sachin Tendulkar india politics Singh sports (9)	Thackeray Sachin Sena Salman sports politics Milkha Singh Kiran More Tendulkar india (12)
Bangala news story (E005)			
	গিরফ্তার, পুলিস, কলকাতা, হুজি (4)	লs র, গিরফ্তার, কলকাতা, লs র-e-তাঃ বা, বাংলাদেশ, বিতর্ক (6)	গিরফ্তার পুলিস কলকাতা হুজি লs র লs র-e-তাঃ বা বাংলাদেশ বিতর্ক (8)

FIGURE 9: Combining audio and visual keywords for indexing. *Kiran More: More (pronounced Moré) is a proper noun and not the English word.

in those individual channels. Finally, the overall indexing performance for the stories is greater than the indexing performances of individual audio/visual channels. This is because of the redundancy of keywords across audio and visual channels.

5.4. *Illustrative Examples.* This section provides some illustrative examples that explain the results in the previous sections. Figure 8 shows the OCR outputs at different stages of processing for examples of English and Bangla ticker text, taken from the stories E004 and B004, respectively. It illustrates the gradual improvement in results through the different stages of image processing and dictionary-based correction.

Figure 9 illustrates improvement in indexing performance by combining audio-visual cues, with an English and a Bangla example. Columns [2] and [3] in the figure show the correctly identified keywords from the ticker text and from speech, respectively. Column [4] depicts the combined keyword list that is used for indexing the story. The combined keyword list is derived as a union of keywords spotted in ticker text and in speech. In these examples, we observe that keywords not detected in speech are often detected in visuals and *vice-versa*. Thus, combining keywords detected in audio and visual forms leads to better indexing performance.

5.5. *Comparison.* While comparing the system performance, we keep in view the unreliability of the language tools for processing Indian transmission. For example, we have observed the average recall and precision values for keyword spotting in speech to be approximately 15% and 47%, respectively for English (see Table 1), as against typical values of 73% and 85%, respectively in [36]. We also observe that use of a constrained keyword list improves the average recall and precision values to 26% and 72%, respectively (see Table 2), which is still significantly below the reported figures. For keyword detection in ticker text, we have achieved an average recall of 59% (see Table 3) without dictionary-based correction; as compared to 70% reported in [50]. With dictionary-based correction, our recall improves to 67% (see Table 4), which is a reasonable achievement considering complexity of Indian Language alphabets.

An experiment to combine text from speech and visual has been reported in [51]. The authors report recall values for speech recognition and Video OCR as 13% and 6%, respectively. While speech recognition accuracy is comparable to ours, we find the poor OCR results surprising. The authors report a recall of 21% after combining audio and video and dictionary based postprocessing. We have achieved an indexing efficiency of 86%. Though the figures do not directly compare, our system seems to have achieved a much higher performance.

6. Conclusion

We have proposed an architectural framework for automated monitoring of multilingual news video in this paper. The basic idea behind our framework is to combine audio and visual modes to discover the keywords that characterize a particular news-story. Our primary contribution in this paper has been reliable indexing of Indian news telecasts with significant keywords despite inaccuracies of the language tools in processing noisy video channels and deficiencies of language technologies for many Indian Languages. The main contributing factor towards the reliable indexing has been selection of a few domain-specific keywords, in contrast to a complete transcription. Use of several preprocessing and postprocessing stages with the basic language tools has also added to the reliability of results. Moreover, use of RSS feeds to derive the keywords automatically results in contemporariness of the system, which could otherwise be a major operational issue. The conversion of English keywords, which are either proper or common nouns, to their Indian Language equivalents helps indexing non-English transmission with English (or any Indian Language) keywords. The complete end to end solution is made possible by integrating or enhancing available techniques in addition to proposing several techniques that make multilingual, multichannel news broadcast monitoring feasible. The experimental results establish the correctness of the system.

While we have so far experimented with English and one of the Indian languages, namely Bangla, we need to extend the solution to other Indian Languages by integrating appropriate language tools, which are being researched elsewhere in the country. Moreover, India is a large country with twenty-two officially recognized languages and many more "unofficial" languages and dialects. Language tools do not exist and are unlikely to be available in foreseeable future for many of these languages. We propose to direct our future work towards classification of news stories telecast in such languages based on their audio-visual similarity with stories in some reference channels (e.g., some channels in English), which can be indexed using the language technologies.

References

[1] G. S. Lehal, "Optical character recognition of Gurumukhi script using multiple classifiers," in *Proceedings of the International Workshop on Multilingual (OCR '09)*, Barcelona, Spain, July 2009.

[2] C. V. Jawahar, M. N. S. S. K. P. Kumar, and S. S. R. Kiran, "A bilingual OCR for Hindi-Telugu documents and its applications," in *Proceedings of the 7th International Conference on Document Analysis and Recognition (ICDAR '03)*, vol. 1, p. 408, 2003.

[3] E. Hassan, S. Chaudhury, and M. Gopal, "Shape descriptor based document image indexing and symbol recognition," in *Proceedings of the International Conference on Document Analysis and Recognition*, 2009.

[4] U. Bhattacharya and B. B. Chaudhuri, "Handwritten numeral databases of Indian scripts and multistage recognition of mixed numerals," *IEEE Transactions on Pattern Analysis and Machine Intelligence*, vol. 31, no. 3, pp. 444–457, 2009.

[5] S. K. Parui, K. Guin, U. Bhattacharya, and B. B. Chaudhuri, "Online handwritten Bangla character recognition using HMM," in *Proceedings of the International Conference on Pattern Recognition (ICPR '08)*, pp. 1–4, 2008.

[6] S. Eickeler and S. Mueller, "Content-based video indexing of TV broadcast news using hidden Markov models," in *Proceedings of the IEEE International Conference on Acoustics, Speech and Signal Processing (ICASSP '99)*, vol. 6, pp. 2997–3000, March 1999.

[7] J. R. Smith, M. Campbell, M. Naphade, A. Natsev, and J. Tesic, "Learning and classification of semantic concepts in broadcast video," in *Proceedings of the International Conference of Intelligence Analysis*, 2005.

[8] J.-L. Gauvain, L. Lamel, and G. Adda, "Transcribing broadcast news for audio and video indexing," *Communications of the ACM*, vol. 43, no. 2, pp. 64–70, 2000.

[9] H. Meinedo and J. Neto, "Detection of acoustic patterns in broadcast news using neural networks," *Acustica*, 2004.

[10] C.-M. Kuo, C.-P. Chao, W.-H. Chang, and J.-L. Shen, "Broadcast video logo detection and removing," in *Proceedings of the 4th International Conference on Intelligent Information Hiding and Multimedia Signal Processing (IIH-MSP '08)*, pp. 837–840, Harbin, China, August 2008.

[11] D. A. Sadlier, S. Marlow, N. Connor, and N. Murphy, "Automatic TV advertisement detection from MPEG bit stream," *Pattern Recognition*, vol. 35, no. 12, pp. 2719–2726, 2002.

[12] T.-Y. Liu, T. Qin, and H.-J. Zhang, "Time-constraint boost for TV commercials detection," in *Proceedings of the International Conference on Image Processing (ICIP '04)*, vol. 3, pp. 1617–1620, October 2004.

[13] X.-S. Hua, L. Lu, and H.-J. Zhang, "Robust learning-based TV commercial detection," in *Proceedings of the ACM International Conference on Multimedia and Expo (ICME '05)*, pp. 149–152, Amsterdam, The Netherlands, July 2005.

[14] K. Ng and V. W. Zue, "Phonetic recognition for spoken document retrieval," in *Proceedings of the IEEE International Conference on Acoustics, Speech and Signal Processing (ICASSP '98)*, vol. 1, pp. 325–328, 1998.

[15] M. Laxminarayana and S. Kopparapu, "Semi-automatic generation of pronunciation dictionary for proper names: an optimization approach," in *Proceedings of the 6th International Conference on Natural Language Processing (ICON '08)*, pp. 118–126, CDAC, Pune, India, December 2008.

[16] J. Makhoul, F. Kubala, T. Leek, et al., "Speech and language technologies for audio indexing and retrieval," *Proceedings of the IEEE*, vol. 88, no. 8, pp. 1338–1352, 2000.

[17] S. Renals, D. Abberley, D. Kirby, and T. Robinson, "Indexing and retrieval of broadcast news," *Speech Communication*, vol. 32, no. 1, pp. 5–20, 2000.

[18] T. Chua, S. Y. Neo, K. Li, et al., "TRECVID 2004 search and feature extraction tasks by NUS PRIS," in *NIST TRECVID-2004*, 2004.

[19] T. Chua, S.-F. Chang, L. Chaisorn, and W. Hsu, "Story boundary detection in large broadcast news video archives: techniques, experience and trends," in *Proceedings of the 12th ACM International Conference on Multimedia (MM '04)*, pp. 656–659, 2004.

[20] A. Rosenberg and J. Hirschberg, "Story segmentation of broadcast news in English, Mandarin and Arabic," in *Proceedings of the Human Language Technology Conference of the North American Chapter of the Association of Computational Linguistics*, June 2006.

[21] M. Franz and J.-M. Xu, "Story segmentation of broadcast news in Arabic, Chinese and English using multi-window features," in *Proceedings of the 30th Annual International ACM SIGIR Conference on Research and Development in Information Retrieval (SIGIR '07)*, pp. 703–704, 2007.

[22] M. A. Hearst, "TextTiling: segmenting text into multi-paragraph subtopic passages," *Computational Linguistics*, vol. 23, no. 1, pp. 33–64, 1997.

[23] X. Gao and X. Tang, "Unsupervised video-shot segmentation and model-free anchor-person detection for news video parsing," *IEEE Transactions on Circuits and Systems for Video Technology*, vol. 12, no. 9, pp. 765–776, 2002.

[24] S.-F. Chang, R. Manmatha, and T.-S. Chua, "Combining text and audio-visual features in video indexing," in *Proceedings of IEEE International Conference on Acoustics, Speech and Signal Processing (ICASSP '05)*, vol. 5, pp. 1005–1008, 2005.

[25] L. Chaisorn, T.-S. Chua, and C.-H. Lee, "A multi-modal approach to story segmentation for news video," *World Wide Web*, vol. 6, no. 2, pp. 187–208, 2003.

[26] L. Besacier, G. Quénot, S. Ayache, and D. Moraru, "Video story segmentation with multi-modal features: experiments on TRECvid 2003," in *Proceedings of the 6th ACM SIGMM International Workshop on Multimedia Information Retrieval (MIR '04)*, pp. 221–226, October 2004.

[27] Anonymous, "F1 Score," *Wikipedia—The Free Encyclopedia*, February 2010, http://en.wikipedia.org/wiki/F1_score.

[28] F. Colace, P. Foggia, and G. Percannella, "A probabilistic framework for TV-news stories detection and classification," in *Proceedings of the IEEE International Conference on Multimedia and Expo (ICME '05)*, pp. 1350–1353, July 2005.

[29] G. Harit, S. Chaudhury, and H. Ghosh, "Using multimedia ontology for generating conceptual annotations and hyperlinks in video collections," in *Proceedings of the IEEE/WIC/ACM International Conference on Web Intelligence (WI '06)*, pp. 211–217, Hong Kong, December 2006.

[30] Anonymous, "News Ticker," *Wikipedia—The Free Encyclopedia*, February 2010, http://en.wikipedia.org/wiki/News_ticker.

[31] D. Winer, "RSS 2.0 Specification," *Wikipedia—The free Encyclopedia*, February 2010, http://cyber.law.harvard.edu/rss/rss.html.

[32] S. Kopparapu, A. Srivastava, and P. V. S. Rao, "Minimal parsing key concept based question answering system," *Human Computer Interaction*, vol. 3, 2007.

[33] P. Gelin and C. J. Wellekens, "Keyword spotting for video soundtrack indexing," in *Proceedings of the IEEE International Conference on Acoustics, Speech, and Signal Processing*, vol. 1, pp. 299–302, May 1996.

[34] Y. Oh, J.-S. Park, and K.-M. Park, "Keyword spotting in broadcast news," in *Global-Network-Oriented Information Electronics (IGNOIE-COE06)*, pp. 208–213, Sendai, Japan, January 2007.

[35] G. Quenot, T. P. Tan, L. V. Bac, S. Ayache, L. Besacier, and P. Mulhem, "Content-based search in multi-lingual audiovisual documents using the international phonetic alphabet," in *Proceedings of the 7th International Workshop on Content-Based Multimedia Indexing (CBMI '09)*, Chania, Greece, June 2009.

[36] D. Dimitriadis, A. Metallinou, I. Konstantinou, G. Goumas, P. Maragos, and N. Koziris, "GRIDNEWS1a distributed automatic Greek broadcast transcription system," in *Proceedings of the IEEE International Conference on Acoustics, Speech and Signal Processing (ICASSP '09)*, 2009.

[37] J. Yi, Y. Peng, and J. Xiao, "Color-based clustering for text detection and extraction in image," in *Proceedings of the ACM International Multimedia Conference and Exhibition (MM '07)*, pp. 847–850, Augsburg, Germany, Sebtember 2007.

[38] J. Sun, Z. Wang, H. Yu, F. Nishino, Y. Katsuyama, and S. Naoi, "Effective text extraction and recognition for WWW images," in *Proceedings of the ACM Symposium on Document Engineering (DocEng '03)*, pp. 115–117, Grenoble, France, November 2003.

[39] Q. Ye, Q. Huang, W. Gao, and D. Zhao, "Fast and robust text detection in images and video frames," *Image and Vision Computing*, vol. 23, no. 6, pp. 565–576, 2005.

[40] J. Gllavata, R. Ewerth, and B. Freisleben, "Tracking text in MPEG videos," *ACM*, 2004.

[41] A. D. Bagdanov, L. Ballan, M. Bertini, and A. Del Bimbo, "Trademark matching and retrieval in sports video databases," in *Proceedings of the International Workshop on Multimedia Information Retrieval (MIR '07)*, pp. 79–86, Augsburg, Germany, Sebtember 2007.

[42] N. Otsu, "A threshold selection method from gray-level histograms," *IEEE Transactions on Systems, Man, and Cybernetics*, vol. 9, no. 1, pp. 62–66, 1979.

[43] R. Y. Tsai and T. S. Huang, "Multiple frame image restoration and registration," in *Advances in Computer Vision and Image Processing*, pp. 317–339, JAI Press, Greenwich, Conn, USA, 1984.

[44] V. H. Patil, D. S. Bormane, and H. K. Patil, "Color super resolution image reconstruction," in *Proceedings of the International Conference on Computational Intelligence and Multimedia Applications (ICCIMA '07)*, vol. 3, pp. 366–370, 2007.

[45] P. Vandewalle, S. Süsstrunk, and M. Vetterli, "A frequency domain approach to registration of aliased images with application to super-resolution," *EURASIP Journal on Applied Signal Processing*, vol. 2006, pp. 1–14, 2006.

[46] M. A. Hasnat, M. R. Chowdhury, and M. Khan, "Integrating Bangla script recognition support in Tesseract OCR," in *Proceedings of the Conference on Language and Technology*, 2009.

[47] S. V. Rice, F. R. Jenkins, and T. A. Nartker, "The fourth annual test of OCR accuracy," Tech. Rep. 95-04, Information Science Research Institute, University of Nevada, Las Vegas, Nev, USA, April 1995.

[48] R. Smith, "An overview of the Tesseract OCR engine," in *Proceedings of the 9th International Conference on Document Analysis and Recognition (ICDAR '07)*, vol. 2, pp. 629–633, September 2007.

[49] M. Gilleland, "Levenshtein Distance, in Three Flavors," February 2010, http://www.merriampark.com/ld.htm.

[50] R. Lienhart and A. Wernicke, "Localizing and segmenting text in images and videos," *IEEE Transactions on Circuits and Systems for Video Technology*, vol. 12, no. 4, pp. 256–268, 2002.

[51] A. G. Hauptmann, R. Jin, and T. D. Ng, "Multi-modal information retrieval from broadcast video using OCR and speech recognition," in *Proceedings of the 2nd ACM International Conference on Digital Libraries*, pp. 160–161, Portland, Ore, USA, 2002.

13

Nonconvex Optimization of Collaborative Multiband Spectrum Sensing for Cognitive Radios with Genetic Algorithms

Michele Sanna and Maurizio Murroni

Department of Electrical and Electronic Engineering, DIEE, University of Cagliari, 09123 Cagliari, Italy

Correspondence should be addressed to Michele Sanna, michele.sanna@diee.unica.it

Academic Editor: Marina Mondin

Cognitive Radio (CR) is a novel technology that permits secondary users (SUs) to transmit alongside primary users (PUs). PUs retain transparent communications whereas SUs perform spectrum sensing and adaptive transmission to avoid collisions. Ultra-wideband sensing is of primary importance for SU to sense and access opportunistically several bands at a time. Reliable detection in wide geographical regions needs collaborative sensing. Optimal collaborative multiband sensing is not analytically solvable unless some approximations and solution domain restrictions are applied for convexity exploitation. In this paper, we demonstrate that convex constraints are deleterious. We propose an alternative optimization technique based on genetic algorithms. Genetic programming performs a direct search of the optimal solution without approximations and solution domain restrictions. As a consequence, collaborative multiband sensing can be consistently optimized without limitations. Additionally the genetic optimization exploits the correlation of time-varying channels for fast adaptive convergence.

1. Introduction

Recent studies have revealed a deep underutilization of the electromagnetic resource due to the static allocation of spectrum band licenses [1]. Large portions of spectrum remain unexploited during certain periods of time and in certain geographical regions, yielding to an average 90% idleness of the licensed bands—the so-called *spectral holes*. The few unlicensed ISM bands are rapidly overloading due to the boom of wireless applications demanding for sporadic access to the spectrum. Cognitive Radio (CR) is a novel technology introduced with the intent of intelligently exploiting the unused spectrum [2, 3]. In a cognitive network, secondary users (SUs) are allowed to operate in licensed bands, under the condition that they do not interfere with the transmissions of the primary users (PUs), legal lessees of the license. Cognitive SUs detect the presence or the absence of transmissions, and identify the unused portions of spectrum. Then they may adapt their time-frequency transmission parameters in order to occupy the detected spectral holes. Some new standards are already adopting this paradigm. IEEE P.1900, for instance, is developing a whole type of ad-hoc wireless network based on Dynamic Spectrum Access (DSA) to the available spectrum [4]. IEEE 802.22 standard is considering the TV bands of the Ultra-High Frequencies (UHFs) for Wireless Regional Area Networks (WRANs) [5, 6].

Spectrum sensing is performed to detect the existing transmissions and identify the spectral holes. Reliable and extensive detection should be performed in order to avoid unwanted collisions and find as much free resources as possible. Observing an ultra-wide range of frequencies at a time is a challenging task since it requires expensive high-speed RF equipment. Although there have been some proposals of wavelet decomposition for multiresolution analysis [7], a common approach is to use tunable bandpass filters and observe one band at a time. Multiband Joint Detection proposed by Quan et al. in [8] applies narrowband sensing techniques to operate an opportunistic optimization of the throughput over multiple independent bands. The channel is divided into K nonoverlapping narrow subbands which may be utilized by distinct primary systems or may be blindly sensed, that is, without knowing who is transmitting there. Energy thresholds for each subband have to be chosen for optimal detection aimed at maximizing the throughput and limiting the interference.

Single CR sensing results can be affected by shadowing or multipath fading [9]. SU may cause harmful interference to the primaries for unreliable decision. Multiple geographically distributed CR can perform collaborative sensing by combining their results and improve performance. In Linear Statistics Combination (LSC), a simple fusion rule of the power levels is applied to perform a reliability-enhanced unique decision. The weights of a linear combination have to be determined by formulating an optimization problem. LSC has demonstrated to noticeably enhance the performance of individual sensors [10].

By applying LSC to multiband detection, Quan proposed the Spatial-Spectral Joint Detection [11]. Multiple independently-sensed levels are bandwise combined in order to increase the reliability in each subband. As a consequence, the useful throughput is increased while further limiting the interference.

Optimal multiband detection is achieved by formulating an optimization problem. Since in general the aforementioned formulations are nonconvex, some methods have been proposed to transform or approximate the problems and limit the solution domain in order to exploit the hidden convexity [8]. Such constraints bind the maximum interference and minimum channel utilization, with a loss of generality in the practical detection configurations.

In this paper we propose at first an alternative formulation of the multiband sensing and then an implementation of the genetic algorithms that solve the presented formulations of detection problems. Our formulation of the multiband sensing interprets the limited interference regime as a bound on the interference caused in each subband, rather than the aggregate disturbance throughout the wideband channel. This yields to a direct solution for the noncollaborative multiband problem. It also reduces the collaborative multiband sensing problem to a set of simple narrowband LSC optimizations, still keeping a controlled interference regime and the aggregate throughput as the objective of the maximization. We then propose the genetic programming as a solving technique that avoids reformulations, approximations, and limitations. Genetic Algorithms (GAs) are extensively used to find true or approximate solutions in different communications engineering applications such as, for instance, network design [12] and adaptive modulations [13]. GAs perform a direct search of the best solution by considering sets of candidates and evaluating them singularly by means of a fitness measure, objective of the maximization. Then they iteratively drop unfit elements and select the fittest ones for combination (reproduction) and random alteration (genetic mutation) [14]. GAs work one step above mathematical analysis, dealing well with nondifferentiable functions as well as functions with multiple local maxima. Exploitation of hidden convexity is not necessary so that no reformulations or approximations of the problem are performed. We show how the genetic programming, by working directly at the root of the problem, can be an efficient and powerful optimization and analysis tool for all possible CR systems. Additionally, GAs demonstrate to exploit the correlation of different detection conditions with time-varying channels. Moving CR senses a channel with

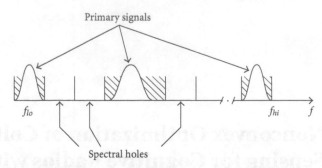

FIGURE 1: Schematic representation of the multiband channel.

variable statistics. GAs exploit the statistical dependence of consecutive sensing events by performing an optimization that starts from the result of the previous instant. The sensing precision is drastically improved as well as the convergence time.

The paper is organized as follows. In Section 2, the multiband detection framework is presented. Section 3 introduces the collaborative sensing within the opportunistic multiband fashion. Section 4 analyzes the genetic algorithms and the possibilities of application. In Section 5 are produced the generic numerical results, whereas Section 6 introduces the results for adaptive optimization and Section 7 concludes the paper.

2. Opportunistic Multiband Sensing

Multiband sensing considers a channel divided into K narrow subbands where one or more primary communication systems may be transmitting. A cognitive SU applies narrowband sensing to each subchannel in order to maximize its own transmission without harm for the PU.

2.1. Narrowband Signal Detection. A CR senses constantly the spectrum to discover which of the K subchannels are free of primary transmissions (Figure 1). Deciding for the condition of the single kth subband means posing the following binary condition [15]:

$$
\begin{aligned}
\mathcal{H}_{0,k} &: X_k = V_k, \\
\mathcal{H}_{1,k} &: X_k = H_k S_k + V_k, \quad k = 1, \ldots, K,
\end{aligned}
\tag{1}
$$

where $\mathcal{H}_0$ represents the absence of primary signal (only Gaussian noise V_k with power σ_v^2) and $\mathcal{H}_1$ represents the presence of primary signal S_k, corrupted by Gaussian noise V_k. Capital letters indicate that we are considering the frequency spectra. H_k is the channel gain between the primary transmitter and the secondary receiver. The presence or absence of the primary signal in each subband is then verified as follows:

$$
Y_k \triangleq \sum_{n=1}^{N} |X_k(n)|^2 \underset{\mathcal{H}_0}{\overset{\mathcal{H}_1}{\gtrless}} \gamma_k, \quad k = 1, \ldots, K,
\tag{2}
$$

where γ_k is the subband energy threshold. The test statistics Y_k can be considered asymptotically normally distributed if

N is large enough (e.g., $N > 10$). The performance of the detection is calculated in terms of

(i) probability of identifying the spectral hole:

$$P(\mathcal{H}_{0,k} \mid \mathcal{H}_{0,k}) = 1 - P(\mathcal{H}_{1,k} \mid \mathcal{H}_{0,k}) = 1 - P_f^{(k)}, \quad (3)$$

(ii) probability of missed detection (interference):

$$P(\mathcal{H}_{0,k} \mid \mathcal{H}_{1,k}) = 1 - P(\mathcal{H}_{1,k} \mid \mathcal{H}_{1,k}) = 1 - P_d^{(k)}, \quad (4)$$

where $P_f^{(k)}$ is the probability of false alarm and $P_d^{(k)}$ is the probability of detecting a primary signal. The random variables Y_k have Gaussian distribution $Y_k \sim \mathcal{N}(\mu_{0,k}, \sigma_{0,k}^2)$ under hypothesis $\mathcal{H}_{0,k}$ and $Y_k \sim \mathcal{N}(\mu_{1,k}, \sigma_{1,k}^2)$ under $\mathcal{H}_{1,k}$.

Thus, $P_f^{(k)}$ and $P_d^{(k)}$ can be calculated as the tail of a normal distribution:

$$P_f^{(k)} = P(\mathcal{H}_{1,k} \mid \mathcal{H}_{0,k}) = Q\left(\frac{\gamma_k - \mu_{0,k}}{\sigma_{0,k}}\right), \quad (5)$$

$$P_d^{(k)} = P(\mathcal{H}_{1,k} \mid \mathcal{H}_{1,k}) = Q\left(\frac{\gamma_k - \mu_{1,k}}{\sigma_{1,k}}\right). \quad (6)$$

Increasing the utilization of the channel implies higher interference to the PU. The thresholds have to be optimized in order to maximize the utilization while limiting the interference.

2.2. Multiband Detection. Opportunistic multiband detection optimizes the aggregate throughput throughout the K subbands while limiting the interference (Figure 1). The design objective is to find an optimal vector of thresholds $\boldsymbol{\gamma} = [\gamma_1, \gamma_2, \ldots, \gamma_K]^T$ such that the free spectrum holes are efficiently exploited and a controlled level of interference is produced. The probabilities of false alarm and detection can be represented compactly as follows:

$$\mathbf{P}_f(\boldsymbol{\gamma}) = \left[P_f^{(1)}(\gamma_1), P_f^{(2)}(\gamma_2), \ldots, P_f^{(K)}(\gamma_K)\right]^T,$$
$$\mathbf{P}_d(\boldsymbol{\gamma}) = \left[P_d^{(1)}(\gamma_1), P_d^{(2)}(\gamma_2), \ldots, P_d^{(K)}(\gamma_K)\right]^T. \quad (7)$$

Given that $\mathbf{1} - \mathbf{P}_f(\boldsymbol{\gamma})$ denotes the probabilities of detecting the free subbands, r_k denotes the achievable throughput over the kth subband and that $\mathbf{r} = [r_1, r_2, \ldots, r_K]^T$, we can express the aggregate opportunistic throughput reached over the K subbands as

$$R(\boldsymbol{\gamma}) = \mathbf{r}^T\left[\mathbf{1} - \mathbf{P}_f(\boldsymbol{\gamma})\right]. \quad (8)$$

Similarly, if $\mathbf{1} - \mathbf{P}_d(\boldsymbol{\gamma})$ is the vector of probabilities of interference and $\mathbf{c} = [c_1, c_2, \ldots, c_K]^T$ is a measure of cost caused by transmitting in the subbands, then the aggregate interference can be expressed as

$$I(\boldsymbol{\gamma}) = \mathbf{c}^T\left[\mathbf{1} - \mathbf{P}_d(\boldsymbol{\gamma})\right]. \quad (9)$$

The maximization of (8) and the minimization of (9) are conflicting tasks. According to the formulation suggested by Quan et al. in [8], we limit the per-band interference $(1 - P_d^{(k)} \leq \alpha_k)$, as well as the aggregate interference (9), and ensure a minimum utilization $(1 - P_f^{(k)} \geq \beta_k)$. The optimization becomes finding the appropriate thresholds $\boldsymbol{\gamma}$ that maximize (8) with the aforementioned bounds [8]:

$$\max_{\boldsymbol{\gamma}} \quad R(\boldsymbol{\gamma})$$
$$\text{s.t.} \quad I(\boldsymbol{\gamma}) \leq \epsilon,$$
$$1 - \mathbf{P}_d(\boldsymbol{\gamma}) \leq \boldsymbol{\alpha}, \quad (P1)$$
$$1 - \mathbf{P}_f(\boldsymbol{\gamma}) \geq \boldsymbol{\beta}.$$

The subchannel interference and utilization bounds can be translated to the linear constraint

$$\gamma_{\min,k} \leq \gamma_k \leq \gamma_{\max,k}, \quad k = 1, 2, \ldots, K \quad (10)$$

to be imposed to (P1), where

$$\gamma_{\min,k} = \mu_{0,k} + \sigma_{0,k}Q^{-1}(1 - \beta_k),$$
$$\gamma_{\max,k} = \mu_{1,k} + \sigma_{1,k}Q^{-1}(1 - \alpha_k). \quad (11)$$

Problem (P1) is convex if the utilization is at least 50% ($\beta_k \geq 0.5$) and the interference at most 50% ($\alpha_k \leq 0.5$). Although these prerequisites are reasonable in many cases, convex maximization is not able to solve (P1) without these impositions.

In Section 4, we introduce the the genetic algorithms to solve the optimization for nonconvex CR systems, including the cases $\beta_k < 0.5$ and $\alpha_k > 0.5$.

3. Collaborative Multiband Sensing

The introduction of cooperative sensing aims at improving the sensing reliability in order to reduce the interference. Let us consider now a set of M CR operating in the primary region (Figure 2). The sensors detect individually the presence of primary transmissions by sensing the surrounding channel in each narrow subband and pose the binary condition (1).

3.1. Reliable Sensing. The receiving conditions of one single CR are subject to fading so that the sensing of only one single terminal can produce unreliable results (Figure 2) [9].

   (i) Hidden terminal: a sensor (CR1) is located behind an obstacle. It senses a low power signal from PTx and may thus decide for $\mathcal{H}_0$ also when the transmission is present, affecting the reception of PRx.

   (ii) Far terminal: a sensor (CR2) lies outside the primary range. It receives a low power level due to the distance and thus decides for $\mathcal{H}_0$. Its transmission can produce interference to PRx, which is inside the primary range.

Space diversity is exploited in CS to increase the reliability of the decision by combining the sensed power levels in a spatially distributed channel.

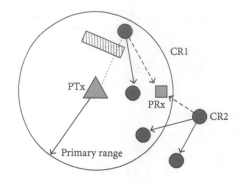

△ Primary transmitter (PTx)
■ Primary recevier (PRx)
● Cognitive radio (CR)
▨ Solid obstacle
⟶ Secondary transmission
--➤ Interference committed

FIGURE 2: Examples of secondary interferences by cognitive sensors.

3.2. Collaborative Detection. Let us consider the signal received by each CR in one single narrow subband. The structure of a narrowband energy detector is (2) for each kth subchannel.

The sensing results are collected channelwise into a vector $\mathbf{Y}_k \triangleq [Y_k(1), Y_k(2), \ldots, Y_k(M)]^T$. Then, for each band, the M sensed levels are linearly combined with a vector of weights $\mathbf{w}_k$ and compared to the subband threshold γ_k [10]:

$$\mathbf{w}_k^T \mathbf{Y}_k = \sum_{i=1}^{M} w_k(i) Y_k(i) \underset{\mathcal{H}_0}{\overset{\mathcal{H}_1}{\gtrless}} \gamma_k, \quad k = 1, \ldots, K. \quad (12)$$

The weight factors $0 \le w_k(i) \le 1$ represent the contributions of the different CR in the respective subchannels. A high weight is more likely to correspond to a sensor with good SNR. The probabilities of false alarm (5) and detection (6) are now expressed as:

$$P_f^{(k)}(\mathbf{w}_k, \gamma_k) = Q\left(\frac{\gamma_k - \mathbf{w}_k^T \boldsymbol{\mu}_{0,k}}{\sqrt{\mathbf{w}_k^T \boldsymbol{\Sigma}_{0,k} \mathbf{w}_k}}\right), \quad (13)$$

$$P_d^{(k)}(\mathbf{w}_k, \gamma_k) = Q\left(\frac{\gamma_k - \mathbf{w}_k^T \boldsymbol{\mu}_{1,k}}{\sqrt{\mathbf{w}_k^T \boldsymbol{\Sigma}_{1,k} \mathbf{w}_k}}\right). \quad (14)$$

Throughput and interference depend now on the weight matrix $\mathbf{W} = [\mathbf{w}_1, \mathbf{w}_2, \ldots, \mathbf{w}_K]$ and the threshold vector $\boldsymbol{\gamma}$:

$$R(\mathbf{W}, \boldsymbol{\gamma}) = \mathbf{r}^T [\mathbf{1} - \mathbf{P}_f(\mathbf{W}, \boldsymbol{\gamma})], \quad (15)$$

$$I(\mathbf{W}, \boldsymbol{\gamma}) = \mathbf{c}^T [\mathbf{1} - \mathbf{P}_d(\mathbf{W}, \boldsymbol{\gamma})]. \quad (16)$$

Coherently with the noncollaborative formulation, the collaborative multiband detection as proposed by Quan et al. in [8] is

$$\max_{\mathbf{W}, \boldsymbol{\gamma}} \quad R(\mathbf{W}, \boldsymbol{\gamma})$$

$$\text{s.t.} \quad I(\mathbf{W}, \boldsymbol{\gamma}) \le \epsilon,$$

$$\mathbf{1} - \mathbf{P}_d(\mathbf{W}, \boldsymbol{\gamma}) \le \boldsymbol{\alpha}, \quad (P2)$$

$$\mathbf{1} - \mathbf{P}_f(\mathbf{W}, \boldsymbol{\gamma}) \ge \boldsymbol{\beta}.$$

The previous considerations apply. This formulation provides further complications for convex optimization. The maximization is not convex and has to be lower bounded with another convex function. This brings loss of performance in terms of achievable throughput [8].

In the next section we introduce an alternative formulation of the multiband detection problem that can be solved by maximizing the LSC.

Then in Section 4 we introduce GA to solve directly the joint detection problem without the limitation of the convexity constraints.

3.3. Multiband Detection without Aggregate Constraint: LSC Optimization. Multiband detection without aggregate constraint can be seen as a collaborative detection with multiband aggregation. This alternative formulation of the multiband detection problem aims at achieving performance optimization with linear collaboration maximization applied to the single bands, still maximizing the aggregate throughput. LSC problem is less complex compared to the aforementioned formulations, which results in a faster and more precise solution with GA.

Let the secondary CR sense K subchannels which are licensed each one to a different primary system. Then the aggregate interference (16) caused by the SU is not a relevant index of caused harm because it is distributed between distinct PUs. It is rather more critical to limit the interference in the individual bands $P_m^{(k)}$ and look for the best weights and thresholds that maximize the throughput (15):

$$\max_{\mathbf{W}, \boldsymbol{\gamma}} \quad R(\mathbf{W}, \boldsymbol{\gamma})$$

$$\text{s.t.} \quad \mathbf{P}_m(\mathbf{W}, \boldsymbol{\gamma}) = \mathbf{1} - \mathbf{P}_d(\mathbf{W}, \boldsymbol{\gamma}) \le \boldsymbol{\alpha}. \quad (P3)$$

No minimum utilization is imposed, given that it may be not always necessary. A weight optimization for the linear statistic combination must be performed in each subband, in order to maximize the subchannel utilization:

$$\max_{\gamma, \mathbf{w}_k} \quad P(\mathcal{H}_{0,k} \mid \mathcal{H}_{0,k})$$

$$\text{s.t.} \quad P(\mathcal{H}_{0,k} \mid \mathcal{H}_{1,k}) \le \alpha_k, \quad k = 1, \ldots, K. \quad (P3a)$$

We can explicit the threshold from the interference constraint by means of (14)

$$\gamma_k = Q^{-1}(1 - \alpha_k)\sqrt{\mathbf{w}_k^T \boldsymbol{\Sigma}_{1,k} \mathbf{w}_k} + \boldsymbol{\mu}_{1,k}^T \mathbf{w}_k, \quad (17)$$

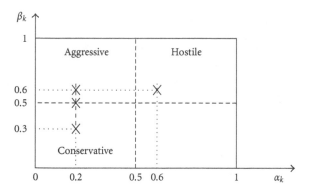

FIGURE 3: Schema of the CR classes plane. Case studies of Figure 5 are indicated with a cross.

and we can solve for $k = 1, \ldots, K$, the following unconstrained maximization:

$$\max_{\mathbf{w}_k} \frac{Q^{-1}(1 - \alpha_k)\sqrt{\mathbf{w}_k^T \mathbf{\Sigma}_{1,k} \mathbf{w}_k} + \left(\boldsymbol{\mu}_{1,k} - \boldsymbol{\mu}_{0,k}\right)^T \mathbf{w}_k}{\sqrt{\mathbf{w}_k^T \mathbf{\Sigma}_{0,k} \mathbf{w}_k}}, \quad (18)$$

where $\boldsymbol{\mu}_{0,k}$ and $\mathbf{\Sigma}_{0,k}$ are the vector of the M average power levels and the matrix of covariances relative to the kth subband in case of $\mathcal{H}_0$, respectively—$\boldsymbol{\mu}_{1,k}$ and $\mathbf{\Sigma}_{1,k}$ in case of $\mathcal{H}_1$, respectively.

Function (18) is again nonconvex in general. Convex maximization is feasible in the case $P_d \leq 0.5$, where hidden convexity is exploitable. Then separate convex subdomains may be considered for the application of techniques such as Semidefinite Programming (SDP), which requires complex reformulations in matrix forms [16]. The eventuality of a system with nonexploitable convexity is not far from reality especially when few CRs collaborate together. Other solving techniques have to be implemented.

3.4. CR Systems Classification. A common classification of CR systems is based on the per-band utilization and interference (Figure 3) [10]

(i) *Conservative System*: A *conservative* CR system has a utilization less or equal to 50% ($\beta_k \leq 0.5$) and a probability of interference smaller than 50% ($\alpha_k < 0.5$).

(ii) *Aggressive System*: An *aggressive* CR system achieves a utilization higher than 50% ($\beta_k > 0.5$) and an interference less than 50% ($\alpha_k < 0.5$).

(iii) *Hostile System*: A *hostile* CR system targets more than 50% of spectrum utilization ($\beta_k > 0.5$), causing at least 50% of interference ($\alpha_k \geq 0.5$).

The Q(x) function is convex if $x > 0$ and concave if $x \leq 0$. Consequently, a necessary condition for (P1) and (P2) to have convex objective with concave constraints is that

$$\beta_k \geq 0.5, \quad \alpha_k \leq 0.5, \quad k = 1, \ldots, K, \quad (19)$$

that is, the system must be *aggressive*. For the problem (P1) this is also a sufficient condition, whereas when considering the weights (P2) the objective throughput is to be additionally lower bounded by a function, for which the aforementioned conditions are sufficient for convexity. The lower bound brings a loss of performance as documented in [8]. The convexity region includes the values from the *conservative* region where $\beta_k = 0.5$ and from the *hostile* systems where $\alpha_k = 0.5$ (Figure 3). The inside of the other regions is in any case not solvable with convex maximization.

The α_k and β_k values are bounds for the minimum and maximum per-band threshold by means of (11), which limit above and below aggregate interference and throughput. An exemplary behavior is that an *aggressive* system may not transmit with low bitrate because a minimum per-band utilization is imposed. It can not either cause less disturbance than a lower implied threshold by the utilization bound.

Section 4 introduces thus the genetic algorithm for solving without convexity limitations these three sensing problems.

(i) Individual Multiband Detection (P1).

(ii) Collaborative Multiband Detection (P2).

(iii) Collaborative Multiband Detection without aggregate interference constraint—LSC (P3).

We show how the genetic approach performs a direct search of the solution that provides the highest throughput by generating, comparing, and discarding various solutions. The advantages of such approach are that it does not need any problem reformulations or mathematical constraints. It is thus suggested as an acceptable way of solving directly the sensing problems for all CR system classes.

4. Optimization Using Genetics

Genetic Algorithms (GA) belong to the class of the evolutionary models for solving optimization and maximization problems (OP) [14]. The natural evolution processes are simulated by means of *natural selection* and *survival of the fittest* in order to find the maximum of a function. GA demonstrated optimum performance with complex multidimensional OP. Nonconvex maximizations (P1), (P2), and (P3) are problems where a lot of methods fail or manage to solve only a subset of cases.

4.1. The Genetic Algorithms. GAs consider a *population* of potential solution vectors to the OP and iteratively select good elements and drop unfits to let the best ones survive from generation to generation. The independent variables are called *genes* and they form a vector called *chromosome* $\mathbf{g}_k^{(n)}$. The numerical realization of such variables (the *genotype*) is a potential solution to the problem—also referred to as an *individuals* or an *element* of a population. The genes are different for the noncollaborative and collaborative problems. Namely the chromosome is

$$\mathbf{g}_k^{(n)} = \begin{cases} \boldsymbol{\gamma}_k^{(n)}, & \text{for (P1),} \\ \left[\mathbf{w}_{1,k}^{(n)}, \mathbf{w}_{2,k}^{(n)}, \ldots, \mathbf{w}_{M,k}^{(n)}, \boldsymbol{\gamma}_k^{(n)}\right] & \text{for (P2),} \\ \mathbf{w}_k^{(n)}, & \text{for (P3).} \end{cases} \quad (20)$$

The genes are the independent variables of the throughput function (8), which is the objective of the maximization. A generation is a set of genotypes at the nth iteration. The subscript $k = 1, \ldots, \text{Pop}_{\text{size}}$ distinguishes the genotypes of a certain generation:

$$G_n = \left\{ \mathbf{g}_1^{(n)}, \mathbf{g}_2^{(n)}, \ldots, \mathbf{g}_{\text{Pop\_size}}^{(n)} \right\}. \tag{21}$$

The index of the generation is $n = 0, 1, 2, \ldots, N_{\text{gen}}$. In order to determine which genotypes fit the problem, a *fitness score* is calculated for each element:

$$\mathbf{s}(n) = \left\{ f\left(\mathbf{g}_1^{(n)}\right), f\left(\mathbf{g}_2^{(n)}\right), \ldots, f\left(\mathbf{g}_{\text{Pop\_size}}^{(n)}\right) \right\}. \tag{22}$$

The fitness function is the objective of the maximization, that is, the throughput (15) in (P1) and (P2) and (18) in (P3). Consecutive generations of solutions and their scores are examined iteratively in order to determine which individuals are suitable for surviving to the next generation as shown in Figure 4.

The generation zero is created randomly, whereas each generation $n + 1$ is created recursively in three steps.

(1) *Selection*: An intermediate population is created by performing the (natural) selection. The individuals with the best fitness scores are duplicated (in a predefined percentage) and the rest are discarded.

(2) *Crossover*: The intermediate population is recombined to simulate the reproduction. Survived elements are taken couplewise and, according to a mixing criterion, a number of children members are created from each couple.

(3) *Mutation*: A percentage of the offspring randomly mutates to create new genotypes. Spreading the search at each generation avoids restraining in a local maximum due to deception (see Section 4.2).

After these steps a new generation G_{n+1} is created from the previous one, with closer elements to the optimal solution (Figure 4). The children elements that do not respect the constraints are dropped. An equal number of elements is regenerated and the constraint is reevaluated, which can increase the computational load.

The evaluation and generation steps are performed iteratively, in order to increase the percentage of fit members. The computation is terminated when the fitness of the population remains unchanged for a sufficient lapse of generations or if the maximum number of generations Max _gen is reached. The genotype with the highest fitness is chosen as the final solution. The convergence precision depends on multiple factors and influences directly the time consumption of the process, as it is discussed in the following Section. For more details about GA refer to [14, 17].

4.2. Feasibility of the Genetic Approach.
GAs are introduced because of the limitations observed when treating the intrinsically nonconvex detection problem with convex optimization methods. There is a single convex domain in (P1) and (P2), with the constraints (19) [8]. LSC (18) has two convex subdomains under a maximum interference bound, to be treated separately. Each one can be optimized with complex methods such as the SDP technique [16]. Other methods like the so-called *hill-climbing* methods need the objective function to be well behaved, that is, it has to be continuous as well as its derivatives. The function also has to be *unimodal*, that is, with only one peak, because with many peaks the search may stop at the first undergone relative maximum.

The main motivation for using GA is that they solve such complex multidimensional problems without in-depth function study, constraints, or reformulations. GAs do not have mathematical limitations such as the convexity requirement. They abstract from the smoothness of the objective function, because they calculate isolated points ignoring discontinuities, cusps, and inflections. GAs also perform well in presence of multiple relative maxima (e.g., in presence of ripples) by spreading the population variety and evaluate as much genotype variety as possible. This way of working one step above the complications of function analysis makes GA suitable for solving the multiband detection problem with any values of α_k and β_k.

Drawbacks of genetic programming are the *deception* and the computational load. The *deception* is the surviving of an apparently fit subpopulation that leads away from the global optimum [18]. This is equivalent to say that local maxima may cause ambiguity that let a GA converge away from the global maximum or not converge at all in reasonable time (slow finishing). Although this is in general not desirable, it has been proven that it is worth using GA if the OP to be solved presents a certain degree of deception, whereas regular-behaved problems are better solved with other methods [18]. In fact, GA have a strong attitude at escaping from local maxima by spreading around the search. Setting up appropriately the parameters of our GA is fundamental to find an optimal configuration for each kind of problem.

GAs also have a characteristic that makes them profitable in time-varying channels, such as the mobile radio channel. The channel statistics $\{\boldsymbol{\mu}_i, \boldsymbol{\Sigma}_i, i = 0, 1\}$ vary due to the movement of the sensors with respect to the PTx. At each sensing instant, reliable cooperation requires an optimization of the weights to adapt to the new statistics. Performing a new optimization procedure at each sensing instant is inefficient, if it is done with SDP or other convex maximization methods. Since the statistics are supposed not to vary too much, the weights of each sensing instant are correlated with the preceding ones. GAs can keep memory of the previous weights and use them as the starting point for the new elaboration. The convergence is faster since the starting vector should be already close to the new optimum.

4.3. Computational Cost.
The computational effort is measured as the number of function evaluations that have to be done to complete a computation. As function evaluations we consider both fitness evaluations and constraints verifications indistinctly, since they have the same form and imply the same number of floating point operations. Comparisons

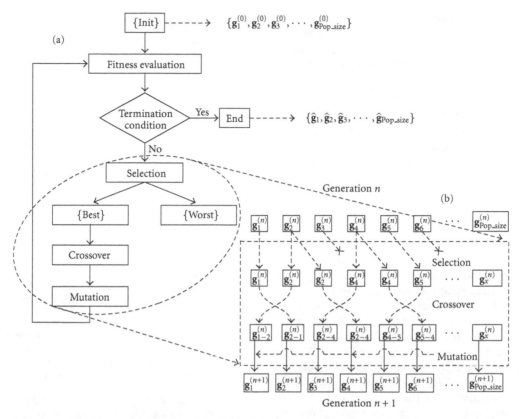

FIGURE 4: Flowchart of the proposed GA (a) and the three steps for the creation of a generation (b).

and data duplications are negligible. In order to converge with a certain accuracy our GA may need big populations and/or more generations, whereas small populations may result in insufficient precision or slow finishing.

The number of computations grows linearly with the population size. Since the aggregate interference constraint cannot be explicited, it has to be computed for each member. Those members that do not respect the constraint are regenerated and a further constraint evaluation is performed. In (P1) the verification of the per-band interference and per-band utilization (10) is made in the genotype space, so they do not yield to other function evaluations and no further increase of the computational load. All constraints in (P2) have instead to be verified for each generation. In general if we name h the total number of function evaluations that have to be computed for each member, then the total number of computations for a genetic optimization is

$$N_{\text{eval}} = h * \text{Pop}_{\text{size}} * N_{\text{gen}}. \tag{23}$$

In unconstrained optimization such as (P3), $h = 1$. In multiband problems (P1) and (P2), $h \geq 2$, because of one fitness and one constraint verification. The value grows as much as how many regenerations are needed in average to find one constraints-fit member. This depends on the crossover criterion, on the random mutation and on the stochastic realizations of the process, as well as on the problem itself. This index of computational effort is quite critical because before establishing a valid offspring the algorithm can undergo several computations.

5. Simulation Results

We analyze now the performance achieved by a multiband collaborative detection framework. The optimization is conducted with variable bounds in order to compare convexity-limited and nonconvex systems. The testbed channel has $K = 8$ subbands, secondary rates between 400 and 1000 kbps, and individual interference costs between 0.8 and 8. The SNR in each band is between -6 and -1 dB. The length of the detection interval is $N = 100$. Throughput-interference characteristics (I-R) are depicted for the three CR classes in Figure 5. The collaborative and noncollaborative systems differ for the LSC in the subbands. Interference and utilization in the single bands are linked together as shown by the curves in Figure 6. The collaborative case has an improved reliability, which corresponds to a smaller interference. On the other hand, (P1) optimizes only the thresholds, whereas (P2) requires the contemporary optimization of a nonhomogeneous set of variables (weights and thresholds), yielding inevitably to a more complex problem. Two procedures have been proposed in [8] to solve (P2).

(1) *Sequential optimization* performs at first a spatial optimization that maximizes the *modified deflection coefficient*:

$$d_{m,k}^2 = \frac{\mathbf{w}_k^T \boldsymbol{\mu}_1 - \mathbf{w}_k^T \boldsymbol{\mu}_0}{\mathbf{w}_k^T \boldsymbol{\Sigma}_{1,k} \mathbf{w}_k}. \tag{24}$$

Then it performs a *spectral optimization* of the thresholds as if there were only one sensing CR. Sequential optimization performs close to the optimal global solution. The spectral optimization is actually the procedure followed to solve also the thresholds optimization in the noncollaborative case.

(2) *Joint optimization* finds directly thresholds and weights for a global maximization of the throughput. It is optimal in a global sense. Exploitation of hidden convexity needs heavy approximations, so that the final performance is compromised [8].

Then single-band weights optimization (P3) is also analyzed by discussing the throughput graphics.

5.1. Analysis of Nonconvex Classes of Multiband Detection Systems.

The multiband frameworks (P1) and (P2) suffer from the same limitations of the convexity constraints. The latter additionally has to be lower bounded when not solved with sequential optimization, which reduces the achievable throughput [8]. The characteristics are analogous for the two problems, because the utilization and interference bounds have the same implications. So the presented results are valid for both frameworks. With the genetic solution the I-R characteristics are calculated for the three CR system classes with the aggregate interference as independent variable. Figure 5 shows four case studies for the problem (P1). The case studies are also presented schematically in Figure 3.

The α_k and β_k values are bounds for the minimum and maximum per-band interference and utilization. By choosing a minimum subband utilization we also impose a minimum interference, and vice versa, for these two quantities are determined by the threshold γ_k. Figure 6 shows the utilization-interference characteristics. If the convexity imposes to operate inside the shaded region then it is impossible to reduce the interference under a certain value, resulting in compromised performance. The region with less utilization but also less unnecessary interference has been excluded before and it is included in the genetic optimization. Convexity exploitation through the utilization constraint $\beta_k \geq 0.5$ is counterproductive for the performance of the system. Therefore comes the importance of a nonconvex maximization tool such as GA.

Different CR systems show different achievable throughput because less or more interference and utilization is permitted in the single bands as shown in Figure 5.

Conservative systems break the convexity with values of utilization β_k below 50%. By reducing β_k we allow transmitting with small bitrates over the subchannels with poor SNR, which are the cause of a high interference. A higher percentage of false alarms is implicitly provoked, but the trade-off is more favorable so that the operative point has a higher throughput and lower interference as β_k decreases. The interested region is mainly for low aggregate interference, whereas, asinthotically, the systems have the same characteristic. The case with $\alpha_k = 0.1$ and $\beta_k = 0.5$ is common in literature for demonstration purposes [8], but it is largely outperformed. *Aggressive* systems with β_k higher

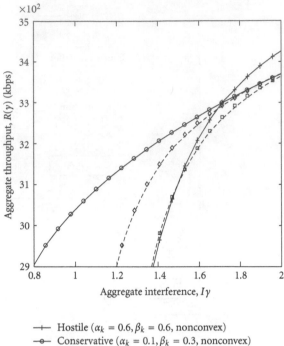

Hostile ($\alpha_k = 0.6, \beta_k = 0.6$, nonconvex)
Conservative ($\alpha_k = 0.1, \beta_k = 0.3$, nonconvex)
Conservative ($\alpha_k = 0.1, \beta_k = 0.5$)
Aggressive ($\alpha_k = 0.1, \beta_k = 0.6$)

FIGURE 5: Aggregate opportunistic throughput versus aggregate interference in multiband detection. Convex systems are plotted in dashed line.

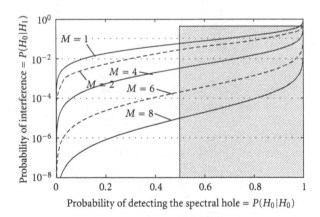

FIGURE 6: Narrowband transmission against interference probability characteristics in LSC, with $M = [1, 2, 4, 6, 8]$ collaborating CR. The shaded region highlights the convexity domain of (P1).

than 0.5 show even less favorable characteristics, with low rates at high interferences.

Hostile systems have a maximum interference α_k beyond 50%. By increasing this value we permit more per-band interference with a gain in the throughput. The missed detections increase, so the bitrate increases with a higher slope, because more disturb on the individual bands is permitted. The other systems with low α_k increase with a poorer slope. This interests mainly the higher interferences, whereas small interferences are largely beyond the bound and the operative point remains similar.

Aggressive systems may not transmit with low bitrate and low interference because a minimum is imposed to both of them. They pay the mild per-band interference and the acceptable per-band utilization with a worse I-R characteristic.

Figure 7 shows the bar diagrams of the thresholds and the per-band average interference and utilization, for one case of each system in the multiband problem. We notice that the limits for convexity are exceeded. On one hand, more interference is caused in some bands, but with a gain in the throughput that is reflected in the I-R characteristics in Figure 5. On the other hand, less utilization is permitted in other bands, especially those with poor SNR (2nd and 5th bands), but with lower interference. Such systems bring an improvement with respect to the *aggressive* case for higher and lower interferences, respectively.

Not all combinations of α_k and β_k are admitted. Some combinations are unfeasible if the utilization limit β_k implies an interference that does not respect the condition on α_k. Low SNR may support the appearance of such cases just by bringing the Gaussian pdfs of the sensed levels one close to each other.

5.2. Analysis of Multiband Detection without Aggregate Constraint.

By removing the constraint on the aggregate interference, the problem of maximizing the utilization with a per-band interference constraint has become a series of independent LSC optimizations. Optimum weights are calculated to provide the maximum probability of transmission in each subband with fixed probability of interference. The thresholds are implicit. LSC provides the graphics of transmission-versus-interference probability in Figure 6. The case with one CR is equivalent to a multiband aggregation problem, but the solution is immediate by means of (17). Then the aggregate throughput is calculated afterwards as a linear combination of the subchannel rates. The total rates against the interference to each subchannel system is plotted in Figure 8, which is a direct result of the reliable detection whose characteristics are shown in Figure 6. Besides, LSC is far more simple to be solved, both for GA, that converge easier, and for convex maximization, when working with interference below 50%.

5.3. Genetic Design.

Setting up the parameters of our GA is important to optimize the computation, from the point of view of the expenditure of resources and the convergence precision.

When using a GA, as well as any iterative solving method, a finite difference between the true maximum and the one computed by the GA is expected, because of the finite number of iterations and individual evaluations. The optimization is considered solved when it approaches a negligible error. An error of tens of kilobits (out of some megabits) on the aggregate throughput is considered acceptable. For the aggregate throughput distance in (P1) and (P2) we use a relative measure, the Mean Absolute Percentage Error (MAPE):

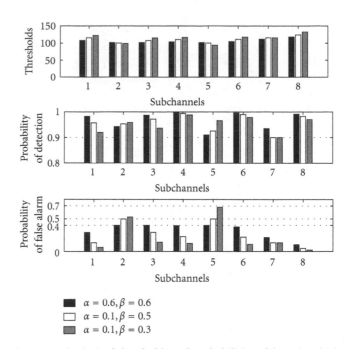

FIGURE 7: Optimized thresholds and probabilities of detection (P_d) and false alarm (P_f) on individual subbands for two of the curves in Figure 5, $\epsilon = 1.3$. SNR = $(-3, -5.2, -3.5, -1.9, -6, -2.2, -4, -1.5)$.

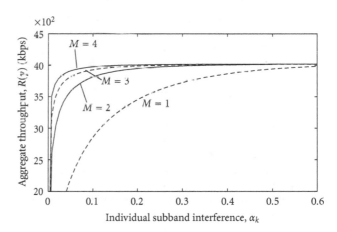

FIGURE 8: Aggregate throughput vs single band interference, with $M = [1, 2, 3, 4]$ collaborating CR.

$$\text{MAPE}(R) = \frac{1}{Z} \sum_{z=1}^{Z} \left| \frac{\hat{R} - R^{(z)}}{\hat{R}} \right|. \tag{25}$$

From the collaborative side, a squared error of around 10^{-6} on the subband fractional utilization (P_f) is also acceptable. The subchannel utilization error is measured with the Mean Squared Error (MSE):

$$\text{MSE}\left(P_f\right) = \frac{1}{Z} \sum_{z=1}^{Z} \left(\hat{P}_f - P_f^{(z)} \right)^2. \tag{26}$$

$R^{(z)}$ and $P_f^{(z)}$ are the value calculated by the GA during the zth experiment and Z is the number of experiments. $\hat{R}$ and

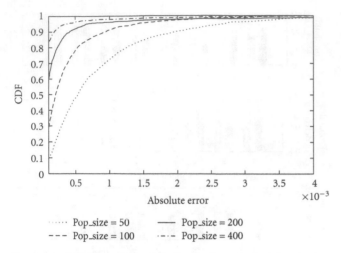

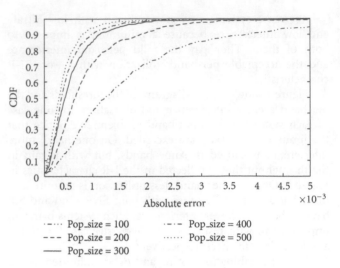

FIGURE 9: CDF (Cumulative Distribution Function) of the absolute percentage error in thresholds optimization with various population sizes.

FIGURE 10: CDF (Cumulative Distribution Function) of the absolute percentage error in joint weights and thresholds optimization with initial points (27) and (28).

$\widehat{P}_f$ represent a solution of the maximization several orders of magnitude more precise than the other optimizations. They are obtained at the expenses of a practically unfeasible algorithm but enough accurate to evaluate the precision of the other computations.

We vary the dimension of ordinary elaborations in order to find a compromise between complexity and accuracy. By setting the value of the population size (Pop_size) we control the dimension of the GA in order to evaluate a wider range of *genotypes* and generate a fitter population. By eventually setting the limit on the maximum number of generations (Max_gen) we avoid the algorithm running for a long time before converging.

The mean number of function evaluations to complete an elaboration (N-eval) is our index of complexity which depends directly on the population size and on the number of generations.

We also examine different crossover functions, for a well-chosen crossover criterion converges faster and with higher accuracy.

5.3.1. Spectral Optimization.
It consists in the optimization of the thresholds for the noncollaborative problem (P1), as well as for the sequential optimization of (P2) with the weights part solved otherwise (modified deflection coefficient or GA applied to LSC). The characteristics for noncollaborative detection are shown in Figure 5. A MAPE less than 0.1% is enough to infer that the algorithm has converged with acceptable precision. Figure 9 shows the convergence precision while varying the population size in terms of Cumulative Distribution Function (CDF) of the relative error.

5.3.2. Joint Optimization.
It consists in the joint optimization of the spatial and spectral variables in (P2). The optimized characteristic is analogous to the one shown in Figure 5. The genes are not homogeneous (weights and thresholds)

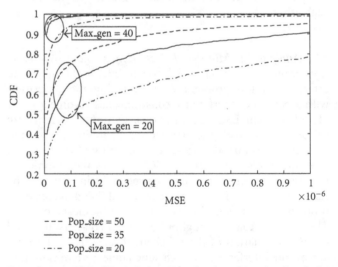

FIGURE 11: CDF (Cumulative Distribution Functions) of the squared error with various population dimensions in LSC weights optimization.

according to (20), so the evolution results more complex. An expedient for helping the convergence is to set some initial points as the starting population of the GA. We first obtain the initial weights from the maximization of the modified deflection coefficient (with a simple GA or with the procedure in [10]):

$$\mathbf{w}_{k,\text{init}} = \arg\max_{\mathbf{w}} d^2_{m,k}, \quad k = 1, \dots . \qquad (27)$$

Then the initial thresholds are uniformly distributed between the minimum and maximum calculated by means of (11):

$$\boldsymbol{\gamma}_{k,\text{init}} = \Big[\gamma_{\min,k}, \gamma_{\min,k} + \text{step}_k, \gamma_{\min,k} + 2 * \text{step}_k, \dots,$$

$$\gamma_{\min,k} + (\text{Pop\_size} - 1) * \text{step}_k, \gamma_{\max,k} \Big]^T, \qquad (28)$$

$$k = 1, \dots, K,$$

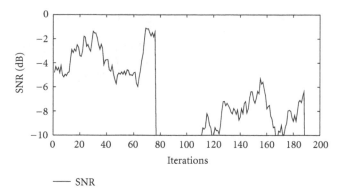

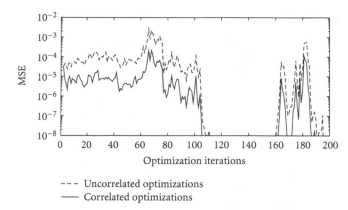

FIGURE 12: Example of time-variation of the SNR received by each sensor.

FIGURE 13: Precision reached with correlated and uncorrelated genetic optimizations of LSC, in terms of Mean Square Error (MSE) with fixed number of generations.

where

$$\text{step}_k = \frac{\gamma_{\max,k} - \gamma_{\min,k}}{\text{Pop\_size}}. \tag{29}$$

With these starting points the GA needs only few generations of joint elaboration to converge to the global optimal solution. Figure 10 shows the CDF of the squared error with different population sizes.

5.3.3. Weights Optimization. It consists in the optimization of the subband weights (18), whose result is shown in Figure 6. It solves the alternative multiband optimization without aggregate constraint (P3). An acceptable convergence is said to be reached with an MSE around 10^{-6}. Figure 11 shows the CDF of the squared error reached by the GA in weight optimization with various dimensions of the population. Since weights optimization is unconstrained, the computational load is exactly $N_{\text{eval}} = \text{Pop\_size} * N_{\text{gen}}$.

6. Variation of the Channel Statistics

Let us consider now the variation of the receiving conditions of the sensors due to the movement. Channel statistics in presence of moving sensors are supposed to vary in time with a certain correlation. A simulated variation in time of the SNR at the radio interface of one CR is shown in Figure 12. The statistic of the received level in presence of transmission μ_1 has lognormal distribution, as it derives from long-term fading and shadowing. The cutoff of the sensor is also simulated, in case of sudden loss of the sensing contribution. A similar variation is followed by each node in the simulation. Measurements correlation is exploited by keeping the result of one elaboration and refining it in the successive instant. Figure 13 shows the precision reached by running the GA for LSC optimization with a fixed number of generations at each instant. The two curves correspond to a genetic optimization from random points every time (memoryless) and from the previous weights as starting vector (with memory). We can see that we gain an order of magnitude of MSE by iteratively updating the objective function (with the channel statistics) and keeping

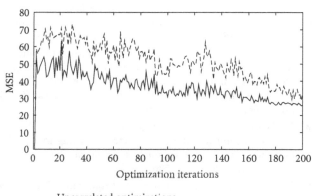

FIGURE 14: Number of generations necessary to achieve a precision of 10^{-6} with correlated and uncorrelated genetic optimizations of LSC, Pop_size = 20.

trace of the previous calculated weights. Figure 14 shows instead the number of generations that are needed to reach a certain precision with memoryless optimization using at each instant the previous weights as starting point. In average, 20 generations less are needed to converge, since the weights are tightly correlated between consecutive instants.

7. Conclusion

GAs were proposed as a valid technique for solving the detection problem efficiently and without convexity constraints. The solution is practically analogous to the true mathematical maximum. GAs are able to exploit the correlation of the mobile channel. Unpractical limits due to mathematically unfeasible problems are avoided. *Conservative* systems demonstrate to outperform *aggressive* systems and the throughput increases as we reduce the minimum subband occupancy. In general the complexity of our GA demonstrates to be sustainable and controllable. The computational load does not increase too much as the sensing problem grows or as the GA dimension increases.

References

[1] I. F. Akyildiz, W.-Y. Lee, M. C. Vuran, and S. Mohanty, "A survey on spectrum management in cognitive radio networks," *IEEE Communications Magazine*, vol. 46, no. 4, pp. 40–48, 2008.

[2] S. Haykin, "Cognitive radio: brain-empowered wireless communications," *IEEE Journal on Selected Areas in Communications*, vol. 23, no. 2, pp. 201–220, 2005.

[3] J. Mitola III and G. Q. Maguire Jr., "Cognitive radio: making software radios more personal," *IEEE Personal Communications*, vol. 6, no. 4, pp. 13–18, 1999.

[4] "IEEE Standards Coordinating Committee 41 (Dynamic Spectrum Access Networks)," http://www.scc41.org/.

[5] "IEEE 802.22 Working Group on Wireless Regional Area Networks," http://www.ieee802.org/22/.

[6] C. Cordeiro, K. Challapali, D. Birru, and N. Sai Shankar, "IEEE 802.22: the first worldwide wireless standard based on cognitive radios," in *Proceedings of the 1st IEEE International Symposium on New Frontiers in Dynamic Spectrum Access Networks (DySPAN '05)*, pp. 328–337, November 2005.

[7] Z. Tian and G. B. Giannakis, "A wavelet approach to wideband spectrum sensing for cognitive radios," in *Proceedings of the 1st International Conference on Cognitive Radio Oriented Wireless Networks and Communications (CROWNCOM '06)*, June 2006.

[8] Z. Quan, S. Cui, A. H. Sayed, and H. V. Poor, "Optimal multiband joint detection for spectrum sensing in cognitive radio networks," *IEEE Transactions on Signal Processing*, vol. 57, no. 3, pp. 1128–1140, 2009.

[9] S. M. Mishra, A. Sahai, and R. W. Brodersen, "Cooperative sensing among cognitive radios," in *Proceedings of IEEE International Conference on Communications (ICC '06)*, pp. 1658–1663, July 2006.

[10] Z. Quan, S. Cui, and A. H. Sayed, "Optimal linear cooperation for spectrum sensing in cognitive radio networks," *IEEE Journal on Selected Topics in Signal Processing*, vol. 2, no. 1, pp. 28–40, 2008.

[11] Z. Quan, S. Cui, A. H. Sayed, and H. V. Poor, "Spatial-spectral joint detection for wideband spectrum sensing in cognitive radio networks," in *Proceedings of IEEE International Conference on Acoustics, Speech and Signal Processing (ICASSP '08)*, pp. 2793–2796, April 2008.

[12] L. Atzori and A. Raccis, "Network capacity assignment for multicast services using genetic algorithms," *IEEE Communications Letters*, vol. 8, no. 6, pp. 403–405, 2004.

[13] M. Murroni, "Performance analysis of modulation with unequal power allocations over fading channels: a genetic algorithm approach," in *Proceedings of the 14th European Wireless Conference (EW '08)*, Prague, Czech Republic, June 2008.

[14] D. Whitley, "A genetic algorithm tutorial," *Statistics and Computing*, vol. 4, no. 2, pp. 65–85, 1994.

[15] S. M. Kay, *Fundamentals of Statistical Signal Processing, Volume 2: Detection Theory*, Prentice Hall, Upper Saddle River, NJ, USA, 1998.

[16] Z. Quan, W.-K. Ma, S. Cui, and A. Sayed, "Optimal linear fusion for distributed spectrum sensing via semidefinite programming," in *Proceedings of IEEE International Conference on Acoustics, Speech and Signal Processing (ICASSP '09)*, pp. 3629–3632, April 2009.

[17] T. Weise, *Global Optimization Algorithms—Theory and Application*, Thomas Weise, 2007.

[18] G. E. Liepins and M. D. Vose, "Deceptiveness and genetic algorithm dynamics," in *Proceedings of the 1st Workshop on Foundations of Genetic Algorithms*, pp. 36–50, July 1990.

14

Unsupervised Segmentation Methods of TV Contents

Elie El-Khoury, Christine Sénac, and Philippe Joly

IRIT Laboratory, Toulouse University, 118 route de Narbonne, 31062 Toulouse Cedex 9, France

Correspondence should be addressed to Elie El-Khoury, elie.el-khoury@irit.fr

Academic Editor: Ling Shao

We present a generic algorithm to address various temporal segmentation topics of audiovisual contents such as speaker diarization, shot, or program segmentation. Based on a GLR approach, involving the ΔBIC criterion, this algorithm requires the value of only a few parameters to produce segmentation results at a desired scale and on most typical low-level features used in the field of content-based indexing. Results obtained on various corpora are of the same quality level than the ones obtained by other dedicated and state-of-the-art methods.

1. Introduction

Nowadays, due to an explosive growth of digital video content (both online and offline and available by means of public or private databases and TV broadcasts), there is an increasing of accessibility for these data. Actually, the wealth of information raises the problem of an adapted access to video content which includes heterogeneous information that can be interpreted at different granularity levels, thus leading to many profiles of requests.

Under these conditions, automatic indexing of the structure, which provides direct access to the various components of the multimedia document, becomes a fundamental issue.

For this purpose, a temporal segmentation of audiovisual is required as a preprocessing operation. Results of this segmentation may be directly used for delinearization purposes such as providing a direct access to the content itself. They can also feed other analysis algorithms aiming at producing synoptical views of the content or exploiting temporal redundancy properties inside homogeneous segments to speed up the processing time.

Basically, temporal segmentation tools work on a low-level feature (or a small set of low-level features) extracted from the content along the time. Commonly, these low-level features express meaningful properties that can be observed or processed directly from the signal, such as spectrum/cepstrum features for an audio signal or color histograms for an image. They are expressed numerically and represented through vectors whose dimensions depend on the number of those features.

Two kinds of segmentation strategies can then be applied. Some algorithms try to gather set of successive values which are supposed to belong to a same homogeneous segment. Some others are focusing on transitions detection between segments.

Such algorithms have been developed independently one with the others for different temporal segmentation problems.

Among the most addressed ones, we find the "audio turn" segmentation. An "audio turn" denotes a homogeneous audio segment related to basic semantic audio classes namely, speech, music, speech superimposed with music, ambient sounds, and silence. This is generally a preprocessing tool. This is also the case for shot segmentation algorithms. The goal here is to identify successive frames in an edited video content which are belonging to a same cinematic take. More recently, some algorithms have been also proposed for TV programs segmentation. They can be used for Electronic Program Guide (EPG) synchronization or simply to provide some entries in recordings.

All those algorithms are dedicated to specific tasks of segmentation. They are based on more or less explicit models and properties of the concepts associated to the segments or to transitions and so cannot be applied to any other segmentation tasks.

In this paper, we develop the idea that, on light processing architectures, a single operator able to produce audio turns, or shots, TV programs segmentation could be of interest if the results are of nearly the same quality than the ones obtained with dedicated tools.

So, after an overview of related works concerning video and audio segmentation methods in Section 2, we present, in Section 3, a generic unsupervised segmentation we firstly developed to process audio contents. Then we show how this segmentation method can be adapted for different granularity levels such as shot detection (Section 4), programs boundaries detection in days of television recordings (Section 5), and speaker segmentation (Section 6).

2. State of the Art of Video and Audio Segmentations

2.1. Video Segmentation. Video segmentation has been studied extensively. Traditionally, a four-layer hierarchical structure is adopted for video structure analysis which consists of a frame layer, a shot layer, a sequence layer, and a program layer. At the bottom of the structure, continuous image frames taken by a single camera are grouped into shots. A series of related shots are then grouped into a sequence. Shot change detection is performed as the first step for video segmentation by most previous approaches.

2.1.1. Video Shot Boundaries Detection. Historically, the first studied video segmentation task is the shot boundaries detection which aims at breaking the massive volume of video into smaller chunks. Shots are concatenated by editing effects such as hard cuts, fades, dissolves, and wipes. A reliable shot detection algorithm should identify such short breaks.

Because it is not an easy task, quite a lot of approaches were proposed in the literature [1–3]. See for example the report of TRECVid for a review and a comparison of state-of-the-art systems and [4] for an overview of the methods and evaluation of shot-segmentation algorithms.

Among the classical algorithms, one can cite the color histogram differences used to detect hard cuts, the standard deviation of pixel intensities for fade cuts, the edge-based contrast for dissolve cuts, and the edge-change ratio for hard, fade, and dissolve cuts. Parameters are often chosen in order to describe color or luminous intensity of the video. However the challenging problem is to distinguish shot boundaries from the following: fast object or camera motion, fast illumination changes, reflections, sudden change to explosion, and flash photography. Each potential artifact leads to develop an adhoc processing tool and explains the myriad of method.

2.1.2. Video Sequence Boundaries Detection. Some works have attempted to find an upper level structuring, mainly by grouping together adjacent shots semantically linked up in scene form [5] using more or less explicit rules used in the audiovisual production domain [6]. This task is tricky for movies because it obeys to subjective criterions. Furthermore

it is difficult to process heterogeneous corpora, but scenes can be detected from special programs having a quite stable structure such as broadcast news or sports [7, 8]. But the implemented methods use a lot of many a priori knowledge.

Reference [9] presented an approach with no models or decision rules to define "story units" according to the following method When two shots are very similar and nearby temporally, they are grouped together with all the intermediary shots in order to form a segment. To calculate the similarity between two shots, intensity histograms of keyframes are used. Similar shots are grouped together in graph nodes form, and nodes are linked up when the two corresponding groups are temporally adjacent. Then segments are produced by partition of the graph, deleting the more minor links.

2.1.3. Program Boundaries Detection. Very few researches have been done for program boundaries detection on TV broadcast. Let us mention here those published by Liang et al. [10], Poli and Carrive [11] and Naturel et al. [12]. Here, a "program" must be understand as a regular television program such as news, weather broadcast, talk show, sports, or sitcoms.

Poli proposes to predict forthcoming TV programs by modelling the past ones in order to boil down the television stream structuring problem to a simple alignment one with the EPG thanks to Hidden Markov Models trained on data about television schedules collected over a full year. The stream is first segmented to find boundaries of programs which are labeled later.

In the same time, Naturel proposes a fast structuring of large TV streams using also program guides to label the detected programs. The method for segmenting a TV stream which is built on the detection of nonprogram segments (such as commercial breaks) uses two kinds of independent information. The first one is a monochromatic frame and silence detector appearing between commercials on French TV. The second kind of information comes from a duplicate detection process. Nonprograms are detected in this way because they are usually broadcasted several times and so already present in a labeled reference video dataset.

Liang proposes a less ambitious work, closer to our proposition, as it only detects programs boundaries without labeling them. He supposes that TV videos have two intrinsic characteristics. On one hand, for a TV channel, programs appear and end at a relatively fixed time every day. On the other hand, for programs of the same type, they have stable or similar starting and ending clips even when they appear in different days. As such, the approach consists of two steps: model construction and program segmentation. The program boundary models for the selected TV channel are constructed by detecting the repeating shots on different days. Then, based on the obtained models, videos recorded from the same TV channel can be segmented into programs. This approach is not valid for more complex streams and can not take into account any possible change of TV schedule.

2.2. Audio Segmentation.

2.2. Audio Segmentation. Auditory scene segmentation is an important step in the process of high-level semantic inference from audio streams, and in particular, a prerequisite for auditory scene categorization.

As opposed to single modal audio (e.g., pure speech in the context of speech recognition task), composite audio of multimedia databases usually contains multiple audio modalities such as speech, music and various audio effects, which can be mixed.

This is why, in the audio indexing context, first works were focusing on music/speech discrimination obtained directly with a set of low-level characteristics [13] or using multi-Gaussian models learned with huge corpora [14].

Other segmentation methods identify key sounds, such as whistle sound, crowd noise, or commentator voice in a soccer broadcast [15]. Here again, segmentation is possible only with the use of a priori knowledge.

In [16], authors first extract audio elements such as speech, music, various audio effects, and any combination of these in order to detect key audio elements and to segment the auditory scene to obtain a semantic description.

Some works, within a musical program, try to identify the musical type [17] or musical instruments used [18]. In [19] a microsegmentation of musical sequences is performed by detecting onsets of notes and percussive events.

This vast number of audio segmentation and classification methods is due on the one hand to heterogeneousness of the content and on the other hand to the aimed semantic level.

Reference [5] presents a method to detect the different audio scenes without a priori knowledge. An audio scene change occurs when a majority of the sources present in the data change. The dominant sources are assumed to possess stationary properties that can be characterized using a few features extracted from the signal [20]. In order to detect scene change, a local correlation function is then used.

2.3. Knowledge-Free and Generic Methods. We have seen that nearly all methods of audio or video segmentation perform with a priori knowledge. These approaches are based on a spatial-temporal modelling of the content and use decision rules. Currently, it is the only way to reach the semantic quality required by search engines. But only recording collections highly structured, such as broadcast videos of news and sports programmes, and homogeneous in terms of production can benefit from such methods. Furthermore, model or decision rules-based methods are limited because, for each new collection, they need either a new learning or a new expertise and often new tools have to be defined.

However some generic methods exist, permitting to process both audio and video documents. Foote and Cooper [21] show that a similarity matrix applied to well-chosen features allows a visual representation of the structural information of a video or audio signal. The similarity matrix can be analyzed to find structure boundaries. Generally, the boundary between two coherent segments produces a checkerboard pattern. The two segments will exhibit high within-segment similarity, producing adjacent square regions of high similarity along the main diagonal of the matrix. The two segments will also produce rectangular regions of low between-segment similarity off the main diagonal. The boundary is the crux of this checkerboard pattern.

A supplementary approach was developed by Haidar et al. [22]. This approach is also generic because it is independent of the size and of the type of the document. Several similarity matrices, each one representing one feature, are accumulated, and the resultant matrix shows the temporal areas homogeneous in terms of the set of the different used features. But automatically inferring a document structure from such a matrix is not easy.

3. The Proposed Segmentation Method

Contrary to the methods seen in the above section, we present a priori knowledge-free segmentation approach relaying mainly on the hypothesis that it is possible to segment at some different granularity levels any audiovisual document and that is equivalent to segment into homogeneous segments at the adequate scale.

The segmentation we propose was firstly designed for audio segmentation in the context of speaker diarization [23]. Because the traditionally used metric approaches (symmetric Kullback-Leibler, Hotteling's T2-Statistic) did not give us sufficient results in presence of multiple simultaneous audio sources, we turned towards approaches based on model selection like the Generalized Likelihood Ratio (GLR) [24] and the Bayesian Information Criterion (BIC) [25]. Though the results are better, we observed that usual GLR and BIC methods present some weaknesses: too many parameters are required to tune the algorithm, and a bad precision is obtained in detecting boundaries when segments are small.

So, we propose some improvements to the general algorithm described hereafter.

3.1. Overview of the Basic Segmentation Algorithm. The basic method for detecting a change between homogenous zones is the GLR applied on a temporal signal in which each sample is a vector of several low-level features.

For genericity reasons, we will describe this method using an unknown signal that may be an acoustic signal, a video signal or an audiovisual signal.

Let $X = x_1, \ldots, x_{N_x}$ be the sequence of observation vectors of dimension d to be modeled, M the estimated parametrical model, and $L(X, M)$ the likelihood function. The GLR introduced by Gish et al. [24] considers the two following hypotheses.

H_0: This hypothesis assumes that the sequence X corresponds to only one homogeneous segment (in the case of audio signal, it corresponds to only one audio source). Thus, the sequence is modeled by only one multi-Gaussian distribution

$$(x_1, \ldots, x_{N_x}) \sim N(\mu_X, \sigma_X). \tag{1}$$

H_1: This hypothesis assumes that the sequence X corresponds to two different homogeneous segments $X_1 = x_1, \ldots, x_i$ and $X_1 = x_{i+1}, \ldots, x_{N_x}$ (in the case of audio signal, it corresponds to two different audio sources or more particularly to two different speakers). Thus, the sequence is modelled by two multi-Gaussian distributions

$$
\begin{aligned}
(x_1, \ldots, x_i) &\sim N(\mu_{X_1}, \sigma_{X_1}), \\
(x_{i+1}, \ldots, x_N) &\sim N(\mu_{X_2}, \sigma_{X_2}).
\end{aligned}
\tag{2}
$$

The generalized likelihood ratio between the hypothesis H_0 and the hypothesis H_1 is given by

$$
\text{GLR} = \frac{P(H_0)}{P(H_1)}.
\tag{3}
$$

In terms of likelihood, this expression becomes

$$
\text{GLR} = \frac{L(X, M)}{L(X_1, M_1) L(X_2, M_2)}.
\tag{4}
$$

If this ratio is lower than a certain threshold Thr, we can say that H_1 is more probable, so a point of change in the signal is detected.

By passing through the log

$$
R(i) = -\log \text{GLR}
\tag{5}
$$

and by considering that the models are Gaussian, we obtain

$$
R(i) = \frac{N_X}{2} \log |\Sigma_X| - \frac{N_{X_1}}{2} \log |\Sigma_{X_1}| - \frac{N_{X_2}}{2} \log |\Sigma_{X_2}|,
\tag{6}
$$

where Σ_X, Σ_{X_1}, and Σ_{X_2} are the covariance matrices of X, X_1, and X_2 and N_X, N_{X_1}, and N_{X_2}, are, respectively the number of the acoustic vectors of X, X_1, and X_2.

Thus, the estimated value of the point of change by maximum likelihood is given by

$$
\hat{i} = \arg \max_i R(i).
\tag{7}
$$

If $\hat{i}$ is higher than the threshold $T = -\log \text{Thr}$, a point of speaker change is detected. The major disadvantage resides in the presence of the threshold T that depends on the data. That is why, Rissanen [26] introduced the Bayesian Information Criterion (BIC).

3.1.1. Bayesian Information Criterion. For a given model M, the BIC is expressed by

$$
\text{BIC}(M) = \log L(X, M) - \frac{\lambda}{2} n \log N_X,
\tag{8}
$$

where n denotes the number of the observation vectors of the model. The first term reflects the adjustment of the model to the data, and the second term corresponds to the complexity of the data. λ is a penalty coefficient theoretically equal to 1. [26].

The hypotheses test of (3) can be viewed as the comparison between two models: a model of data with two Gaussian distributions (H_1) and a model of data with only one Gaussian distribution (H_0). The subtraction of BIC expressions related to those two models is

$$
\Delta \text{BIC}(i) = R(i) - \lambda P,
\tag{9}
$$

where the log-likelihood ratio $R(i)$ is already defined in (6) and the complexity term P is given by

$$
P = \frac{1}{2}\left(d + \frac{1}{2}d(d+1)\right) \log N_X,
\tag{10}
$$

d being the dimension of the feature vectors.

The BIC can be also viewed as the thresholding of the log-likelihood distance with an automatic threshold equal to λP.

Thus if $\Delta \text{BIC}(i)$ is positive, the hypothesis H_1 is privileged (two different speakers). There is a change if

$$
\left\{ \max_i \Delta \text{BIC}(i) \geq 0 \right\}.
\tag{11}
$$

The estimated value of the point of change can also be expressed by

$$
\hat{i} = \arg \max_i \Delta \text{BIC}(i).
\tag{12}
$$

A well-known BIC segmentation method was proposed by Sivakumaran et al. to detect multipoints changes in audio recordings [27]. In our work we applied this method, and we figure out some limitations. Although the amount of parameters to be tuned is important, the penalty coefficient is not as stable as expected, and there is a possible cumulative error due to the sequential segmentation process: if a point is erroneously detected, the next point might be affected by this error and might not be detected correctly. All those limitations encouraged us to propose a new segmentation based on GLR and BIC.

3.2. Proposed Improvements. The proposed method for signal segmentation follows four main steps as explained below and in Figure 1.

Row a is a time line on which the expected segmentation points are shown.

(1) This time line is split into fixed size temporal windows (shown on row b) of duration d. On each window, a GLR point detection is performed independently. Doing so, one potential segmentation point P_i^0 on each window W_i^0 is so obtained. Row c shows these intermediate results. At this step, actual segmentation points closed to a temporal window boundary have a poor probability to be detected. Furthermore, some of the candidate segmentation points may have only a local significance in their temporal window but not at a larger scale.

(2) To overcome these problems, we now consider overlapping temporal windows whose boundaries correspond to one candidate segmentation point over two, obtained during the previous step of the process.

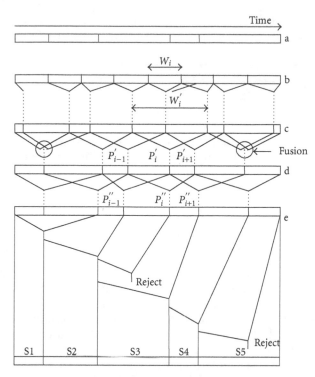

FIGURE 1: The proposed segmentation.

At the first iteration of the process, the first window W_1^1 goes from the beginning to point P_2^0; the second window W_2^1 goes from point P_1^0 to P_3^0; ...; the ith window W_i^1 goes from point P_{i-1}^0 to P_{i+1}^0. On each window, a new GLR point detection is performed. We obtain after this step a new set of potential segmentation points P_i^1. More generally, we note P_i^k the GLR point detected over the window W_i^k whose temporal boundaries are defined by points P_{i-1}^{k-1} and P_{i+1}^{k-1} at the kth iteration.

(3) We then go for a readjustment step where the closest segmentation points are merged (two points are closed if the distance between them is less than 3 samples). Step (2) and step (3) are iterated until stable results are obtained, that is we look for k so that $P_i^{k+1} = P_i^k$.

(4) At the last step, all the candidate segmentation points, obtained during the last iteration, are tested against the BIC Criterion.

One may have noticed that if there is N fixed size temporal window defined at the beginning of this process, we will obtain M segmentation points at the end with $M \leq N$. This means that the size of the window must be a priori fixed at a lower value than the minimal length of segments expected as a result.

Moreover, we found that a bidirectional segmentation of the signal (i.e., both forward and backward) may be useful in some cases where the transitions between two homogeneous regions are not very discriminative (interactive acoustic regions, fade or dissolve transition effects between shots,

etc.). Indeed, due to the shifted variable size window introduced in the segmentation method, processing from "left to right" may detect different points of change than processing from "right to left", and therefore, there is a chance that a missed boundary in the first direction can be detected in the other direction and vice versa.

The purpose of all those steps is to generate an as stable as possible segmentation that gives homogeneous zones in terms of features distributions.

4. Application to Shot Boundaries Detection

We formulate now the hypothesis that shots are homogeneous video segments and that we may find features that can at the same time be modelled by Gaussian distributions. If we can assume that it exists a large range of such features, the first hypothesis (shot are homogeneous segments) is far from be always observed. Some lighting effects (such as flashes) or fast moving objects are strong limitations to this hypothesis. To take this specificity into account, once we have applied the previously described segmentation algorithm, we go for a rather simple postprocessing step aiming at removing false detections generated by those kinds of effects.

In this present work, a feature vector is extracted as follows. Each image provided every 40 ms (25 images/second) is divided into 4 equal parts.

The mean values of R, G, and B colour space descriptors are computed in each part. Therefore, the feature vector of dimension d ($d = 3 \times 4$) is composed of those values.

Then, the segmentation algorithm is applied as explained in Section 2. The window size W is fixed equal to 50 feature vectors because we took the assumption that the minimum duration in which a point of change can be detected is greater than 2 seconds. The penalty coefficient λ was tuned to 3.

In order to eliminate some false alarm detections due fast motion and lighting effects, a final step of histograms comparison is applied on the detected boundaries using the Manhattan (or City-Block) distance.

Suppose the video is composed of frames $I_1, I_2, I_3, \ldots, I_n$ and the segmentation step returns the following frames $I_1, I_{k_1}, I_{k_2}, \ldots, I_n$ as boundaries. For each boundary frame I_{k_j}, we consider the window of frames $[I_{k_{j-a}}, I_{k_{j+a}}]$ (a is fixed experimentally to 6), and we compute all the Manhattan distances between the histograms of the frames I_{p-1} and I_{p+1} where $p \in [k_{j-a+1}, k_{j+a-1}]$. Then, if all the distances are lower than a threshold, the frame I_{k_j} is withdrew from the boundaries set.

4.1. Experiments

4.1.1. The Corpus. We experiment our method on the corpus of the French ARGOS campaign [28]. The content set of the ARGOS campaign was made of various TV recordings, gathering TV news programs as well as commercials, weather forecast, documentaries, and fiction.

We used the two files of development (about 1 hour) to tune parameters. Then test was performed on 10 other hours.

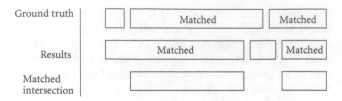

FIGURE 2: Identification of matched segment intersections.

TABLE 1: Shot boundaries detection: evaluation of the proposed system with the two types of metrics.

	Recall	Precision	F_measure
ARGOS metrics	0.935	0.931	0.933
TRECVid metrics	0.893	0.918	0.905

4.1.2. The Metrics. Two types of metrics both from ARGOS and TRECVid campaign (http://www.nlpir.gov/projects/tv2007/tv2007.html) were used. The TRECVid metric highlights the ability to localize transitions in opposition with the ARGOS metric which highlights the ability of the segmentation tool to gather units belonging to a same segment.

(a) The TRECVid Metric. This is the traditional F_measure computed from precision and recall as follows:

$$precision = \frac{number\_of\_correctly\_detected\_boundaries}{total\_number\_of\_detected\_boundaries}$$

$$recall = \frac{number\_of\_correctly\_detected\_boundaries}{total\_number\_of\_boundaries\_to\_be\_detected}$$

$$F\_measure = \frac{2 \times precision \times recall}{precision + recall}$$

(13)

(b) The ARGOS Metric. The reference and system outputs are transformed into a list of continuous segments. Each segment of the ground truth is matched with the longest overlapping segment obtained as a result. A segment of the results can be matched only once. The temporal intersection between matched segments is then identified (cf. Figure 2).

Dynamic programming is used to find an optimal matching. Once the optimal matching is found, the F_measure is defined as

$$F\_measure = \frac{2 \times |matched\_intersection|}{|Ground\_truth| + |Results|},$$

(14)

where $| \cdot |$ represents the overall duration of the segments.

4.1.3. Results. Table 2 shows the results (with ARGOS metric) of the proposed system compared to the average system and the best system of the campaign. We can see that our system and the best system of ARGOS give quite similar results. The method of the best system is specific

TABLE 2: Shot boundaries detection: the proposed system versus the average one and the best one at the ARGOS campaign (ARGOS metric).

	Proposed Sys.	Average Sys.	Best Sys.
ARGOS metrics	0.933	0.87	0.94

to the task: it detects cuts by image comparisons after motion compensation. Then gradual transitions are detected by comparing norms of the first and second temporal derivatives of the image

5. Application to Program Boundaries Detection

We consider here that hypotheses made for shot detection can be extended to program segmentation. It means that a selected set of features during a program behave in an homogeneous manner so that their values distribution can be modelled by a Gaussian law and that features of two consecutive programs follow two rather different Gaussian laws. The last hypothesis is that a segment is of a minimal duration (in order to fix the size of the window used at the beginning of the algorithm and to determine when fusion of boundaries must be operated—see Figure 1(d)).

In our work, the goal is to check if typical video and audio features could validate the above hypotheses.

5.1. Program Boundaries Detection Using Visual Features. Each TV program has a certain number of visual characteristics that make this program different from the others. For example, the luminance, the dominant colors, and the activity rate in a soap episode are different from those observed on a TV game or a TV News program.

As input for the system, a vector of features is originally provided as follows. Every k seconds where k denotes the approximate value of the most frequent shot duration in seconds (experimentally $k = 8$) for the tested content set, a frame is extracted and then, the three corresponding 2^m-dimension color histograms (R, G and B) are computed and their 3×2^m ($m = 8$ if the images are 8-bit images) values are concatenated in a vector. Furthermore, the Singular Value Decomposition (SVD) is applied in order to reduce the vectors dimension. Experimentally, an inertia ratio higher than 95% is reached with a vector dimension reduced to 12.

Finally, the segmentation method explained above is applied on the sequence of these 12-dimension feature vectors. Results in table 3 show a precision of about 78% on 5 days of television (120 hours).

The major errors appear when there are commercial breaks: it may be typically explained because in this type of programs, in addition to their short duration, the homogeneity hypothesis is not still verified.

The variation and the distribution of the first "video" feature (after SVD) on 3 consecutive programs are given on Figures 3 and 4. Figures 5 and 6 show the same phenomena for the third "video" feature obtained after SVD.

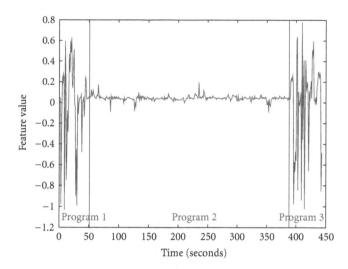

FIGURE 3: Variation of Feature F1 for 3 consecutive programs.

We can verify that both variation and repartition are different for the three programs.

5.2. Program Boundaries Detection Using Acoustic Features.

In this subsection, we evaluate the ability of our segmentation method to detect program boundaries using only audio features.

The input feature vectors are provided as follows. The first p Mel Frequency Cepstrum Coefficients ($p = 16$) are extracted every 10 ms using a sliding window of 20 ms. Those coefficients are then normalized and quantified between 0 and $D - 1$ ($D = 48$). Every k seconds ($k = 8$), histogram vectors are computed for each MFCC coefficient and concatenated to build a super-vector of dimension $p \times D$. Then, the SVD is applied in order to reduce the dimension of those vectors. Practically, an inertia ratio of about 90% is obtained for a resulting vector dimension of 40. Finally the segmentation is applied.

Table 3 shows that scores are lower with the acoustic features (75%) than with the visual features.

5.3. Program Boundaries Detection Using Audiovisual Features.

In order to exploit the complementary information brought by the two different modalities, the previous audio and video features are simultaneously used. Because we took the same temporal sampling to produce feature vectors ($k = 8$) with the same dimensions value ($3 \times 2^m = p \times D$) reduced by the same processing (SVD, histograms) for the above two methods, it is very easy to combine them using two kinds of fusion: fusion at the decision level and fusion at the feature level.

At the decision level, the fusion was done by computing

$$\Delta\text{BIC}_{AV} = \Delta\text{BIC}_A + \Delta\text{BIC}_V, \quad (15)$$

where ΔBIC_{AV} corresponds ideally to a change between two TV programs.

TABLE 3: Results of the program boundaries detection (120 hours of test).

	Visual System	Audio System	AV System
F_measure	78.04%	75.16%	80.72%

At the feature level, the early fusion aims to concatenate the visual vector of features (dimension $= 3 \times 2^m$) and the acoustic vector of features (dimension $= p \times D$). SVD is then applied: a resulting vector of dimension 60 is obtained for an inertia ratio of about 90%. Finally, the segmentation is processed to detect the frames of change. Experimentally, the early fusion at the features level gives (about 80.7%) better results than the fusion at the decision level (about 78.5%).

5.4. Experiments.

Tests were carried out on 120 hours of TV videos recorded continuously from a general French TV channel during 5 days (including various kinds of programs such as news, weather forecast, talk shows, movies, sports, and sitcoms) with a rate of 25 frames/second. The size of the programs is very variable: from few minutes for weather forecast to 3 hours for a film.

For the segmentation step, we had to define the length of the fixed size window W, the penalty coefficient which depends on W, and the dimension of the feature vectors (12 for video features, 40 for audio features and 60 for audio/video features). We chose a window size of 4 minutes (corresponding to 30 vectors) as the hypothesis on the minimal duration of a program. The penalty coefficient λ was tuned to 5 for the Video system, to 1.2 for the Audio system, and to 1 for the AV system.

To evaluate those systems, the ARGOS F_measure metric, described above, was used. It highlights the ability of the segmentation tool to gather units belonging to a same segment.

Results in Table 3 show that the visual system is better (about 78%) than the audio one (about 75%). With audio features, the majority of errors appear especially when there are commercial breaks. This might be explained typically because this type of program does not follow the homogeneity hypothesis. We can see that the two modalities audio and visual bring complementary information because the results are better than those obtained with only one modality.

Many improvements can be done while taking into account some knowledge already identified in the state of the art. For example, on French TV, commercials are separated by a sequence of monochrome images (white, blue, or black). As this kind of effect can be easily detected, improvements of about 9% (F_measure $= 87.34\%$) can easily be reached while gathering advertisements in a single program.

Comparison of the above results with those obtained by the state-of-the-art systems is a difficult task because corpora, units, and metrics are different for each experience and cannot be shared. To our knowledge, there is no international campaign addressing this topic. In this case, the evaluation we provide here should be considered as a basic reference which can be used later to evaluate improvements of this method or to compare with other future approaches.

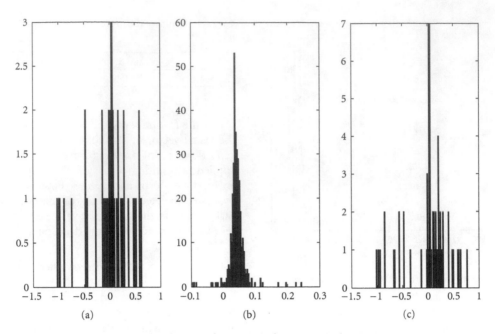

FIGURE 4: Distribution of Feature F1 for 3 consecutive programs.

As our system is almost knowledge-free, it can process any kinds of TV content without any prior training phase. In this way, it can be seen as a useful preprocessing step in the context of video indexing for example.

As part of the project ANR EPAC (http://www.epac.univ-lemans.fr/), the program boundaries detection was applied on 1700 hours of TV and Radio contents: the processing took less than 16 hours (lower than (recording duration $\times 10^{-2}$) with a nonoptimized version written in Matlab on a classical PC architecture.

6. Application to Speaker Diarization

In the context of speech processing on meeting data, with high interaction between speakers, one of the most difficult and unsolved problems is "speaker diarization". Speaker diarization is the process that detects speaker turns and groups those uttered by the same speaker. It is based on a first step of segmentation that consists in partitioning the regions of speech into segments: each segment must be as long as possible and must contain the speech of only one speaker. The second step is speaker clustering which consists in giving the same label to all the segments corresponding to the same speaker.

6.1. Experiments. In order to evaluate our method applied on speaker segmentation, we compare it to a well-known state-of-the-art method based only on BIC as described in [27, 29, 30].

The test set is the one used in ESTER 2009 evaluation competition (http://www.afcp-parole.org/ester/index.html). This set contains 20 shows for a total duration of about 7 hours recorded from 4 French radio stations.

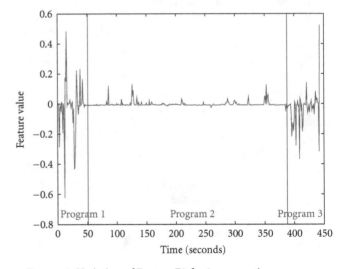

FIGURE 5: Variation of Feature F3 for 3 consecutive programs.

In these experiments, a centisecond approach is used that is, the soundtrack is firstly decomposed into 10 ms frames: the feature vectors used are the first 12 Mel Frequency Cepstrum Coefficients (MFCCs). The bidirectional segmentation is then directly applied on these vectors by fixing the size of the window equal to 2 seconds, and the penalty coefficient λ is tuned to 1.

As part of the speaker diarization task, the segmentation step is followed by a clustering step which consists in grouping all segments corresponding to the same speaker. The clustering step we use, presented in [31], allows adjusting the boundaries previously detected by the segmentation. Therefore, an additional improvement of 2.77% is

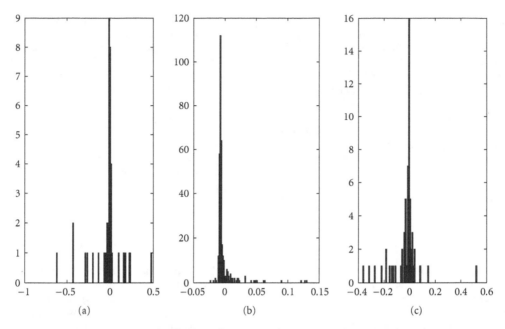

FIGURE 6: Distribution of Feature F3 for 3 consecutive programs.

TABLE 4: Evaluation of the output segments provided by the state-of-the-art segmentation method, our segmentation method, and our diarization system.

	Recall (%)	Precision (%)	F_measure (%)
State-of-the-art method	74.25	71.62	72.91
Our segmentation method	**85.36**	**85.37**	**85.37**
Our diarization method	87.95	88.26	88.10

obtained when we take into consideration this clustering process.

7. Conclusions

We have presented in this paper a temporal segmentation algorithm aiming at detecting stable boundaries between homogeneous segments. The parameters of this algorithm allow adapting it in order to address different types of segmentations problems. The size of temporal windows used at the first step of the algorithm allows controlling the size of the generated segments and the algorithm complexity. The penalty coefficient used in the DBIC criterion allows to adapt the decision sensitivity to the given problem parameters.

Applied on typical audiovisual data, the performances of this algorithm can only be compared with state-of the-art methods if we apply the same kind of postprocessing tools which are already involved in these methods (lighting effects or fast motion detection, dedicated commercial breaks detection, etc.). This algorithm can be applied on a light processing architecture (such as a set top box for example) in order to produce segmentation results on a large variety of content and for a large variety of applications.

References

[1] B. T. Truong, C. Dorai, and S. Venkatesh, "New enhancements to cut, fade, and dissolve detection processes in video segmentation," in *Proceedings of the 8th ACM International conference on Multimedia (ACM '00)*, pp. 219–227, New York, NY, USA, 2000.

[2] A. Hanjalic, "Shot-boundary detection: unraveled and resolved?" *IEEE Transactions on Circuits and Systems for Video Technology*, vol. 12, no. 2, pp. 90–105, 2002.

[3] Z. Liu and Y. Wang, "Major cast detection in video using both speaker and face information," *IEEE Transactions on Multimedia*, vol. 9, no. 1, pp. 89–101, 2007.

[4] A. M. A. Ahmad, "Multimedia content and the semantic web: methods, standards and tools: book reviews," *Journal of the American Society for Information Science and Technology*, vol. 58, no. 3, pp. 457–458, 2007.

[5] H. Sundaram and S.-F. Chang, "Video scene segmentation using video and audio features," in *Proceedings of the IEEE International Conference on Multi-Media and Expo (ICME '00)*, vol. 2, pp. 1145–1148, Beijing, China, 2000.

[6] P. Aigrain, P. Joly, and V. Longueville, "Medium knowledge-based macro-segmentation of video into sequences," in *Intelligent Multimedia Information Retrieval*, pp. 159–173, MIT Press, Cambridge, Mass, USA, 1997.

[7] M. Bertini, A. Del Bimbo, and P. Pala, "Content-based indexing and retrieval of TV news," *Pattern Recognition Letters*, vol. 22, no. 5, pp. 503–516, 2001.

[8] G. Piriou, P. Bouthemy, and J.-F. Yao, "Extraction of semantic dynamic content from videos with probabilistic motion models," in *Proceedings of the 18th European Conference on Computer Vision (ECCV '04)*, vol. 3023, pp. 145–157, 2004.

[9] M. Yeung, B.-L. Yeo, and B. Liu, "Extracting story units from long programs for video browsing and navigation," in *Readings in Multimedia Computing and Networking*, pp. 360–369, Morgan Kaufmann Publishers, San Francisco, Claif, USA, 2001.

[10] L. Liang, H. Lu, X. Xue, and Y.-P. Tan, "Program segmentation for TV videos," in *Proceedings of IEEE International Symposium on Circuits and Systems (ISCAS '05)*, pp. 1549–1552, Kobe, Japan, May 2005.

[11] J.-P. Poli and J. Carrive, "Modeling television schedules for television stream structuring," in *Proceedings of the 13th International Multimedia Modeling Conference (MMM '07)*, vol. 2, pp. 680–689, Singapor, 1996.

[12] X. Naturel, G. Gravier, and P. Gros, "Fast structuring of large television streams using program guides," in *Proceedings of the 4th International Workshop on Adaptive Multimedia Retrieval (AMR '06)*, vol. 4398 of *Lecture Notes in Computer Science*, pp. 222–231, Paris, France, 2007.

[13] E. Scheirer and M. Slaney, "Construction and evaluation of a robust multifeature speech/music discriminator," in *Proceedings of the IEEE International Conference on Acoustics, Speech and Signal Processing (ICASSP '97)*, vol. 2, pp. 1331–1334, Munich, Germany, 1997.

[14] J. Pinquier and R. André-Obrecht, "Audio indexing: primary components retrieval: robust classification in audio documents," *Multimedia Tools and Applications*, vol. 30, no. 3, pp. 313–330, 2006.

[15] S. Lefevre, B. Maillard, and N. Vincent, "Deux niveaux et deux outils d'analyse pour une meilleure segmentation de données audio," in *Proceedings of the 19th Colloque GRETSI sur le Traitement du Signal et des Images*, Paris, France, September 2003.

[16] L. Lu, R. Cai, and A. Hanjalic, "Audio elements based auditory scene segmentation," in *Proceedings of the IEEE International Conference on Acoustics, Speech and Signal Processing (ICASSP '06)*, vol. 5, pp. 17–20, Orlando, Fla, USA, May 2006.

[17] G. Tzanetakis and G. Essl, "Automatic musical genre classification of audio signals," in *Proceedings of the IEEE Transactions on Speech and Audio Processing*, pp. 293–302, New York, NY, USA, 2001.

[18] T. Heittola and A. Klapuri, "Locating segments with drums in music signals," Tech. Rep., Tampere University of Technology, Tampere, Finland, August 2002.

[19] O. Gillet and G. Richard, "Comparing audio and video segmentations for music videos indexing," in *Proceedings of the IEEE International Conference on Acoustics, Speech, and Signal Processing (ICASSP '06)*, vol. 2, pp. 873–876, Toulouse, France, May 2006.

[20] J. Saunders, "Real-time discrimination of broadcast speech/music," in *Proceedings of the IEEE International Conference on Acoustics, Speech and Signal Processing (ICASSP '96)*, vol. 2, pp. 993–996, Atlanta, Ga, USA, 1996.

[21] J. T. Foote and M. L. Cooper, "Media segmentation using self-similarity decomposition," in *Storage and Retrieval for Media Databases*, vol. 5021 of *Proceedings of SPIE*, pp. 167–175, Santa Clara, Claif, USA, January 2003.

[22] S. Haidar, P. Joly, and B. Chebaro, "Style similarity measure for video documents comparison," in *Proceedings of the 4th International Conference on Image and Video Retrieval (CIVR '05)*, vol. 3568 of *Lecture Notes in Computer Science*, Springer, Singapore, July 2005.

[23] E. El Khoury, C. Sénac, and R. André-Obrecht, "Speaker diarization: towards a more robust and portable system," in *Proceedings of the IEEE International Conference on Acoustics, Speech, and Signal Processing (ICASSP '07)*, vol. 4, pp. 489–492, Honolulu, Hawaii, USA, 2007.

[24] H. Gish, M.-H. Siu, and R. Rohlicek, "Segregation of speakers for speech recognition and speaker identification," in *Proceedings of the IEEE International Conference on Acoustics,*

Speech, and Signal Processing (ICASSP '91), vol. 2, pp. 873–876, Toronto, Canada, 1991.

[25] S. S. Chen and P. S. Gopalakrishnan, "Clustering via the Bayesian information criterion with applications in speech recognition," in *Proceedings of the IEEE International Conference on Acoustics, Speech and Signal Processing (ICASSP '98)*, vol. 2, pp. 645–648, Seattle, Wash, USA, May 1998.

[26] J. Rissanen, *Stochastic Complexity in Statistical Inquiry Theory*, vol. 2, World Scientific Publishing, River Edge, NJ, USA, 1989.

[27] P. Sivakumaran, J. Fortuna, and A. Ariyaeeinia, "On the use of the Bayesian information criterion in multiple speaker detection," in *Proceedings of the 7th European Conference on Speech Communication and Technology (Eurospeech '01)*, vol. 2, pp. 795–798, Aalborg, Denmark, 2001.

[28] P. Joly, J. Benois-Pineau, E. Kijak, and G. Quénot, "The ARGOS campaign: evaluation of video analysis and indexing tools," *Signal Processing: Image Communication*, vol. 22, no. 7-8, pp. 705–717, 2007.

[29] A. Tritschler and R. Gopinath, "Improved speaker segmentation and segments clustering using the Bayesian information criterion," in *Proceedings of the European Speech Processing (Eurospeech '99)*, vol. 2, pp. 679–682, Budapest, Hungary, 199.

[30] P. Delacourt, D. Kryze, and C. J. Wellekens, "DISTBIC: a speaker-based segmentation for audio data indexing," *Speech Communication*, vol. 32, no. 1, pp. 111–126, 2000.

[31] E. El-Khoury, C. Sénac, and J. Pinquier, "Improved speaker diarization system for meetings," in *Proceedings of the IEEE International Conference on Acoustics, Speech, and Signal Processing (ICASSP '09)*, pp. 4097–4100, Taipei, China, 2009.

15

A Cross-Layer Location-Based Approach for Mobile-Controlled Connectivity

T. Inzerilli,[1] A. M. Vegni,[2] A. Neri,[2] and R. Cusani[3]

[1] *Dipartimento per le Comunicazioni, I.S.C.T.I., Ministero dello Sviluppo Economico, Viale America 201, 00144 Rome, Italy*
[2] *Department of Applied Electronics, University of Roma Tre, Via della Vasca Navale 84, 00146 Rome, Italy*
[3] *Department of Information Engineering, Electronics and Telecommunications (DIET), University of Rome "Sapienza", Via Eudossiana 18, 00184 Rome, Italy*

Correspondence should be addressed to A. M. Vegni, amvegni@uniroma3.it

Academic Editor: Stefania Colonnese

We investigate into the potentiality of an enhanced Power and Location-based Vertical Handover (PLB-VHO) approach, based on a combination of physical parameters (i.e., location and power attenuation information), for mobile-controlled connectivity across UMTS and WLAN networks. We show that the location information in a multiparameter vertical handover can significantly enhance communication performance. In the presented approach a power attenuation map for the visited area is built and kept updated by exploiting the information sharing of power measurements with other cooperating mobile devices inside the visited networks. Such information is then used for connectivity switching in handover decisions. The analytical model for the proposed technique is first presented and then compared with a traditional Power-Based approach and a simplified Location-Based technique. Simulation results show the effectiveness of PLB-VHO approach, in terms of (i) network performance optimization and (ii) limitation of unnecessary handovers (i.e., mitigation of *ping-pong effect*).

1. Introduction

Current heterogeneous wireless networking scenarios include multimode Mobile Terminals (MTs) equipped with multiple wireless Network Interface Cards (NICs) and providing Vertical Handover (VHO) capability to autonomously select the best access. VHO allows switching from one access technology to another thus offering additional functionalities with respect to horizontal handover, where MTs move from an Access Point (AP) to another without changing the serving access network [1, 2].

A VHO process aims to guarantee seamless connectivity between heterogeneous wireless networks inside areas where simultaneous coverage from multiple networks is provided [3, 4]. Selection of the serving network can be based on optimality criteria which balance different factors including, for instance, monetary cost, energy consumption and end-user Quality-of-Service (QoS) [5]. In order to obtain an optimal tradeoff among these factors, while assuring high service continuity, fast and reliable procedures for the selection of the serving network have to be designed in the case of link degradation or loss of connectivity.

Various wireless networks exhibit quite different data rates, link errors, transmission range and transport delay. As a consequence, a direct comparison between heterogeneous wireless links in order to select the best network to attach to is not always straightforward. In general, a VHO strategy requires a preliminary definition of performance metrics for all the networks providing access in a visited environment, in order to compare the QoS offered by each of them and to decide for the best one [2, 5].

VHO decisions can be based on wireless channel state, network layer characteristics, as well as on application requirements when required. In this respect, various parameters can be taken into account, such as the type of the application (e.g., conversational, streaming, interactive, background), minimum bandwidth, tolerable maximum delay, bit error rate, transmitting power, current MT battery status, as well as user's preferences [1, 5].

In this paper is presented a novel mobile-controlled VHO scheme, in the following denoted as PLB-VHO. PLB-VHO is based on an integrated approach using two main procedures, that is, (i) a *Distributed Attenuation Map Building* (DAMB) and (ii) an *Enhanced Location-based* (ELB) *VHO* based on the calculated attenuation maps. PLB-VHO aims to select the best wireless access network in real-time and improve the overall network performance.

The paper is structured as follows. In Section 2 basic concepts on vertical handover mechanism are discussed. Section 3 describes the main procedures of the proposed PLB-VHO, that is, *Distributed Attenuation Map Building* and *Enhanced Location-based VHO*. Section 4 is dedicated to a performance comparison between the proposed PLB-VHO approach with a Power-Based VHO technique (i.e., PB-VHO) and a simplified Location-Based VHO solution (i.e., LB-VHO, where no attenuation map is considered for vertical handover decisions). Finally, conclusions are drawn in Section 5.

2. Related Work

In this section we propose an overview of the main criteria behind a vertical handover mechanism and describe how our technique results are innovative with respect to the related works.

Handover procedures typically fall into two main classes *Mobile-Controlled Handover* (MCHO) and *Network-Controlled Handover* (NCHO), depending on whether a handover is both initiated and controlled either by the MT or by the network, respectively [6]. In horizontal handover management, MCHO is the most common case, especially for WLAN environments, while NCHO is generally the preferred choice for cellular networks where resource optimization and load management are centralized. When a handover across different networks is considered—Vertical Handover—the MCHO appears a more practical approach, as handover decisions do not require interaction between heterogeneous networks and distinct network providers, which should interact to perform a handover across the two networks. In this work we are then focusing on an MCHO approach.

Furthermore, VHO schemes can be classified on the basis of the criteria and parameters adopted for initiating a handover from a Serving Network (SN) to a new Candidate Network (CN). Namely, we can enlist the following main schemes differing on the metrics driving handover decisions:

(1) *Received Signal Strength- (RSS-) based VHO algorithms*: this technique is native for horizontal handover mechanisms, specially for GSM system, which mainly considers RSS as the only decision metric. A drop of the RSS below the receiver sensitivity denotes lack of connectivity, which necessarily requires the execution of a handover [7–9]. The evolution of criteria for handover decisions provides for cost of services, power consumption, Quality-of-Service, positioning, and velocity of the mobile terminal,

which are mainly oriented to maximize user requirements;

(2) *Signal-to-Noise and Interference ratio- (SINR-) based VHO algorithms*: SINR directly impacts achievable goodput in a wireless access network [10, 11]. (The goodput [Bps] defines the amount of useful information per second. Such definition does not consider dropped packets or packet retransmissions, as well as protocol overhead.) In some wireless access technologies the transmission rate is dynamically adapted to the channel state condition. For instance, in the HSDPA network the modulation and the channel coding schemes vary versus the measured SINR, and both schemes influence the actual communication goodput;

(3) *multiparameter QoS-based VHO algorithms*: VHO algorithms can be based on the overall quality assessment for the available networks obtained by balancing various parameters [12, 13]. In order to improve the perceived communication quality, these approaches mostly consider the user connectivity to be switched to a candidate network, whenever the bandwidth is higher than the currently experienced in the actual serving network;

(4) *speed-based VHO algorithms:* in vehicular environments where users move fast at different speeds, seamless connectivity results in a challenging issue. Handovers should be performed on the basis of specific factors as vehicle mobility pattern and locality information, rather than currently perceived QoS, which might change rapidly over time. Speed-based VHO approaches combine the user location information, the measured vehicle speed, and the currently perceived QoS to make predictions and perform handovers [14]. In [15] whenever the vehicle speed falls below a given threshold, a vertical handover is executed in order to maintain a required QoS level and a seamless connectivity;

(5) *location-based VHO algorithms*: the location information can drive handover initiation allowing an MT to select that network which currently assures the best performance—network QoS parameters—on the basis of MT proximity to the nearest AP [16, 17]. In general, a location-based VHO technique consists in a preliminary handover initiation phase triggered on the basis of MT's location; handover is then carried out by following a QoS estimation phase. For instance, in [18] the MT's location information is exploited to initiate a goodput assessment, followed, if necessary, by a vertical handover execution. In [19] the prototype of a dual mode UMTS-WLAN mobile terminal for seamless connectivity and location-aware service is presented.

Notice that in general a vertical handover mechanism is oriented to maintain a seamless connectivity and limit the well-known *ping-pong effect* [20]. Unwanted and unnecessary vertical handovers often occur, especially when a mobile terminal moving back and forth between the two neighboring wireless networks—or in general around a corner that involves three or more wireless networks—triggers handover attempts repeatedly. This leads to excessive location and registration updates (i.e., network resource consumption), frequent connectivity interruptions, as well as seriously affection to mobile terminal's QoS (i.e., decreasing battery life). Typically, the *ping-pong effect* is a consequence of fluctuations of signal strength received by the mobile terminal from adjacent cells, causing unwanted handovers between neighboring wireless networks.

In addition, from the user perspective, frequent handovers can be experienced as numerous unpleasant transients of service interruption, while they might also produce excessive battery consumption. It follows that the minimization of the number of VHOs is a key issue in handover management [8, 9, 11, 14, 15, 18, 20, 21]. For this purpose, many handover algorithms incorporate a hysteresis cycle within handover decisions so as to prevent unnecessary and unwanted handovers. As an alternative, a precise constraint to handover frequency might be encoded in the VHO algorithm so as to assure a minimum permanence time in a wireless network. This last approach can reduce the algorithm complexity and the overall scalability of the vertical handover algorithm.

However, a deep discussion on the possible techniques to limit the *ping-pong effect* is out of the scope of this paper.

The detailed descriptions of the behavior of the above vertical handover approaches are discussed in Sections 2.1–2.5, respectively.

2.1. RSS-Based VHO Algorithms.

The conventional method to initiate a handover (both horizontal and vertical) is by monitoring the mean value of RSS against a predefined acceptable threshold for entry in a candidate network [7]. Since the RSS value suffers from severe fluctuations due to effects of shadowing and fading channels, filtering techniques (i.e., exponential smoothing average [8] and FFT-based methods [9]) should be considered to estimate the trend of RSS signal. In an RSS-based VHO approach, when the measured RSS of the SN drops below a predefined threshold, the RSS of the monitored set of CNs is evaluated in order to select the best network to migrate to. Although the RSS-based VHO method does not aim to optimize communication performance, but only focuses on maintaining a seamless connectivity, it represents the simplest and traditional handover mechanism.

2.2. SINR-Based VHO Algorithms.

In the SINR-based approach, Yang et al. [10] compare the received power against the noise and the interference levels in order to obtain a more accurate performance assessment, which brings about a slight increase of computational cost. SINR factor is considered for VHO decisions, as it directly affects the maximum data rate compatible with a given Bit Error Rate (BER). Therefore, when the SINR of the serving network decreases, the data rate and the QoS level decrease too. As a consequence, a SINR-based VHO approach is more suitable to meet QoS requirements, as described in [10, 11], and can be used to implement an adaptive data rate procedure. Again, the SINR parameter is also assumed as handover decision metric, combined with traditional RSS factor in order to improve efficient handover executions [11]. RSS-based and SINR-based schemes are both *reactive approaches*, which means that they aim to compensate for performance degradation when this occurs, that is, whenever either the RSS or the SINR drops below a guard threshold.

2.3. Multiparameter QoS-Based VHO Algorithms.

This class of vertical handover takes a connectivity switching decision on the basis of QoS parameters, coming both from the user requirements and the network performance [12, 13]. In [12] a multiparameter QoS-based VHO scheme is described. This technique is representative of a *proactive approach* based on the regular assessment of the QoS level offered by the current SN, as well as by other CNs. The proposed method attempts to select the best CN at any time, thus preventing performance degradation and sudden lack of connectivity. It can be based on the simultaneous estimation of a set of parameters—throughput and BER—and in the subsequent evaluation of an objective QoS metric, which is a function of such parameters. Its effectiveness is directly dependent on the ability of the objective QoS metric to mimic subjective Quality-of-Experience of the end-users and on the accuracy of the assessment of the parameters on which the metric is based.

As illustrated in [12], QoS-based VHO is well suited for multimedia applications like real-time video streaming. As a drawback, preventive approaches may lead to high handover frequency and hence lead to algorithmic instability. If numerous unwanted handovers may be executed in order to pursue QoS metric optimization in a proactive fashion, however low reliability in parameter assessment can be the cause of instability even when using a simpler reactive approach. For example, in an RSS-based VHO, the fluctuations of signal strength associated with shadow fading might cause a session to be handed over back and forth between available networks repeatedly. A hysteresis cycle [22], as well as a time constraint on maximum handover frequency (i.e., *waiting time* parameter [s]) [8, 11, 14, 18, 19], represents a solution to prevent an MT to trigger repeatedly undesired handover attempts from one network to another—*ping-pong effect*.

2.4. Speed-Based VHO Algorithms.

The speed-based VHO approach is mainly addressed on Vehicular Ad hoc Networks (VANETs), where users moving at high speeds are hardly able to maintain a service. In this scenario a vehicle-controlled VHO represents the mostly preferred solution, since innovative vehicles, equipped with smart *on-board* computer, and GPS (Global Positioning System) connectivity, are able to decide whether to make an handover or not [14]. This approach is based on both vehicle speed and handover latency, while in [15] the focus is a jointly improving of three QoS metrics (i.e., delay, jitter, and throughput), while keeping limited the number of vertical handovers.

In high-mobility environments, either QoS or RSS-based VHO procedure may fail due to the speed and the time that a vehicle is going to effectively spend in a candidate network, compared with the handover latency. It follows that handover algorithms in VANETs should be based on specific factors as vehicle mobility pattern [23] and speed. As a matter, Chen et al. in [23] consider how to reduce both handover delay and packet loss rate by proposing a novel network mobility protocol in VANETs, by exploiting vehicular communications and multihop procedures.

2.5. Location-Based VHO Algorithms. In location-based VHO solutions, the knowledge of location information is exploited to assess the quality of the link between the SN and the MT and to predict its future evolution to some extent on the basis of the MT's estimated path. User's position can be determined in several ways [16], including Time-of-Arrival, Direction-of-Arrival, RSS, and Assisted-GPS techniques.

Examples of location-based VHO algorithms are discussed by Wang et al. in [16], though their proposed technique shows a computational complexity of the handover decision that is rather high, as establishing and updating a lookup table to support a handover margin decision turns out to be time-consuming. In contrast, Kibria et al. [24] develop a predictive framework based on the assumption that the random nature of user mobility implies an uncertainty on his/her future location, which increases with the extension of the prediction interval.

The above descriptions have shown the main vertical handover approaches, mainly based on single metrics (i.e., RSS, SINR, QoS, speed, and location). Still, many handover techniques are based on the combination of two or more handover metrics, which generate most effective VHO decisions, but increase the computational load, since the handover decision exploits a rich set of input criteria. Such techniques are called *hybrid* (or combined) vertical handover approaches [25]. An example of hybrid approach is given in [11], as described in Section 2.2. Moreover, in [26] Hasswa et al. present a multiparameter VHO decision function, based on monetary cost, power requirements, security parameters, MT's preference, network conditions, and speed. No simulation results are reported for such approach.

Table 1 collects and highlights the main aspects, metrics, and performance parameters of the above discussed VHO approaches, listed in terms of decision metrics (i.e., RSS, SINR, QoS, speed, and location).

This paper proposes a novel vertical handover algorithm—called Power and Location-based Vertical Handover. It is a combined approach, which includes both RSS measurements and a location-based VHO algorithm. In particular, an RSS-VHO approach is used in order to decide on handover execution, while acquiring knowledge on the current environment (i.e., through received power levels, and network channel estimations) [8]. Then, the location information (i.e., the distance from the MT to an access point) is used to estimate QoS parameters (i.e., goodput) and decide for handover executions.

Leveraging such considerations, it follows that our proposed technique can be classified as (i) MCHO, (ii) hybrid approach, and (iii) based on RSS and location information. Its main goals are (i) a maximization of throughput and (ii) a limitation of *ping-pong effect*.

3. Proposed Power and Location-Based Vertical Handover (PLB-VHO)

In this section we shall introduce the Power and Location-based Vertical Handover (PLB-VHO) technique. In Section 3.1 some basic assumptions are given, regarding the main functionalities of considered dual-mode MTs and APs. A first overview of PLB-VHO approach is presented in Section 3.2, while more detailed descriptions of its two phases, that is, the *Distributed Attenuation Map Building* (DAMB) and the *Enhanced Location-based mode* (ELB), are presented in Sections 3.3 and 3.4, respectively.

3.1. Basic Assumption. Without loss of generality, in the illustration of the proposed PLB-VHO scheme, we will consider a dual-mode MT provided with UMTS and WLAN NICs—though the approach we are presenting can be extended to other types of networks—which exploits both RSS and its location measures to assess achievable goodput levels in the WLAN and UMTS networks.

As basic hypothesis, we consider the following assumptions:

(i) the MT moves within an area with double UMTS and WLAN coverage. As it often happens, while UMTS coverage is complete in the considered area, WLAN access is available only in some *hot-spot zones*;

(ii) the MT is able to determine its location through some auxiliary navigation aid, like GPS, while moving in a visited area;

(iii) both the MT and the APs in the visited network include an *application-layer service* to calculate a power attenuation map of the visited environment, which can be used to drive handover decisions through a *cross-layer approach*; (Note that for the sake of simplicity, we will use the generic term access point to indicate a network node providing access to the wireless network for both the WLAN, and the UMTS technologies.)

(iv) the AP includes a *server application*, while the MTs attached to it a *client application*. Client applications regularly deliver to the server application RSS samples linked to location information. The server application calculates an attenuation map from the received samples and broadcasts it to all MTs attached to the network.

3.2. PLB-VHO Overall Operation. The PLB-VHO scheme includes two procedures, that is, (i) a *Distributed Attenuation Map Building* (DAMB) and (ii) an *Enhanced Location-based Vertical Handover* (ELB-VHO), exploiting the calculated attenuation maps for the WLAN and the UMTS networks.

TABLE 1: Classification of handover algorithms on the basis of decision metrics and performance results.

VHO Decision Metric	VHO algorithm	Main aspects	Performance
RSS	Ayyappan and Dananjayan [7]	This technique considers both hard and soft MCHO version between WLAN and CDMA networks. The RSS parameter is monitored against unwanted power level fluctuations.	Throughput
	Inzerilli and Vegni [8]	This approach is an MCHO technique between WLAN and CDMA networks. It focuses on the minimization of *ping-pong effect* by channel estimation techniques and *waiting time* parameter.	Throughput and handover frequency
	Xie and Wu [9]	The algorithm makes handoff decisions after analyzing the signal strength fluctuation caused by slow fading through FFT. The method strongly reduces the number of handovers. It can be applied to both horizontal and vertical handovers.	Handover frequency and delay
SINR	Yang et al. [10]	This technique results in a QoS oriented VHO, since the SINR factor is strictly affecting the QoS level.	Throughput
	Vegni et al. [11]	It is an MCHO technique between WLAN and CDMA networks. The goal is to limit the *ping-pong effect* by preventive vertical handovers. Since the SINR factor is combined with RSS parameter, the technique results in combined-metric based VHO approach for preventing unnecessary VHOs.	Throughput and handover frequency
QoS	Vegni et al. [12]	In this technique the QoS parameters are both subjective and objective. This approach is an MCHO and network-assisted VHO technique between WLAN and UMTS networks, in an IEEE 802.21 network architecture.	Seamless connectivity
	Jesus et al. [13]	The handover technique is QoS-oriented and is based on context-aware information coming from both the network and the user. The handover decision is negotiated by both the MT and the network (i.e., UMTS and WLAN) in an IEEE 802.21* network architecture.	Maximum allowed number of active users
Speed	Vegni and Esposito [14]	This technique is a vehicle-controlled VHO, based on speed and handover delay. It addresses on VANETs.	Throughput and handover frequency
	Esposito et al. [15]	This approach results in a vehicle-controlled VHO for improving QoS metrics.	Throughput, jitter, delay and handover frequency
	Chen et al. [23]	This is a novel network mobility management protocol for VANETs, by exploiting traditional vehicle-to-vehicle communications.	Handoff delay and packet loss rate
Location	Wang et al. [16]	This technique is limited on a horizontal handover approach, for both hard and soft versions. The MT's location is exploited for adaptive handovers.	Dropped calls and outage probability
	Kibria et al. [24]	It is an MT controlled VHO technique, based on MT's location information to predict handovers.	Hysteresis margins
	Inzerilli et al. [18]	This method is driven by MT's location in order to prevent vertical handovers between WLAN and UMTS networks. The limitation of *ping-pong effect* is acted by the use of the *waiting time* parameter.	Throughput and number of vertical handovers

*The IEEE 802.21 standard provides quick handovers of data sessions across heterogeneous networks with small switching delays and minimized latency [27]. The handover procedures could become more flexible and appropriate with this standard, by exploiting the Media Independent Handover (MIH) functional model. The IEEE 802.21 focuses on protocol aspects rather than handover algorithms. In this table the IEEE 802.21 is not investigated since it is out of the scope of this paper.

Namely, an MT switching on in the visited environment is initially unaware of the signal power spatial distribution (i.e., no knowledge of access point's location and associated power levels is available) for the available UMTS and WLAN networks. The MT will enter the DAMB-mode and interrogate the serving APs for each network being visited, in order to obtain the attenuation maps. The attenuation maps can be returned immediately if available in the AP, as a result of the interaction of the AP with other MTs previously roaming in the network and collaborating to the *Attenuation Map Building*.

Once provided with both the attenuation maps from both the WLAN and UMTS networks, the MT can select the best network and enters the *Enhanced Location-based* (ELB) mode. While roaming it will then exploit the received attenuation maps along with the current location information to assess achievable goodput in both the UMTS and WLAN networks and take handover decisions to optimize goodput. Namely, knowledge of the expected spatial distribution of the power attenuation in the surrounding area of the current location allows taking more accurate and stable estimates of the achievable goodput. The handover algorithm used in this phase is then called as *Power and Location-based Vertical Handover* (PLB-VHO).

In the ELB-mode the MT will continue collecting RSS samples and deliver them to the serving AP, which will contribute to the update of the attenuation maps in the serving access points. When the MT moves towards new unvisited zones, requiring for instance change of serving access point in the same network, new attenuation maps might have to be built and hence the MT re-enters the DAMB-mode. It will transit to the ELB-mode again once the updated attenuation maps have been created.

Figure 1 depicts the essentials of the PLB-VHO, highlighting the two modes just described. In the DAMB-mode the MT exploits an interrogating-phase with the nearest access point. In the ELB-mode the MT relies on a more elaborate VHO algorithm, while it keeps refining its knowledge of the visited environment (*Attenuation Map Update*).

Figure 2 shows an example scenario with a mesh network of five MTs (i.e., MT1, MT2, MT3, MT4, MT5) with dual WLAN and UMTS NICs, two WLAN access points (i.e., AP1 WLAN, AP2 WLAN), and one UMTS access point (i.e., AP1 UMTS). The five MTs roam in an area covered by the two WLAN APs and a single UMTS AP. Namely, MT2, MT3, MT5 roam in the AP1 WLAN area, while MT1 and MT4 roam in the AP2 WLAN area.

In Figure 2 we use dotted lines for time scales in the intervals of DAMB-mode, while continuous lines are used in the intervals of ELB mode. The picture shows only the messages of map requests from the MTs and map replies by the APs, while delivery of RSS samples from MTs to APs are neglected. The dynamics of message exchange are the following:

(i) MT1, MT2, and MT3 have already issued a map request to AP1 WLAN, AP2 WLAN, and AP1 UMTS prior time $t = 0$;

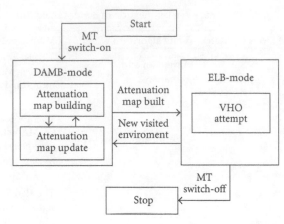

FIGURE 1: Finite state machine for the PLB-VHO algorithm.

(ii) at time $t = 0$ an attenuation map becomes available at AP1 UMTS and it is issued to MT1, MT2 and MT3;

(iii) MT2 and MT3 will instead wait for time $t = 9$ to receive a map from AP1 WLAN, while MT1 will wait for time $t = 12$ for the map;

(iv) MT4 and MT5 enter the area following $t = 0$ and hence receive the attenuation map from AP1 UMTS immediately, after their request. On the contrary, reception of WLAN maps for MT4 and MT5 occurs in times $t = 9$ and $t = 12$, respectively, that is, as soon as they become available.

3.3. Distributed Attenuation Map Building (DAMB-Mode). From mobile switch-off up to the completion of both UMTS and WLAN *Attenuation Map Building*, the mobile terminal uses the DAMB procedure to obtain attenuation maps and works jointly with the other neighboring mobile terminals.

During the DAMB-mode each MT selects and interrogates the nearest access points of the UMTS and WLAN networks, collects a set of RSS samples for the *Attenuation Map Building* process, and delivers them to the selected access points. Availability of a power attenuation map derived from RSS measures makes it possible to apply a more sophisticated method for handover management and optimization of goodput without waiting for severe performance degradation prior handover initiation.

The spatial distribution of the power attenuation associated to the monitored UMTS and WLAN access points are calculated by each AP simply as the difference between the access point transmission power and the RSS samples received by the MTs connected to the AP, that is, by taking the difference between the nominal transmitted power and the short-term time average of the RSS. Averaging is required in order to smooth fast fluctuations produced by multipath signal reflections and can be performed by means of a mean filter applied to the attenuation sample series multiplied by a sliding temporal window.

Let us assume that an access point governs an area partitioned into a lattice of $\widetilde{M}_H \times \widetilde{M}_V$ square zones, each of them with a width w_{zone}. In general, this parameter is

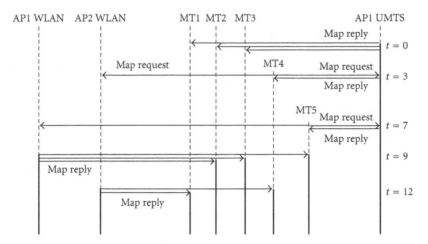

FIGURE 2: DAMB procedure in a mesh network example scenario.

different for UMTS and WLAN networks, in accordance to the maximum rate of change of the received power signals. While moving in that area, an MT measures the attenuation in each visited zone, associates it with its current location, and delivers it to the serving access point.

Let n be the discrete time index, and let $a_j[n]$ be the attenuation measured in the jth zone at time n. Then, the Moving Average (MA) attenuation estimation (i.e., $A_j^{\text{MA}}[n]$) on a sliding window of length K is

$$A_j^{\text{MA}}[n] = \frac{1}{K} \sum_{i=n-K+1}^{n} a_j[i], \quad n \geq K. \tag{1}$$

Averaging over the last K samples allows reducing the impact of instantaneous power fluctuations in attenuation detection and reduces the power error estimation. On the other hand, as the mobile terminal is assumed to be moving, the length of the moving window cannot be too large. As an alternative, an Exponential Smoothing Average filter with time constant t can be applied, so that

$$A_j^{\text{ESA}}[n] = \alpha \cdot A_j[n-1] + (1-\alpha) \cdot a_j[n], \tag{2}$$

where $\alpha = \exp(-(t_n - t_{n-1})/\tau)$.

Although (1) and (2) have the same computational cost and similar performance, (2) requires smaller quantity of memory to store the measured time series $\{a_j[n]\}$. Furthermore, since Moving Average filters are prone to outliers, a more robust estimate can be computed by replacing the linear mean filter with a (nonlinear) median filter.

When each zone of the lattice has been visited at least once by an MT, the attenuation map is completed. However, it is possible that a complete visit of all the zones of the map can take a long time, and perhaps it never accomplishes. As a consequence, in order to speed up the *Attenuation Map Building* process it is possible to resort to interpolation in order to assign an attenuation value to locations that have not yet been visited.

Namely, let us assume that the jth zone, with center in (x_j, y_j), has not been assigned a power value yet, and let j_1, j_2 and j_3 be the nearest three locations whose attenuation has

already been measured. We can estimate the attenuation A_j of zone j by applying linear algebra and using the equation of a plane passing through three points

$$\det \begin{pmatrix} x_j - x_1 & y_j - y_1 & A_j - A_1 \\ x_2 - x_1 & y_2 - y_1 & A_2 - A_1 \\ x_3 - x_1 & y_3 - y_1 & A_3 - A_1 \end{pmatrix} = 0. \tag{3}$$

Through simple manipulation of (3), we can easily obtain a direct formula for interpolation of A_j, such as

$$\begin{aligned} A_j &= \frac{A_2 \left(x_3 y_1 - x_j y_1 - x_1 y_3 + x_j y_3 + x_1 y_j - x_3 y_j \right)}{x_3 (y_1 - y_2) + x_1 (y_2 - y_3) + x_2 (-y_1 + y_3)} \\ &+ \frac{A_1 \left(-x_3 y_2 + x_j y_2 + x_2 y_3 - x_j y_3 - x_2 y_j + x_3 y_j \right)}{x_3 (y_1 - y_2) + x_1 (y_2 - y_3) + x_2 (-y_1 + y_3)} \\ &+ \frac{A_3 \left(x_j y_1 + x_1 y_2 - x_j y_2 - x_1 y_j + x_2 \left(-y_1 + y_j \right) \right)}{x_3 (y_1 - y_2) + x_1 (y_2 - y_3) + x_2 (-y_1 + y_3)}. \end{aligned} \tag{4}$$

It is worth highlighting that linear interpolation through (3) brings some errors in the attenuation map. In general, a sufficient number of visited zones have to be achieved prior completion of the attenuation map. Such a number is also dependent on the actual path of the MT in the lattice.

Let $VZ[n]$ be the set of visited zones by an MT up to time n at time n. Then, in order to evaluate the degree of reliability of the attenuation map at time n, we employ a *Map Reliability Index (MRI)* at time n, defined as follows:

$$\text{MRI}[n] = \frac{\|VZ[n]\|}{\widetilde{M}_H \cdot \widetilde{M}_V}, \tag{5}$$

where $\widetilde{M}_H$ and $\widetilde{M}_V$ represent the number of horizontal and vertical zones in the neighborhood, respectively.

We can empirically set a threshold value MRI^{TH} for the index in (5) beyond which the knowledge of the visited environment is regarded as acceptable. Only when this threshold is exceeded, interpolation is applied. Thus, the attenuation map will be filled in partially with measured attenuations and partially through linear interpolation, respectively.

Even after *Attenuation Map Completion*, when the MT enters the ELB-mode (see Figure 1), power samples continue being collected and used as in (2) in order to increase the accuracy of each map. Conversely, when for the current location the MRI falls below MRI^{TH} a transition from the *ELB*-mode to the *DAMB*-mode is performed (see Figure 1).

3.4. Enhanced Location-Based (ELB) Mode.

A more significant parameter than measured RSS for comparing performance of two wireless links is the expected goodput, that is, the net transmission throughput out of the percentage of service outage.

In general, the goodput experienced by an MT in a wireless cell depends on the bandwidth allocated to the MT for the requested services and on the channel quality. When inelastic traffic (e.g., real-time flows over UDP) is conveyed the goodput (i.e., GP [Mbps]) can be approximated to the net traffic received out of channel errors and given by

$$\text{GP} = \text{BW} \cdot (1 - P_{\text{out}}),\qquad(6)$$

where BW [bps] is the bandwidth allocated to the MT and P_{out} is the service outage probability in the considered channel. Instead, when elastic traffic is conveyed (typically when TCP is used for data downloading/uploading), throughput tends to decrease with increasing values of P_{out} as an effect of the TCP congestion control algorithm.

The parameter BW is in general a function of the wireless link nominal capacity and is conditioned by the Medium Access Control algorithm that is used and sometimes of the experienced P_{out}, for example, in those technologies using adaptive modulation. In the UMTS network P_{out} can be theoretically calculated [28], using the following formula:

$$P_{\text{out}}^{\text{UMTS}} = \Pr\left\{\frac{E_{b,\text{Tx}}^{\text{UMTS}}}{\sigma_{N_{\text{UMTS}}}^2 + \gamma I_{0_{\text{UMTS}}}} \cdot \frac{1}{A^{\text{UMTS}}(d_{\text{UMTS}})} \le \mu_{\text{UMTS}}\right\},\qquad(7)$$

where $E_{b,\text{Tx}}^{\text{UMTS}}$ is the transmitted bit energy, μ and γ are parameters dependent on the signal and interference statistics, respectively, and σ_N^2 is the receiver noise power. I_0 is the inter- and intracell interference power, and can be calculated in terms of the number of effective interfering users (i.e., N_{interf}) as follows:

$$I_0 = \frac{N_{\text{interf}}}{G_{\text{spread}}} E_{b,\text{Tx}}^{\text{UMTS}},\qquad(8)$$

where G_{spread} is the WCDMA spreading factor. Finally, the parameter $A^{\text{UMTS}}(d_{\text{UMTS}})$ is the overall power loss, expressed as

$$A^{\text{UMTS}}(d_{\text{UMTS}}) = \frac{P_{\text{Tx}}}{P_{\text{Rx}}} = \left(\frac{4\pi}{\lambda}\right)^2 \frac{d_{\text{UMTS}}^\beta}{G_{\text{Tx}}^{\text{Ant}} G_{\text{Rx}}^{\text{Ant}}},\qquad(9)$$

which depends on the MT's distance d_{UMTS} from the UMTS base station.

Let us initially assume for simplicity that all wireless cells have an isotropic behavior [20]. Expected goodput is then calculated as a function of a single variable, that is, the MT's distance from the access point of the network cell the mobile device is visiting.

The service outage probability for a WLAN network $P_{\text{out}}^{\text{WLAN}}$ can be theoretically calculated in a similar fashion to (7), using the following formula:

$$P_{\text{out}}^{\text{WLAN}} = \Pr\left\{\frac{E_{b,\text{Tx}}^{\text{WLAN}}}{\sigma_{N_{\text{WLAN}}}^2} \cdot \frac{1}{A^{\text{WLAN}}(d_{\text{WLAN}})} \le \mu_{\text{WLAN}}\right\}.\qquad(10)$$

We remark that, with respect to the UMTS W-CDMA case, cochannel interference effects are not present due to the different structure of the physical layer. For compactness of notation we observe that (10) can be formally seen as a special case of (7) obtained for $\gamma = 0$.

Let us define as the range of an isotropic cell the distance R_{cell} from the cell centre beyond which the outage probability exceeds the maximum acceptable value $\tilde{P}_{\text{out}}$. R_{cell} can be obtained resolving the above equations or empirically, through measurement on the network. As an alternative, typical value for well-known technologies can be used, for example, [29, 30].

Let $\tilde{\mu}$ be the threshold corresponding to signal to a given QoS level based on (7) for UMTS networks and on (10) for WLAN cells, respectively. Then, as the path loss $A_d(d)$ for a link of length d is approximately proportional to d^β, the received *Signal-to-Noise and Interference ratio* (i.e., SINR(d)) can be written as (see [31])

$$\text{SINR}(d) = \tilde{\mu}\left(\frac{R_{\text{cell}}}{d}\right)^\beta.\qquad(11)$$

For a given location at distance $d^{\text{WLAN}} < R_{\text{cell}}^{\text{WLAN}}$ from a WLAN access point, and at distance $d^{\text{UMTS}} < R_{\text{cell}}^{\text{UMTS}}$ from an UMTS base station, since in free space $\beta = 2$, while in more complex environments $\beta > 2$, the goodput GP(d) at distance d from the access point can be computed as a derivation from (6), with the following approximated formula:

$$\text{GP}^{(k)}(d_{(k)}) = \text{BW}_{\text{max}}^{(k)} \cdot \Pr\left\{d_{(k)} < R_{\text{cell}}^{(k)}\right\},$$
$$k \in \{\text{UMTS, WLAN}\}\qquad(12)$$

whose value is set to zero if the distance is greater than the cell range, while $\text{GP}^{(k)}(d_{(k)}) = \text{BW}_{\text{max}}^{(k)}$, when the mobile terminal is lying at the center of the wireless cell.

Handover can be initiated when the estimated goodput of the Serving Network (SN) is lower than that of the Candidate Network (CN). Namely, in the case of vertical handover from WLAN to UMTS, the following condition holds:

$$\text{GP}_{\text{max}}^{\text{UMTS}}(d_{\text{UMTS}}) < \text{GP}_{\text{max}}^{\text{WLAN}}(d_{\text{WLAN}}).\qquad(13)$$

It is worth noticing that when handovers are too frequent, the quality as perceived by the end-user can significantly degrade in addition to the waste of battery charge. Then it can be useful to limit handover frequency by imposing a minimum time interval between two consecutive

```
Input { T_{W/U-wait}; n_{VHO} = 0; P_W }
Output { n_{VHO}; CRB }
If P_W > P_{W-min}
  | WLAN access
  | CRB = GP_N^{UMTS};
  | cont = T_{W-wait};
  |   If cont == 0
  |     | If GP_max^{WLAN} > GP_max^{UMTS}
  |     | | Soft VHO attempt
  |     | |   If GP_N^{UMTS} > GP_N^{WLAN}
  |     | |     | UMTS access
  |     | |     | n_{VHO} = n_{VHO} + 1;
  |     | |     end
  |     | end
  |   end
else
  | UMTS access
  | CRB = GP_N^{UMTS};
  | cont = T_{W-UMTS};
  |   If cont == 0
  |     | If GP_max^{WLAN} > GP_max^{UMTS}
  |     | | soft VHO attempt
  |     | |   If GP_N^{WLAN} > GP_N^{UMTS}
  |     | |     | WLAN access
  |     | |     | n_{VHO} = n_{VHO} + 1;
  |     | |     end
  |     | end
  |   end
end
```

FIGURE 3: Pseudo-code for vertical handover algorithm in ELB-mode.

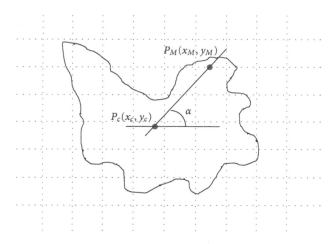

FIGURE 4: Anisotropic cell model.

handovers (i.e., applying the *waiting time* constraint [s]), possibly different for the cases of UMTS-to-WLAN handover and WLAN-to-UMTS handover, as in [8, 14, 15, 18]. As an alternative, also a hysteresis cycle in handover initiation process can be introduced. We remind from [15] that the waiting time parameter has been defined as an *interswitch time period*, during which the handover process enters an idle mode. For instance, if a mobile terminal moves at 0.5 m/s, a 10-second waiting time results in 50 meters covered by the user, before the handover process is reactivated. This approach results are necessary to avoid a high handover frequency.

Figure 3 depicts the pseudocode for the *Enhanced Location-based* (ELB) process, which uses (13) to drive handover decisions and exploits a *waiting time*, different for WLAN and UMTS (i.e., $T_{W/U\text{-wait}}$ [s] for WLAN, and UMTS, resp.) between consecutive handovers to limit the number of executed handovers (i.e., handover frequency).

In the location-based approach presented so far the goodput is estimated simply on the basis of the distance d from the center of a wireless cell. This method is applicable when the coordinates of the center of the cells and the cell range are known *a priori*. In addition, this goodput model assumes an isotropic access point source and no obstacles between the MT and the access point.

In this section we will exploit the *Distributed Attenuation Map Building* phase in order to derive a more realistic estimate of the goodput by relaxing the hypothesis of isotropic cells.

In order to exploit the PLB-VHO approach, it is first necessary to obtain (i) a goodput estimation approach adapted for anisotropic cells, and (ii) a method to derive wireless cell geometry from the *Distributed Attenuation Map Building*.

We assume a generic-shape cell model and estimate goodput as a function of the MT's line of sight direction α, (i.e., the direction of the line drawn from the access point's location $P_c = (x_c, y_c)$ to the MT's current position $P_M = (x_M, y_M)$, as shown in Figure 4). Namely, α is calculated as follows:

$$\alpha = \arctan\left(\frac{y_M - y_c}{x_M - x_c}\right). \tag{14}$$

For a cell with access point placed in P_c, we define the radius of the cell R_{cell} as a function of the line of sight α, which represents the distance $R_{\text{cell}} = R_{\text{cell}}(\alpha; P_c)$ from the cell centre along the line of sight α beyond which the outage probability exceeds the maximum acceptable value $\tilde{P}_{\text{out}}$.

Hence, the goodput $\text{GP}^{(k)}(d_{(k)}, \alpha_{(k)})$ at distance $d_{(k)}$ along the line of sight α can be calculated for each zone with the following approximated formula, which replaces (12) for the case of anisotropic cells:

$$\text{GP}^{(k)}(d_{(k)}, \alpha_{(k)}) = \text{BW}_{\max}^{(k)} \cdot \Pr\left\{d_{(k)} < R_{\text{cell}}^{(k)}(\alpha; P_c)\right\}, \tag{15}$$

where, as in (12), k is the index denoting the corresponding wireless network, that is, $k \in \{\text{UMTS}, \text{WLAN}\}$. Handover decisions are still taken on the basis of (13).

We can calculate the function $R_{\text{cell}}^{(k)}(\alpha; P_c)$ by using the *Attenuation Map*. In fact, for a given direction α, we can consider the set of zones lying along the corresponding line of sight. Using (3) the attenuation profile along the line of sight can be easily computed. Then, the cell range along direction α can be set to the distance for which the attenuation equals to the maximum attenuation $A_{\max}$, beyond which the outage probability exceeds the maximum acceptable value $\tilde{P}_{\text{out}}$.

In addition, in zone Z_j with center in (x_j, y_j) characterized by an attenuation $A_j^{(k)}$ the average goodput can be evaluated as

$$\text{GP}^{(k)}(d_{(k)}, \alpha_{(k)}) = \text{BW}_{\max}^{(k)} \cdot \text{Pr}\left\{A_j^{(k)} < A_{\max}^{(k)}\right\}, \qquad (16)$$

where $\text{Pr}\{A_j^{(k)} < A_{\max}^{(k)}\}$ is obtained as an analogy from $\text{Pr}\{d_{(k)} < R_{\text{cell}}^{(k)}(\alpha; P_c)\}$.

4. Performance Evaluation and Comparisons

Simulation results for PLB-VHO technique are now presented and compared with other vertical handover schemes. Namely, a multiparameter vertical handover—that is, DRI-VHO, Data Rate, and Interference-based Vertical Handover, [11]—is considered along with the two single-parameter vertical handover approaches, such as (i) a traditional Power-Based Vertical Handover (PB-VHO) [8] and (ii) a simple Location-Based Vertical Handover (LB-VHO) [18], from which PLB-VHO is derived. Basically, simulated trends for all four algorithms—PB, LB, DRI, and PLB—represent different realistic cases in a dual-mode WLAN/UMTS MT using in turn one of the four algorithms.

As described in [8], PB-VHO uses power measurements in order to initiate VHOs, while LB-VHO employs mobile location information to optimize MT's goodput [18]. PLB-VHO integrates then power estimations and location information in order to enhance the use of location information and apply it to anisotropic cells. Finally, DRI-VHO—also referred to as C-VHDF (Combined-Vertical Handover Decision Function) in [11]—is a VHO hybrid approach, whose purpose is goodput optimization, as well as in PLB and PB. In DRI-VHO, RSS measurement is used to drive VHO in a first phase (i.e., handover initiation), while data rate estimation from SINR guides the handover accomplishment phase (i.e., handover execution). The DRI-VHO aims to maximize throughput, through the optimization of *Data Rate gain* parameter [Bps], defined as the increment of data rate resulting from the execution of a vertical handover. More details of DRI-VHO technique are given in [11].

In the scenarios simulated using Matlab 7.6, an MT moves in a heterogeneous network grid with 3 UMTS and 20 WLAN cells. One hundred network scenarios have been generated, where the location of the WLAN access points and UMTS base stations are randomly varied. In each scenario the MT moves with a constant speed (i.e., 0.5 m/s, corresponding to a pedestrian speed) along a random path inside the heterogeneous grid for a simulated time around 1 hour and 20 minutes.

The Okomura-Hata model for the signal power attenuation [32] has been employed together with an AWG (Additive White Gaussian) channel model. In addition, the following parameter set has been employed, as well as in [8, 18]: (i) the transmitted power in the middle of UMTS cells equal to 43 dBm and (ii) UMTS/WLAN receiver sensitivities $P_{\text{U/W-min}}$ and $P_{\text{U/W-TH}}$ threshold equal to -100 dBm.

During the walk, the MT moves in an area totally covered by UMTS, which means that UMTS coverage is always guaranteed, though with different levels of throughput. Occasionally the MT enters some WLAN cells, which are hotspots where the MT can reach higher levels of throughput.

In Figure 5(a) performance of the four algorithms is evaluated in terms of the number of the executed vertical handovers versus the *waiting time* parameter, as introduced in Section 3.4. As expected, the number of VHOs obtained with the PB-VHO is significantly lower than that for all the other techniques (i.e., LB-VHO, PLB-VHO, and also DRI-VHO) whose curves are roughly overlapping, except for that relative to LB-VHO, which is significantly higher, when the waiting time is set to 0. This means that performance optimization pursued by the LB, PLB, and DRI is achieved at the expenses of an increase handover frequency, though PLB-VHO results as more effective than DRI-VHO and LB-VHO, in terms of a decreasing average of handover occurrences, independently on the specific values considered for the *waiting time* parameter. In contrast, the worse performance is given by LB-VHO particularly for low values of the waiting time. This is probably due to the fact that the location-based handover decision scheme is less precise in LB-VHO than in PLB-VHO as it does not consider the actual shape of the wireless cells and approximates them to simple circles.

Table 2 shows, in more detail, the collected statistics of the number of VHOs experienced with the PB, LB, DRI, and PLB approaches, respectively. For each of them two columns are given. In the first column the mean values of the number of VHO, also depicted in Figure 5(a), are reported for different values of *waiting time* (i.e., from 0 up to 120 s). These are calculated by averaging the total number of VHO values registered at the end of each simulation over the considered 100 scenarios for each value of the waiting time. In the second column the so-called *Dispersion Index* (i.e., defined as the ratio between the standard deviation and the mean value over the considered 100 scenarios) is reported for different values of *waiting time* (i.e., from 0 up to 120 s).(The Dispersion Index represents the relative variation of the collected samples with respect to the mean value.) It is observed that the number of vertical handovers with DRI-VHO is on average two times greater—equal to 104% increment—than that obtained with PB-VHO, while DRI-VHO increases the handover occurrences with respect to PLB-VHO (i.e., on average 21% increment). In contrast, DRI-VHO shows on average a low number of handovers—equal to 11% decrement—with respect to LB-VHO approach, while PLB-VHO has a higher number of vertical handovers—equal to 68% increment—than that for PB-VHO. Finally, PLB-VHO results on average in 26% reduction of the number of vertical handovers, with respect to the LB-VHO approach.

In order to evaluate the effectiveness of a vertical handover technique along with the number of VHOs, the total number of data, that is, Cumulative Received Bits (CRBs), is also considered. Such statistics has to be regarded as more important in the evaluation the VHO performance, as the number of VHOs, when these are an issue, can be explicitly limited by setting the waiting time parameter properly.

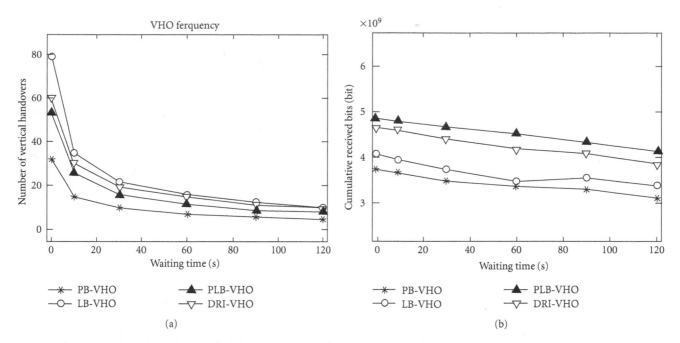

FIGURE 5: (a) Average of number of vertical handover occurrences for PB, LB, DRI, and PLB. The handovers are performed by a MT during its path, for different values of *waiting time* constraints. Performances have been obtained over 100 simulation scenarios. (b) Average of CRBs performance for PB, LB, DRI, and PLB-VHO versus different values of *waiting time* parameter. Performances have been obtained over 100 simulation scenarios.

TABLE 2: Statistics for the number of VHO occurrences for PB, LB, DRI-VHO, and PLB-VHO approaches.

Waiting time [s]	PB mean	PB disp. index	LB mean	LB disp. index	DRI mean	DRI disp. index	PLB mean	PLB disp. index
0	31.8	81.58%	79.2	24.29%	60.1	36.98%	53.1	51.28%
10	14.6	65.23%	34.6	25.42%	30.2	40.39%	25.8	50.29%
30	9.6	62.73%	21.4	31.16%	19.2	34.09%	16	42.08%
60	6.8	68.20%	15.8	49.72%	15.1	34.54%	11.6	44.36%
90	5.6	64.76%	12.3	49.97%	11.2	36.88%	8.8	37.42%
120	4.6	76.82%	10	55.17%	9.4	24.67%	8	39.08%

In Figure 5(b) the CRBs versus the *waiting time* parameter is displayed. The PLB-VHO has visibly the best performance of all the four approaches. Namely, PB-VHO does not aim at goodput performance optimization but it rather limits computational cost and simply aims to recover from connectivity loss. LB-VHO performs a rough estimation of the achievable goodput assuming circular cells, unlike PLB-VHO which estimates cell shapes more accurately. Finally DRI-VHO, which aims at goodput optimization on the basis of SINR estimation, turns out to be less accurate in handover decision than PLB-VHO, still as it does not exploit location information. This is evident from the fact that DRI-VHO experiences both a higher number of handovers and results into lower values of goodput.

Table 3 provides the statistics for the CRBs of the four considered algorithms. As in Table 2, two columns for each algorithm are provided. Analogously, The first column reports the mean value of the CRBs parameter versus the waiting time parameter, while the second column reports the

relevant Dispersion Index versus the waiting time parameter. The CRBs mean values for PLB-VHO and DRI-VHO at 0 second waiting time are around 4.90 Mbit and 4.67 Mbit, respectively, while for LB-VHO and PB-VHO it reaches 4.08 Mbit and 3.71 Mbit, respectively. Again, these numbers confirm how PLB focuses on goodput maximization and is able to deliver the highest CRBs among the four approaches thanks to the combination of power samples and location information.

From Table 3 we notice that DRI-VHO shows a higher curve for CRBs, with respect to PB-VHO and LB-VHO (i.e., 26.32% and 17.32% higher, resp.) while lower values of CRBs are obtained with respect to PLB-VHO (i.e., 5.84% lower). In contrast, PLB-VHO presents the highest CRBs trend, that is, (i) 5.98%, (ii) 24.64%, and (iii) 34.17% higher than DRI, LB, and PB-VHO, respectively. This is justified by the fact that DRI-VHO does not exploit the location information for goodput estimation, then resulting in a higher number of handover attempts and a lower CRBs trend.

TABLE 3: Statistics for the CRBs for PB, LB, DRI-VHO, and PLB-VHO approaches.

Waiting time [s]	PB mean [Mbit]	PB disp. index	LB mean [Mbit]	LB disp. index	DRI mean [Mbit]	DRI disp. index	PLB mean [Mbit]	PLB disp. index
0	3.71	49.80%	4.08	59.58%	4.67	45.75%	4.90	38.49%
10	3.64	48.92%	3.94	59.46%	4.63	45.57%	4.84	37.39%
30	3.45	48.51%	3.71	60.53%	4.44	44.47%	4.71	38.06%
60	3.33	48.25%	3.44	58.90%	4.19	41.60%	4.55	35.40%
90	3.26	45.84%	3.53	57.28%	4.10	43.29%	4.36	44.80%
120	3.07	47.51%	3.34	57.29%	3.84	42.10%	4.13	44.37%

As a conclusion we can summarize the following results:

(i) PB-VHO makes the lowest number of vertical handovers and provides the lowest CRBs trend (i.e., in the range [3.07, 3.71] Mbit). It is suitable for *ping-pong effect* avoidance, but not for throughput maximization. It does not require high values of waiting time (i.e., <15 handovers executed at waiting time >10 s);

(ii) LB-VHO makes the highest number of vertical handovers and provides a slight increment of CRBs trend (i.e., in the range [3.34, 4.08] Mbit). It is suitable for low-QoS services, and the limitation of *ping-pong effect* occurs only for high values of waiting time (i.e., <15 handovers executed at waiting time >90 s);

(iii) DRI-VHO makes vertical handovers in the range [10, 79.2] and shows high values of CRBs in the range [3.84, 4.67] Mbit. It is suitable for high-QoS services; its best performance is obtained for high values of waiting time parameter (i.e., <15 handovers executed at waiting time >60 s);

(iv) PLB-VHO makes vertical handovers in the range [8, 53.1] and presents the highest CRBs trend (i.e., in the range [4.13, 4.90] Mbit). It is suitable for high-QoS services requiring throughput maximization and limits the *ping-pong effect*. Its best performance is for medium values of waiting time (i.e., <16 handovers executed at waiting time >30 s).

5. Conclusions

A novel hybrid vertical handover approach—PLB-VHO—for WLAN and UMTS networks has been presented. It is mainly oriented to ensure service continuity and avoid unnecessary/unwanted handover occurrences. The PLB-VHO develops an enhanced location-based approach to build and maintain a power attenuation map, which provides an updated description of the wireless cells in a visited environment. The attenuation map building and update phases are processed by the aid of cooperating mobile terminals within a local area network. RSS samples are then exchanged between mobile nodes, whenever a mobile terminal enters a visited network.

Performance results have been reported to compare PLB-VHO technique with a multiparameter vertical handover

scheme [11], a traditional power-based [8], and a location-based [18] vertical handover approach, respectively. We validated the effectiveness of PLB-VHO approach, in terms of (i) a maximization of Cumulative Received Bits and (ii) limitation of the number of vertical handovers. The use of combined location and power information to drive handover decisions brings about goodput enhancements while assuring controlled VHO frequency with respect to both simple single-parameter, as well as multiparameter approaches, considered in the paper.

Acknowledgments

The authors are grateful to the anonymous reviewers for their valuable comments and to the journal editor Professor Colonnese for her kind availability. This work was supported in part by RADIOLABS CONSORTIUM.

References

[1] S. Balasubramaniam and J. Indulska, "Vertical handover supporting pervasive computing in future wireless networks," *Computer Communications*, vol. 27, no. 8, pp. 708–719, 2004.

[2] G. P. Pollini, "Trends in handover design," *IEEE Communications Magazine*, vol. 34, no. 3, pp. 82–90, 1996.

[3] J. McNair and F. Zhu, "Vertical handoffs in fourth-generation multinetwork environments," *IEEE Wireless Communications*, vol. 11, no. 3, pp. 8–15, 2004.

[4] M. Stemm and R. H. Katz, "Vertical handoffs in wireless overlay networks," *Mobile Networks and Applications*, vol. 3, no. 4, pp. 335–350, 1998.

[5] M. Kassar, B. Kervella, and G. Pujolle, "An overview of vertical handover decision strategies in heterogeneous wireless networks," *Computer Communications*, vol. 31, no. 10, pp. 2607–2620, 2008.

[6] H. Cho, J. Park, W. Ko, K. Lim, and W. Kim, "A study on the MCHO method in hard handover and Soft handover between WLAN and CDMA," in *Proceedings of the International Conference on Consumer Electronics (ICCE '05)*, pp. 391–392, January 2005.

[7] K. Ayyappan and P. Dananjayan, "RSS measurement for vertical handoff in heterogeneous network," *Journal of Theoretical and Applied Information Technology*, vol. 4, no. 10, pp. 989–994, 2008.

[8] T. Inzerilli and A. M. Vegni, "A reactive vertical handover approach for WIFI-UMTS dual-mode terminals," in *Proceedings of the International Symposium on Consumer Electronics (ISCE '08)*, pp. 1–4, Vilamoura, Portugal, April 2008.

[9] S. Xie and M. Wu, "Adaptive variable threshold vertical hand-off algorithm," in *Proceedings of the IEEE International Conference Neural Networks and Signal Processing (ICNNSP '08)*, pp. 366–369, Zhenjiang, China, June 2008.

[10] K. Yang, I. Gondal, B. Qiu, and L. S. Dooley, "Combined SINR based vertical handoff algorithm for next generation heterogeneous wireless networks," in *Proceedings of the 50th Annual IEEE Global Telecommunications Conference (GLOBECOM '07)*, pp. 4483–4487, Washinton, DC, USA, November 2007.

[11] A. M. Vegni, G. Tamea, T. Inzerilli, and R. Cusani, "A combined vertical handover decision metric for QoS enhancement in next generation networks," in *Proceedings of the 5th IEEE International Conference on Wireless and Mobile Computing Networking and Communication (WiMob '09)*, pp. 233–238, Marrakech, Morocco, October 2009.

[12] A. M. Vegni, M. Carli, A. Neri, and G. Ragosa, "QoS-based vertical handover in heterogeneous networks," in *Proceedings of the 10th International Wireless Personal Multimedia Communications (WPMC 2007)*, pp. 1–4, Jaipur, India, December 2007.

[13] V. Jesus, S. Sargento, D. Corujo, N. Sénica, M. Almeida, and R. L. Aguiar, "Mobility with QoS support for multi-interface terminals: combined user and network approach," in *Proceedings of the 12th IEEE International Symposium on Computers and Communications (ISCC '07)*, pp. 325–332, July 2007.

[14] A. M. Vegni and F. Esposito, "A speed-based vertical handover algorithm for VANET," in *Proceedings of the of 7th International Workshop on Intelligent Transportation (WIT '10)*, Hamburg, Germany, March 2010.

[15] F. Esposito, A. M. Vegni, I. Matta, and A. Neri, "On modeling speed-based vertical handovers in vehicular networks "Dad, slow down, I am watching the movie"," in *Proceedings of the Annual IEEE Global Telecommunications Conference (GLOBECOM '10)*, Miami, Fla, USA, December 2010.

[16] S. S. Wang, M. Green, and M. Malkawi, "Adaptive handover method using mobile location information," in *Proceedings of the IEEE Emerging Technology Symposium on Broadband Communications for the Internet Era Symposium*, pp. 97–101, Richardson, Tex, USA, September 2001.

[17] D. B. Lin, R. T. Juang, H. P. Lin, and C. Y. Ke, "Mobile location estimation based on differences of signal attenuations for GSM systems," in *Proceedings of the IEEE International Antennas and Propagation Symposium*, vol. 1, pp. 77–80, June 2003.

[18] T. Inzerilli, A. M. Vegni, A. Neri, and R. Cusani, "A location-based vertical handover algorithm for limitation of the ping-pong effect," in *Proceedings of the 4th IEEE International Conference on Wireless and Mobile Computing, Networking and Communication (WiMob '08)*, pp. 385–389, Avignon, France, October 2008.

[19] A. M. Vegni and F. Esposito, "Location aware mobility assisted services for heterogeneous wireless technologies," in *Proceedings of the IEEE MTT-S International Microwave Workshop Series on Wireless Sensing, Local Positioning and RFID (IMWS '09)*, Cavtat, Croatia, September 2009.

[20] W. I. Kim, B. J. Lee, J. S. Song, Y. S. Shin, and Y. J. Kim, "Ping-pong avoidance algorithm for vertical handover in wireless overlay networks," in *Proceedings of the 66th IEEE Vehicular Technology Conference (VTC '07)*, vol. 3, pp. 1509–1512, September-October 2007.

[21] X. Yan, Y. A. Şekercioğlu, and N. Mani, "A method for minimizing unnecessary handovers in heterogeneous wireless networks," in *Proceedings of the 9th IEEE International Symposium on Wireless, Mobile and Multimedia Networks (WoWMoM '08)*, pp. 1–5, June 2008.

[22] N. Zhang and J. M. Holtzman, "Analysis of handoff algorithms using both absolute and relative measurements," *IEEE Transactions on Vehicular Technology*, vol. 45, no. 1, pp. 174–179, 1996.

[23] Y. S. Chen, C. H. Cheng, C. S. Hsu, and G. M. Chiu, "Network mobility protocol for vehicular ad hoc networks," in *Proceedings of the IEEE Wireless Communications and Networking Conference (WCNC '09)*, Budapest, Hungary, April 2009.

[24] M. R. Kibria, A. Jamalipour, and V. Mirchandani, "A location aware three-step vertical handoff scheme for 4G/B3G networks," in *Proceedings of the IEEE Global Telecommunications Conference (GLOBECOM '05)*, vol. 5, pp. 2752–2756, St. Louis, Mo, USA, November-December 2005.

[25] X. Yan, Y. A. Şekercioğlu, and S. Narayanan, "A survey of vertical handover decision algorithms in Fourth Generation heterogeneous wireless networks," *Computer Networks*, vol. 54, no. 11, pp. 1848–1863, 2010.

[26] A. Hasswa, N. Nasser, and H. Hassanein, "Generic vertical handoff decision function for heterogeneous wireless networks," in *Proceedings of the 2nd International Conference on Wirelessand Optical Communications Networks (WOCN '05)*, pp. 239–243, March 2005.

[27] "IEEE 802.21 Media Independent Handover Services—Media Independent Handover," Draft Text for Media Independent Handover Specification.

[28] J. Laiho, A. Wacker, and T. Novosad, *Radio Network Planning and Optimisation for UMTS*, chapter 3, Wiley, New York, NY, USA, 2nd edition, 2005.

[29] "IEEE Standard for Information technology Telecommunications and information exchange between systems. Local and metropolitan area networks. Specific requirements," Part 11: Wireless LAN Medium Access Control (MAC) and Physical Layer (PHY) Specifications.

[30] J. Laiho, A. Wacker, and T. Novosad, *Radio Network Planning and Optimisation for UMTS*, chapter 6, Wiley, New York, NY, USA, 2nd edition, 2005.

[31] J. Laiho, A. Wacker, and T. Novosad, *Radio Network Planning and Optimisation for UMTS*, chapter 3, Wiley, New York, NY, USA, 2nd edition, 2005.

[32] Y. Okumura et al., "Field strength and its variability in VHF and UHF land-mobile service," *Review of the Electrical Communication Laboratory*, vol. 16, no. 9-10, pp. 825–873, 1968.

16

A Software-Defined Radio System for Intravehicular Wireless Sensor Networks

Xiangming Kong, Deying Zhang, and Mohin Ahmed

Information & System Sciences Lab, HRL Laboratories, LLC, Malibu, CA 90265-4797, USA

Correspondence should be addressed to Xiangming Kong, ckong@hrl.com

Academic Editor: Ronan Farrell

An intra-vehicular wireless sensor network is designed and implemented on a software-defined radio system. IUWB signal is chosen to carry the data packets. The MAC layer of the system follows the specification of the IEEE802.15.4 standard. The transceiver design, especially the receiver design, is detailed in the paper. The system design is validated through lab test setup.

1. Introduction

Modern vehicles are equipped with a multitude of sensors to collect data that are essential for proper operation of the vehicle. These sensor data include vital information such as exhaust quality and lateral velocity which affect driving safety and environment friendliness, as well as information for improving the comfort and convenience of passengers. As a trend, more and more sensors will be added in the future to make automobiles "smarter". Currently, these sensors are connected to the Electronic Control Unit (ECU) via cables. By 2002, the length of these cables has already added up to over 1000 meters and weighed more than 50 kg, and the cable length still increases rapidly [1]. These cables not only adversely affect the cost and fuel economy, but also increase the complexity of the vehicle design. Another major drawback brought by the cables is the scalability issue. Whenever a new sensor is added to a car, a cable has to be added and routed properly inside the car body. The cable may interfere with other components. In this case, much more redesign work is necessary than simply adding the sensor alone. One way to reduce the undesirable effect caused by the bundle of wires is to connect sensors with the ECU wirelessly. Hence, ElBatt et al. proposed a wireless sensor network for intra-vehicular sensor data transmission [2].

Since some sensor data are essential for the safety of the vehicle, it is important for the intra-vehicular wireless sensor network (IV-WSN) to provide the same level of reliability and transmission latency as offered in the current wired system. This requirement differentiates the IV-WSN from the existing sensor networks and imposes a big challenge in the design of the WSN, especially at the physical layer, which determines the data integrity and data rate. Another factor to be emphasized in the WSN design is the power consumption. Removing wires means removing not only the data cables but also power supply cables. The sensors have to rely on other power sources. Vibration energy can be one viable source [3]. Energy harvesting for wireless sensors is by itself a hot research topic and will not be discussed further here. We only note that since the existing energy harvesting techniques cannot provide a large amount of power to the sensors, there is a strict limit on the power budget for transceivers.

In addition to the two major requirements mentioned above, many other issues are needed to be addressed in the design, including, but not limited to, cost, sensor heterogeneity, wireless channel variation, modulation waveform, and networking. Without prior experience, a flexible platform such as a software defined radio (SDR) system is proper in the early design phase to carry out different experiments.

The importance of removing the cables in vehicles has begun to attract attention only recently. Although some research has been done to study the viability of an IV-WSN [4, 5], to our knowledge, our system is the first SDR for IV-WSN. It will be very useful for future development of IV-WSN. Moreover, our SDR can handle very broadband signals and will be found useful in many applications.

FIGURE 1: The transceiver board.

2. System Overview

The IV-WSN has to coexist with narrowband communication devices such as cell phones and should not add much interference to the narrowband system nor should it be susceptible to the interference from the narrowband systems. Moreover, some sensors have to send data at a rate that can only be serviced by relatively large bandwidth. Several short range wireless technologies are compared as the first design step, including RFID, Bluetooth, Zigbee, and UWB. The data rate and transmission range of RFID technology are both small and not suitable for our application. A Bluetooth network supports up to seven slave devices. This network size is too small to handle many sensors. Furthermore, Bluetooth and Zigbee both use the crowded ISM band of 2.4 GHz and are vulnerable to interference from signals coexisting in the same band, reducing the system reliability. To reduce interference, a low-power wideband technique is much more preferable. One choice is the ultrawideband (UWB) technology.

Two important types of UWB techniques exist: impulse UWB (IUWB) and OFDM UWB. IUWB signals are easily generated with simple hardware and widely used in WSN. Another valuable feature of the IUWB technology is its high time resolution. Like many indoor environments, the intravehicular communication channel is rich in multipaths [6]. An IUWB signal can easily differentiate the line-of-sight path and the reflection paths. This feature greatly simplifies the receiver design and reduces hardware cost. Since one receiver is needed for each sensor or at least each group of sensors that are positioned together, a low-cost receiver is highly desirable for the IV-WSN. Based on the above consideration, IUWB is our first choice as the media to carry information.

A software defined system is called so because many fixed hardware components in it are replaced either by software or reconfigurable firmware running on computing devices. Unlike the analog devices that handle analog signals directly, computing devices can only process digital signals. Hence, the analog signal received by an antenna has to be digitized before it can be further processed. Due to the limitation imposed by current analog-to-digital converters (ADCs), most existing SDRs only replace the baseband or at most intermediate-frequency (IF) hardware components

and leave the radio frequency (RF) front end components unchanged. This configuration limits the system in two ways. First, we have to restrict ourselves to baseband experiments. Any change made in the RF components has to be done in the traditional way, that is, designing a brand-new RF board. Secondly, and more importantly, we cannot try out the IUWB signal most suitable for our system through those SDRs. Therefore, an SDR that digitizes the signal in the RF band is necessary for our system. To address this requirement, we adopt the testbed from Virginia Polytechnic Institute and State University in our system [7, 8].

For a simple WSN, a network stack made of a physical (PHY) layer and a media access control (MAC) layer is enough. There has been a lot of effort devoted to the MAC layer protocol design [9, 10]. IEEE802.15.4 standard also specifies the control and implementation of the low-rate Wireless Personal Area Network, which can also be applied to a WSN. To simplify the system, we follow the IEEE802.15.4 specification for MAC layer design. However, to accommodate the high data rate required by some sensors in our application, we replace the OQPSK modulation specified in the standard by IUWB in the PHY layer. Hence, the system is not compatible with IEEE802.15.4 devices.

3. System Architecture

3.1. Transceiver System. The major components of the transceiver include a simple RF front end, eight ADCs that can take up to 10^9 samples per second each, a Field-Programmable Gate Array (FPGA) embedded with a CPU, and some peripherals. The transceiver board is shown in Figure 1. Its corresponding functional block diagram is given in Figure 2.

The CPU is responsible for data handling, MAC layer processing, and hardware control. To keep the system flexible, the RF front end only consists of the most basic elements: a transmitter/receiver switch, filters, and amplifiers. At the transmitter side, a transmission controller reads in the data packetized by the MAC layer and generates a positive/negative pulse for each 1/0 bit accordingly through a diode. The pulses are then passed to the RF front end and sent out through an antenna. At the receiver side, the signal from the RF front end is first digitized by eight MAX104 ADCs. Each ADC offers an input bandwidth of 2.2 GHz with a maximum sampling rate of 1 GHz. Interleaving sampling techniques as in [7, 8] are applied to combine the samples from different ADCs. The total maximum sampling rate is thus 8 GHz. The samples from the ADC are fed into the FPGA. The transmission controller and the remaining receiver blocks are all designed using VHDL in RTL level and implemented in Xilinx FPGA (xc2vp70ff1704-7).

3.2. Signal Structure. Before jumping to the design detail, it is useful to first explain the signal structure because some design issue is closely related to the signal structure.

The data from sensors are first wrapped into a packet with the following structure see Table 1.

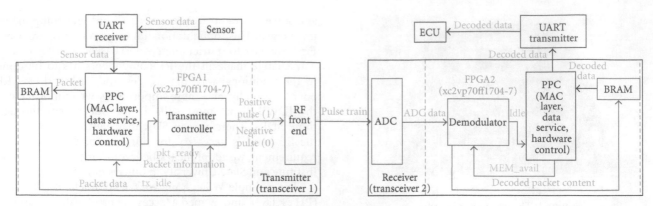

FIGURE 2: Transceiver block diagram.

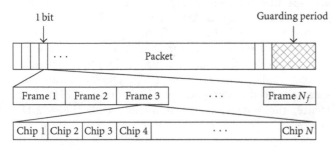

FIGURE 3: Signal structure.

TABLE 1

Bits: 32	8	8	Variable
Preamble	SFD	Frame Len	Payload

The preamble bits are all "1"s and are known at the receiver. The preamble is used as a pilot to learn the wireless channel. The Start of Frame Delimiter (SFD) is a byte of fixed value. The frame length byte records the length of the payload in bytes. The payload comes from the MAC layer which contains the sensor data and the MAC header.

At the signal level, each bit is made of N_b frames. Each frame is further divided into N_f time slots called chips. The duration of a chip equals the length of a transmitted pulse. Within each frame, only one chip contains a pulse. Other chips are empty. The index of the chip containing the pulse varies from one frame to the next and follows the pattern of a time-hopping (TH) sequence of length N_{th}. N_f can be equal to or greater than N_{th}. The large N_f is useful for removing any intersymbol interference (ISI). The signal structure is given in Figure 3. According to this structure, the transmitted signal can be written as

$$s(t) = \sum_i b_{\lfloor i/N_b \rfloor} p\left(t - iT_f - c_{\lfloor i/N_f \rfloor} T_c\right), \qquad (1)$$

where b_n is the bit sequence, $p(t)$ is the transmitted waveform, T_f is the frame duration, T_c is the chip duration, and c_n is the time-hopping sequence.

3.3. Receiver Design.
Each multipath attenuates and delays the transmitted signal differently. Assuming there are L paths, the received signal can be represented as

$$r(t) = \sum_{l=1}^{L} a_l s(t - \tau_l), \qquad (2)$$

where a_l and τ_l represents the path amplitude and delay, respectively.

We use a coherent receiver in our system. A coherent receiver demodulates the signal by correlating the received signal with a local template and determining the bit value based on the correlation result. Letting $g(t)$ be the local template, the correlation result is

$$R(\tau) = \int_0^{T_f} r(t)g(t, \tau)dt. \qquad (3)$$

As explained in the next two sections, different templates are used in the timing acquisition phase and the demodulation phase.

The digitized signal from the ADCs passes through five-phase processing: energy detection, timing acquisition, bit demodulation, packet synchronization, and packet demodulation. When the receiver powers up, after initialization, it enters an idle state. Once the CPU informs it that the upper layer is ready, it begins to detect energy on the channel by comparing the square of the received signal with a threshold value. This procedure is realized through a correlator where the received signal itself is used as the local template. If energy is detected on the channel, the receiver enters timing acquisition phase. The timing acquisition process determines the channel delay. If correct delay is acquired, future absolute correlation value should be larger than a given threshold. Only if this condition is met can the receiver move on to the next phase. Otherwise, it returns to the energy detection phase. In the next phase, the receiver first generates the local template for demodulation purpose. Then, it demodulates each bit and begins to search for the SFD pattern from the demodulated bits. When the SFD field is found, it means that the packet level synchronization is reached. The next byte after the SFD should be the payload length. This value dictates the number of bytes the receiver should demodulate before it notifies the upper layer of the incoming packet and returns to idle state, waiting for a new signal from the upper layer. The whole process is illustrated in Figure 4.

When the demodulator receives a command from the CPU to begin receiving packets and enters the energy detection state, there may be a node already sending on the channel. Even if the receiver is not receiving the preambles, it may still pass the timing acquisition phase and begin to demodulate bits. However, since there is no byte in the payload that has the same pattern as SFD (this is ensured by the software), the demodulator never reaches packet synchronization and may get stuck. To avoid this scenario, a guarding period is added at the end of a packet. Since a packet sent from one node will be received by all nodes, every node knows when the guarding period is. During this period, no sender will transmit a packet. While the demodulator searches for the SFD, it also monitors the absolute correlation value. If this value drops below a threshold, it means that the end of a packet has been reached. The demodulator automatically stops SFD search and jumps back to the energy detection phase. (In fact, even if a node fails to detect the previous packet and transmits during the guarding period, the channel it goes through will be different from the previous sender. Since the demodulation template is one frame of the signal from the previous sender, with high probability, this template would not have high correlation with the current received signal and the correlation value test would fail. The receiver then goes back to the energy detection phase).

3.4. Timing Acquisition. The narrowness of a pulse and the low duty cycle of the pulse period of an IUWB signal impose a stringent requirement on the time accuracy at the receiver side. The fine timing resolution in IUWB systems results in a large search space, making timing acquisition a very challenging problem. Long spreading sequences employed in typical IUWB systems further complicate the acquisition problem. Acquisition can be achieved by a noncoherent energy detection scheme [11]. Since this scheme is more sensitive to noise, we focused only on coherent receivers. In general, the search space in the acquisition process is made up of two subspaces: the one for the delay of the pulse within a chip and the one for the phase of the spreading sequence. The existing paper addresses only one aspect of the problem. Either the spreading code is assumed to be absent [12], or the channel delay is assumed to be an integer number of pulse width [13]. There are two typical searching schemes: serial search and parallel search. Serial search scheme requires very simple hardware. However, its searching time is long. Multiple searches can be done in parallel to reduce the search time, but the hardware complexity increases a lot. Many techniques have been proposed to speed up the searching process without increasing hardware cost. However, they either require large computational complexity [14] or are not suitable for the environment rich in multipaths [15, 16]. In our system, a new acquisition scheme is developed to meet our needs [16].

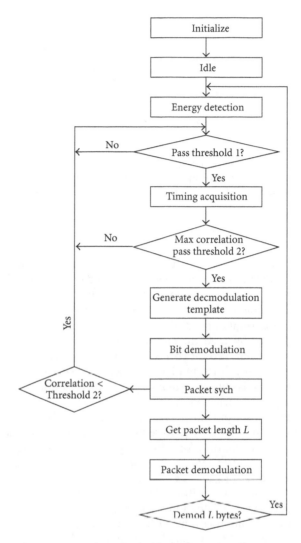

FIGURE 4: Receiver physical layer processing diagram.

The template used at the timing acquisition phase is the transmitted signal received in the free space. This template incorporates the characteristics of both transmitter antennas and receiver antennas without being affected by multipaths. Such a template can resolve the time delay of the channel very well. Since this template is fixed, it is hardcoded in the receiver.

In our new scheme, the timing acquisition process is carried out in two steps: delay search and code search. Delay search determines the delay at the chip level. The received signal is correlated with the local template and sampled at the end of each chip. After every $N_d = N_f + \max_{i,j} |c_i - c_j|$ sample has been obtained, the template is delayed by $\Delta\tau$, where $\Delta\tau$ is the predefined search resolution and $|c_i - c_j|$ represents the number of chips between two pulses in the transmitted signal. The delay search stops when the maximum value of the N_d samples is above a given threshold Th_1. This happens when the received signal and the template are aligned on the chip boundary.

The code search follows the delay search and further locates the phase of the TH sequence. When the code search

tc	1	2	3	4	5	6	7	8	9	10	11	12	13	14	15	16	17	18	19	20	21	22	23	24
Phase 1	1	2	3	4			1	2	3	4			1	2	3	4			1	2	3	4		
Phase 2		1	2	3	4			1	2	3	4			1	2	3	4			1	2	3	4	
Phase 9			1	2	3	4			1	2	3	4			1	2	3	4			1	2	3	4
Phase 14		1	2	3	4			1	2	3	4			1	2	3	4			1	2	3	4	
Phase 22	4			1	2	3	4			1	2	3	4			1	2	3	4			1	2	3

FIGURE 5: Illustration of the code search process. Assume that the TH sequence is $\{4,1,3,2\}$, $N_{th} = 4$, and $N_f = 6$. Let the code search start from chip 1. The chips in yellow correspond to when there is a received pulse at the receiver. The shaded chips are the chips when there should be a pulse for the corresponding phase. The red chips represent the bit starting positions.

starts, the chip index is set to 1. At the end of each chip, the correlation between the received signal and the local template is sampled and compared with the threshold Th_1. When the sample value is above Th_1, a pulse is detected in that chip. The pulse count of the phase which allows a pulse in the chip is increased by 1. At the end of a bit, the phase having the maximum pulse count corresponds to the correct phase. In this way, many different phases are searched simultaneously. This process is illustrated in Figure 5. In this example, assume that a pulse is detected in chip 4. Phase 1 expects a pulse in this chip four, but not phase 2. Hence, the pulse count of phase 1 is increased by 1. To reduce the number of counters, pulse counts are only kept for the possible phases after the first pulse is detected. In the above example, the possible phases are 1, 9, 14, and 22.

The entire acquisition algorithm can be implemented through one correlator and N_{th} counters. However it finishes the acquisition process in N_f frames. This search time is the same as the traditional parallel search scheme, which requires $N_{th}N_f$ correlators in total. More detail about the acquisition algorithm can be found in [16].

3.5. Demodulation. While the template of one transmitted pulse is good for the timing acquisition purpose, it does not capture all the received energy and can result in poor signal-to-noise ratio (SNR). Therefore, we use the received signal within a frame period captured after timing acquisition phase as the template in the demodulation phase. As long as the wireless channel is stationary during a packet period, this template can combine the energy from multipaths coherently and improve the SNR. Such a receiver is suboptimal compared to the RAKE receiver. However, its hardware complexity is much lower too. Since the received signal is noisy, directly using the received signal as the template increases noise and degrades the receiver performance. To reduce the noise in the template, the received pulses from multiple frames are averaged and used as the template. When a frame is long compared to the chip duration, even in rich-multipath environment, the useful signal only occupies a small portion of a frame period. In this case, only the portion of the frame that contains the useful signal is used to generate the template.

3.6. Software Infrastructure. Since this is a data transfer system, the application layer is very simple. The major task at this layer is data handling, including collecting data from sensors and passing data to the ECU.

At the physical layer, the software is also relatively simple. In addition to driving transmitter and receiver hardware and handling the physical layer header in the packet, it also performs bit staffing/removal operation to ensure that no byte in the payload has the same pattern as the SFD.

The MAC layer follows the MAC sublayer specification in the IEEE802.15.4 standard. A superframe is composed of a mixture of contention access period (CAP) and collision free period (CFP). For sensors whose data are very delay-sensitive, one or more guaranteed time slots (GTS) are allocated to it. Other sensors will compete for slots in the CAP.

To reduce system complexity and cost, the software system is designed to be event driven without an operating system. When an event happens, such as when a packet is to be received or to be sent out, a task is created and added to the task queues. Tasks can have high, medium, or low priority. Tasks at one priority level are all finished before any task at the next lower priority level can be processed.

A main timer controls the handling of the tasks. It times out every one unit of the back-off period. Since the backoff period is aligned with the boundary of a slot, using this time period ensures that no slot will be missed. When the timer times out, tasks are processed following the order determined by their priority levels and the time when it is added to the queue. Once all the tasks in the queue are processed, the processor gets into the idle state again until the next timeout happens.

The entire software is partitioned into modules. There are four major modules: a timing module, a radio management module, a service module, and a device driver module. Depending on the complexity of each module, there may be one or more state machines maintained within the module. The timing module is the heart of the MAC sublayer. It fulfils the basic functionality of an operating system and controls the flow of the entire sublayer. The radio management module is responsible for communication handling and provides the interface between the service module and the physical layer. The service module includes two major

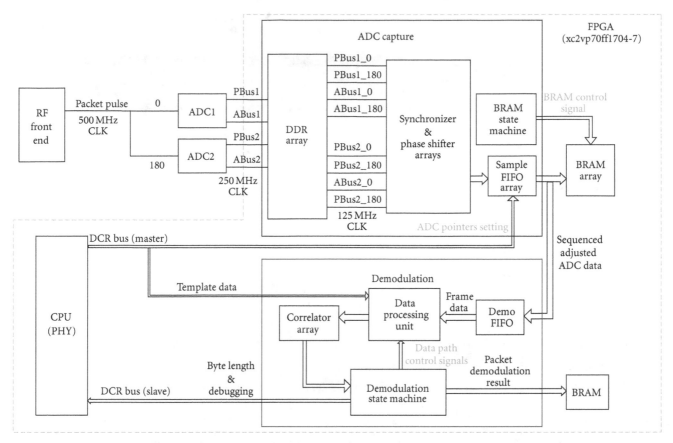

FIGURE 6: Receiver hardware blocks.

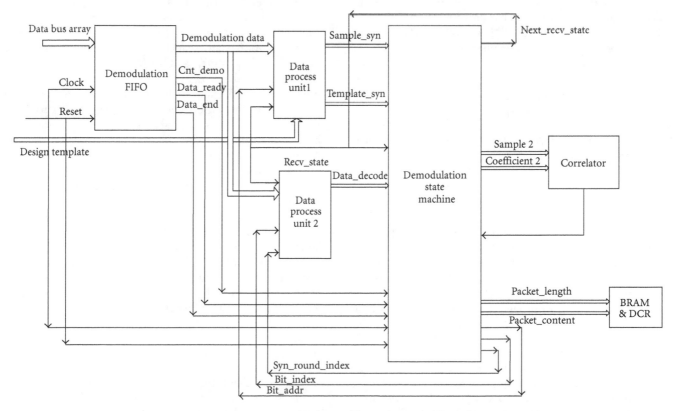

FIGURE 7: Demodulation unit internal structure.

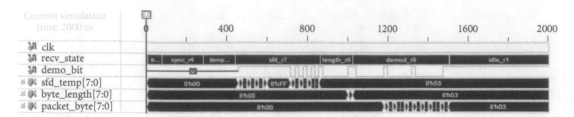

FIGURE 8: Timing sequence of signals in the receiver.

Packet Decoding Result

```
BIT_SYNC: Ox 8
bit_max_corr: OxECOO
syn_round_index: Ox 4
bit_index: Ox 2

Decoding Template:
Template_decode[0]: Ox 1; Template_decode[1]: Ox 1; Template_decode[2]: Ox 1; Template_decode[3]: Ox 1
Template_decode[4]: Ox 2; Template_decode[5]: Ox2B; Template_decode[6]: Ox2B; Template_decode[7]: Ox2F
Template_decode[8]: Ox2F; Template_decode[9]: Ox2F; Template_decode[10]: Ox2E; Template_decode[11]: Ox2E
Template_decode[12]: Ox2E; Template_decode[13]: Ox2E; Template_decode[14]: Ox2C; Template_decode[15]: Ox 3

Byte_length: Ox B

Demodulation Result in BRAM5 --
i = 00000000 D[02010000]=08070605   005   006   007   008   05   06   07   08
i = 00000001 D[02010004]=04030201   001   002   003   004   01   02   03   04
i = 00000002 D[02010008]=00000000   000   000   000   000   00   00   00   00
i = 00000003 D[0201000c]=000b0a09   009   010   011   000   09   0a   0b   00
```

FIGURE 9: Packet data decoding result printed from HyperTerminal.

components: (1) the MAC common part sublayer (MCPS) responsible for the data handling of the upper layer, (2) the MAC layer management entity (MLME) that manages other services generally more internal to the MAC layer. The device driver module includes all the low-level interfaces to the physical devices and the I/O peripherals.

4. Receiver Hardware

The transmitter in an IUWB system is very simple. However, this often means more weight would be lifted by the receiver whose design is detailed next.

Since the design of eight-ADC channels is very similar to that of two-ADC channels, the design and implementation details of a two-ADC system are presented in this section. As shown in Figure 6, The ADC capture unit consists of a DDR array, a synchronizer, and phase shifter arrays, a sample FIFO array, and a BRAM state machine. The DDR array in the FPGA reduces the data rate in the ADCs by a factor of 2 to match that of the internal bus in the FPGA. The synchronizer and phase shifter arrays make sure that each internal bus in the FPGA is synchronized with the global clock and there is a fixed phase shift between two buses. The data on each internal FPGA bus will be combined sequentially to form the final data stream. These data are also stored into the BRAM array for debugging purpose. At power up, the order of the output data sequences from the ADCs does not necessarily follow the sequential order. For example, ADC2 may sample first while ADC1 may take the second sample. Through a testing signal, the CPU determines the order of the ADC

output data sequence and assigns a pointer to data sequences for them to be combined correctly for future use.

The internal structure of the demodulation unit is given in Figure 7. The demodulation unit consists of a demodulation FIFO, a data processing unit, correlators, and a demodulation state machine. The demodulation FIFO serves as a data buffer and stores the samples from the PLB bus as well as distributes the stored data to data processing units. Data unit1 takes in the received data (from the demodulation FIFO) and the template data (from the memory) and adjusts the data format for the correlation procedure. Data unit2 handles the template reconstruction, SFD searching, and packet demodulation. The demodulation state machine generates the control signal for data processing and computation, as well as controlling the receiver to go through states based on the state machine diagram in Figure 4. The correlator is made of adder trees. It carries out the correlation computation for timing acquisition and bit demodulation.

To help readers understand the receiver state transition, the timing sequence of some signals inside the receiver is shown in Figure 8. The content of the packet is "FFFFFFFF5503010203", where "FFFFFFFF" is the preamble, "55" is the SFD, "03" is the byte length, and "010203" is the payload. All numbers are given in hexadecimal format. The "recv_state" signal tells the receiver state. Soon after the receiver finishes the template generation, valid result begins to appear on "demo_bit" (demodulation bit) and SFD search begins. Once the SFD byte shows up in the "demo_bit", the receiver finds it and the state transfers to the packet length-reading state. The packet length value is one byte long and is correctly read as "03" in the "byte_length" signal. The packet demodulation phase then begins. After 3 bytes are demodulated, as shown in the "packet_byte" signal, the receiver transitions into the idle state again.

In addition to validating the system through simulators, we also tested the entire system in the lab setup. The first test only checks the physical layer. One transmitter sends out the data packet containing "FFFFFFFF550B 01020304050607008090A0B". The demodulated packet from a receiver is printed out on a computer screen, as shown in Figure 9. (The data bus in the receiver is eight bytes wide, and the data bus in the memory is only four bytes wide. When the data is stored in the memory, the first four bytes and the second four bytes are stored in reverse order. MAC layer handles this problem. Since the MAC layer is not involved in this test, the data in the screen print is shown in reverse order). No MAC layer processing is involved in this test.

The second test checks both the PHY layer and the MAC layer. A hyperterminal simulates a sensor and generates data to be sent out. The data are correctly received at a receiver and printed out.

Since we still have some problem in the antenna design, the tests are carried out through two units connected by a cable. Hence, rich-multipath environments, low-SNR scenarios, and network handling functions in the MAC layer cannot be tested.

5. Conclusion

The design of an intra-vehicular wireless sensor network is presented in this paper. Due to the high reliability required by the automobile sensors and the lack of prior experience, we need a flexible system so that parameters, such as transmission waveforms, and power budgets, can be optimized through tests in real environments. Hence, an SDR system is chosen to implement the design. Our system also proves the concept that a software radio can be realized at the RF band without using any mixers. This proof is useful in the expansion of the application areas of SDR systems and hopefully can also promote the development of SDR systems.

Acknowledgments

This paper is supported by the General Motor's research fund. The authors wish to thank Cem Saraydar and Tim Talty for their support of the project, Daniel Zehnder for sharing his expertise in VHDL design, Hooman Shirani-Mehr for his simulation effort, and David Shu and Simon Han for many useful discussions. The authors would also like to thank the reviewers for their insightful comments.

References

[1] G. Leen and D. Heffernan, "Vehicles without wires," *Computing and Control Engineering Journal*, vol. 12, no. 5, pp. 205–211, 2001.

[2] T. Elbatt, C. Saraydar, M. Ames, and T. Talty, "Potential for intra-vehicle wireless automotive sensor networks," in *Proceedings of IEEE Sarnoff Symposium*, Princeton, NJ, USA, March 2006.

[3] S. Roundy, P. K. Wright, and J. Rabaey, "A study of low level vibrations as a power source for wireless sensor nodes," *Computer Communications*, vol. 26, no. 11, pp. 1131–1144, 2003.

[4] O. K. Tonguz, H.-M. Tsai, T. Talty, A. Macdonald, and C. Saraydar, "RFID technology for intra-car communications: a new paradigm," in *Proceeding of IEEE Vehicular Technology Conference (VTC '06)*, pp. 3008–3013, Montreal, Canada, September 2006.

[5] H.-M. Tsai, C. Saraydar, T. Talty, M. Ames, A. Macdonald, and O. K. Tonguz, "ZigBee-based intra-car wireless sensor network," in *Proceedings of IEEE International Conference on Communications (ICC '07)*, pp. 3965–3971, Glasgow, UK, June 2007.

[6] W. Niu, J. Li, and T. Talty, "Ultra-wideband channel modeling for intravehicle environment," *Eurasip Journal on Wireless Communications and Networking*, vol. 2009, Article ID 806209, 12 pages, 2009.

[7] C. Anderson, *A software defined ultra wideband transceiver testbed for communications, ranging, and imaging*, Ph.D. thesis, 2006.

[8] T. Van Dam and K. Langendoen, "An adaptive energy-efficient MAC protocol for wireless sensor networks," in *Proceedings of the 1st International Conference on Embedded Networked Sensor Systems (SenSys'03)*, pp. 171–180, 2003.

[9] G. Lu, B. Krishnamachari, and C. S. Raghavendra, "An adaptive energy-efficient and low-latency MAC for data gathering in wireless sensor networks," in *Proceedings of the 18th International Parallel and Distributed Processing Symposium (IPDPS '04)*, p. 224, 2004.

[10] B. Miscopein and J. Schwoerer, "Low complexity synchronization algorithm for non-coherent UWB-IR receivers," in *Proceedings of the 65th IEEE Vehicular Technology Conference (VTC '07)*, pp. 2344–2348, April 2007.

[11] E. A. Homier and R. A. Scholtz, "Rapid acquisition of ultra-wideband signals in the dense multipath channel," in *Proceedings of IEEE Conference on Ultra Wideband Systems and Technologies*, pp. 105–109, May 2002.

[12] S. R. Aedudodla, S. Vijayakumaran, and T. F. Wong, "Timing acquisition in ultra-wideband communication systems," *IEEE Transactions on Vehicular Technology*, vol. 54, no. 5, pp. 1570–1583, 2005.

[13] H. Zhang, S. Wei, D. L. Goeckel, and M. Z. Win, "Rapid acquisition of ultra-wideband radio signals," in *Proceedings of the 36th Asilomar Conference on Signals Systems and Computers*, pp. 712–716, November 2002.

[14] S. Gezici, E. Fishier, H. Kobayashi, H. V. Poor, and A. F. Molisch, "A rapid acquisition technique for impulse radio," in *Proceedings of IEEE Pacific RIM Conference on Communications, Computers, and Signal Processing*, vol. 2, pp. 627–630, 2003.

[15] L. Reggiani and G. M. Maggio, "A reduced-complexity acquisition algorithm for UWB impulse radio," in *Proceedings of IEEE Conference on Ultra Wideband Systems and Technologies*, pp. 131–135, November 2003.

[16] X. Kong and M. Ahmed, "A rapid acquisition method for impulse ultra-wideband signals," in *Proceedings of the 12th IEEE International Conference on Communication Technology (ICCT '10)*, Nanjing, China, November 2010.

Permissions

The contributors of this book come from diverse backgrounds, making this book a truly international effort. This book will bring forth new frontiers with its revolutionizing research information and detailed analysis of the nascent developments around the world.

We would like to thank all the contributing authors for lending their expertise to make the book truly unique. They have played a crucial role in the development of this book. Without their invaluable contributions this book wouldn't have been possible. They have made vital efforts to compile up to date information on the varied aspects of this subject to make this book a valuable addition to the collection of many professionals and students.

This book was conceptualized with the vision of imparting up-to-date information and advanced data in this field. To ensure the same, a matchless editorial board was set up. Every individual on the board went through rigorous rounds of assessment to prove their worth. After which they invested a large part of their time researching and compiling the most relevant data for our readers. Conferences and sessions were held from time to time between the editorial board and the contributing authors to present the data in the most comprehensible form. The editorial team has worked tirelessly to provide valuable and valid information to help people across the globe.

Every chapter published in this book has been scrutinized by our experts. Their significance has been extensively debated. The topics covered herein carry significant findings which will fuel the growth of the discipline. They may even be implemented as practical applications or may be referred to as a beginning point for another development. Chapters in this book were first published by Hindawi Publishing Corporation; hereby published with permission under the Creative Commons Attribution License or equivalent.

The editorial board has been involved in producing this book since its inception. They have spent rigorous hours researching and exploring the diverse topics which have resulted in the successful publishing of this book. They have passed on their knowledge of decades through this book. To expedite this challenging task, the publisher supported the team at every step. A small team of assistant editors was also appointed to further simplify the editing procedure and attain best results for the readers.

Our editorial team has been hand-picked from every corner of the world. Their multi-ethnicity adds dynamic inputs to the discussions which result in innovative outcomes. These outcomes are then further discussed with the researchers and contributors who give their valuable feedback and opinion regarding the same. The feedback is then collaborated with the researches and they are edited in a comprehensive manner to aid the understanding of the subject.

Apart from the editorial board, the designing team has also invested a significant amount of their time in understanding the subject and creating the most relevant covers. They scrutinized every image to scout for the most suitable representation of the subject and create an appropriate cover for the book.

The publishing team has been involved in this book since its early stages. They were actively engaged in every process, be it collecting the data, connecting with the contributors or procuring relevant information. The team has been an ardent support to the editorial, designing and production team. Their endless efforts to recruit the best for this project, has resulted in the accomplishment of this book. They are a veteran in the field of academics and their pool of knowledge is as vast as their experience in printing. Their expertise and guidance has proved useful at every step. Their uncompromising quality standards have made this book an exceptional effort. Their encouragement from time to time has been an inspiration for everyone.

The publisher and the editorial board hope that this book will prove to be a valuable piece of knowledge for researchers, students, practitioners and scholars across the globe.

List of Contributors

Jiaqi Zhang, Molin Jia, Noriyoshi Yamauchi and Takaaki Baba
Graduate School of Information, Production and Systems, Waseda University, 2-7 Hibikino, Wakamatu-ku, Kitakyushu-shi, Fukuoka 808-0135, Japan

Zhengyi Li, Lin Liu and Chi Zhou
Department of Electrical and Computer Engineering, Illinois Institute of Technology, Chicago, IL 60626, USA

T. H. Szymanski
Department of Electrical and Computer Engineering, McMaster University, Hamilton, ON, Canada L8S 4K1
Bell Canada Chair in Data Communications, McMaster University, Hamilton, ON, Canada L8S 4K1

D. Gilbert
Department of Electrical and Computer Engineering, McMaster University, Hamilton, ON, Canada L8S 4K1

Maziar Nekovee
BT Innovate and Design, Polaris 134, Adastral Park, Martlesham, Suffolk IP5 3RE, UK
Centre for Computational Science, University College London, 20 Gordon Street, London WC1H 0AJ, UK

Dongyu Qiu
Department of Electrical and Computer Engineering, Concordia University, Montreal, QC, Canada H3G 1M8

S. B. Musabekov
ZTE Investment LLC, Oybek Street 14, Tashkent 100015, Uzbekistan
Ahmadabad Earth Station, Space Applications Centre (SAC), Headquarters, 4 Kalidas Road, Dehradun, 248001, India

P. K. Srinivasan and A. S. Durai
Indian Space Research Organization (ISRO), Ahmedabad, 380015, India

R. R. Ibraimov
Tashkent University of Information Technology (TUIT), 108, Amir Temur Street, Tashkent 100084, Uzbekistan

Nimbe L. Ewald-Arostegui and Gorry Fairhurst
School of Engineering, University of Aberdeen, Aberdeen AB24 3UE, UK

Ana Yun-Garcia
Thales Alenia Space, C/Einstein 7, Tres Cantos-Madrid 28760, Spain

Massimiliano Laddomada
Electrical Engineering Department, Texas A&M University-Texarkana, Texarkana, TX 75505, USA

Fabio Mesiti
DELEN, Politecnico di Torino, 10129 Torino, Italy

Kamran Arshad, Muhammad Ali Imran and Klaus Moessner
Centre for Communication Systems Research, University of Surrey, Guildford GU2 7XH, UK

Lukasz Kondrad, Vinod Kumar Malamal Vadakital, and Moncef Gabbouj
Department of Signal Processing, Tampere University of Technology, 33720 Tampere, Finland

Imed Bouazizi
Nokia Research Center, 33720 Tampere, Finland

Miika Tupala
Nokia, 24100 Salo, Finland

Andreas Merentitis and Dionysia Triantafyllopoulou
Department of Informatics and Telecommunications, University of Athens, Panepistimiopolis, Ilissia, 15784 Athens, Greece

Hiranmay Ghosh, Ashish Khare, Sujal Subhash Wattamwar and Amarendra Gorai
TCS Innovation Labs Delhi, TCS Towers, 249 D&E Udyog Vihar Phase IV, Gurgaon 122015, India

Sunil Kumar Kopparapu and Meghna Pandharipande
TCS Innovation Labs Mumbai, Yantra Park, Pokhran Road no. 2, Thane West 400601, India

Tanushyam Chattopadhyay
TCS Innovation Labs Kolkata, Plot A2, M2-N2 Sector 5, Block GP, Salt Lake Electronics Complex, Kolkata 700091, India

Michele Sanna and Maurizio Murroni
Department of Electrical and Electronic Engineering, DIEE, University of Cagliari, 09123 Cagliari, Italy

Elie El-Khoury, Christine Sénac and Philippe Joly
IRIT Laboratory, Toulouse University, 118 route de Narbonne, 31062 Toulouse Cedex 9, France

T. Inzerilli
Dipartimento per le Comunicazioni, I.S.C.T.I.,Ministero dello Sviluppo Economico, Viale America 201, 00144 Rome, Italy

A. M. Vegni and A. Neri
Department of Applied Electronics, University of Roma Tre, Via della Vasca Navale 84, 00146 Rome, Italy

R. Cusani
Department of Information Engineering, Electronics and Telecommunications (DIET), University of Rome "Sapienza", Via Eudossiana 18, 00184 Rome, Italy

Xiangming Kong, Deying Zhang and Mohin Ahmed
Information & System Sciences Lab, HRL Laboratories, LLC, Malibu, CA 90265-4797, USA